# FORWARD

C000052300

*TO MY CHILDREN AND GRANDCHILDREN*

*Remy, Jared, Markus and Anya*

*and*

*all of this world's children*

# FORWARD!

## – YORICK BLUMENFELD –

Printed and bound in England by www.printondemand-worldwide.com

http://www.fast-print.net/bookshop

Forward!
Copyright © Yorick Blumenfeld 2018

ISBN: 978-178456-593-0

All rights reserved

No part of this book may be reproduced in any form by photocopying
or any electronic or mechanical means, including information storage
or retrieval systems, without permission in writing from both the
copyright owner and the publisher of the book.

The right of Yorick Blumenfeld to be identified as the author of this work has
been asserted by him in accordance with the Copyright, Designs and
Patents Act 1988 and any subsequent amendments thereto.

A catalogue record for this book is available from the British Library

First published 2018 by
FASTPRINT PUBLISHING
Peterborough, England.

# CONTENTS

# FORWARD !

## VENTURES FOR GLOBAL IMPROVEMENT

A Selection of Yorick's Blogs from 2013 through 2017

BEING an idealist in the age of blogs and the social media is not exactly fashionable. The entire globe, from Venezuela to North Korea, and from Afghanistan, Libya and the Middle East to Myanmar, is engulfed by daily horrors. The current US President, Donald Trump, regrettably exemplifies the various forces of greed, stupidity, mediocrity, celebrity, & blindness which threaten to engulf us. I feel it is my duty in this state of affairs to present positive alternative aspects for what ails us. My personal goal is to contribute to the improvement of our human collective.

If we consider how swiftly we have progressed from the condition of the cavemen- only some 15,000 years ago- we should feel encouraged to evaluate our prospects! It took only a couple of hundred years to transform the world with the contagious ideals of Jeffersonian democracy. Consequently, in my blogs I try to suggest some advancements we could make in the coming generations.

In this context I am enormously encouraged to see how today's youngsters swiftly adopt new perspectives. Ecology, for example, had hardly entered the teen-age consciousness in the 1980's. Today it is globally endorsed by each successive generation. The development of the arts, of language and the breakthroughs in science and technology are all powerful elements intrinsic to such advances. Despite the setbacks caused by some inept as well as retrograde politicians, multiculturalism and globalization are ultimately inevitable.

Nearly all of us would like to control aspects of our future. Our common challenge is to imagine, anticipate and assist in the process of transformation. We can reconnect our private aspirations with the larger human hopes of which we all partake, like survival and improvement of the planet. At the same time I recognize that a substantial fragment of humanity resist the application of any blue-prints worked out by thinkers and intellectuals. Serious social problems, such as inequality and poverty, resist broad solutions, such as universal health care could offer. Alas, the current surge of populism undermines the very goals of policy development.

I have been faced with numerous challenges while writing these blogs in trying to suggest possible improvements. There are strongly held beliefs that society itself is a process with its own life and development and that interfering with such a process could serve to stunt the natural course of events. My response is that one must view society much as one views the education of children: With the right education and approach there are many ways in which it can be directed. If you encourage children, if you give them selected praise, if you develop self-esteem and aspiration, there is a far better chance of achieving  desired results than if they are left to roam unwittingly believing that 'life' itself can fatalistically determine their future.

The multi-faceted approach of these blogs attempts to promote the need for diversity and integration. Diversity enriches the concept of wholeness as an underlying principle: it endorses the "unity of differences." You will soon observe that I tend to adopt an holistic approach. This prefers embracing cooperation and harmony rather than advocating the advancement of the ego and competition as  frameworks for our future development.  I have highlighted the importance of striving towards the greater exercise of individual responsibility, but I have not viewed this as a social or political panacea. Alas, the folly of ultimate conclusions is widespread. The demand for "final goals," is an illusion, similar to that of 'perfection.'  However, hopefully the creation of an open and better human community is plausible.

This volume suggests that a large number of politicians in the democracies are only marginally concerned with the future . Partially this is because they are focused more immediately on their re-election.

However, 'conservatives' , by the very nature of their outlook, do not offer any programmed alternative to the direction in which their nations may be moving. They are opposed to both the speed and the direction of change. They tend to romanticize the past. However neither nostalgia nor foot-dragging can serve as a program for our future. The market-driven economists, on the other hand, have no idea where rapid changes could lead us, and simply suggest to let "the market" 'run its course.

I started writing blogs on basic issues like Restoring Trust, Forgiveness, Leisure, Loneliness, Respecting the Truth and the like, in the hope that personal issues could encourage us to alter our current perspectives.

I have also expressed my sense that the physical sciences may yet provide us with a sense of direction which philosophy has failed to offer. Perhaps physicists will one day find a 'final theory' of such compelling beauty that its truth will be undeniable. Such a unified field theory might somehow relate the destiny of mankind to that of the universe. However, it is also plausible that there may be no such 'final theory' which would reunite all the different strings, just as there may be no ultimate social formula to unite all human beings. What we cannot do is to turn our backs on the search itself. It is such searching which constitutes our noblest effort and provides us with a sense of development. We are all comforted in the knowledge that each and everyone of us is part of a greater whole which we assume is universal.

I launched my blog early in 2013 with a picture and a statement of what I hoped to offer:

**About Yorick's Blog**

### Enhancing, Provocative, and Future Tense

*Are your prospects likely to improve in the next decade?*

*How can the state create more jobs?*

*Is our embrace of democracy realistic?*

*Does the survival of our race on this planet worry you?*

*Is capitalism really the best way?*

*How might the introduction of Internet education affect you?*

In an age where the surfeit of information is beginning to clog our brains, this blog will focus on what is not being offered or suggested elsewhere. It will examine what is taboo and where denial prevails. Hopefully it will also be engaging.

We live in a world where capitalism is accepted by most advanced societies and its inhabitants are offered no alternative possibilities; a planet in which no serious politician opposes growth; a time in which the unfettered advance of electronic communication is regarded as sacrosanct; where profits and efficiency prevail over jobs and employment. Ultimately the course being followed is one which daily diminishes the chances of human survival on this environmentally threatened planet. All too many people refuse to accept this final evaluation to humanity's ultimate peril.

It is with this perspective in mind that I am launching yet another blog to the already 80 million blogs around the world!

This hopefully "Enhancing, Provocative and Future Tense" effort will look with a different slant at areas which the media may have tackled. And I am not going to pretend that a perfectible electronic future is in store for us.

CHANGE, with all its uncertainties, seems threatening to the well being of most of us. Yet change is inevitable although its speed is not. We cannot stand still on this rapidly spinning planet. In this unusual era of rapid change we must accept that the new also can be for the better. It has been in this spirit that I edited a series called *Prospects for Tomorrow*, and have written such books as *Towards the Millennium: Optimistic Visions for Change* (1996) and *Dollars or Democracy* (2004)

Global economics have particularly shifted in direction in this new century. Economics seem to "have gone off the rails!" The inability to deal with the facts of economic life was largely confirmed at the meeting this January in Davos of the more than 2,500 leading figures in global economics. These leaders refused to confront that the Internet and computers are fundamentally transforming our economic lives with unknown consequences.

In the 19th Century corporate capitalism delivered new jobs, new opportunities, new resources, and put an end to the bases of the feudalistic structure.

In the 20th Century despite two world wars and a massive global depression, the standard of living for several billions improved substantially.

In the 21st Century we are now faced with a widespread recession and an end to the economic promises that corporate capitalism once offered. Tax avoidance/evasion on a global scale is making the funding of social welfare programs unsustainable. Companies like HSBC, SONY, GE, and Shell have become such giants that for fear of the consequences governments cannot allow these corporations to fail. The desire for ever greater profits through the advance of technology has forced the development of mobiles, social networks and communication without any consideration for the possible effects on the younger generation nor for the well-being of society itself.

The vast gap growing between the hyper-rich and the rest of humanity threatens to de-stabilize the semblance of economic equilibrium of the past two centuries.

The ever-growing demands, as well as the expectations of seven+ billion people on this planet, are now threatening the prospect of survival of future generations. Our economic perspective itself has become overwhelmed by its short-termism. Most corporations think in three-year terms, politicians in four or five year terms, and few economists dare to look ahead beyond that. The only plausible conclusion is that the time has come to examine positive and imaginative changes to the darkening prospects currently on offer.

(For a summary of my book on economics, Dollars or Democracy, see the excellent summary which has just been produced by Randy Hayes at Foundation Earth:

http://www.fdnearth.org/essays/capitalism-cant-be-reformed-try-the-incentive-economy/

:

## Hope

Posted on June 16, 2014

Hope, that invisible, intangible, and optimistic word, almost seems wired into our psyche. No one knows when the idea of hope first surfaced in human consciousness. It appeared in ancient Greek mythology with Hesiod's story of Prometheus, mankind's great benefactor, who stole the secret of life from Zeus. This so infuriated the supreme god that in revenge he created a great vase (now incorrectly called "Pandora's Box") which he filled with misery and every manner of affliction which would fly out if opened. The beautiful but untrustworthy Pandora, (the first woman, created at Zeus's command by Hephaestus) was unaware of the contents, but had been warned never to take off its cover. When curiosity eventually got the better of her, all kinds of troubles flew out into the world, except for hope, which remained at the very bottom of the vase. Thus the first woman unwittingly introduced disease, despair, pain and other miseries into the world. So much for hope's introduction to the ancient Greeks.

Two centuries after Hesiod and Homer has spread this complex and wonderful myth, Thales of Miletus, often credited with being the first of Greek philosophers, wrote that "Hope is the only good that is common to all men; those who have nothing else possess hope still." Those Greeks who followed him, like Plato and Aristotle, considered hope to be connected to the gods and something akin to a waking dream.

The Old Testament recognized, we are all "prisoners of hope." As one of our most frequently used expressions, hope is what keeps much of humanity going. Hope refuses to accept despair, so it is actively embraced by all religions. Hope is one of the three theological virtues of Christianity. In the Bible hope has entailed a strong and confident expectation of an afterlife. It is thus a source of ultimate salvation. The founder of Protestantism, Martin Luther, wrote, "faith without hope is nothing worth, for hope endures and overcomes misfortune and evil." Like so many Church fathers, Luther believed transcendental hope was at the basis of everything, including religion, because it kept the future

# I  NEW POTENTIALS

## Hope

Posted on June 16, 2014

Hope, that invisible, intangible, and optimistic word, almost seems wired into our psyche. No one knows when the idea of hope first surfaced in human consciousness. It appeared in ancient Greek mythology with Hesiod's story of Prometheus, mankind's great benefactor, who stole the secret of fire from Zeus. This so infuriated the supreme god that in revenge he created a great vase (now incorrectly called "Pandora's Box") which he filled with misery and every manner of affliction which would fly out if opened. The beautiful but untrustworthy Pandora, (the first woman, created at Zeus's command by Hephaestus) was unaware of the contents, but had been warned never to take off its cover. When curiosity eventually got the better of her, all kinds of troubles flew out into the world, except for hope, which remained at the very bottom of the vase. Thus the first woman unwittingly introduced disease, despair, pain and other miseries into the world. So much for hope's introduction to the ancient Greeks.

Two centuries after Hesiod and Homer had spread this complex and wonderful myth, Thales of Miletus, often credited with being the first of Greek philosophers, wrote that "Hope is the only good that is common to all men; those who have nothing else possess hope still." Those Greeks who followed him, like Plato and Aristotle, considered hope to be connected to the gods and something akin to a waking dream.

The *Old Testament* recognized, we are all "prisoners of hope."[1] As one of our most frequently used expressions, hope is what keeps much of humanity going. Hope refuses to accept despair, so it is actively embraced by all religions. Hope is one of the three theological virtues of Christianity. In the *Bible* hope has entailed a strong and confident expectation of an afterlife. It is thus a source of ultimate salvation. The founder of Protestantism, Martin Luther, wrote, "faith without hope is nothing worth, for hope endures and overcomes misfortune and evil."[2] Like so many Church fathers, Luther believed transcendental hope was at the basis of everything, including religion, because it kept the future open. Thus Thomas Aquinas regarded hope as that which is "possible of attainment."[3] Modern philosophers like Jacques Ellul have come to regard hope as man's response to the silence of God.[4]

Hope looks forward with desire, reasonable confidence and expectation. The philosopher Ernst Bloch attempted to articulate a philosophical approach to hope and also treated hope as a cosmological principle. "The striving, yearning, and anticipation of something 'not yet' that characterizes human hope is also a fundamental feature not just of non-human life, but of the universe itself. This yearning and striving is the key to understanding not just human nature but nature as such. The hope principle is thus not a confined but an open process."[5]

Today we recognize that hope can take us beyond ourselves, our limitations and our predicaments. Humanity appreciates that hope expands our horizons and our potentialities. The "advance" or progress of mankind requires hope, realistic hope in the possibility of improvement. Such hope ultimately has to be based on planning, scientific research, and social endorsement if it is to be effective. Hope encompasses both utopian and communitarian dreams as well as our spiritual needs. Jean-Paul Sartre said: "I think that hope is built into man. Human action is transcendent. It places its goal, its realization in the future. There is hope in the very manner of action — in the fixing of a goal to be reached."[6] Although sometimes on the edge of despair, as a philosopher Sartre came to respect hope as 'the nerve of moral action.' I profoundly believe that although we can harbor deep unease about the way things are, we must have hope about how things could be. From the very first this has been at the basis of my blog.

President Obama gave us great hopes for change when he was elected and now that such changes have not come about we feel disappointed and somehow cheated. Obama himself hoped that with bi-partisan support in Congress he could bring about substantive changes. His profound hopes, based on a long history of political party cooperation in American history, were not realistic. Racism and political radicalization turned compromise into a dirty word. No matter what the President proposed, the Republicans denounced it. In such a narrow-minded atmosphere, hope for change began to evaporate.

Some political figures have given people hope in important ways: Churchill, Roosevelt, Atlee, Kennedy, Reagan and Clinton all filled us with hope at different moments in their careers. Others, like Baldwin and Nixon, never were convincing. It is difficult for us to accept that hope also can be an escape from the harshness of the present, that it can be a denial of reality. This may lead some to disparage hope as an extension of the predominantly wishful thinking of childhood. The rejection of hope is recognized by psychologists as a child's method of avoiding disappointment.

While recognizing that we cannot live without hope, most people today live without optimism because of the vast scale of the problems facing us at every level. Our destiny is no longer manifest as was believed before WWI. The desirability of advancing from hope to optimism is not even a notion subscribed to by all. A dystopian and fatalistic outlook has spread around the world. Such fatalism purports that as it is impossible to know what is going to happen, we should pray that the worst is not going to consume us. Spiritually this debilitating outlook tends to rob life of its potential for meaning. What progress we can make depends in large measure on our willingness to risk possible improvements.

It should give us hope that we can creatively adapt ourselves and change just as all other existing life forms have done through evolution. Positive feedback has been one of the basic mechanisms of life. It should fill us with hope that bit-by-bit we are unravelling the secrets of the universe and that this will make our own existence more comprehensible. Hope cannot be excluded from scientific empiricism because science itself is based on the continuing hope that the experiment will succeed and the hypothesis will be proven.

Optimism is frequently criticized because it exceeds strictly reasonable, 'realistic' boundaries. I am all too aware of Machiavelli's warning that "Men commit the error of not knowing when to limit their hopes." However, I believe that hope should have no limit. We must let our imagination soar with our hearts and let the best in our minds prevail. A vision of what could be is of the essence, for we cannot move from hope to optimism without it. As the *Bible* says: "Where there is no vision, the people perish."[7]

I fervently believe that our hopes, ideas and ideals can ultimately be translated into actions to bring about a far greater degree of social harmony. I do not believe that capitalism is guiding us towards that goal. The fabled 'market' does not provide us with a sense of social direction. We must meet our enduring human needs in new ways. Envisioning a different economic structure constitutes one of our greatest challenges, but one, which we must embark upon with hopes for a more sustainable and viable future. The wholeness and unity of humanity is of the essence as well. Each one of us must do what we can to further an environment in which our collective hopes could develop into optimism. For optimism itself can turn life into a more brightly lit vision. As the metaphysical poet George Herbert wrote some four hundred years ago: "He that lives in hope dances without music."

---

[1] Zechariah IX, 12.c.520 B.C

[2] Martin Luther, *Table Talk* I, 1598.

[3] Thomas Aquinas, *Summa Theologica* trans. Fathers of the English Dominican Province, (1971) p.17-18.

[4] Yorick Blumenfeld, *Towards the Millennium*, (1996) p.596

[5] Ernst Bloch,'*Philosophisches Jahrbuch*, vol. 95, 1988, p.326

[6] Jean-Paul Sartre, "Where I got it wrong on despair," in a talk with Bernard Levy, *The Observer*, April 20, 1980.

[7] *Proverbs*, 29:18 (King James Version).

## The Unacceptable Face of Change

Posted on March 13, 2013

There are days when I don't think I can face the highly intrusive pace of change anymore. And then *The Economist* (usually a right of center magazine) places a parody of Rodin's thinker sitting on a toilet seat on its cover suggesting that "Modern science has failed to make anything with such a powerful impact, and that is why a growing band of thinkers claim that the pace of innovation has slowed." I only wish this were true.[1]

The day has started with my mobile ringing just as I was opening the morning flood of Yahoo emails. Then the landline rings and while I am pleased to hear breathing at the other end, the incoming tide of communications, like the pace of daily life, is overwhelming. I cannot be alone in worrying how this on-line flood will affect billions of people around the world.

The editors of the *Economist* seriously under-estimate the scale of the computer revolution. Not only is it changing our ways of payment and banking, of sending information, and of shopping, but it also is deeply affecting our daily lives. Our personal privacy is diminishing, our free time is being infringed upon, and our imaginations are being corrupted. All this is happening without any genuine public or political discourse. The all-powerful corporate world propagates the belief that the technological advances pushed by market forces are both inevitable and benign.

The daunting question arises: how much longer can we keep up this pace of ever faster and more invasive and intrusive communications? The challenge is enormous because the impact is already taking its toll and the long-term effects are not only unknown, but are not even seriously considered.[2]

Who is responsible for the avalanche of verbal messages to my brain? Not the government. Not some subversive brainwashing group. One cannot place all the blame on Network Orange or Yahoo, Wikipedia, Facebook, Linked-in or Twitter. All companies not even in existence a few years ago. And now I am even launching my own blog. Am I abetting this electronic tsunami of technology? What surge of new devices and apps will come next?[3]  I hate even to think about it.

More important than the yet unstudied effects of the Internet is the concern that this new technology is undermining our mental processes, such as memory, imagination and attention spans. The Internet is also making dramatic intrusions into our personal lives, diminishing our traditional forms of communication — like eye-to-eye contacts and — yes — smell.

While the introduction of computers, mobiles, texting, the Internet and global communications are all changing the daily lives of adults at an unprecedented pace, the new formats are accepted as normal by the younger generation. An emerging teenager cannot even recognize that the nature of her or his friendships is changing. The visual introduction of sexuality is coming at ever-earlier stages. 10- and 12-year-olds are 'sexting' and transmitting images of their genitals to each other.

Social relations for those who are now in their twenties and thirties are equally disrupted by the ease with which new relationships can be entered through thousands of contact sites. Making new acquaintances in pubs or parks or museums is becoming distinctly unfashionable.

And the pace (or should I say "threat"} of change is far from diminishing: we may soon be faced with another radical industrial revolution with unknown consequences, namely nanotechnology. This will use molecules as our building blocks and create computers the size of a blood vessel. The implications of the immense potential for military, medical and commercial applications are staggering.

Indeed, nanotechnology may eventually overwhelm the next stage of civilization. However, this will be at a microscopic level and will not create any new employment opportunities. Some may come to see it as a chance to insert truly micro-devices into our brains.

As it is, I find the excess of information being produced for consumption alarming. There is no way I can keep up. Much of this material can swiftly be classified as "rubbish" but I see it as gradually overwhelming our human capacity to think with clarity and perspective. There will be little space for the development of wisdom — not to mention insight or the establishment of priorities. Might trying to pass on wisdom on the Internet become something of an oxymoron?[4]

We are rapidly moving further and further away from the natural world of which we used to be a part. We are now in almost constant touch with the mechanical world at our fingertips.[5] Even if we were to stand still in terms of further technological breakthroughs we can only guess how long it would take future generations to acclimatize to the social changes brought about by the mobile electronic communications of the past thirty years?[6]

How can we slow down the advance of ever more intrusive technology? Canute could not stop the waves; mass protests on the streets could not affect the speed of the impending advances in technology.

A decisive global slow-down could come from a shift away from capitalism towards a less money/profit driven economic system. But alas, a less greedy, less commercialized, less unequal, less competitive and also less environmentally polluting economy is not being seriously contemplated.

I tried to present such an option with an alternative I named the "Incentive Economy" in my book, *Dollars or Democracy*. However, this more cooperative and less corporate controlled system has yet to be considered by the hordes of micro-economists and election-focused politicians.

Change also could come through any number of possible catastrophes: Like an accidental nuclear war, an unstoppable pneumonic plague, or a major flare coming from the sun which would down all our electrical appliances. But when I see quite another form of communication in trouble, namely the endemic congestion on our roads, I feel there may be different natural ways in which advances in technology might "slow down." Perhaps the congestion of the various forms of electronic communication could eventually overwhelm our Internet and its storage capacity as well. Luddites please take note.

[1]*The Economist*, January 12, 2013

[2]*"Where's IT Going?"* Ian Pearson & Chris Winter

[3]http://gizmodo.com/5976659/what-happened-on-the-internet-in-2012-in-numbers

[4]"Digital Revolution" *The Observer*, March 10,2013, p.40

[5] *"Scanning The Future,"* (1997) Edited by Yorick Blumenfeld

[6] *Towards the Millennium,* Optimistic Visions for Change, (1996) Yorick Blumenfeld

**Fears of Change**

Posted on May 28, 2013

The fear of change is a fickle one. At one moment people are excited and want change and the next instant they are most fearful of it. Individually, men and women seek to cultivate something new and different and at the very same time want to save their familiar image in the mirror.

Fear of the dark unknown, of the possible disaster lurking, is as old as mankind. The threat of an economic meltdown makes people yearn for the *status quo*. They want to say, "STOP" to change. However, change is both inevitable and all around us. We live in a rapidly transforming and globalizing time in which scientific and technological breakthroughs are overwhelming not only our past traditions but also our very mood and thought patterns. The French proverb, "The more it changes, the more it remains the same," is in many ways being turned on its head. The more discoveries are made in biotechnology or advances are made in robotics, the more we are affected; the more our lives change.

Lucretius, one of my heroes from antiquity, wrote back in 57 BC (at a time of rising Roman power) that "One nation rises to supreme power in the world while another declines, and in a brief space of time the sovereign people change, transmitting, like Marathon racers, the torch of life to some other that is to succeed them."[1] In this way little has changed: The British are becoming accustomed to their fall from Imperial grace, the Chinese are looking forward to global predominance, and Americans are beginning to feel insecure about their iffy-place in the world.

The United States, being a relatively youthful nation, has always been led by people optimistically seeking improvement. However, at present they are expressing anxiety about their direction and the prospects of change: for example, the birth rate of Latino-Americans is altering demographics … which may ultimately alter politics. No matter how the ultra-conservatives oppose such change, in a few years the Latino vote is likely to switch Texas into the democratic column and the Republican Party will be facing radical change. Some observers may contend that it already is doing so.

The United Kingdom (which is likely to remain united despite the forthcoming vote on Scottish independence) is an old but rapidly changing country whose citizens prefer to look back nostalgically — even if life in the time of Dickens was far harder for the Brits of that era. A large proportion of the Tory party members are upset by the inflow of workers from Eastern Europe and by the large number of new citizens from India and Pakistan who are not adapting to the British way of life. These conservatives are unsettled by gay marriage and find the speed of change produced by the Internet hard to follow. Sites like YouTube, Facebook, Tumblr, not to mention the plethora of pornographic options, have arrived too quickly for a nation to digest. Ultimately, even in terms of the physical state of this island, they find the steady erosion of what had made England a "green and pleasant land" unacceptable.

In the US, on matters demanding change, like gun control, the rising prison population, fracking, or even sorting out health care, there is little in-depth debate. Great effort is made to avoid contentious issues in social discourse. Americans want to avoid the confrontations that inevitably accompany change. The media, as they pursue the "new" and the "different", also do not like doubt and are fostering an "all or nothing", "with us or against us" mentality. FOX news with its generally slanted approach, for example, is out to get an audience rather than informing one.

I have long been intrigued by the extent to which Americans are exposed to intentional distortion of the facts on issues to which certain groups are opposed, such as global warming or health care. When Obama was trying to push through ways to change the spiralling costs of the health care industry, he was opposed by a most formidable array: the insurance companies, the pharmaceutical industry, a vast assemblage of lawyers protecting the hundreds of thousands of private doctors, Washington's lobbying industry which was spending well in excess of $150 million a year on this particular issue, large sections of the media controlled by the wealthy opponents to change, and not only the Republican Party but even Democrats in Congress who were in the pay of lobbyists. Faced with such anti-change forces, it seemed incredible that Obama even got a diluted version of his Health Care bill passed.

It was no surprise that given the vociferous scale of these opponents, every effort was made to malign Britain's National Health Service. The goal was to instil the fear of "godless" socialism creeping in via socialist medical practices. The outright distortions, misrepresentations, and falsehoods of the media as well as those of politicians were astounding. The NHS was portrayed as the home of eugenics, death panels, euthanasia, and a rampant state bureaucracy controlling every aspect of medical care. The forceful negative campaign was not only based on the propaganda techniques of Dr Joseph Goebbels — it copied them outright. The danger of such practice is that the opposition to change becomes so distorted that this itself introduces change in the national perception.

In this time of economic uncertainty, the same scenario holds true. Criticism capitalism is taboo. Fear of capitalism's possible collapse simply freezes the possibility of presenting alternatives which it is feared would inevitably lead to massive change.

So ambivalence triumphs: the need for change, whether it be in the environment, economics, or politics is evident, but the fear of change pervades. So does the uncertainty which presently accompanies the subsequent lack of clear decisions. And the situation is not going to improve. We are moving into an ever more artificial, electronic and computerized world which conflicts with our basic physiological and psychological evolution over the millennia. Irrespectively, the fundamental curiosity, rebelliousness, and the almost built-in desire for change on the part of the young will continue to divide coming generations. Whatever the ultimate outcome, it is unlikely that we shall be able to resolve the wired fears in our genetic make-up as human beings.[2]

---

[1]Lucretius, *"De rerum natura II"*
[2]See: Yorick Blumenfeld, *Towards the Millenium: Optimistic Visions for Change*, (1996)

**Blinkers**

posted on August 14, 2013

I continue to be deeply troubled by the long list of challenges which politicians are unwilling to confront with any degree of honesty in this increasingly imperilled planet. I consider it imperative to answer the questions which the following challenges raise:

- The myth of perpetual growth. (I have yet to note any politician holding office who does not see growth as the way out of socio/economic problems.)
- The dire implications of a projected upcoming world population of 9 billion plus.
- The refusal to admit that the "War on Drugs" has been a disaster. (Nearly four generations ago the US abandoned Prohibition — without any of the predicted disastrous effects. Why can politicians not abandon the equally harmful War on Drugs?)
- The dismal failure to take effective steps to provide jobs for the under 30 population.
- The inability to abandon the prison system for those who are mentally ill. (And the continued growth of the Prison Industry?)
- The unwillingness to tackle global migration problems.
- Placing "the market" in the forefront of tackling our economic problems. (Accepting capitalism as the only way forward in terms of the global economy.)
- The inability to face up to the long-term. (And the attendant resort to short-termism.)
- The introduction of technology without considering the consequences of robotics, genetically altered foods, space exploration, and nanotechnology.
- The unwillingness to recognize that religion has in many ways been a destabilizing force for humanity.
- A failure to impose a global ban on nuclear weapons.
- Inaction on the effects of chemistry on nature, specifically the increasing disappearance of species and the devastating

consequences of spraying on bees, birds, frogs. (Not to mention the unrecognized effects of these chemicals on human beings).

- The hostility to permitting workers to have adequate protection and union representation.
- The growth of extreme inequality between rich and poor worldwide.

The questions which these challenges immediately raise are inevitable:

- Is the inability to face the future in democracies due to politicians having to face elections every four or five years?
- Is the irresponsible corporate system of economics based on shareholders getting their return on investment not threatening the continuity of human life on this planet?
- Is the lack of effective means of protest preventing the resolution of any of these major challenges?
- Is this impasse aided by a prevailing orthodoxy that "the market" should decide our direction and that state control is the principal danger facing us?
- Is the current breakdown of codes, traditions, values and morals irreversible?
- Is the sum of all these challenges not a prelude similar to what has been called CCD, or Colony Collapse Disorder, which is affecting bees around the world but whose cause remains to be diagnosed?
- CAN THIS PREVAILING STATE OF BLINKERS BE ALTERED? I welcome your perspective on this host of challenges.

## An appreciation of greater needs

Posted on September 23, 2013

"What really motivates or drives you?" I asked my friends at an end of summer luncheon.

"Need arouses my inner being and sustains it," volunteered finance manager Janice with considerable intensity. "My need for a kind of spiritual affirmation demands a deeply inward search on my part," she confessed. "I need to have a sense of where I am going. Above all, I have a need to accept my own uncertainties."

"I like your honesty, Janice." retorted James who spends much of his time in Southern Africa helping native groups to modernize their agricultural practices. "Of course we all have a need to know where we are going in this overly revved-up world. The people I work with have seemingly unending material and physical needs — but their social needs and acceptance are richly met in their families and the solidarity of their relationships."

"Needs. Needs! I'm dealing with weeds all week-end", joined in Anne, a sun-tanned neighbor desirous of lightening the conversation. "They're much more real to me than all that psychologizing and social anthropology."

Fred, the oldest of the group, could not resist inserting a limerick:

> *There was once a bloke in dire need*
> *Whose thoughts had slowed with his seed*
> *He considered jumping the Niagara*
> *But instead chose the latest Viagra*
> *And is now celebrating in deed.*

We all chuckled at Fred, but I was determined to bring the discussion back on track. "The experts on happiness point out that it is not money nor goods nor travels that fulfil our innermost needs. I agree with James that in the tribal communities, like those of New Guinea, the communal life of these so-called primitives provides a much simpler and comparatively more satisfying life for its members than we create for ours."

"Yes they do," agreed James. " their tribal ties, their close family connections, their lack of sexual inhibitions, their spiritual contact with their ancestors, their closeness with nature, the expressiveness of their art all serve to fulfil their what you called their innermost needs."

"They enjoy significant primary relationships with other," added Janice, revealing her own inner needs, and then continued "but they are involved in something higher than the material world. They accept the need for self-esteem."

"Janice you read your own concerns into those of New Guinea natives," observed Fred. "I prefer to deal with real needs."

"What do you mean by real needs? Are some unreal to you, Fred?"

"Real needs are those basic ones like thirst, hunger and sex. Less real ones like support and commitment — which concern you — I think of as secondary needs," countered Fred who could sense Janice was becoming increasingly irritated.

I decided to try and defuse the discussion by bringing in Karl Marx. This tactic has worked for me for years. "Marx defined humans as 'needy creatures' who experienced suffering in the process of their hard labors when trying to meet their physical needs. Marx recognized that their efforts also helped to meet their emotional, moral and intellectual needs. But in this process of meeting such diverse needs, humans developed new needs. This implied that, to a certain extent, we humans can make and remake our own nature."

"I prefer to skip Marx," responded Fred. "I see needs defined according to our having, doing and interacting. This means: nourishment, good health, security, affection, participation, understanding, identity, creativity, autonomy and freedom."

I had to admit to myself that this old codger had his feet solidly planted on the ground. Mary-Lee, however, swiftly retorted. "Sure, Fred, but how do these needs depend on human qualities like a sense of humor, passion, care, adaptability, achievement, respect, or receptivity?"

"Our individual needs are representative of all the efforts and interactions involved in being members of society," tersely replied Fred.

"I'm glad none of you have confused needs and wants," interjected James. "In Ethiopia I have remarked that ordinary people want what they see on TV and end up feeling needy."

"Needs are more urgent, intensive and imperative than mere wants," rejoined Janice. "humans keep on redistributing their wants but seldom their needs."

"There I have to agree with you, Janice. Wants are often spread by greed. I have come to see capitalism itself as the collectivity of wants and the denial of the real needs of the poor, the sick, the old, the weak and so forth," said Anne who had been remarkably silent.

"The accompanying word to "want" is the almost infantile 'MORE'," added Fred. "That is also the by-word of capitalism."

"I guess I need to be needed," admitted Janice. "I also suspect my needs are driven by internal dissatisfactions, unrest and a kind of imbalance."

Agreeing with her, I concluded: "We all have a powerful need to be needed, that others want us and need us. We must develop an awareness of our feelings as indicators of the needs that are alive within us. I think that is what we have been doing in this lively lunchtime discussion: arriving at some agreement on the importance of the individual needs of each of us. Identifying our needs, met or unmet, as Janice has been trying to do, is the most vital step in this process. Thank you all."

## Dire Straights for the Oceans

Posted on October 14, 2013

Water, air and soil are all basic to our survival on this planet and yet, to my bewilderment, we are dramatically failing to protect them. Commercial exploitation, pollution and greed are all major factors, but I find it embarrassing how persistently we don't get our priorities right even when the warning signals from our bees, trees, fish as well as our own health are so clear. Indeed the whole system of planet earth is being undermined irrespective of the mounting evidence. We don't like the scientific facts or the necessary conclusions, coldly observes ecologist Thomas Lovejoy.[1]

Our oceans are now more acidic than they have been for 300 million years — affecting the vast number of species in them. This is in part due to the emissions of carbon dioxide produced by burning coal and oil for electricity, heating, manufacturing and transportation. Several decades pass between the carbon dioxide being emitted and the effects being recordable in the oceans. This implies that further acidification and warming of the seas is inevitable as the greenhouse gas emissions continue.

More than a third of the carbon dioxide that we have been producing are absorbed by and dissolved in the oceans. Prof Alex Rogers of Oxford University says "The health of the ocean is spiralling downwards far more rapidly than we had thought. We are seeing greater change, happening faster, and the effects are more imminent than previously anticipated."[2]

Overfishing is also contributing to the crisis in the combination of destructing forces imperilling marine life on which a large proportion of the world's population depends for its nutrition. But not a single nation is really tackling the problem of overfishing according to the latest reports. Are we going to end up with:

"Water, water everywhere but no longer any fish to eat."

Three-quarters of the world's edible fish populations are being over-exploited. Controlling the use of mile-long fishnets, huge inboard freezers, and other destructive fishing equipment on the subsidized, large commercial vessels are all seen as critical. This also would give the large number of small-scale operators a better chance of survival.

The "Critical State" of the Oceans is the headline of a scientific report out this month. The bad news extends from the cumulative impact on the entire spectrum of marine life, starting at the base of the food chain, marine phytoplankton.[3]

Most phytoplankton are invisible to the naked eye. This extraordinary species, of which there are 5,000 known varieties, sustain the aquatic food web, and they are responsible for 50% of the Earth's oxygen. Half of each breath you take comes from these microorganisms!

Marine phytoplankton can be sensitive to the rising $CO_2$ level and lowered pH. Only of late, however, have oceanographers begun to examine how these trends affect the phytoplankton species. A 2010 study by Dalhousie University in Canada published in *Nature* found a 40 per cent decline since 1950 in phytoplankton. More recently, and in concert with the continual warming up of the open seas, studies analysing 1.5 million plankton DNA sequences show temperature plays a critical role in the chemical cycles of these organisms altering them by changing the natural cycles of carbon dioxide, nitrogen, and phosphorous. This negatively affects their reproduction, making them scarce, and thus impacting life all the way up the food chain.[4]

The list of growing problems begins with ocean acidification, a direct result of burning fossil fuels. This acidification is occurring at a rate 10-to-100 times faster (depending upon the area) than ever recorded, with some estimates that by the end of the 21st century, the surface waters in some areas of the ocean may not be able to support shell-bearing plankton.[5]

The IPSO report claims coral is especially at risk because acidity dissolves calcium carbonate skeletons, which create reef structure. As well, increasing warmth leads to bleaching, causing corals to lose symbiotic algae. The report claims current governmental plans to cut emissions do not go far enough, nor fast enough, to save the world's reefs. Corals are vital to the health of fisheries because they serve as the nurseries for the young fish and provide nourishment for the larger varieties.

The IPSO report also states that the carbon dioxide absorbed by the seas is higher than previously anticipated, The world's oceans, by absorbing carbon dioxide and heat from the atmosphere, have shielded or slowed the rate of climate change on land. Accordingly, to a large extent, the potential harm associated with climate change has been hidden underwater.

Acidification diminishes development, i.e., growth and reproduction, of coral reefs, shellfish and plankton. According to Jane Luchenco, former director of the US National Oceanic and Atmospheric Administration, the effects of acidification are already present in some oyster fisheries, like those of the West Coast of the U.S. According to Luchenco, "You can actually see this happening … It's not something a long way into the future. It is a very big problem."[6]

90% of all life on the planet is in the ocean, a body of water so vast that scientists are only beginning to grasp the full extent of anthropogenic-caused degradation as a result of burning fossil fuels. I must add here that pollution has added to the disaster scenario: Our seas have become a dumping ground for a wide variety of pollutants, including pesticides and nutrients from aquaculture, sewage, industrial discharges, urban and industrial run-off, accidents, spillage, sea dumping by ships, mining, waste heat sources, and radioactive discharges like the Fukushima disaster.

Plastic marine debris poses a particularly severe threat: an estimated 90% of floating debris is plastic which can take centuries to break down. A section of the Pacific (the North Pacific Gyre) is home to the world's largest floating "island" of trash, known as the "Great Pacific Garbage Patch". The polluted area covers millions of square miles in an area larger than the entire United States. Ideas for dealing with this abound but little is actually being done as this is in international waters.

Mankind finds it hard to accept the scientific evidence that the upper 150 feet of the oceans have warmed by a full degree centigrade over the past 50 years and that there are no indications that the speed of such increase is changing. As the water temperature rise, so do the water levels because not only does ice around the poles melt but the water itself expands.[7]

Trevor Manuel, co-chair of the Global Ocean Commission, pronounced that its latest report this month was a "deafening alarm bell on humanity's wider impacts on the global oceans." He contends that governments "must respond as urgently as they do to national security threats." Will our short-term politicians now take heed of the longer-term disaster threatening our oceans and in turn our very survival?

---

[1]Thomas Lovejoy, "Let Science set the facts," *International Herald Tribune*, October 3, 2013.

[2]Fiona Harvey, "Mass Extinction feared over acidic oceans," *The Guardian*, October 3, 2013.

[3]The International Programme on the State of the Ocean (IPSO) State of the Ocean Report. October 3, 2013.

[4]A. Toseland, et al, "The Impact of Temperature on Marine Phytoplankton Resource Allocation and Metabolism," *Nature*, 2013.

[5]See: C L Dybas, "On a Collision Course: Oceans Plankton and Climate Change," *BioScience*, 2006.

[6]Fiona Harvey, "Ocean Acidification due to Carbon Emissions is at Highest for 300M Years," *The Guardian*, October 2, 2013.        [7]"Climate Science," *The Economist*, October 5, 2013, p.12

## In The Public Interest

Posted on April 7, 2014

The ideals implicit in the term "in the public interest," have been with me ever since I left my teens. The writings of John Stuart Mill and the British utilitarians, with their concern about the greatest good for the largest numbers, were at the basis of my original curiosity about this complex social concept. In the early age of television when color was first introduced, I was particularly appalled by the intrusion of commercials and sponsorship in American broadcasting when compared to the paternalistic controls of the airwaves being promulgated by Lord Reith at the BBC. Now there was my role model of an organization being run for and in the public interest.

I must confess that coming from an artistic family, I had little but contempt for banks, commerce, and the stock market (which I regarded as a professional high-stakes gambling den.) I saw corporations as carefully structured legal ways for investors and directors to escape liabilities and all responsibilities except for making profit. And in my mind, a profit by one party always entailed a loss by another. While capitalism seemed a frail system, state socialism as practiced by the Russians seemed to blend control, compulsion and terror. American democracy, however, seemed to hold ideals full of promise but often remiss in the actual fulfilment of commitments to "the public interest."

One of my heroes during that era was the essayist Walter Lippmann who wrote that "the public interest may be presumed to be what men would choose if they saw clearly, thought rationally, acted disinterestedly and benevolently."[1] In his time the term "in the public interest" was central to politics, policy debates and the proper functioning of government. While there was general consensus that furthering the well being and general welfare of the people was a positive goal, little agreement existed on exactly what constituted the public interest.

Another scholar at that time, Pendleton Herring, wrote, "The concept of public interest holds the ultimate ethical justification for the demands that the state makes on the individual. The high value placed upon freedom and justice calls for the readiness of the citizen to make sacrifices if necessary and to share responsibility for sustaining the values of the polity."[2] Indeed, the public interest demanded considerations that transcended the immediate, the selfish and the merely expedient. The collective impulse of human beings and the need for social bonding and community were implicit in Herring's concept of the public interest. The principles of justice, caring, health, education as well as economic interdependence were also fundamentally involved.

I think I reflected that spirit in my first book, *One Viewer* (1959) which examined the violation of 'the public interest' by the nascent industry of that time. I quoted one spokesperson, Richard Salant (who later became President of CBS) to the effect that, "We've let ourselves get pushed into agreeing that the words 'public interest' in the Communications Act really mean that kind of programming in which not much of the public seems to be very interested."

Since then politicians in Washington and London have steadily undermined the public interest by selling a variety of airwaves (which rightly belong to the nation) to corporations and individuals, to the overall detriment of the people. The way commercials began to dominate what Americans saw on their television screens remains both a national scandal and a national tragedy. Other natural resources, such as water, oil, gas and coal, began to be sold by the state to corporations and even to foreign nations. Usually the excuse given by politicians was that the sale helped reduce (temporarily) the national deficit. As a consequence the Chinese, French, Germans and Americans now own most of the water rights and much of the power supply in the UK. For whose long term interest is this?

Today neo-conservatives believe that the public interest is best served when there is none. Some libertarians believe that when the public service is driven by government then authoritarianism or even totalitarianism could result. Both these extremists hold that government should get out of the way of corporations if well-being is to be attained.[3] When it comes to the decline of concern about "the public interest" over the last 50 years, the lobbying and pressure exerted on both Congress and Parliament have come from the legally irresponsible global corporations whose driving motivation is profit. Just about the only demands shareholders of the corporations ever make concern profits (and their gains are always taxed at much lower levels than the earnings of the workers resulting in gross inequalities of wealth) with consequent losses for the state of a nation's common good. There has been increased concern about the evasive corporate tactics in offshore havens to shelter their gains and avoid taxation so instrumental to the functioning of the state in furthering the well being of the population.

So where are we headed? Is profit truly the be-all and end-all of our species? I can't believe we don't have higher social, cultural and spiritual aspirations. That is why I am writing this blog.[4] Like the public interest, our common good is not static. It shifts — both with our understanding and with scientific advances — our attitudes on what is possible, what we as human beings can create. In one word: progress. Continuing technological and scientific breakthroughs in communication are increasingly connected to the demands of the public interest. Crucial elements such as population increase, social inequalities and environmental considerations all have an impact on changes in the public interest. So do such commonly enjoyed services as transportation, water supply and energy distribution. Few people are prepared to sacrifice their current comforts for the potential risks involved in the construction of more nuclear reactors as a source of cheap energy. We now recognize threats posed by Chernobyl and Fukushima. Is it for the Common Good or in the Public Interest to proceed with building more?

Is the continued fervor for "privatization" of the few remaining publicly owned resources truly for the Common Good or is it for the enrichment — as it has proven to be — of a select group of the wealthy? Transportation, education, prisons, health and childcare are all under consideration for private outsourcing. This despite the revelations of Blackwater, KBR and Wackenhut in the US and G4, Atos and other groups in the UK. Many American States (16 so far) have introduced legislation to rein in the reckless outsourcing of public services to for-profit corporations and private entities. This will help to keep taxpayers in control of their services and increase both accountability and transparency. Nevertheless some states like Georgia have been considering such follies as the outsourcing of that state's foster care system. In the UK the practices of miscreant outsourcing groups has proved to be an increasing embarrassment to the coalition government.

There are currently many ideas and groups debating new organizational forms for public services offering alternatives to the current impasse between profit and non-profit organizations. The possibility of such innovation has appealed to the British government and new arrangements have been made for the railway infrastructure (Network Rail) and through high performance NHS trusts in Foundation Hospitals. The government itself has come out in favor of a Community Interest Company to encourage social enterprise in the Public Interest.

The Gubelkian Foundation has assisted in establishing bodies not only looking at the design and potential of such new organizations but also to project the obstacles and difficulties these might face in delivering effective services. These include: How much autonomy would the organization have, including independence from government and political control? To what extent could the public purpose of such an organization be assured? Could private profit be made from its public service? Who would own the assets of the organization and how could these assets be disposed of? Who would be responsible for the direction and probity of this body? How would it raise capital to provide its service to greater numbers of groups or people? Indeed, how would efficiency be determined and achieved? The range and scope of these crucial questions is impressive indeed.

In democracies, the private-interest view of government assumes that politicians want to be elected (or re-elected). This is the public sector equivalent to the private sector assumption that businessmen try to maximize profit. Further, just as businessmen must respond to customers, and thus often are forced to do those things that the customers want, so politicians must respond to voters. This need to respond to voters has led politicians to enact socially beneficial programs which are sometimes greater than the economy can support. Following a decade of rather excessive spending by the Labour government, the aim of George Osborne at the Treasury has been to drastically reduce spending. The UK has cut public services by 8% since the coalition came to office but plans for the future are that the cuts by 2018 will total a reduction of 20% in eight years. The adverse affects of this will be on all but the richest and are unlikely to be 'in the public interest.'

As opposed to the public-interest economic view, the **private-interest** of economic theory holds that those who are involved in government have the same motivations as those in the private sector; that is, they are motivated by a narrow concept of self interest: wealth, fame and power. If what is in the public's interest is also in the private interest of government decision-makers, the public interest will be served. If there is a conflict between the public's interest and the private interest of governmental decision-makers, the public's interest will lose. It is the incentive structure that determines behavior, suggest these economic theorists. A poor performance by government indicates a bad incentive structure, not a problem with motives.

Even if we know everything and the rules for it, to paraphrase Wittgenstein, "the public interest" remains a puzzle. It has been called "the central concept of a civilized polity. Its genius lies not in its clarity but in its perverse and persistent moral intrusion upon the internal and external discourse of rulers and ruled alike." Thus, as a value-laden concept, "the public interest" is to be much admired for its utility as a myth. I recognize it as more than just that: I view it as a basic recognition of our interdependence which encompasses the scope and diversity of our humanity for the good of our species in the years ahead.

---

[1]Walter Lippmann, *Essays in the Public Philosophy*, (1955) p.42

[2]Pendleton Herring, "Public Interest", *Encyclopedia of the Social Sciences*, (1968) Vol.13, p.171

[3]Marcus G. Raskin, *The Common Good*, (1986) p.24.

[4]Yorick Blumenfeld, *Dollars or Democracy*, (2004)

[5]Stephen K. Bailey, "The Public Interest: Some Operational Dilemmas" (1962)

## Outsourcing Part I: Security

Posted on May 14, 2014

When a single individual can expose the contents of an entire secret, hidden and somewhat illicit intelligence network involving different agencies, corporations and separate government departments, it is easy for some of my patriotic but naïve friends, as well as a vast number of politicians, to focus the blame on that scapegoat 'traitor.' The real challenge is not to punish the wrongdoer but to recognize that the problem is much larger: it is systemic. It encompasses not only the whole intelligence community but our security. As an extremely well-researched article in *Vanity Fair*[1] made clear to me, not only has a lateral, "dark" intelligence network developed, but also, while one level of operations is driven by the critical security needs of government, another, which has been outsourced and privately owned, is also driven by money and profit.

Tackling such a large subject in one relatively short blog was overwhelming, so I have divided it into three separate submissions: The first deals with the overall challenges of outsourced and privately owned security, the second is focused on the operations of one of the largest of these secretive groups, and the third concentrates on the associated but curiously parallel security operations of the privately owned prison industry. Government outsourcing of security now encompasses such diverse areas as Information technology (IT), border controls, prisons and intelligence gathering. A few of the larger outsourced security groups, like Serco and G4S that are involved in our protection, hire thousands of public servants to work in their private, for-profit endeavors.

I will be asking three basic questions:

- Is outsourcing government functions to privately owned groups the way to make the state and its inhabitants more secure?
- Does outsourcing security save money for the state?
- Who actually benefits from the outsourcing of security?

The annual spending of billions of dollars and pounds on outsourced security is not being seriously examined in neither the United States nor the UK. In large measure this is because there is an ethical and political as well as economic division between those who fear and deplore "big government" and those who believe that an efficiently run government – irrespective of its size – can provide effective security for the nation. Another factor not often considered, is that outsourcing to private corporations provides those in government, and in particular the intelligence groups like the CIA and the NSA, with an easy way out of responsibility or being held to account.

There are also those ideologues and politicians in Wall Street and the City (of London) who want government to falter so that private enterprise (read: profits) can take over. There appears to be no limit to Republican machinations in Washington to privatize governmental functions regardless of the risk and danger this might pose for the nation. Republican strategy entails starving the governmental agencies of resources so as to give the impression to the electorate that agencies like the EPA (Environmental Protection Agency) are failures. They want to convince voters that everyone would be better served by private enterprise. Ergo: outsource security.[2]

In large measure outsourcing governmental functions is a considerable source of wealth for those with political connections like the Carlyle/Booz group (to be examined in the next blog), for the vast network of lobbyists, the huge corporations like IBM and Dell, and the ever growing group of security operators like Serco and G4S in both the US and the UK. Little attention is paid to the fact that 70% of the entire US intelligence budget is spent on hiring private contractors. And here we are considering billions of dollars. According to the *Washington Post*, just the NSA's 'black budget' (allocations to covert operations) is over $10 billion (£6 billion). The private companies that have been outsourced by the government's intelligence agencies vastly increased in numbers and in profits after the terror attacks of September 11, 2001.

"Especially since 9/11, the NSA has increasingly outsourced much of its core mission, relying on private contractors to do the dirty work of government," said a former employee of the agency and a Booz Allen Hamilton contractor. Edward Snowden, who worked for the same contractor said in an interview for a German television channel that 'Anyone who has the skills – who can convince a private company that they have the qualifications to do so – will be empowered by the government to do that; and there's very little oversight – there's very little review."

Many companies were involved in building the NSA and CIA's internal telephone and computer networking systems, their data networks, and expanded into operational areas which had not previously been open to outside contractors. They included SAIC (Science Applications International Corporation), L-3 Communications, Northrop Grumann, Lockheed Martin, Palantir, Raytheon Intelligence and Information Systems, Narus, The Analysis Corporation, Verizon, Boeing Integrated Defense Systems, Serco and many others who played a role in the 'shadow' NSA and its new surveillance operations like Muscular, Prism, ThinThread and Trailblazer. These were all part of a legally questionable metadata collection program.

While allowing its own workforce to slowly atrophy, the government was all too willing to outsource to private contractors much of the security operations for which it used to be responsible. The result was minimal oversight. The development of closely-knit financial relationships between the NSA and its contractors extended to a 'revolving door' where former spooks became CEO's of surveillance companies and the executives of private contracting firms who held top-secret clearance landed high ranking jobs with NSA.[3] However, the increasingly convoluted history of the intertwined relationship in security matters between the private and governmental sectors was kept largely hidden from the public until exposed by Snowden.[4]

END PART 1

---

[1]Suzanna Andrews, Brian Burrough and Sarah Ellison, "The Snowden Saga," *Vanity Fair*, May 2014 p.158

[2]Richard McGregor and Geoff Dyer, "Too much information," *Financial Times*, November 2, 2013

[3]David E. Sanger, "NSA Nominee," New York Times, March 12, 2014, p. A18

[4]Glenn Greenwald, "They have gone too far," *The Guardian*, June 8, 2013, p.7

## Outsourcing Part II: Privately Operated Intelligence

Posted on May 20, 2014

The privatization of government functions, like the airwaves, the post office, water, and health care has disturbed me for decades and was at the core of my book, Dollars or Democracy (2004). However, I never even considered the privatization of portions of the national intelligence services. Now it turns out that spying on anyone and everyone for profit is something that unaccountable, privately owned corporations have been doing for years.

At the forefront of these high technology outsourcers who were getting large contracts from the National Security Agency (NSA) was a secretive intelligence group called Booz Allen Hamilton. (BAH). This elusive outfit, which was concerned with the improvement of surveillance equipment, also served as a guide and training ground for the Intelligence Community's revolving door interchange of high ranking government positions. My curiosity was aroused by how BAH managed to achieve this special position in Washington's restricted intelligence community.

Booz Allen Hamilton (BAH) was founded in Chicago one hundred years ago by three businessmen who gave the firm its name. In 1940, after almost three decades of consulting for such major companies as Goodyear Tire and Montgomery Ward, its management contractors were called in to help the vast restructuring of the US Navy after the Japanese attack on Pearl Harbor. As patriotic contractors, BAH prided themselves for soon having a representative in each of the Navy's many wartime departments. This infiltration of contractors was to set the pace for its future defence work in intelligence and national security.

As the cold war intensified after WWII, BAH became increasingly involved in intelligence matters. It hired a dazzling board of former CIA and security officials forging strong links with the intelligence community and its military defence clients. The company gradually involved itself in virtually every aspect of intelligence gathering.

By the summer of 2001 it had become an important external consultant of the National Security Agency (NSA) with its advisory role in the integration of internal communications systems called Project

Groundbreaker. This position enabled BAH to capture a flood of intelligence contracts in the aftermath of the 9/11 attacks. Christopher Ling, a BAH vice-president said later, "An entire analytic production system geared to detect large-scale cold war adversarial capabilities was suddenly required to transform." The budgets for outsourcing grew dramatically in the Bush administration, which felt it essential to reshape the NSA's covert communications capabilities without attracting the attention of the media or the public.

BAH's strategic role also changed. A CIA operative, Joan Dempsey, said: "I like to call Booz Allen the shadow intelligence community" because it has "more former secretaries of this and directors of that" than any government department. On its website BAH described its intelligence work as integral to its broadening expertise in information technology: "Whether dealing with homeland security, peacekeeping operations, or the battlefield, success depends on its ability to collect, safeguard, store, distribute, fuse, and share information." BAH did not mention its equally important ability to cover up, hide, or even on occasion, to distort.

The more security was outsourced the more difficult accountability became for those overseeing intelligence in the US Congress. Increasingly BAH had become crucial in advising top officials on how to integrate the 16 agencies within the American Intelligence Community (IC). Questions began to arise from members of Congress about who was really in charge of any given operation: The head of the government Agency or Department, the managers of operations, the contractors or the highly trained and skilled workers/operatives? Rep. Henry Waxman (D-CA) chairman of the House committee on Government Oversight, charged in 2007 that BAH had a significant conflict of interest over its contract to oversee an $8 billion initiative to Secure America's borders with Mexico and Canada by means of a "virtual fence" of cameras, radar, satellite observation and sensors that would transmit imagery and data to border patrol agents. At the hearing, Rep. Waxman pointed out that although 98 people had been hired to oversee the contract, "the problem is that 65 of these people don't work for the government, they work for the contractor (BAH). You're relying on them to do the function that the government ordinarily would do." The Department of Homeland Security official responded by asserting that BAH had been hired for advice not oversight.

Early in 2007 BAH also began to work on the Cryptographic Modernization Program, one of the most important intelligence initiatives of the final years of the Bush administration. By the end of 2007 BAH, owned and run by a group of 300 vice-presidents, had become a key adviser and prime contractor to all of the major U.S. intelligence agencies. Most of these BAH executives had deep experience in the intelligence community and had even begun to serve as a training cadre for senior positions when they got back to government.

These board members all gathered at company headquarters in McLean Virginia in the late autumn of 2007 for an extraordinary two day meeting at which the vice presidents signed off on a "new strategic direction" which involved separating BAH's commercial and government units into two separate private companies. It therefore came as something of a surprise, after its efforts to shed its image as an equity firm specialized in defence, to learn that the Carlyle Group, a flourishing private investment firm, had bought a majority stake in the intelligence branch of the now divided Booz Allen Hamilton firm for $2.5 billion. The Carlyle unit retained the name of Booz Allen Hamilton and each of its Vice-Presidents was reportedly rewarded with the equivalent of more than a million dollars in cash, shares, or dividends.

Carlyle, which had been launched barely two decades earlier by four enterprising fundraisers, had already gained status as an asset management firm specialized in acquiring businesses related to the defence industry. Using its powerful political as well as economic connections, Carlyle completed the acquisition and resale of various military electronic systems in the early 1990s. Its most notable defence industry investment came in 1997 with the $850 million acquisition of United Defence Industries which it then sold in stages until April 2004 when it started to downplay its focus on defence industry investment which, in effect, had been turning secretive government work into private profit..

BAH today is part of the internationally diversified Carlyle group where it continues to make large profits of close to $3 billion in government intelligence contracts it lands every year. The strategically created toxic brew of secrecy surrounding the intertwined activities of BAH, Carlyle and the National Security Agency were exposed by the intelligence revelations of Snowden a year ago.[1]

As evidence of BAH's close relationship with US administrations, Obama's chief intelligence official James R. Clapper Jr. is a former Booz Allen executive. The executive who held that position in the Bush administration, John M McConnell, now works again as a director of Carlyle's BAH.[2]

When buyout firms like Carlyle, which now has close to $200 billion in assets and offices in more than 30 countries, combine with a firm like BAH, the enforcement of tax reporting requirements inevitably becomes more opaque. The opportunities of executives to create offshore tax avoidance schemes also are easier. Their loyalty to their shareholders exceeds what they might owe to the nation. When private companies like Carlyle's BAH become a substitute for genuine checks and balances on the government's surveillance activities, a nation's security is compromised. When profit becomes the driving force behind its intelligence communications, a nation's security is further compromised. There are those who may contend that capitalism itself is all about profits and that the basic security of the economy – and consequently of the nation – depends on profits. This raises basic questions about what has happened to our values under capitalism and, indeed, challenges our priorities regarding our genuine desires for security.[3]

---

[1]Andrews, Burrough and Ellison "The Snowden Saga" *Vanity Fair*, May 2014, p. 111

[2]Many of the facts in this article were cross-checked on the internet. Hours after I entered the name of James R. Clapper Jr. my computer went into an unexplained spin causing material to be displaced and drafts of this blog to be deleted from my Microsoft file. A chance accident or surveillance?

[3]Yorick Blumenfeld, *Dollars or Democracy,*2004, pp. 165, 222

## Outsourcing Part III: Domestic Security

Posted on June 4, 2014

Outsourcing domestic security is a costly and risky way to "reduce" governmental expenditures on the military, the police, the penal system and even health care. The truth is, as I have analyzed in the first two blogs on national security, that outsourcing is driven in part by the profit motive but also by politicians driven by ideological positions. The outsourcing of prisons, air traffic controls, or even policing military facilities by such giant companies as G4S and Serco ultimately tends to undermine our security rather than consolidate it.

These companies, whose executives are far more skilled at winning highly profitable government contracts than in providing acceptable levels of service, appear ready to take on any activity, irrespective of their qualifications. For example, in the UK an outsourcing group has been offering investors an 18% return on their money on the care of disabled, disturbed, or needy children in residential homes. As the writer Polly Toynbee observed: "Now troubled children are an investment opportunity."[1]

The increasingly contentious relationship between the Police Federation and Prime Minister David Cameron's party has been driven in part by the ever-greater desire to reduce the power and the costs of those doing the policing. London's police force is paying £500 million ($800 million) a year for back office functions which have been transferred to private sector groups. The police contend that their federation has been subjected to a Tory-led campaign of denigration. Cameron insists he wants to "release the grip of state control," but he is in danger of giving up his nation's security to a few firms that may become "too big to fail" and will run out of anyone's ability to control them.

The speed of the outsourcing revolution in both the UK and the US has been phenomenal: Outsourcing deals in the public sector in the UK went up by 168% in the first quarter of this year.[2] The companies involved focus more on the contract they want to win than on implementing its fulfilment. Those hired at the lowest fees available often lack training, skills or the understanding essential for security. Let us look at the growing trend to outsource the penal system in both countries:

The very idea that privatizing prisons, so that corporations can make money from those being incarcerated, seems patently immoral. I am not alone in this: The U.S. Presbyterian Church, the United Methodist Church and the Catholic Bishops of the South have all called for a moratorium on the construction of private prisons or for their outright abolition. (Admittedly, a few people exploiting society's larger social problems for their own gain is also part of the deeper problem underlying the entire capitalist steamroller.) The influence of this for-profit prison industry in the US has now come to be described as the "prison industrial complex." Its power has been attacked by criminologists, economists, religious and community leaders, human rights activists, and even correctional officer unions. The privatizing of prisons has led to a revolving door between public and private correctional institutions which minimizes the usually required disclosure of public-private ties.

Critics claim that private prisons don't save the state money because, like any other business, they try to maximize their profits. This leads to a reduction of essential services within the privatized institution. Staff costs, medical care, clothing and food are all kept to a minimum — affecting the inmates, the staff, and the correctional aspects of the institution itself. Studies suggest that the smaller staff levels and inadequate training at these prisons has led to increases in violence, riots, and escapes. Assaults on guards by inmates were almost 50 per cent more frequent in private prisons than in government-run ones, according to a nationwide US study which claimed that assaults on fellow inmates were 65 per cent more frequent in these outsourced prisons. Apparently correction officers may also be in charge of smuggling drugs and even weapons into their prison in order to earn more money. This is hardly the way to improve national security!

A 2014 study[3] revealed that minorities make up a greater percentage of inmates in private prisons than in public ones. Privatizing (outsourcing, in effect) of prisons threatens to re-institute the link between race and commerce of slave-trading days: 50% of prisoners today are African-American, 35% are Latino and only 15% are White. In part this may be because it is cheaper and more profitable to incarcerate blacks than whites! The for-profit prison operators, like the GO and CCA groups, are able to select these lower cost inmates "through explicit and implicit exemptions written into contracts between these private prison management companies and state departments of correction."

Perhaps one of the most corrupting aspects of the private prisons in the southern states is the historically racist practice of "Convict Leasing." The historian Alex Lichtenstein pointed out that "only in the South did the state entirely give up its control to the contractor; and only in the South did the physical "penitentiary" become virtually synonymous with the various private enterprises in which convicts labored."[4]

Cindy Chang, a reporter for *The Times–Picayune* wrote in May 2012 that Louisiana now had the highest per capita incarceration rates in the world. The hidden engine behind the state's growing private prison machine has been profit. A majority of Louisiana inmates are housed in for-profit facilities which must be supplied with a constant influx of human beings or the prison industry in Louisiana would go bankrupt. If inmate counts fall, profit is reduced and the state's powerful prison lobby ensures this does not happen by thwarting nearly every reform that could result in fewer blacks being convicted.

Meanwhile, Louisiana's prisoners subsist in dire conditions. Each inmate is worth about $25 a day in state money and sheriffs trade them like horses, loaning any surplus inmates to colleagues whose prisons may not be not full. Thus a prison system that leased its convicts as plantation labor in the 1800s has come full circle and is again a nexus for profit. This is a national disgrace. In the past two decades, Louisiana's prison population has doubled; costing taxpayers billions while New Orleans continues to lead the US in homicides.

This sordid account shows how public officials profit from prison privatization as it allows them to act with minimal accountability. It also reveals that private prisons do not make those that vote for them more secure. A 2011 report by the American Civil Liberties Union pointed out that private prisons are more costly, more violent and less accountable than public prisons and contribute significantly to the extraordinary increases of incarceration in the US.

Among the leading players in providing a wide scope of outsourced security is Serco with 120,000 workers in the US, the UK and 37 other countries. Serco has more than £4 billion in contracts with Britain's Ministry of Defence. It jointly runs crucial security operations at Britain's nuclear weapons facility at Aldermaston, trains pilots for the RAF in Lincolnshire, manages the UK's ballistic early warning system on the Yorkshire moors, monitors traffic on England's motorways as well as much of its air traffic control.[5]

However, Serco is still dogged in the UK by revelations that it had billed the government for electronically tagging prisoners who had died, were back in jail or did not exist. For this security "lapse" it had to repay around £70 million ($110 million) to the government. Britain also cancelled the projected privatization by Serco of three Yorkshire prisons. Serco's latest embarrassment has been the way it tried to keep secret allegations that one of its male care workers at Yarl's Wood, Britain's largest immigration detention center for women, had sexually assaulted a Pakistani. Lawyers for Serco, arguing for keeping the story out of the public sphere, insisted there was a public interest in not disclosing the confidential report on the case.[6]

G4S ("S" standing for the controversial Securicor Corporation) is the principal outsourcer in the UK, where it employs 45,000 workers out of a global total of some 650,000. Its last minute failure to provide sufficient security guards to patrol the 2012 Olympics in London, forcing British armed servicemen to be brought in as replacements, badly stained its reputation and that of the surveillance industry. It is significant that three of G4S's top executives in the UK have departed in the past two years over scandals which have rocked the world's biggest security firm. Keith Vaz, chairman of the House Affairs select committee in Parliament said, "We should not be giving out contracts to companies that have let the country down."

The larger question is: Does any government really need to outsource the security of the nation and its inhabitants? My answer in these last three blogs is a loud "NO!" Security matters should be out of bounds for outsourcing companies. There are powerful political groups in both the US and the UK that are driven by the belief that private is always better than public and have persistently denigrated the basis of public service.

These forces, like the right wings of the Republican Party and of the Conservative Party, are also motivated by the fact that there are substantial profits to be made by outsourcing and almost none in maintaining an effective public service. In conclusion: outsourcing security has meant higher costs to the taxpayers, substantial profits to the outsourcers, and less security and worse service for the state. The time has come to end it.

---

[1]*The Guardian,* May 13, 2014, p.29

[2]The Arvato UK Quarterly Outsourcing Index.

[3]Holland, Joshua "Higher Profits Explain Why There Are More People of Color in Private Prisons," *Moyers & Company,* February 7, 2014

[4]Lichtenstein, Alex, *Twice the Work of Free Labor: The Political Economy of Convict Labor in the New South',* Verso Press, 1996, p. 3

[5]Jill Treanor, "Outsourcing," *The Guardian*, May 2 2014, p. 35

[6]Mark Townsend, "Serco," *The Observer*, May 18, 2014, pp. 8-9

## Is Order to be Created along the Western Image?

Posted on November 24, 2014

The peoples of this planet desire both peace and order, but we have become gridlocked in our thinking about how to achieve this: The European and North American nations have simply assumed that the world would naturally adopt westernization as the way forward; Islam has been locked for over a thousand years in its faith that the Koran is the only way for global unity and peace; and the Chinese have traditionally viewed themselves at the center of civilization. How to proceed? The outspoken Indian writer, Pankaj Mishra, has observed that many now doubt "that western institutions of the nation state and liberal democracy will be gradually generalized around the world, and that the aspiring middle classes created by industrial capitalism will bring about accountable, representative and stable government. In short, that every society is destined to evolve just as the west did."[1]

The evaluation of this educated scholar demands a careful examination of both how the current state of global disorder has come about and why "westernization" is not necessarily the answer. Many nations are still eager to catch up with the living standards of the more advanced states in Europe and North America and peoples of divergent cultures are being swayed by the external pressures to make them conform to an alien socio-economic outlook.

Can states like Nigeria, Myanmar, Pakistan or Thailand overcome the inner contradictions incorporated in nationalism, democracy, globalization, and economic instability? Its populations do not accept the driving force of western "rules" for the world, namely market capitalism, with its impact and outlook on time, speed, way of life, as well as on work, energy and pollution of the environment. They see this economic system being imposed on them as very much at odds with their local as well as traditional social and political structures. Some also fear that the era of rapid growth may now be at an end and that consequently they may be on the edge of a descent into chaos.

Even members of the more "advanced" societies find it difficult to accept that our "humanism" and civilization have been founded on the back of centuries of wars, conquests, slavery and the exploitation of peoples and resources. There is concern that, with its emphasis on human rights, as well as on equality and democracy, "westernization" cannot be something that can be exported effectively with swift results. Cultural and political concepts such as legal frameworks, rationality, democracy, constitutions and legitimacy, when combined with economic forces such as increasingly freer trade, have taken centuries to develop.

The United States, ever since its inception, has been at the forefront of spreading democratic principles. With great insight, the fathers of the American Revolution instituted the separation of church and state. From the first, Americans believed the world would progress if it could follow or emulate its example. Theodore Roosevelt was the first President to deal systematically with both the responsibilities and implications of America's increasing world role. He declared that when it came to interference in Latin America: "All that this country desires is to see the neighboring countries stable, orderly and prosperous."

Woodrow Wilson went further in expressing this desire when declaring war against Germany in 1917, saying: "We have no selfish ends to serve. We desire no conquest, no dominion ... We are but one of the champions of the rights of mankind." President Wilson's outlook was in tune with the aspirations of an electorate of diverse migrants eager to spread democracy beyond its borders. Since the end of WWII, Presidents have insisted that the United States had global interests while most other countries merely had national interests. Former Secretary of State Henry Kissinger, in his latest book *World Order*, defined the "American Consensus" as "an inexorably expanding cooperative order of states observing common rules and norms, embracing liberal economic systems ... and adopting participatory and democratic systems of government."[2]

Such a position is diametrically opposed to that of the Muslim world. There is no "Islamic Consensus," just an obligation binding on every Muslim to expand his faith through struggle by means of "his heart, his tongue, his hands, or by the sword."[3] This is now known globally as "Jihad." The Muslim approach bypasses that of most western leaders and politicians seeking pragmatic and rational solutions as an alternative to conflict. Islam's universal vision is that the overthrow of "foreign legitimacy" (that is, western legal, political and economic practices) is mandatory. The incompatibility of the western forms of international order with the ruthlessness of Jihad has been recognized by Europeans for over a thousand years.

In Islam's universal concept of world order, which has hardly evolved over the past thousand years, a single divinely sanctioned governance rules and unites all parties that have either accepted the Koran or have been forced into submission.[*] Sultan Mehmed the Conqueror, who proclaimed his people as "the shadow of God on earth," was to declare in the 15th Century that "There must be only one empire, one faith, and one sovereignty in the world." This dictum remains in Muslim hearts to this day. Even the brutal leaders of Isis and al-Qaeda believe that what the Koran prescribed in the building of the social order has been historically tested and is therefore valid and will ultimately bring Islamic unity. How the bitterly divisive struggle between Shias and Sunnis, which has raged for 1,300 years, can be resolved into a united faith remains unclear.

The Post WWI creation of European style secular states in the Middle East, such as Egypt, Iraq, Jordan, Lebanon, Palestine, Turkey and Saudi Arabia, by French and English cartographers, civil servants and politicians was a blueprint for trouble. The leaders of certain tribal factions used the concepts of statehood and sovereignty imposed on them for their own ends. While the "Pan Arabists" continued to view the region as a single linguistic and cultural entity, such as it had been under the Ottoman Empire, the political Islamists saw their common religion as the best way forward in creating a modern Arab identity without having to abandon their historic cultural values, that is, without becoming westernized.

Towards the end of the 20th Century, the excesses and failures of the secular rulers in Iraq, Syria and Egypt led to a more religiously inspired governance backed by opportunistic terrorism for those seeking to fulfil their own universal mission. Groups like Hamas, al Qaeda, Isis, and Hezbollah all regarded the nation state as a secular institution and thus illegitimate. The United States and other western powers tried to hold the artificially created nation of Iraq together when it was really a number of different groupings of Kurds, Shias, Sunnis and others who regarded each other with open hostility.

Christendom, by comparison, has never become a strategy for imposing international order. Christians have made a clear distinction between what is Caesar's and what is God's. This has enabled the evolution towards a secular, pluralistic nation-based international system. Kissinger's endorsement of the Westphalian system of the balance of power between nation states was based on their acceptance as being legitimate units in search of a common creation of order.

Other societies, such as that of China, never historically engaged in the creation of order with other nations. For millennia the Chinese inhabited their own ordered world surrounded by "barbarians" whom they disdainfully dismissed. To this day China does not accept the proposition that international order is fostered by the spread of democracy or human rights. They firmly believe that any international effort towards a balance of power must be combined with the concept of partnership. Order and freedom have yet to be understood by them as interdependent in a pluralistic world.

Our era is intensely pursuing a working concept of a world order (which thus far has been no more than a phantom). National interests have to gradually accept second place to universal interests in such areas as the environment, economic stability, and the long-term future. But it is hard for new nations like India, Indonesia and South Africa to maintain an internal political consensus when faced with privatization of their water and energy as well as the exploitation of their land and mineral resources by foreign companies. Western prescriptions for what is ailing their societies are not appealing.

The EU has already made some progress in transcending narrow national interests through a structure of pooled sovereignty. The EU as well as the English-speaking world have been striving to curtail mounting international chaos by creating a network of international economic, legal and organizational structures dealing with free trade and market capitalism. However, unstable economics now dominate the world, not religion, science, technology, ideology, morals nor even rationality. As two outspoken editors of *The Economist* warn in their latest book[4] the western way is in danger of being left behind. They suggest that it is unclear which political values will triumph in the 21st Century. The battle is between the liberal values of democracy and freedom versus the authoritarian power of command and control.

Indeed, where has western progress led us? It has forced billions off the land into stiflingly overcrowded cities; it is producing such levels of pollution that survival itself has come into question; it is robbing the land and the seas of its resources; and it has produced a scientific and technological revolution which may be separating mankind from its humanity.

Widening voter disaffection in the US, the UK, France, Italy and most democracies reveals that the realities of our disordered world do not match the ideals of yesteryear. Pankaj Mishra claims, "The time for grand Hegelian theories about the rational spirit of history incarnated in the nation-state, socialism, capitalism or liberal democracy is now over."[5] Indeed current political leadership in the western world seems unable to tackle their rapidly growing economic inequalities, the millions of young people without employment and the vanishing prospects of continued growth.

The nations of the world have yet to accept that a long-term strategy based on careful consideration of the needs as well as the prospects of all its inhabitants is essential. We must begin to understand where we want such strategy to lead us and how it could meet humanity's basic aspirations.

---

[1]Pankaj Mishra, "Once Upon a time in the West," *The Guardian*, October 14, 2014.
[2]Henry Kissinger, World Order, 2014, p.1
[3]Majid Khadduri, War and Peace in the Law of Islam, (1955) p.56
[4]John Micklethwait and Adrian Wooldridge, The Fourth Revolution, 2014.
[5]op.cit. Mishra
*Note: "The first deliberate attempt in history to unite heterogeneous African, Asian and European communities into a single organized international society" was formulated by the Persian Kings in the 6th Century BC. (Kissinger. op cit., p.5)

## Whither the "intellectual elite?"

Posted on February 16, 2015

What's become of the intellectual elite? Have they gone the way of stenographers, elevator operators and social secretaries? I look back longingly (or is it just nostalgically?) to the 1960's when intellectuals were concerned with the Civil Rights movement, the nuclear showdown with Russia (climaxing with the Cuban missile crisis), the horrors of the war in Vietnam and the student revolution of 1968. In my bookcases I still keep copies of the *Encounter* magazines of that era: There were marvellous letters of Evelyn Waugh, quality essays by Henry Miller, Jorge Luis Borges and George Steiner (who wrote so brilliantly about language). I also have copies of *Partisan Review* whose editor, Irving Howe, for years was one of America's most respected dissidents. Under duress, Howe's commitment to socialism demanded what he admitted was "a capacity of living with doubt, revaluation and crisis." Those were the days!

The post WWII intellectuals seemed to exude non-conformism, a devotion to a kind of Thomas Paine idealism, and they were possessed by a streak of rebellious embattlement against the conventional politics of their time. Raymond Aaron one of France's more right wing intellectuals of that era, wrote that the theme of material prosperity "fails to give 'meaning to life' and some price has to be paid for it. The individual has the feeling (and it can actually agonize) that in becoming master and owner of nature, man has enslaved himself to an inhuman scheme of things." Aaron recognized that the left did not ignore "the inhumanity of personal relations, the desiccating effect of specialization in the field of work, the alienation of the producer in and by the things that he produces."[1]

Today's intellectuals have not been able to give up sniffing capitalist cocaine. Indeed, what attracts intellectuals in search of a faith? Science? Certainly not a whiff of radical utopianism. In the United States the anti-intellectual triumphs of order and conformism are evidenced by the decline of argument (marked by the taboo of argument at dinner tables), and the popular mass disdain of intellectual analyses. "Revolutionists" or intellectuals who aspire to a purer or better world have almost disappeared. There are narrow experts who are concerned about the growing economic and social inequalities, the environmental threats, the lack of charismatic leadership, as well as such specific global challenges as the Ukraine and ISIS. This reflects the enormous increase in the specialization of function in all fields.

Specialization has narrowed the vision of most scientists, doctors, economists, teachers, researchers and administrators. This has also affected the possibility of existence for the free-lance writer or journalist and that of the non-academic philosopher, sociologist or historian. I write this even though there now are some 230 million blogs available on the Internet. Many of these, like *Amor Mundi* of the Hannah Arendt group at Bard College, could easily be included in the category of any "intellectual elite." *The Dish, a highly professional blog, lists some 230 other blogs which could join most intellectual sets. All of these have their own supporters and enthusiasts but these have yet to be linked under a more comprehensive intellectual umbrella on the Internet.*

The lack of socially committed intellectual elites is accompanied with a distrust of intellectuals by the masses. Part of this is undoubtedly due to the abuse of the socialist ideals by the Bolsheviks and the Russian "communist" dictatorship. The failure of contemporary intellectuals to concern themselves with interpreting society's conflicted heritage or instructing the youth in history's mistakes, or in defining the legitimacy and responsibilities of authority, also should be held to account. The very idea of tradition, which still held sway in the sixties, is rapidly diminishing — weakening the forces which formerly held society together. Meanwhile, the gap between the ideals of democracy and the reality of the ever-increasing power of capitalism continues to grow.

The global expansion of different forms of communication also opens more questions about our roles in society. The challenge of "who is an artist today?" also affects intellectuals. The popular response has become: Anybody. Who can be a writer? On the Internet: Anyone. The Internet is now the keeper of memory and many of the abilities which used to be held by the human brain. The historical community of any period or era was defined by the communication of its intellectuals. Now the question arises whether in forthcoming generations this intellectual community will become obsolescent. As it is, the younger generation is no longer used to asking questions: If they want to find out something they will go to Google or Wikipedia. No reason to respect an elder with a good memory — never mind an outstanding one. The solitude and isolation of the rare, spontaneously individual intellectual in a world of conformist philistines has become ever more evident.

From the social perspective, government by an intellectual elite has not developed since the time of the ancient Greeks. No civilization has been able to produce a Platonic Republic. In his *Republic* Plato warned, "the ills of the human race will never end until those who are sincerely and truly lovers of wisdom come into political power." For the Greek intellectuals, however, social status was the prerequisite of true knowledge and goodness. Almost all their philosophers, such as the Pythagoreans and members of the Academy, came from the aristocracy. The Greek populace, however, treated their philosophical elites with a blend of indifference and humor. Aristotle advised that the philosophic elite, rather than seeking power, should restrict themselves to become advisors to the rulers.[2]

I have always admired the emergence from the Middle Ages of the intellectual elite which flourished in the Renaissance. These were writers, philosophers and artists who were not of one voice but who believed in intellect and education rather than birth or station. Most were distrustful of unproven concepts and despised the prevailing society of corrupt priesthoods, warring aristocrats, rich merchants and an ignorant peasantry. They admired quality in the arts and aspired to it.

While this intellectual elite did much to alter the old order, its leading figures disdained the new world where those with wealth were replacing the aristocrats as arbiters of the social order. Thomas Jefferson, himself an elitist, believed that government should be run by a trained elite and that young men who possessed exceptional talent should be selected from the poor as well as the rich and should receive the highest levels of education to enable them to serve in responsible positions. "Instead of an aristocracy of wealth, of more harm and danger than benefit to society, to make an opening for the aristocracy of virtue and talent, which nature has wisely provided for the direction of the interest of society... (is) essential to a well-ordered republic."[3] This elite should be chosen to run the government, but in no case was confidence be placed to the extent of giving them unlimited power. This was to be a government of the people and not an aristocracy of talented and capable experts. "Our Constitution has accordingly fixed the limits to which our confidence in man may go... but bind him down from mischief by the chains of the Constitution."

Jefferson believed that no one was to be trusted with the powers of government independently of oversight by the people, who were his only hope for good government. However, he recognized that there were many functions for which the people were not competent. That is why they had to choose representatives to whom they could delegate those responsibilities. To this day, there is a sense that the will of the people restrains government by intellectual elites who may disregard that will.

It is feared that, driven by the advances in science in the modern world, elite bureaucracies might tend to underestimate the weaknesses of human character. "The Best and the Brightest" were the intellectual elite of the sixties that gave Americans the Vietnam War and much of the current Welfare System. Although the leaders of this elite were confident of their own abilities, many Americans grew distrustful of their lack of common sense (or character) in controlling national policies. The foreign correspondent, David Halberstam, characterized the White House intellectuals as arrogantly insisting on "brilliant policies that defied common sense" in Vietnam.[4] I believe that American anti-intellectualism was based not on the fear of intelligence but the fear of narrow "brain trusts" exercising undue powers.

The student uprisings of 1968 had the effect of splitting intellectuals into various groups. The "author intellectuals" made a choice to withdraw from exerting direct influence on governance and withdrew into their specialized environments. Specialized intellectuals from the academic, scientific and economic domains started to directly collaborate with those in political power. Harvard's Henry Kissinger and Richard Pipes were to be at the forefront of those helping to guide policies from the inside rather than being academic intellectuals attacking government from the outside.

Notwithstanding Jefferson's efforts, all organized societies are and have been ruled by an elite. A mixture of political, economic and military elites manage our contemporary nations and each of these has its own intellectual experts. The outstanding contemporary theorists on elitism agree that the intellectuals working within the state do play influential and highly esteemed roles. Robert Michels (1876-1936) posited that all organizations were elitist because they were run by a few individuals. The bureaucratic structure of the modern state demanded a need for leaders with specific psychological attributes as well as specialized staffs. G. William Domhoff in his book, *Who Rules America?* maintains that an elite class, not an intellectual one, which owns and manages large income-producing properties, such as corporations and banks, dominates the American power structure politically and economically.

While the intellectual elite is both essential and an adornment for a civilized state, any intellectual elite ruling on its own is not held to be desirable. Brilliant academics lacking people skills most often are inept at such forms of social organization as running the military or the government. Writers of exceptional conceptual capacity may not have any skills in economics or personnel management. As advisors, those with great intellectual capacity are most beneficial. Totalitarian governments, like that of Russia or China, that had first hoped to build a new society by purging all its intellectual freethinking elite, laid the foundation for their own self-destruction.

Intellectuals of the past few centuries have been the ideologists of movements ranging from Marxism to market capitalism. We can only hope that the future stance of the intellectual elite will be of a more civil nature. Moderation has never been one of the manifestations of the intellectual elite.[5] Ideological expression (as dubious as that often may be) also can have fruitful consequences. The creative force of such intellectuals as authors, teachers, comedians, journalists and even bloggers in influencing social change can be surprising.

Will the major vocation of the intellectual elite of tomorrow still be in the expression and pursuit of the ideal? Will they be able to form any kind of consensus, for example, in denouncing the swiftly rising inequalities in society? Will we observe any renewal of "amenities" or "the public interest?" Could there be an effective intellectual opposition to the political extremism of groups like the "Tea Party?" Focus may rapidly shift to the Internet with enormous effects on its expressive social practices. Forms of consensus of the past century may disappear with globalized digitalization.

I see hope in new intellectual figures like Pankaj Mishra, for example, coming from other backgrounds (in his case, the Indian sub-continent) who scan the state of the world and bring together endless connections in a manner which arouses a greater comprehension of the global state of affairs for the reader without necessarily coming to any resolution or solution of the problems being considered. But more must be done to strengthen the intellectual elite as opposed to the economic elite. Civil society institutes, The McArthur Fellowships, TED, *The New Yorker*, The Ford Foundation, *The New York Review of Books,* The Hannah Arendt Center, *The Atlantic*, n + 1, and *Harper's* are just a random sampling of the groups and magazines furthering public intellectuals in an era when the media are obsessed with personalities and entertainment. Of course, academia at colleges and universities all over the world must be at the forefront of the changes which will affect tomorrow's intellectual elite: Perhaps by 2030 there may even be an elite of "Republican Intellectuals." Don't hold your breath!

---

[1]Raymond Aaron, "The exaltation of Folly and Reason," *Encounter*, August 1969, p. 60.

[2]Frank L. Vatai, *Intellectuals in Politics in the Greek World,* (1984).

[3]Thomas Jefferson, *Autobiography*, (1821).

[4]David Halberstam, *The Brightest and the Best*, (1972).

[5]Peter Vireck, Shame and Glory of the Intellectuals, (1963).

## Arousing Empathy

Posted on September 14, 2015

The word "empathy" is increasingly in use following the horrific scenes of Syrian refugee children sleeping on the concrete floors, lost and exhausted, begging for food, and swept along by incomprehensible events. I vividly associate with these young ones because I was in similar situations in France in 1940-41 while my parents were trying to escape from the clutches not only of the Germans but also from the French fascists — not so different from the vicious Hungarian fascists today. Memory and empathy hurl me into the contemporary scenes and I profoundly wish I could save some of the youngsters in the way I was rescued by a humanitarian group.

I remember holding on to my mother for security during our narrow escape from the fast advancing Nazis in France during WWII. It was a harrowing time, but I never realized how close we were to death. I only suffered much later when, during our confinement in a detention camp, I was infected with a usually fatal recurrent fever (which killed many of the children around me.) While interned, I was semi-conscious, lying in a cot for a few weeks and only realizing that I was getting better when I saw the much-relieved faces of my parents.

Family relationships at that age are crucial in the development of one's capacity for empathy. Nicholas Kristof, in his column this week in the *New York Times*, writes: :"If you don't see yourself or your family members in those images of today's refugees, you need an empathy transplant."[1] I suspect that is exactly what all exceptional narcissists, like Donald Trump, need because they spend so much time and energy promoting themselves that their brains have no space for empathy. However, I also wonder whether our feelings of empathy are not being over-stretched by the media and the Internet? It is impossible for us to relate to all those suffering around the globe. Empathy relates to the feeling: "That could be me!" We are presented with ever more distressing images of suffering refugees from all too many quarters. Genuine empathy for those outside our own realm of experience is rare.

Are the multitude of daily horrors beginning to erode our capacity for empathy?

In the first week of September, a "roving" Empathy Museum opened in London, dedicated to helping visitors to develop their capacity to put themselves into the shoes of others. Roman Krznaric, its founder and cultural thinker, believes that empathy can be a guiding light for the art of living and a powerful tool for social change.[2] Krznaric wants us to rethink our priorities in life and tackle social problems from violent conflicts to everyday prejudice. His desire to create a global revolution in human relationships through empathy is certainly an ideal. Turning the idea of "Empathy" into yet another museum is more problematic. Empathy adds a dimension to our spiritual lives which we can only appreciate as we experience it. Stuffing the idea into a museum is unlikely to enrich us.

Because human nature is so complex, individuals do not respond uniformly to the same set of circumstances. Consequently, empathy must be seen as a set of constructs rather than a single unipolar social response. The English word is derived from the classical Greek word 'empatheia', which incorporated both passion and suffering.[3] It has a number of differing definitions ranging from having a desire to help others and caring for them, to having emotions that somehow match those of another being. The word can also incorporate the way we reduce the differences between the self and the other. It can also discern what another may be experiencing.

Empathy is distinct from pity, compassion, and sympathy. Pity is "feeling sorry" for another who may be in trouble and in need of help. Compassion and sympathy incorporate feelings of concern *for* another, of shared humanity. In empathy the feelings are "with" another in a spontaneous sharing of affect. We may be mirroring the emotional state that another may be experiencing. It is important to accept that empathy is always a distinctly positive and sympathetic relation. Empathy leads to altruistic action and to sympathy and is never turned off by extremes of another's distress. Empathy is one of the deep ways we connect with others, saying:" We are in sync." Alas, not all of us are capable of feeling and sharing another's emotions.

Our ever-increasing understanding of the nature of empathy started in the research of psychotherapists and now encompasses the expanding explorations of molecular neurology. Carl R. Rogers pioneered research in effective psychotherapy in mid-20th century. This led to promoting empathy for those helping patients in care. Today neuro-empathy has become a growing field with neurologists examining its functioning in the brain. Laboratory measures of empathy show that mirror neurons are activated during the arousal of sympathetic responses. Yes, the researchers believe empathy can be re-enforced; that we could become more empathic.

The issue of gender differences in empathy is also being examined. On average, women score higher than males on what is known as the "Empathy Quotient" (EO.) Research suggest that we are more willing and able to empathize with those most similar to ourselves, in particular when it comes to gender but extends to those with similar socio-economic backgrounds. Women have found that empathy promotes their social relationships and permits them to relate more intimately with others. Effectively, empathy plays an important role in raising their children. The actress Judy Garland affirmed this ability to relate when she said: "Wouldn't it be wonderful if we could all be a little more gentle with each other, a little more loving, have a little more empathy, and maybe we'd like each other a little bit more."[4]

Women have been more frequent readers of novels than men and as Barbara Kingsolver has written, "Good fiction creates empathy,. A novel takes you somewhere and asks you to look through the eyes of another person, to live another life." Fictional characters can become almost as real as the thoughts of the reader. The ability to situate yourself in the position of the character in a novel is a sophisticated imaginative process, but it can be improved through reading and unconsciously enhanced.

Both sexes recognize that eye contact is important in augmenting our feelings of empathy. As Henry David Thoreau observed: "Could a greater miracle take place than for us to look through each other's eyes for an instant?" We seem to make a corresponding immediate connection between the tone of voice and the inner feelings of the speaker. This is evident in the way we react to the characters portrayed in theatrical performances. "Our job as actors is empathy," said Natalie Portman.

"Our job is to imagine what someone else's life is like. And if you can't do that in real life, if you can't do that as a human being, then good luck as an actor!"[5]

Not all of us are capable of such positive emotions as empathy or gratitude. Research has shown that people with Asperger's syndrome often have problems understanding the perspective of others. Reduced emphatic concern also is frequently evident in those on the autism spectrum. Prof Simon Baron-Cohen of Cambridge University has studied the phenomenon extensively and suggests that those with classic autism often lack both cognitive and affective empathy. Hostility can also develop through a lack of regard for another's feelings. Perhaps, instead of resorting to anger or bullying, those suffering from a lack of empathy should be encouraged to "walk a mile in another's shoes" and learn to relate to the challenges facing the other.

"If it is not tempered by compassion and empathy, reason can lead men and women into a moral void," wrote that incisive thinker Karen Armstrong.[6] The problem with David Cameron, the Prime Minister, is that he continues to put political tactics and terrorist threats ahead of any feeling of empathy he may have in dealing with the tragedy of millions of refugees fleeing from the brutal civil war in Syria. This attitude towards desperate asylum seekers will not serve him well. Politicians are well aware that a manifest lack of empathy is generally regarded as an antisocial form of behavior, while the unselfish, pro-social behavior of those with empathy is generally applauded.

The philosopher Iain King has been using empathy as the basis for a system of ethics.[7] He reasons that empathy is the "essence" or "DNA" of right and wrong. For King, "Empathy for others really is the route to value in life." He believes that moral motivation should stem from the basis of an empathic perspective. "I feel your pain," is one of the ways we express our desire to respond to another's needs.

"Not even one's own pain weighs so heavy as the pain one feels with someone, for someone, a pain intensified by the imagination and prolonged by a hundred echoes," wrote the novelist Milan Kundera in his memorable novel, *The Unbearable Lightness of Being*. I believe that considering matters from another's perspective is crucial to one's identity as a human being. Empathy's influence extends beyond relating to another's emotional state; it transforms us into an active mode of helping or aiding another. That must be at the core of resolving the asylum crisis now facing all of us.

---

[1]Nicholas Kristof , "Refugees who could be us," *The New York Times* (International), September 7, 2015

[2]Roman Krznaric, *Empathy: Why It Matters, and How to Get It*, (2015) see: http://www.empathymuseum.com

[3]The Greek term was adapted in the 19th century by two Germans, Hermann Lotze and Robert Vischer, who created the Teutonic notion of "feeling into" (*Einfuhlung*) which was then translated by Edward Titchener into "empathy."

[4]Judy Garland, quoted in *Little Girl Lost* by Al DiOrio (1974) p.9

[5]Natalie Portman, *Inside the Actor's Studio,* in an interview with James Lipton, November 21, 2004.

[6]Karen Armstrong, *Twelve Steps to a Compassionate Life*, (2010), p.52

[7]Iain King, *Solving the Riddle of Right and Wrong,* (2008).

**Optimistic Directions**
Posted on February 10, 2016

It is hard some mornings to get back on track. Hearing a recording of Louis Armstrong this morning urging me to step "On the sunny side of the street" delivered a powerful surge of optimism. Yes, change is inevitable and some of it is distracting and painful, but the optimistic approach to life remains essential. If we are bent on redefining the boundaries of the possible, as is much of Silicon Valley, then optimism is one defining source of energy.

Martin Seligman, a psychologist who pioneered the study of positive psychology, examined the ways optimism improves the immune system, prevents chronic disease, and helps us to cope with bad news. There is now recognition that changes in the level of optimism can lead to more positive results. It can improve our entire approach to life.

In the twentieth century, parents living in the technologically advanced nations were assisted by the hopeful expectation that the life of their children would be an improvement on their own. Indeed, they had expectations well beyond those of previous generations, but these improvements occurred on such a scale that in many ways they began to transform our planet. Indeed, our outlook now is recognizing the importance of increasing such optimism:

- We are no longer in denial: the gravity of the impact of pollution is finally being accepted and genuine steps, such as the commitments made in Paris in December, are being taken seriously in order to try and reduce threats to the environment.

- Greater economic equality for women is now high on the agenda. Today it is being promoted in much of the world. In areas like education and medicine, women are at the forefront of their professions. Many are now in top executive positions. Hurrah!

- The internet has exploded as a revolutionary agent of communication. It has become the driving force behind globalization, information, understanding, reporting, economics and even education. Its overwhelming power is such that we are not yet able to fully comprehend all the implications. It is transforming not only our lives but our entire culture. Optimists now hope that it will successfully introduce transparency in areas where secrecy has been the rule.

- Capitalism is no longer seen as our economic future. It is coming under increasingly serious attack from the younger generation. This has been demonstrated by the victory of Corbyn in the UK and the vote in New Hampshire for Bernie Sanders. At long last capitalism is being recognized as a threat not only in terms of inequality or jobs, but also in terms of its effects on the environment and its corruption of the democratic process. The young clearly see that capitalism's focus on profits at the expense of morality, ethics, justice, and equality have had serious consequences not only on our political foundations but even on eroding family life. Capitalism's materialism has proved neither satisfying nor sustainable. I am filled with optimism because the aspirations of the young will be at the forefront of tomorrow's impending changes. A more cooperative and less competitive economic system is in the making. I outlined such an alternative, which I described as a technology-driven 'Incentive Economy' in my book *Dollars or Democracy*, (2004).[1] The world will have to learn how to live without capitalism.

Understandably, political 'conservatives' have become increasingly opposed to both the speed and direction of change. However, because of their philosophical outlook — which is about going back to previous stages of our socioeconomic/technological development, they cannot offer any programmed alternative to the direction in which mankind is moving. Looking backward is not the way to move forward. It does not promote optimism. Conservatives see the state as an ever-growing and threatening octopus which will strangle liberty, freedom and choice. As the sociologist Daniel Bell, observed ironically "The nation-state is becoming too small for the big problems of life, and too big for the small problems." Optimists like myself counter that big and small must be brought together in a more cooperative manner.

Technology has advanced beyond nearly everyone's expectations over the past two decades (or indeed over the past two centuries!) It continues to promise unending marvels for tomorrow, but here I contend optimistically that we must not let it runaway at such a speed as to destroy everything we hold dear, starting with ourselves. In terms of our physical and cranial make-up we are genetically identical to our ancestors of 10,000 BC, but perhaps not for much longer. Optimism must incorporate rational thinking. Technology will make genetic modifications feasible in this century. I don't propose halting technological advance, but we must balance it with a vision of a future in which our social and physical structures are not overwhelmed.

There is a strong conviction among free-market advocates that society resembles an organic process with its own life and development. Interfering with such a process could serve to stunt the natural course of events and might end in disaster. My answer to such objections is that I see society much as I see children: with the right education and positive and optimistic approaches there are many ways in which they can be directed. If you encourage them, praise them selectively, and develop their self-esteem and aspirations, they will have a far better chance of achieving their advancement than if you simply leave them to fend for themselves. The same perspective applies for the positive advancement of mankind.

If we look back at how swiftly the world has progressed in the last century, in which the contagious ideals of 'liberal democracy' swept the world, imagine how far we could move in the next two generations if we could accept the ideal of cooperation over that of competitive capitalism. It is possible for us to reconnect our personal desires and aspirations with a larger human purpose of which we are all a part. This means that while we improvise along the way, we also must introduce a more planned approach. (Alas, much of humanity seems to resist the application of any blueprints worked out in advance by thinkers and intellectuals.) Piecemeal or patchwork reforms to our social services have typically led to unexpected problems that have made the systems more difficult and costly to fix. For example, in both the US and the UK, we need a more comprehensive vision of how best to deliver the medical services we need. I am optimistic we can do this.

I firmly believe we can best relate to the world as optimists, not as pessimists, jokers, nor as rationalists or mere realists. The joker can turn things around or upside down with a laugh. Some pessimists may indeed be capable of shrugging-off the worst news with: "I knew this was going to happen!" The realist does not see events in terms of positive or negative and operates with a minimum of pre-set expectations — which can then be met. The optimist can view the world through rose-tinted glasses and will interpret most events from a positive perspective. In doing this the optimists not only believe this will turn things around in their favor but will actually be inspired to make them succeed. The power of optimism is enormous. It helps to counter our fears and assists us in developing essential longer-range perspectives.

Most of us now accept there is a strong link between optimism and psychological well being. This does not mean that it can or should stop us from worrying about threats like environmental pollution, jihad terrorism, or nuclear errors. Optimists look beyond the here and now and accept the need to take action to prevent the worst from happening. When trying to achieve such goals optimism does not always demand success. Optimists accept failures and learn from what went wrong and why. This means, we believe in trying again.

Finally, the strong links between optimism and psychological well being must be exploited: Love, gifts of tenderness, caring, compassion, mothering and understanding are there within us. With every act of kindness and charity, with every virtue, we become stronger and develop. With every meaning we give to expressions of love, we help to make our world more humane. Understanding shown to a child, praise given to a colleague, kindness rendered to a stranger, or a promise kept to a friend, all touch those with whom we are in contact and may in some way uplift them. Ultimately, all such positive acts can assist in feeding our capacity for optimism.[2] Let us all lend a hand in making this happen.

---

[1] Yorick Blumenfeld, *Dollars or Democracy*, A Technology Driven Alternative to Capitalism (2004)

[2] Yorick Blumenfeld, *Towards the Millennium, Optimistic Visions for Change* (1997)

## Optimism versus Pessimism in Our Rapidly Evolving World

Posted on November 4, 2016

Optimism is essential. It starts from a belief in oneself, which gradually extends to a belief in others. Optimism is at the basis of a belief in the future. If the future is to be more than mere hope, it demands an active and engaged commitment in which risk is almost always involved. This risk taking demands self-confidence, and a willingness to take chances and pay the price.

My earliest expressions of optimism were certainly nourished by the influential way it was expressed by both my mother and father. My optimism was aroused by a realization that I could amuse others. My facial expressions could even change the mood in a room. This, in turn, affected me and gave me a sense of confidence to continue. Eventually, such expression of the positive, of hopes, was to lead to a more generalized personal optimism.

But in a world infected by pessimism this was not easy. Escaping from the horrors of a detention camp in WWII and arriving with my family as a refugee in New York at the age of ten could have led to highly negative reactions. Just learning to speak English was both frustrating and exhausting, but the affirmative American diet strengthened my determination to succeed.

Decades later I had gathered enough courage to write my most serious book, *Optimistic Visions for Change*. This did not do much to change the world, but it sufficiently intrigue the Astronomer Royal Sir Martin Rees to invite me to a series of lunches at which he tried to find out more about the nature of my optimism: where it had come from, how solid it was, and what could it lead to. This great scientist truly sought to enhance his optimism about the challenging world in which we live.

The power of optimism is enormous, as is the power of pessimism. It is evident how an optimistic mood in the stock market can spur advances on a broad front while a pessimistic trend can result in a plunge. As human beings we prefer to act in unison with others rather than to cope alone or in isolation. Because this holds true for both optimists and pessimists, it has a strong impact on politics, economics, and our social contacts. We have seen this most recently in the economic consequences of the Brexit vote in the UK and the extraordinary swings in the electoral process in the US.

The basically negative approach by Donald Trump depended on arousing popular fear, hatred, and the desire for revenge, while Hillary took the optimistic path of change for the better. The competition of the two approaches was wrenching, but it is also universal. Writing in the *Economist*, "Schumpeter" suggested that the business world is also divided between pessimists and optimists: "Some of the world's best business people are giddy with optimism. They live in a world of digital wonders where every problem has a solution and every scarcity is yielding to abundance. Others are haunted by pessimism. They live in a world of "secular stagnation", jobless growth, zero-sum completion and stability-threatening inequality."[1] The truth is that pessimists expect their nightmares to come true while the optimists hope for their dreams to be realized.

Ever since grade school I have found pessimism a repulsive social position, but I admit to being intrigued in later years to understand philosophical pessimism. It is true that throughout history the approach of pessimism has had an impact on all trends of thought. However, the scepticism which pessimists hold, that our efforts cannot actually improve the human condition, goes against my most firmly held beliefs. Pessimists contend that every step forward has been followed by a step back and that such oscillation is basically unfruitful. Philosophical pessimists have often turned into existential nihilists who doubt that life has intrinsic meaning.

One of the greatest philosophic pessimists was Friedrich Nietzsche who called his more life-affirming view a "Dionysian pessimism." He developed this approach from the pessimism of the pre-Socratic Greeks which was at the core of their great tragedies. Nietzsche viewed the optimism of Socratic philosophy as an optimistic refuge for those Athenians who had come to reject the overdose of the tragic. To the Socratic proposition that wisdom could lead to happiness, Nietzsche in his *Birth of Tragedy* (1886) responded that this was "morally speaking, a sort of cowardice... amorally, a ruse." To counteract this kind of escapism, Nietzsche proposed a total embrace of the nature of this world, a "great liberation" through a "pessimism of strength" which "does not sit in judgment of this decision." To achieve this status, such "creative" pessimism had to be used like a hammer, attacking the basis of old beliefs and moralities, so that our philosophers could fly with "a new pair of wings." Such Nietzschian pessimism would say "yes" to the forever changing nature of life on this planet and urged us to suffer joyfully while embracing Wagnerian destruction. My reaction to first reading about this was: No wonder the Nazis loved Nietzsche!

More recently, the campaign of Donald Trump made me realize that pessimists generally do not take to facts. Pessimists are likely to see negative events as permanent, pervasive and uncontrollable, while optimists tend to see downturns as temporary and changeable. Martin Seligman in his book, *Learned Optimism* (1990) explained that pessimistic thinkers generally take negative positions to heart. Some environmentalists who, like James Lovelock, are not philosophical pessimists do believe that our planet's ecology has already been irretrievably damaged and that no revolutionary shift in politics can save it. The existence of 7 billion people, all aiming for the comforts publicized on their mobiles, is not compatible with the economy, the homeostasis of climate, or the chemistry and biology of this planet. As Lovelock said: "humans overpopulate until they do more harm than good." His perspective is not far from those technological pessimists who believe that advances in science and technology will not lead to any improvement in the human condition.

While I recognize the pessimism of Lovelock, as well as that of technological pessimists, I have found that being optimistic usually allows me to pursue my own goals more successfully. Positive thoughts help me to enhance the activities in which I may be engaged with a broader optimism. Studies by various sociologists suggest there is a strong link between optimism and psychological well being. A close correlation between optimism and happiness, life satisfaction and physical well being is now broadly accepted. Optimists apparently smoke less, drink alcohol more moderately, and eat more fruit, vegetables, and whole grain breads. As a consequence optimists enjoy increased life expectancy, greater recovery rates from heart operations, and increased success in sports.

Psychologists like Professor Suzanne Segerstrom claimed in 2006 that about 80% of people could be classified as optimistic, but back in 1990 a sociologist, Martin Seligman held that only 60% of people were somewhat optimistic.[2] Both of these were in sharp contrast to past centuries in which only a very few people were able to hope that their future ever would be any better. It should increase our general optimism that in the past generation more than a billion people world-wide have been hauled out of extreme poverty. For those living in Europe and North America, medicine and technology combined to conquer diseases and extend life spans.

I have found it increasingly challenging to evoke my basic belief in optimism in a world steadily being changed by the advancing technologies in robotics, mobiles, computer engineering and bio-genetics. The advances are both undeniable and so fast that they are hard for many of us to manage. Indeed, one must ask whether this is ultimately good for humanity? Optimists still think "yes" but a column in *The Economist* suggested that the sunny outlook which swept in after World War II is now turning pessimistic.[3]

I have to face up to it: Our destiny is no longer manifest. The desirability of advancing from hope to optimism is no longer self-evident. A dreary, somewhat fatalistic and dystopian outlook is spreading around the economically advanced nations of the world. Fatalists purport that as it is impossible to know what is going to happen, we should simply do our best and pray that the worst is not going to engulf us. Spiritually this debilitating outlook tends to erode the potential meaning of life.

For human beings, hope and meaning have become intertwined like the rings of the double helix. The sociologist Lionel Tiger, in his book on *Optimism* (1979), wrote that "As a mood, attitude and mode of perceiving life, optimism has been central to the process of human evolution; it determines to a degree not yet charted to the way humans think, play, and respond to birth and death." Even though we can harbor enormous unease at the way things are turning out, we must have hopes about how things "could be." Optimistically, we should open ourselves to the potentials of a new and brighter vision.

Optimism is frequently criticized because it exceeds reasonable boundaries, but that is exactly what we must do: Take a leap with our imaginations, soar with our hearts, and let what is finest in our spirits prevail. It should give us hope that we can creatively adapt ourselves to change, just as all other existing creations have through evolution. Positive feedback has been one of the very basic mechanisms of life. It should fill us with hope that bit-by-bit, we are unravelling the secrets of the universe as well of biology and that this ultimately will make our own existence more comprehensible.[4] Optimism, however, does assume a belief in programmatic change. To those who deny this, a faith in the potential of amelioration appears unfounded.

In a world of 7 billion people, there will inevitably be a considerable percentage who find they share similar hopes, hold like-minded optimistic visions and who would be willing to take risks and endure hardships for the fulfilment of those dreams — if only they could unite and draw up a set of blueprints and manifestos. Science plays a large role in this. "What man does today and will do tomorrow is determined to a large extent by the techniques that expert knowledge puts at his disposal, and his dreams for the future reflect the achievements and promises of the scientists."[5] And one might add, to the promises offered by tomorrow's robots... but will these ever be able to idealize?

The writer Irving Singer proposed, "Man would not be man unless he idealized, unless he constructed ideals of deliberate and imperative character that guide his life and give it a feeling of urgency as well as direction."[6] In this respect, both pessimists and optimists can use their differing viewpoints to motivate themselves. Pessimists can help people reduce their natural anxiety and to perform better. Pessimists, who may be preoccupied with safety and security, also like to hear what the problems are so that they can work towards making corrections.[7]

I have often wondered why, when so many of the younger generation take euphoriants to improve their moods, governments have not shown greater interest in upgrading the levels of social optimism? Aldous Huxley suggested as much in his *Brave New World* (1932). Indeed, certain contemporary observers perceive optimism as a kind of dopamine which makes us see our own actions in a favorable, purposeful light. It is true that optimists tend to ignore the darker aspects of life and often attribute wrongdoing to ignorance.

My own optimistic vision is that in this new millennium a higher proportion of people could develop their own capacities to a far greater measure. Our hopes may be fragmentary but our optimism must be whole. We must do what we can to further an environment in which our hopes could collectively be transformed into optimism:

> *Whither is fled the visionary gleam?*
> *Where is it now, the glory and the dream?*
> *The Prelude,* William Wordsworth (1770-1850)

So to conclude this blog entry, I will go back to where I started, my own childhood — some 2000 words back! Critics may disparage both hope and optimism because they regard hope as the extension of the predominantly wishful thinking of childhood. Ironically, their rejection of hope then becomes a return to childhood's way of sparing ourselves disappointment. I now see society much as I see the child: with the right education and approach there are any number of ways in which optimism can be realized. If you encourage the child, if you give selected praise, if you develop self-esteem and aspirations, you have a far better chance of achieving your goal than if you simply leave children to their own devices and let 'life' determine their fate. In this context, I find it optimistically encouraging to note how rapidly new generations can pick up an entirely new perspective: Ecology, for example, had hardly entered teen-age consciousness in the sixties, by the seventies it was being taught at the primary school level and today the supreme importance of clean air is finally recognized at a governmental level around the world. Yes, pessimists are moaning that it may well be too late.

---

[1]*The Economist*, January 31, 2015, p.66
[2]Martin Seligman, *Learned Optimism* (1990)
[3]Schumpeter, "Techno Wars", *The Economist*, October 22, 2016, p.64
[4]Yorick Blumenfeld, *Towards the Millennium, Optimistic Visions for Change* (1996)

[5]Rene Jules Dubos, *Mirage of Health* (1959) p. 214
[6]Irving Singer, *The Meaning of Life* (1992) p.93
[7]Abigail Hazlett et al., *Social Cognition* (2011).

**II**

# DRAMATIC PROSPECTS FOR CHANGE

These blogs have not been an exercise in prognostication. I am not a futurologist and do not pretend to know what are the prospects for a calmer, more stable and peaceful world in the 21st Century, much as I might desire this for homo sapiens.

I have long held that there have been two prevailing views about the relationship between human beings and nature. The first was that nature was there to be mastered and exploited, the second was that nature itself was of intrinsic value and had to be preserved. I calculate that it must take less than a century to resolve the ecological salvation of this planet or there will be little left to save.

I have cautioned that the world's population has to stabilize if we desire a greater modicum of security and universal well being.  Towards that end I believe our ethical imperatives should include:

l. You shall leave the Earth in better shape than when you arrived.

2. You shall try to protect the environment just as you would like it to protect you.

It has been said that the real test of civilization is the number of things it takes for granted. The ethic of care transcends economic rationality. Caring for ourselves, for each other, and for our environment are imperative for the sustainable improvement of the quality of life. The forces of capitalist greed and the advance of a select elite must be overcome. However, just because I am advocating a social equilibrium does not mean that I expect that we will actually get there. I do believe that what is important is that we can be energetic in getting "on the way" and "in the process" of such advances. Tomorrow's desires are also likely to manifest themselves in the creative relationship between intimate consciousness and a playful Artificial Intelligence. Even before this occurs in our imaginations, we are just beginning to recognize that our emotional interaction with the wide range of living species may be almost  as important to our well-being as our  relationship with other human beings. Sentiment, shared feelings and personal communion can all play major roles to counter-balance the new world of satellite matrixes, electronic hallucinations, and 'smart' social security cards which now engulf us.

## Creating Millions of New Jobs – Enhancement through Youth Mentoring

Posted on February 18, 2013

I first came across mentoring as a ten-year-old refugee at a summer camp in the U.S. when a councillor took pity on me because I could hardly speak English and seemed totally lost. This young blonde mentor was to guide me through all four weeks of what would otherwise have been sheer hell. Ten years later, in the summer of my sophomore year at Harvard, I myself took to guiding teenagers in a New England summer camp and found the mentoring most rewarding.

Today I am haunted by the knowledge that this global economic crisis is hitting the younger generation particularly hard.[1] Young adults around the world between the ages of 16-26 are finding it hard to find any employment while youths between 10 and 18 are struggling with difficulty to find their bearings. There are no statistics for the 10-16 year olds in terms of what they need, but the Mayor of Los Angeles has said that 600,000 youngsters in that city alone are in dire need of guidance. I believe that in terms of the social wellbeing of any society such conditions are not acceptable. In London, which has also been affected by youth-

fuelled riots, Mayor Boris Johnson, a strong supporter of mentoring programs in the inner city, said on January 8th: "For many, mentoring can have a dramatic and positive effect, helping teenagers turn their backs on the lure of gangs or criminality."

Numerous forms of mentoring exist for business, academia, health and prison reform. My proposal is to turn mentoring for the young people into a job opportunity for the slightly older ones.[2] Mentoring, coaching, guidance and teaching jobs which desperately need to be created for those under 25 are currently being lost. My proposal is to create millions of entirely new jobs for those in need. As mentoring is a form of personal counselling, training and qualifications are essential.[3]

Our young people in the age group from 12 to 18 are bewildered by the worlds opening up before them, are in need of guidance and one-to-one contact. Parents are often too busy or absent and frequently youthful rebellion makes the new generation look elsewhere. Harassed teachers are often unavailable for such personalized attention. The peer group of these youngsters is unhelpful because they are themselves exploring and insecure with a sense of being isolated and stressed. They feel they don't know where to turn for questions regarding their mood swings, intimacy, puberty, sex and drugs. Their issues range from the lack of part-time jobs to the future of our environment.

At the same time, those in the northern hemisphere nations finishing college or university or even high school have a different set of challenges facing them, mostly surrounding work and finding both meaning and direction. In an era when education itself is facing all kinds of cuts and challenges, I believe that a vast program of Enhancement through Mentoring would be a direct way of catering to the needs of both groups described above as well as to the needs of a society which is desperately searching for new ways to create meaningful employment.

Mentoring already plays a major role in the voluntary sectors of the U.S. and the UK. Look at the Internet and there are hundreds of different mentoring groups scattered around our countries catering to all ages.[4] Because by its very definition its "remit' is so wide-ranging, mentoring has not received official recognition. This proposal suggests that to alter the status of mentoring from a voluntary into a state approved one is essential.

In my innovative approach, our young, starting at the age of about 10, would be given mentors to help them in the non-cognitive aspects of life.[5] Yet few of these vital aspects are seldom, if ever, covered in school for so many youngsters faced with the challenges of belonging and identity. All children, even at the pre-adolescent stage, greatly need and seldom receive much guidance and advice from an older person. [6] They often are in search of role models.

Mentoring could be done by all those who have finished high-school (for the younger ones) or who have finished college (to help guide teenagers.) Mentors also could identify those youngsters with special scientific skills as well as those with creative ability and imagination.

Each "mentor" could be paid for this assistance on a commensurate basis including transport and hours spent mentoring. For example those mentoring 6 students for four hours at $10 (£7) per hour could earn $240

(£160) per week. Those mentoring 12 students could earn more. Even a modest program could lead to several million "mentors" being employed and sponsored by the state.

Those kids entering their second decade would see rapid improvements in their self-confidence, determination, self-control, and resilience. They would experience delayed gratification and ways to accept or overcome disappointment and failure. They would increase their attention spans and planning skills. All too many children in the 21st Century are not getting support in crucial areas like character building.[7] The time is truly ripe for a breakthrough in providing such a fundamentally essential program.

All of us must begin to recognize that in the age of the Internet with its built-in remoteness from real human contact, mentoring must gradually become an integral part of the educational systems as they have developed and are now being revolutionized. Al Gore has pointed out in his brilliantly insightful new book, *The Future*, "the resulting explosion of thought and communication has stimulated the emergence of a new way of thinking about the legacy of the past and the possibilities of the future."[8]

The personal, one-to-one relationships in mentoring are often challenging. One recent mentor at an historic private school in England explained how some of the older boys in this establishment were upset that the new guidance being provided to the first year entrants was contrary to the historic traditions of "fagging."(as this hazing is called.) One senior protested that, "I went through it all so why should it stop now, when it's my turn?"

I can hear voices of Tea-Party ilk yelling, "Mentoring? Yet another instance of state intervention when we need less" and "Where's the money for this coming from?" Paying for new endeavors is a subject which I shall deal with in blogs to come. The problems immediately at hand are to recognize the human and educational challenges faced by young people. A launch of such a program would offer vast new opportunities for coming generations. In discussions I have had on his subject it has even been suggested that national Mentor "drafts" could be considered as an approach.

Mentoring of the young has been around since the days of the ancient Greeks, but it has generally been a voluntary activity and not a community or state funded one. My hope is that this blog will help to change the public attitude. Much is being written about mentoring but very little is being done to assist those most in need: the younger generation.

Enhancement through Youth Mentoring thus represents a bold and challenging proposal to help both the young and those out of work. To succeed it will take massive public support and this can come in part through your potentially viral contacts on the Internet.

---

[1] http://blog.euromonitor.com/2013 key-facts-about-global-youth-unemployment.html

[2] http://www.state.gov/i/gyi/

[3] www.mentoruk.org.uk

[4] www.mentoring-uk.org.uk

[5] This would include such specific aspects as: curiosity, memory, expression, persistence, competition, cooperation, efficiency, friendship, patience, endurance, failure and success, concentration, imagination, desire, denial, inhibitions, frustration, efficiency, priorities, accepting differences, risk, respect, self-fulfilment, self-expression, harmony, commitment, sacrifice and excellence.

[6] www.youthmentoring.org

[7] See: How Children Succeed, Paul Tough, (2012)

[8] Al Gore, The Future, (2013) p. 51

## The Future

Posted on February 27, 2013

Al Gore's latest book, *The Future,* is an ultra-sobering work which anyone concerned with the prospects for planet Earth should read. Gore's dispassionate approach to the dire consequences which face our children and grandchildren bowled me over. The world he describes seems bent on self-destruction but also appears to be spinning out of control.

The first 201 pages offer a stiff-upper lip recitation of what is going wrong, not only in America but also in the world. Gore's deeply felt insights of the takeover of democracy by corporate interests in America must be taken seriously. The remaining 176 pages of text address the possible ways of dealing with the environmental calamity facing us.

Gore's coverage of lobbyists and corporations, the growing inequality of incomes and wealth in the US, and even the counter-productive indicators of the GDP (Gross Domestic Product) as well as the lack of leadership and our diminished ethical concerns are all painfully commendable. As opposed to most politicians currently in high office, Gore does not advocate growth as a cure-all. Instead he devotes enormous energy to warn us about the growth of: population, mega-cities, joblessness, pensioners, migrations, robotics, technology, inequality, corporations, waste and, of course, of the increased pollution of both air and water. This is just a partial listing of a torrent of the compelling challenges facing us. These range from increases in obesity (he himself is overweight) to the depletion of topsoil on a global scale.

Although Gore is weak in proposing solutions and in particular in offering us alternatives, there is no sensible alternative to reading his book. Gore strongly urges from the first chapter that capitalism must become sustainable and suggests that to do this the short-term perspective of those managing corporations, banks, and investment must be altered. He writes "the only policies that will prove to be effective in restoring human influence over the shape of our economic future will be ones that address the new global economic reality on a global basis." (p.35) Such words of wisdom are hardly instructive.

When faced with this challenge a decade ago, I wrote *Dollars or Democracy*, and proposed solutions which no one at that time wanted to hear! NPR (National Public Radio) executives refused to give me/or the book air-time because they explained that its radical approach would cause Republicans to further cut the already reduced funds for National Public Radio. As future blogs will explain, my proposal for an Incentive Economy was predicated on the restructuring of all corporations into cooperatives. I also presented a plan how to replace capitalism with a less competitive, less profit motivated, less corrosive and far more collaborative socio-economic system — see: http://www.fdnearth.org/essays/capitalism-cant-be-reformed-try-the-incentive-economy/

A takeover by universal cooperatives would have major consequences: it would slow down the pace of change dramatically. (This is essential because technological advances have moved faster than either societies or individuals can safely handle- and this ranges from nuclear weapons/reactors to the introduction of robots, nanotechnology, and the computer generated age of the global internet.) The commitment of cooperatives to long-term planning as well as to the immediate surroundings of its members, would give a tremendous boost towards protecting the clearly embattled environment. Cooperatives would not put an end to growth, but would effectively reduce both output and the growth of demands. As one can observe in cooperatives like the much-vaunted John Lewis Partnership in the UK, UPS in the US, or Mondragon in Spain, their members share in the profits and are protected in their jobs.

Perhaps Gore, a man now worth hundreds of millions of dollars, can afford to be generous about capitalism in the 21st Century. I am concerned that his wealth may cloud his otherwise sharp vision of how capitalism is perverting the course of humanity. As I pointed out in an earlier work, *Towards the Millennium,* (1996) capitalism was instrumental in taking us out of the feudalistic agricultural era and ushering us it into an industrial one. However, in the over-populating world of 2013 which is hurtling us unprepared into the new era of global communications and nanotechnology, capitalism is no longer the right economic system

I do not view the United States of America as a failed democracy as polymath Gore does. I recognize that it certainly is a struggling one. If the glaring inequalities forced on the American people by the corrupting force of corporate driven capitalism do continue then a systemic economic breakdown seems inevitable. Perhaps that would be a first cataclysmic step towards a Braver New World.

---

Al Gore, *The Future* (2013)

Yorick Blumenfeld, *Towards the Millennium: Optimistic Visions for Change.* (1996); Dollars or Democracy (2004)

Joseph Stiglitz, *The Price of Inequality*, (2012)

**Opposite Sex Economics**

Posted on May 15, 2013

I am writing this entry because I believe women might really be good at rethinking the very basis of our failed economic system. A new approach to resolving our current economic problems is essential. We have to get out of the box into which we have packed ideological economics.

Women endorse a more socially just way of living in harmony with the natural world. They try not to let economic problems rule their lives or dictate their choices. They frequently give voice to greater income equality and sharing. They generally endorse sustainability, a greener economy and embrace life support systems not only for children but also for air, water and land. Above all they are more flexible in their positioning.[1]

Men have proven themselves to be excessively rigid. Perhaps this is just a physiological inevitability? In the UK, for example, David "Bedroom Tax" Cameron has been unable to shift his stance on austerity despite the widespread criticism of economists and the widespread suffering of the population.

Women, as opposed to men, are not opposed to a larger role for the government in managing the economy. They generally do not consider the economy as being over-regulated. But they are troubled by the fact that such an economic power-house as Goldman Sachs has almost no women at top levels of management and at the same time can place these men at the top levels of government and banking not only in the United States but in many other countries as well.

The general lack of acceptance by men of the views of women when it comes to economics is rather startling. Contentious females, like Naomi Klein and Naomi Wolf, both of whom write wonderful books (which I openly admire) analyzing the dangerous direction in which our global societies are moving, are not listened to (or read) by many men. Neither of these Naomis is an economist — they are more into sociology — but both believe the overly intense focus by elected officials on economic policy to resolve problems of population changes, global warming, or growth is not tenable.

Curiously, although open market trading has often been dominated by women and still is in countries like Nigeria, men — starting with Adam Smith — have dominated economics since its very beginning as a dismal science. Back in 1898, the American sociologist and writer Charlotte Perkins Gilman suggested "the economic independence and specialization of women as essential."[2] Gilman proclaimed "When the mother of the race is free, we shall have a better world, by the easy right of birth and by the calm, slow, friendly forces of evolution."

Two generations later, Joan Robinson one of the foremost female economists of the 20th Century (whom I had the honor to know in Cambridge) asserted somewhat cynically "The purpose of studying economics is not to acquire a set of ready-made answers to economic questions, but to learn how to avoid being deceived by economists." Being a devoted Marxist, which caused her to be dismissed by the predominantly American-dominated schools of economic scholarship, she claimed that "The fundamental differences between Marxian and traditional orthodox economics are, first, that the orthodox economists accept the capitalist system as part of the eternal order of Nature, while Marx regards it as a passing phase in the transition from the feudal economy of the past to the socialist economy of the future.[3]

A generation later, Naomi Klein, writing from her outlook as a Canadian observed "A term like capitalism is incredibly slippery, because there's such a range of different kinds of market economies. Essentially, we've been debating over what parts of the economy are not suitable to being decided by the profit motive." She pointed out that in the United States, Canadian ideas on unsuitable areas for the profit motive, like fire fighting, were simply absent from male dominated discussion.[4]

A broader female perspective on our global economic structure has been given by the sociologist Naomi Wolf: "The economics of industrialized countries would collapse if women didn't do the work they do for free: According to economist Marilyn Waring, throughout the West it generates between 25 and 40% of the gross national product."[4]

Christiane Lagarde, as the first female head of the IMF, has said "The financial industry is a service industry. It should serve others before it serves itself." But then she was never an economist. Discussing global finance she has said "left to themselves men are apt to make a mess of things."

The male dominated world finds it hard to accept the logical consequence of such female declarations. Re-directing the economy to accommodate these positions would require more radical rethinking than they are willing to contemplate.

I also want to make it clear that I am not suggesting that women collectively or individually cannot make grave economic errors. Margaret Thatcher was as inflexible as any man. She shifted the UK economy from being a manufacturing and merchandising one into one which became dependent on the banking strength of The City (of London). She also privatized large sectors of the economy such as the railroads, British Airways, British Telecom etc., and crippled Britain's mining industry. The UK is now suffering because of her often brash and narrowly motivated political decisions.

Generally women, unlike men, try not to let economic problems rule their lives or dictate their own choices. They are eager to express their appreciation of joy in life. Perhaps that is ultimately what is most missing in the continuing gray-suited image of all those long-faced males still directing the global mishandling of economic policies. Consequently I am proposing that one of the truly radical economic alternatives open to us is to give women the opportunity to bring a breath of fresh air into the global economic atmosphere.

---

[1] www.fdn.earth.com
[2] Charlotte Perkins Gilman, "The Yellow Wallpaper."
[3] Joan Robinson, *Essays in the Theory of Economic Growth,* 1963, p. 1.
[4] Naomi Klein, *The Shock Doctrine: The Rise of Disaster Capitalism,* 2007
[4] Naomi Wolf, *The Beauty Myth: How Images of Beauty are Used Against Women,* 1991

## Time out

Posted on June 4, 2013

I am disturbed by the global obsession with time. Driven as it is by capitalism, which depends on borrowing time, the pressures exerted by time on us seem overwhelming; our beings seem obsessed by it. Our minds are restricted by the literal ticking of the clock; locked into the irresistibility and irreversibility of time.[1] But difficult as it is to find the minutes to meet my daily commitments, the challenges of time as a construct to be explained by physics have steadily increased.

Such a quandary over time is not new. Human time and cosmic time are our inventions. We created the idea of time in our earliest cultures. Today the most pertinent question might be: what could make us less dependent on time? Meditation? Dreaming? Sleep? Drugs? Or an end to the economic system which prevents us from following an easier and more desirable way of life?

Focused energy has been devoted to measuring time since our earliest records — mostly by priests in such diverse cultures as those of ancient Egypt, China, India, Peru and Central America. The Hindu Vedas, written two millennia before Aristotle, proposed that the Universe goes through repeated cycles of creation, destruction, and rebirth, with each cycle lasting 4,320,000 years.

Many of the ancients held beliefs about time which were based on intelligent speculation: The Incas regarded space and time as a single concept, named **"pacha"**. The ancient Greek philosophers believed that the universe had an infinite past with no beginning. And *The Bible* reads: "A thousand years in thy sight are but as yesterday when it is past."[2]

Two thousand years later time remains a profound unknown, a construct which would appear to be closest to metaphysics. We struggle to understand how time will pass for those cosmonauts traveling in future generations who will age less swiftly than those humans living on earth.

And if speed is the determining factor in this difference, what is the impact – if any – on our own longevity from the high speed at which our planet is spinning as it rotates around our sun which itself is circling around our galaxy?

Modern Science has made notable breakthroughs in measuring time, including atomic clocks, digital time-keeping, calibrating the rate of decay of radioactive material, and discovering the speed of light itself which enabled cosmologists to estimate the very existence of the universe at around 13.5 billion years. I ask myself: Are the photons reaching our telescopes on earth actually the physical leftovers from that "Big-Bang" billions of years ago?

Personally, I remain disturbed by the many fundamental questions which have arisen over the past few decades about time. Not only are there different forms of time: like Cosmic time, quantum time and our Earth-bound time, but in physics and astronomy it is also very hard to specify with any exactitude the time in space-time itself: How and when did time begin? Why is the arrow of time tipped forward? (And, it is speculated, goes backwards in black holes?) Could time be sped up or slowed down, or even stopped? Could time take different forms in other universes? If our universe of galaxies ultimately implodes, might that end time?

The theoretical astrophysicist, Prof Adam Frank, has speculated that if there is more than a single universe, then in this "multiverse" there might not be any time because there might be no universal flow to time in any direction."[3]

Paul Dirac, the great physicist credited with predicting the existence of the black hole, asked the provocative question: "What is time itself?" And astrophysicists and other scientists have been trying to come up with answers ever since. One young student, Julian Barbour, was so disturbed by Dirac's challenge that he spent thirty years pondering the question before coming up with an answer in his book, *The End of Time*.

His ultimate conclusion was: There is no such thing as time. Instead he regarded each individual moment as a distinct unit, a "now", the sequence of which he called "nows" which exist in a Platonic realm where "time" does not exist. Past and future simply vanished in Barbour's vision.[4]

The concept of time as a measure of change was not challenged by Einstein in his formulation of "space-time" into a single four-dimensional entity which was blind to any distinction between past and future. In today's cosmological formulations one must ask which part of the equation that describes space-time is arbitrary? Time is not treated as a separate entity. The implications for basic physics are disturbing for they imply that its laws are not fixed but variable.

In quantum physics particles, such as electrons, have no definitive properties and, strange as it may seem, the electrons can co-exist in many places at the same time. This challenges the very notion of space-time itself. Those scientists engaged in quantum cosmology have gone on to try and explain the entire universe as a quantum object. For example, Stephen Hawking in his celebrated *A Brief History of Time* proposed a model of the universe in which no origin of time appears.

Prof Adam Frank suggests, "by recognizing that we have invented and are re-inventing time, we give ourselves the opportunity to change it yet again."[5]

I would add: That's just like any myth. Most myths are attempts to explain or elucidate our human role on this planet. Alas, the complexities of time seem to make our life passage harder to understand. Frequently the layering and overlapping of the various interpretations of time seem of such a daunting order that, perplexed as I am, I should like to shout: "Time Out! NOW."

---

[1]Paul Davies, About Time, (1995) p. 28
[2]*Psalms* xc, 4.
[3]Adam Frank, *About Time*, (2011) p. 292
[4]Julian Barber,*The End of Time*, (1999) p. 47
[5]*About Time* (2012) p. 319

# Chaos

Posted on July 17, 2013

CHAOS is in the news everywhere: on the internet, in traffic, in the Arab world, banking, the National Security Agency, the Republican party, Britain's National Health Service. The word is being used to describe global phenomena. "Chaos" instantly brings up mental images of confusion, uncertainty and instability leading to potential panic. However, chaos is also the word economists, politicians, and even weather forecasters fear.

For the ancient Greeks, Chaos was at the origin of all things. The word referred to the formless or void state preceding the creation of the universe. Chaos was the first of all the Greek primordial deities. Philosophers like Heraclitus regarded Primal Chaos as the true foundation of reality. Today theoretical physicists as well as contemporary philosophers, agree that metaphysically the creators of this mythology were not that far off the mark in separating void and matter and placing chaos before the creation of the earth itself.

Yes, the irrational, the unpredictable, the totally confused, the unexpected, and particularly the uncontrollable, must be viewed with a certain caution. Of course these aspects of chaos are what makes it completely unacceptable to every control freak in our midst. And these obsessives surround us!

Naturally there can be serious dangers accompanying chaos as well: On the eve of the military takeover in Egypt, a young Muslim in Cambridge told me that he feared chaos because it inevitably ends with the conservative forces winning and restoring the old order.

Physicists recognize that in the "Chaos theory," which is the study of nonlinear dynamics, seemingly random events in complex systems and interactions are often predictable. The French physicist Henri Poincare discovered in the early 20th century that some astronomical systems, consisting of three or more interacting bodies could become highly unpredictable if there were minute errors in the initial measurements. Such unpredictability was far out of proportion with what mathematicians could expect. Physicists have declared, "Fundamental randomness has come to be called chaos."[1]

Two decades ago an enthusiastic prize-winning professor of theoretical engineering wrote with extraordinary enthusiasm: "Never in the annals of science and engineering has there been a phenomenon so ubiquitous, a paradigm so universal, or a discipline so multidisciplinary as that of chaos. Yet chaos represents only the tip of an awesome iceberg, for beneath it lies a much finer structure of immense complexity, a geometric labyrinth of endless convolutions, and a surreal landscape of enchanting beauty … [This] is the omnipresent nonlinearity that was once wantonly linearized by the engineers and applied scientists of yore, thereby forfeiting their only chance to grapple with reality."[2]

Beauty and chaos are seen by some as contradictory, but what theoreticians are after is principles whose simplicity is such that the consequences seem inevitable. We all recognize that there are turning points in the weather, in our lives, and in history. What the chaos theory highlights is that turning points are all about us. The smallest changes can unleash a chain of events that result, most literally, in a hurricane or a revolution.

Order can come out of chaotic fluctuations. It has been clearly established through fractals that there are patterns — there is order in chaos. The fractal geometry inherent in chaos has a clear connection to the harmonious arrangements found in crystals, snowflakes, clouds, flowers, trees and humans.

Computer specialists, mathematicians and physicists working on Chaos continue to seek the natural laws about systems at the point of transition between the orderly and disorderly.

While we all like ordering, neat categories, progressive layerings and rational explanations, the random factor of chaos also is immensely appealing to our complex, divided and interactive minds. Our intellect sorts through the chaos of our perceptions and stores or pigeonholes impressions in the brain with astounding precision.[3]

Our thinking patterns reflect the conflict between our attraction to order, structure and stability on the one hand and our fear of the unpredictability of anarchy on the other. What we don't always grasp is our continuing dependence on change, variation and innovation to enrich our lives.

I think chaos can be transformative. It is really one of the few ways humanity ultimately can sort itself out of its global economic mess. Chaos may be able to triumph where scheming politicians, greedy bankers, and hoodwinked economists fail to come up with the basic changes necessary to create a more cooperative, more equal, more ecologically based and more spiritually aware system. The secret of chaos is that creativity begins when controls break down.

---

[1]Peitgen Jurgens, *Chaos and Fractals* (1992) p. 10
[2]Leon O. Chua in *Chaos and Fractals* (1992) p. 655
[3]Yorick Blumenfeld, *Towards the Millennium: Optimistic Visions for Change,* (1997) p. 87

# Surveillance

Posted on August 6, 2013

Where on this surreal planet is surveillance taking us?

Some three generations ago Aldous Huxley in *Brave New World* and George Orwell in *1984* vividly described nightmarish alternatives which their readers might face in the future. Their warnings and predictions had impact — but these visionaries never imagined mobile phones, computers, nor the Internet.

Today's authors are not providing us with vistas of what surveillance might look like a few decades hence. Will entire populations be tracked? And to what effect or purpose? Perhaps future generations simply won't give a damn.

A while back I had a nightmare in which I was being interrogated by intrusive intelligence agents trying to read my mind via needle-like probes inserted into my brain. Initially I was enormously disturbed during this dream because I recognized that my most secret thoughts could be read, but then I rationalized that these agents would never be able to decode my ability to create new secret thoughts! The secret of my creativity would remain intact. This was a most comforting revelation: the core of my being would remain mine alone. End of dream. Perhaps in the future microchips will be introduced enabling all kinds of transmissions to take place to and from the brain. That truly will be one micro-leap into BigBrotherLand.

The era into which we have plunged unwittingly over the past two decades is one of increasingly intrusive overt and covert surveillance. The new spy cameras already in operation can pick out a face in a crowd half a mile away. Cameras as small as our finger nails are being developed which will make it possible to capture images without being seen or noticed. Our consent will not be asked: the privacy of our encounters will be eroded as we are being recorded in different ways.

When I complain that the swift advance of surveillance technology itself is overwhelming our ability to manage the complex attendant challenges, critics retort that the history of technology shows there is always opposition at first and, as Guttenberg's press illustrates, no one can predict the ultimate social consequences of new inventions.

In a concerted governmental effort to reduce crime and increase protection against terrorism, the UK has spent more than a billion pounds ($1.5 billion) in capital funding for the development of CCTV. The result is that there are 6 million CCTV cameras in operation in the UK — about one for every 12 inhabitants. Only one in twenty of these are to aid the police. Most are used in shopping malls, schools, offices, factories, airports, rail stations, and hospitals. The UK has become the most advanced surveillance society in the world with little understanding of how this will affect all those subjected!

There have been positive results from surveillance: street crime is down, fewer banks are robbed, and even classrooms in the school system suffer from less disruption. There are also great benefits to be had in providing diagnostics in old age homes where the well-being of the residents demand round-the-clock watch by monitor systems. Similarly, monitoring babies through such CCTV cameras is welcomed.

Worrying, however, is the unregulated and ad hoc introduction of CCTV. Indeed, there is not even a clear idea how different private and public CCTV groups can coordinate their resources to best resolve the desired ends.[1]

In the United States the war against terrorism has been used as justification for the ever-increasing numbers of CCTV. Some 78% of Americans polled by CBS News/New York Times said that having more surveillance cameras, which remain relatively rare on American streets, was "a good idea." Their responses came after private CCTV footage from a local shop helped the FBI identify the Tsarnaev brothers who killed three people and wounded more than 200 at the Boston Marathon. Michael Bloomberg, the mayor of New York City, said soon after this that the bombings were "a terrible reminder" of why investing in "camera technology" could be essential in preventing future attacks.

Surveillance made its appearance well before 2011 or even Big Brother. Optical surveillance was popularized more than 200 years ago by Jeremy Bentham, the English philosopher (founder the school of Utilitarianism) and prison reformer who designed the model of the famed "Panopticon." This was based on his belief that if the prison inmates thought they were being watched from a central control tower, they would refrain from violence.

It is most ironic that 200 years later Britain's prisons are one of the rare places without CCTV even though there is a great deal of violence behind the walls. The prison staff don't want to be held responsible for all the wrong-doing on their watch. The former Inspector of Prisons in the UK, Lord Ramsbotham, told me that the reason there is no CCTV in Britain's prisons was that the wardens would go on strike if efforts to do so were ever made to install such cameras by lawmakers.

The arguments ranged against CCTV generally are weak, abstract and emotional as compared to the solid law and order arguments of the CCTV industry and governments. Psychologists tend to point out that the inevitable effects of the growth of surveillance will be to make us, who are being watched, more self-aware and self-conscious. At the same time, "People tend to like CCTV well enough in a public place where it makes them feel protected. But a camera trained on their front gate feels like an invasion of privacy, even if that privacy cloaks nothing more than regular, legitimate comings and goings."[2]

My own perspective on the rapidly evolving surveillance scene is that we are rushing headlong without examining the ramifications or the unintended consequences which our progeny will have to face. Government representatives on both sides of the Atlantic tend to dismiss warnings of Big Brother voiced by libertarians. Author David Brin, analyzing the situation, suggests that we should "adapt with resilience" to the unprecedented intrusions of surveillance in the years ahead.[3] Adapt? To unwarranted unwanted and threatening intrusions? Better to resist, block and undermine unauthorized and excessive government surveillance. Before passively adapting, would it not be preferable to examine and debate the serious challenges that surveillance now presents.

---

[1]See http://www.le.ac.uk/oerresources/criminology/msc/unit8/

[2]"Deborah Orr, "Is domestic violence a private matter because there's no CCTV at home? *The Guardian*, July 13, 2013, p.29

[3]David Brin, "If you can't hide from Big Brother, adapt," *The International Herald Tribune*, July 25, 2013

## Overwhelmed by Data

Posted on September 4, 2013

One of the earliest sayings I can remember is: "Don't put all your eggs in one basket." In the years that followed I learned the benefits of diversification and the dangers of single strand resolutions to many human problems. Now I am frightened how mindlessly we are putting all our info into one gigantic electronic basket.

But how long will the information stored by friends and family, by banks and the tax people, by Google and Yahoo, by the intelligence services as well as such social network as Facebook or Twitter remain accessible? Five years? A decade? 25 years? Unlikely. And what will this do for the historical understanding of future generations? For now this seems of negligible concern.

Ever since the mass production of silicon chips and computers as well as the accompanying development of the Internet, most of those living in the advanced technological nations have focused on both the ever-increasing speed of communications, its use in all applicable areas, and the conversion from different forms of calculation, classification, and storage to labor-saving computers. Most of the younger generation never learned penmanship and many have never written a letter!

The revolutionary consequences of the past thirty years have overwhelmed economics, markets, airline travel, research, information communication, as well as our daily lives. This has led to far more comprehensive and intensive change than the introduction of printing or even the much more gradual transformations of the industrial revolution.

From the globalization of corporations to the globalization of credit cards, the ease of networking communications, and the immense social impact on the younger generation, the scope of this revolution is so overwhelming that it has become difficult for us to digest. "Progress" in the form of hi-tech is moving humanity in so many new directions and at such an accelerating speed that we are at the point of losing control.

Our taxes, bank accounts, credit card transactions, police records (including fingerprints, health records including DNA files, car licenses and driving records, CCTV recordings, NSA and GCHQ spying on our communications, are only some of the areas affecting our lives and which are now dependent on the storage of what is being called "Big Data." Is this new information structure sufficiently resilient to cope with yet unknown threats ranging from intentional sabotage, solar flares or simply the inability to deal with the congestion caused by incredibly rapid growth? Indeed, when will the sheer volume of traffic that all these servers process become so overwhelming it causes a systemic global black-out?

The Guardian (UK), in a front-page story pegged to major computer crashes on the Nasdaq stock market, Google, and insurance companies, warned that "governments, banks and big business are over-reliant on computer networks that have become too complex."[1]

Jaron Lanier, the author-creator of the concept of virtual reality, went further in writing that the digital infrastructure was moving beyond our control: "When you try to achieve great scale with automation and the automation exceeds the boundaries of human oversight, there is going to be failure." (Not only in the breakdown of specific servers but also of entire systems, such as the global stock exchanges and the banking system.)

And there seem to be no boundaries: Cisco the California based manufacturer of communication equipment predicts that in four years it will be possible to transmit in a three-minute burst over the internet the data equivalent to all the films ever produced.

At the same time, greed, as evidenced by the extreme demands of high-frequency computer trades of shares by hedge funds and banks, is triggering ever more mini-crashes on the stock markets. In May 2010 one such incident following a false report caused close to a trillion dollars to be erased in 20 minutes from the value of US shares. (Most of this was swiftly recovered.) Once a stock fell to an automated "Sell" level, it was impossible to halt all the other computers from executing their sell commands and across-the-board selling spread with lightning speed.

Amazon, Google, Yahoo, and such social sites as Facebook, Flicker, and Twitter, all need to process and store immense quantities of data. Twitter alone has to grapple with 500 million tweets a day! When glitches occur, and this seems inevitable, the "dirty" entities — sometimes simply garbled or confused ones and occasionally intentionally corrupting ones from hackers or alien sources, such as North Korean or Syrian military saboteurs, can corrupt files and communications which could ultimately bring down the entire system.

At this level, there is a rising awareness of the problem. Google alone is investing around £4 billion ($6 billion) a year on network data centers. Annual global spending on such centers will rise to close to £100 billion ($150billion) this year.[2]

The rise of big data has resulted in many traditional data warehousing companies, such as Teradata, continuously updating their products and technology. The Teradata product encompasses a massively parallel processing system referred to as a "data warehouse system" which stores and manages data. The data warehouses use a "shared nothing architecture," which means that each server node has its own memory and processing power. Adding more servers and nodes increases the amount of data that can be stored. The database software sits on top of the servers and spreads the workload among them. [3]

Speed has also become a factor, as has the surging demand for storage. Consider that almost three quarters of all trades on the American stock exchanges are being executed by machines which process transactions in less than a millionth of a second via fiber-optic connections. As a necessary consequence Teradata is also used as a series back-up during downtime. The systems work to balance the workload of big data which has arisen exponentially from new media sources, such as social media.

Storing increasingly immense quantities of data also has become a challenge by placing a limit on the number of years most of it is (or can be) stored. At the same time, more steps are being taken to prevent disasters from occurring. A prime example is Microsoft's Exchange ActiveSync (commonly known as EAS). This is a protocol designed for the synchronization of email, contacts, tasks, and notes from a messaging server to a smartphone or other mobile device. But such efforts also illustrate how the global system has grown along market-driven choices and corporate decisions — not according to any plan nor oversight nor set rules or regulations. This does not seem like a comprehensive way to proceed globally. Alas, the possible consequences of the fantastic expansion of Big Data may not be recognized until a comprehensive meltdown suddenly occurs with the most dire results for all but the most undeveloped societies like those of Papua New Guinea or Bhutan. You have been warned!

---

[1]Juliette Garside, "Warning over data meltdown," The Guardian (UK) 24 August, 2013, p. 1

[2]Charles Arthur, "The Cost," The Guardian, 24 August, 2013, p. 7

[3]See the Teradata entry in Wikipedia

# Extremism

Posted on October 7, 2013

I have never been an admirer of political or religious extremism. Adolph Hitler was my introduction to extremism and initially I mistook him for a clown and laughed. That was in the days of Charlie Chaplin's great impersonations. Perhaps laughter is the strongest weapon we possess against political extremists but it is very hard to laugh at someone so inept as Sen.Ted Cruz of Texas filibustering the Senate floor for 21 hours. I now understand that extremism spells: Danger!

Some friends have argued that it takes two to tango in a democracy: the right and the left, the Tories and Labour, the capitalists and the socialists, those for downsizing government and those opposed. I have felt that unless the contenders in these divisions had some degree of civility, displayed a readiness for dialogue and were ultimately willing to compromise, the only solution was to vote the extremists out of office or expel them from whatever group or party they belonged and to replace them with "tolerants."[1]

The complexity of the problem is illustrated by President Obama strongly denouncing Congressional extremists while he himself is viewed as an extremist by his Tea-Party opponents. For these radicalized members of the Republican Party bringing down the entire governmental process would be a triumph — even when they have no idea of what might follow. As President Theodore Roosevelt declared over a century ago: "Every reform movement has a lunatic fringe."

It is significant that no political party ever calls itself "extremist," or that its most radical members ever call each other, to the right or left, extremists. Tea-Party members see themselves as "true" conservatives and ardent patriots. They do not even accept being called "radical" because in America that word is regarded as pejorative. Earlier on in this series I wrote about "obstructionism".[2]

The two terms are not exclusive. Obstructionists can be extremists and vice-versa. Obstructionists are frustrated and want to block change; extremists are protesters and want reform. The economist Ronald Wintrobe has noted that many extremist movements, even though they might have opposing ideologies, share a common set of characteristics: They are against any compromise, are entirely sure of their position, are intolerant of dissent within their group, and demonize the "other side."

Robert F. Kennedy noted: "What is objectionable, what is dangerous about extremists is not that they are extreme but that they are intolerant. The evil is not what they say about their cause, but what they say about their opponents." In Kennedy's unfortunate case the extremist who shot him was not only intolerant but murderous.

I find it difficult to acknowledge that politics are rarely rational: race, religions, class are all factors in determining political allegiance in a democracy. Many southern and right wing Republicans have not been able to come to terms with the election and re-election of the first African-American president. They also have emotional problems with any form of gun control legislation, environmental protection, and science — all of which could undermine their basic beliefs. Part of their growing extremism is furthered by the provocation of the host of right-wing think tanks funded by such extreme billionaires as the Koch brothers and Rupert Murdoch.

The Heritage Foundation and its spin-off, Heritage Action for America, aided by lobbyists, teams of organizers and social media specialists are sponsors of most of the current extremist efforts. Heritage Action has taken to ranking members publicly according to how they vote and exposing them when these members of Congress do not follow the 'conservative' party line. Ultimately they threaten rebels with challengers in the party primaries. "When you are spending $550,000 attacking Republicans and not the Democrats who voted for Obamacare, it is entirely fair to question what your motives are," said Brian Walsh."[3]

Heritage Action has been effective in advancing its own power in Washington and has focused for several years on ways to defund the Obamacare health program which they view as more toxic than any government shut-down. Its place as the leader of America's think tank extremists was confirmed in 2012 by its selection of the former senator and southern bigot, Jim DeMinto, to oversee its subversive operations in Washington.

But extremism in the United States has spread far beyond the corridors of power in the Congress. Media coverage has encouraged the polarization of extremes. Fox News, for example, presents the news as seen by the right — any other perspective is ignored. The so-called rebuttals are phony. The impact of broadcasters of venom, like Rush Limbaugh, is pronounced. It reinforces the prejudice and emotions of those on the right and succeeds in producing extreme views in an audience which no longer tolerates dissent. But then common forms of communication, such as debate, discussion, and disagreement, are no longer tolerated by most Americans.

I ask myself, where are the left-wing extremists of yesteryear? There are no effective ones that stand out! I have been surprised by the lack of focused anti-extremists for the very soul of the United States of America. I deem it high time for a national revulsion to be expressed against the distinctly narrow, anti-democratic, nihilistic practices of the Tea-Party extremists. If such revulsion ultimately takes hold, perhaps the voters can obliterate this highly destructive and dangerous grouping of obstructionists in November 2014.

---

[1]Don't bother to look for it in the dictionary — it is not there.
[2]See Blog #16 *Oust the Obstructionists!*
[3]Former communications director the National Republican Senatorial Committee.

## PROTESTS

Posted on October 28, 2013

It seems paradoxical to me that in the age of the web popular protest has become ever more difficult. This blog is an effort to enhance the effectiveness of mass demonstrations in a time of overwhelming technological advances in communication. We have seen serious demonstration in Turkey, Brazil and Indonesia this past summer resulting in minor positive changes and a major one in Egypt resulting in the full return of military dictatorship. Minor improvements are indeed occurring through the efforts of groups like www.change.org. However, wider themed protests like those on immigration, debt ceilings, youth unemployment, poverty, banking reform, and growing inequality seem impotent. The resulting mass frustration is evident at all levels – particularly in the under twenty-fives.

Truly aroused by the launch of the Occupy movement in New York in 2011, I was thrilled by the openness, scope and perspective of those launching the protests: banking, money, capitalism, third world poverty, corruption, unemployment and more were all being questioned and attacked.  As this wide-ranging protest paralleled my thinking in *Dollars or Democracy* (2004), I briefly participated in the Occupy movement at St Paul's Cathedral, London. I was immediately struck by the good will of the participants and their loquaciousness. I admired their commitment to nonviolence. These demonstrating neophytes were seething with a desire for change.

Aside from such fundamental challenges as the ever increasing gap in attention spans and all-around diminished retentiveness, the good protesters of 2011 failed to have effective organization, lacked experienced leaders, had far too wide and divergent goals, and had no tactical program beyond occupying very tiny open spaces adjacent to large institutions or buildings. (Wall Street, St. Paul's etc.)  Simply staying in one location could not encompass such a real issue as student debt! The result was that by the spring of 2012 the media had just about forgotten their encampments.

Only rarely have the contributions of contemporary protest movements equalled the impact of past marches for trade unionism, women's suffrage, civil rights, or the vast anti-war gatherings. The Arab spring has been the first and major 21st century exception. Thanks to the Internet there has been increasing resort to protests by relatively powerless groups. "Spontaneity gives the protests an intoxicating sense of possibility," wrote *The Economist*.[1] Although the protesters have the ability to quickly change tack and pick up other winds to increase their numbers, their lack of solid agenda or well structured organization means that encirclement by the police or the military and the opposition of entrenched and well-funded economic and political forces swiftly put an end to their efforts.

Commentators in the press often criticize protesters for failing to have clearly defined demands, but the protesters contend that issuing rigid demands could prove counter-productive. Many protest groups have an "overriding commitment" to participatory democracy in which decisions are made by consensus. Meetings increasingly use hand signals to augment participation and "discussion facilitators" tend to replace the usual role of leaders whom "security forces" could swiftly arrest.

In the past unaddressed protests have led to insurgency, civil resistance, riots, as well as social and/or political revolutions such as the American Revolution of the 1770's and the French Revolution of 1789. More recently the Tiananmen Square protests of 1989, the Palestinian intifada, and the revolution in Egypt have not led to greater freedom. Indeed, the political demonstrations in Paris in May 1968 and that of the "*indignados*" in Spain in 2011-12 saw the return of rightists.

Many protests in the 21st Century seem to have become political substitutes for opposition. Protester rallies are in many ways shaped by the social media on the Internet. In Brazil, for example, the protesters have come to regard traditional organization and political parties as redundant in the age of Twitter and Facebook. "They don't even use loudspeakers to get their message across with thousands of people on the streets," wrote one observer.[2]

New forms of social and political organization are essential so that the discontented and despairing can express their anger or channel their resentment without violence. Protest leaders, who could effectively control demonstrations, are usually sought out by police or intelligence forces and sequestered. As a consequence the leaderless crowds don't know which way to turn and often get sidetracked by infiltrated provocateurs.

Globalization and the Internet thus call for the invention of new forms of protest so that the voice of the people on this planet can become more effective. Joining a march can create a special feeling which signing a petition on the Internet does not. A substitute for marches and rallies which gives protesters a sense of power has yet to be imagined or designed. Live, camera-produced social rallies might be a possibility, but are not likely to be as effective as the real thing: elected officials or dictators would not be seriously challenged. The threats and uncertainties posed by huge numbers on the streets, all demanding change, exert a power which a petition signed by 100,000 electronic signers does not! Until a new way is found much of the global electorate, unwilling to face tear gas and water-canon, will continue to feel voiceless, frustrated, isolated, impotent and desperate for change.

---

[1]"The march of protest," *The Economist*, June 29, 2013.
[2]Simon Romeo, "Mass protests take on a life of their own in Brazil", *International Herald Tribune,* June 22, 2013.

## 21st Century Sexual Mores

Posted on December 17, 2013

The extraordinary rapidity of change in our lives over the past two generations has not left our sex-lives unaffected. A handful of factors reign supreme: The birth control pill, the Internet, our extended life spans, greater sexual equality, and the resulting openness on our sexual behavior — although not necessarily in that disorder. In 2013 both the social concern and the changing outlook have led to massive over-exposure as evidenced by the stream of daily media coverage: features on gay marriage, sexting, restrictions on prostitution, paedophilia and pornography are complemented by the exploitation of sexuality in advertising.

One of the foremost challenges facing the older generations is how to deal with the sexual education of the young. It is said that Internet pornography has become the leading educator for children between the ages of 10 and 15.[1] The effects of this are evident when a vast number girls in the UK between the ages of 13 and 16 shave their public hair because they think boys expect this as all women in porn films are shaven. Alas, for many youths spending hours on end glued to their screens, life on the Internet is their first life and real life comes second.

Many parents find it difficult to acknowledge that sex is an aspect of the process of maturing for which they deserve to be educated. Few can admit that sex begins even before birth: In the womb unborn males may experience erections. Both genders often masturbate while babies and toddlers harbor a natural interest in their genitals as they do in all other basic activities.[2] It is impossible to deal with the sexual education of children by sweeping the facts of life under the carpet as the Victorians attempted to do. We are all sexual beings — the product of mating. To accept this means recognizing the various forms our sexual drives may take. It also demands open-mindedness and understanding which many religions have denied.

Acceptance is not always easy. Even Romans struggled with the problem of incest, for example. My descriptions of father-daughter incest in the Augustan age proved painful for many readers. Yet it mirrored this recurrent theme in Ovid some 2000 years earlier![3] The promiscuity of the Roman gods was driven by the sexual desires and drives of the creators. Divine communion was often portrayed as sexual intercourse between gods disguised as animals and humans. Romans were also fascinated by sexual duality. When gender identity is ambiguous, as in hermaphrodites, it challenges our conceptions of who we are writes psychiatrist Coline Covington.[4] In part this is because it can also "trigger anxieties about our own unconscious homosexual fantasies."

Rapidly many of us in the western world are catching up with the Romans in the acceptance of homosexual relations. This has certainly been one of the most reported advances in the United States and Europe in the past few years. Even the new Pope is bravely trying to cope with the complexities this problem presents for the Catholic Church. Here the younger generation has been much more open than their elders.

There is now far greater tolerance of sexual experimentation than two generations ago. The recognition of the elements of bisexuality in our being has become more widespread. The National Survey of Sexual Attitudes and Life Styles has revealed that in the UK the population has become increasingly accepting of sexual diversity. For example, Growing numbers of women in the UK have had some kind of homosexual experience.[5] Censorship of sex scenes in motion pictures has also become far more relaxed. Even sexually explicit S&M in the film being shot of *Fifty Shades of Grey* is most likely to pass censorship.

The desire of large numbers of both men and women to express themselves through exhibitionism has become evident on the Internet. Some would seem far more eager to display their private parts than their faces!  Pushed by the glamour of the young film stars, many women, desirous of being admired for their bodies, are having their lips, breasts, buttocks and even their labia enhanced. But there is also protest here from the older generation. (I receive dozens of unsolicited emails every week for male enhancement!) The still youthful actress Lynne Segal writes: I see the media's endless production of eroticized young female flesh as feeding a sense of shame attached to older women's bodies."[6]

The extended lifespan of both men and women has created its own set of sexual challenges. Many women in their seventies and eighties still have strong sexual yearnings but fewer opportunities for relations with men. A discouraging 70% of women over 65 in the UK now live alone. I did not come across a figure for the number of men over 65 in a similar position.

All too many members of society sit uneasily with the notion that when it comes to sex, "anything goes." The extreme levels of narcissism are increasingly matched by the practice of sex without attachment. Sexual mores no longer seem be keeping up with the unprecedented advances in communication. The rapid decay of any sexual boundary in the 21st century disturbs both editors and readers. They see pornography with its often-brutalizing images as dehumanizing the pleasurable vistas of sex.

So where is sex going? The institution of marriage is suffering in part because of the greater economic and social equality for women. They have become breadwinners as well as wives, mothers and lovers. A fundamental change has been the equalization of desire between women and men for sexual satisfaction. Women have become open about their wants and sexual needs. The "cougars" of tomorrow are likely to be far more public. However, excessive exposure could swiftly lead to boredom before turning into fatigue!

It is likely that marriage rates will continue to decline for a while before the sexes reach a truer equality and the decision to have and raise children will become steadier. For the destiny of sexual desires resides with our children. Those now in the ages between 25 and 50 look back on their divorced parents and grandparents with their serial or "open" marriages and their sexual betrayals and say: "No, thanks. We don't want more of that!"

The "Bad Sex" awards by the Literary Review (UK) are getting more tawdry with very passing year. Perhaps in the not-too-distant future there finally will be a "Good Sex" award … and a reward for its many joys to all of us as humans.

---

[1] See Cindy Gallop in a TED talk promoting her web site www.makelovenotporn.com

[2] Hannah Betts, "We can't shelter kids from sex completely," *The Guardian*, June 22, 2013, p.19

[3] Yorick Blumenfeld, *The Waters of Forgetfulness* (2009)

[4]Coline Covington, *Shrinking the News* (2013) p.115.
[5]"Love in a cold climate," *The Economist*, November 30, 2013
[6]Lynne Segal, "Growing old erotically," *The Guardian*, December 16, 2013

## US "reefer madness" continued…
Posted on January 15, 2014

The raging incongruity of US efforts to control the use of marijuana is no longer irrational, it is insane. The complexity of the overlapping controls by local communities, states, the judicial system, the criminal system, and the federal government has left me flabbergasted. However, I have yet to come across an American who believes that it serves such dubious purposes as keeping young male blacks in jail, maintaining employment in the "prison industry," keeping the Mafia in business or subsidizing the ever growing numbers dealing with the surrounding legal issues. All these interests, opposed to the decriminalization of marijuana, have contributed to political gridlock on the issue in Washington.

The US now has experienced almost 80 years of prohibition on Marijuana which, after alcohol and tobacco, is the third most popular natural substance consumed nationally. It is important to compare this with the prohibition of alcohol which lasted only 14 years from 1919 to 1933. It took the 21st Amendment to the Constitution to repeal the prohibition on alcohol. Is it not high time to end the folly of the ineffectual prohibition on marijuana with an amendment to the Constitution which would decriminalize production, transportation, sale and consumption of this "drug?"

The patchwork of prejudice, fear, ignorance and phony medical expertise stitched together by a range of politicians stretching over generations is truly awesome. The origins of such folly seem quite beyond the fantasy of even the best of Hollywood scriptwriters. During the depression of the mid-1930's when a number of Americans were wondering what could fill the vacuum created by the end of prohibition, one rather bizarre administrator, Harry Anslinger, the first head of the Federal Bureau of Narcotics detested jazz to such an extent that he wondered how to stop such degenerate sounds from further undermining the sensibilities of young Americans. Investigating the background of those playing jazz, he noted correctly that most of the gifted musicians smoked marijuana. Blocking the drug could stop the music! And so the campaign of fear focused on "reefer madness" was launched to frighten the American electorate into gradually banning marijuana. The propaganda of the 1930's portrayed cannabis as the killer weed which could turn average American youths into a homicidal, suicidal and crazed maniacs. So by the mid-1930s cannabis was declared a drug in every state.

And so where are we 75 years later? The US is spending well over $50 billion a year in its war on drugs. In the thriving black market, more than 750,000 Americans are arrested by the police every year in connection with the use of marijuana. One in six of Americans serving time in one of the over-crowded federal prisons is there for having violated the laws regarding cannabis. An even larger number is held in state and local prisons.

The first ray of good news on this issue in a long time is that since January 1st recreational use is permitted in Colorado and the state of Washington and that 20 states and the District of Columbia now allow some form of medical marijuana to be used. Any resident of Colorado over the age of 21 can now buy up to an ounce of cannabis at one of the 40 stores ("dispensaries") open to retail customers. A rolled joint costs $10 (£7). Out of state visitors can buy just a quarter of an ounce but must use it within the state as carrying "pot" across state lines remains a federal offense.

There is big money to be made in cannabis and the prospect of an open market in cannabis may serve to drive much needed reforms. Investors are watching whether the legal sales of cannabis in Colorado and Washington will match the optimistic predictions of a windfall for the state budgets? Those behind the reforms in these states are motivated by the need to have more money flowing in from the taxes, but also from the money to be made by the growers and distributors who will no longer have to pay the Mafia, the police and the lawyers in order to stay out of jail.

The war on marijuana, like any war, results not only in casualties but also deeply affects all those involved in fighting it. Under current drug laws, some criminals escape long prison sentences by informing and also earn up to 25% of the assets that are forfeited by those convicted of growing, buying, selling, or using marijuana. So a substantial number of professional informers have developed a direct interest in lying for profit.

Few marijuana cases commence without an initial tip from an informant. Some power company employees, who may be allowed to trespass in order to read meters or repair equipment, have made informing a second (and more profitable) career. Employees of various shipping companies, such as UPS and FedEx also can earn extra cash by informing on anything suspicious. Such activities by informers tend to undermine the social fabric of any society.

There is growing public recognition in the US "that prohibition (of marijuana) has been a fiasco that has led to needless imprisonment and fiscal waste."[1] As the *Financial Times* concluded editorially "Blanket prohibition has failed and cannot be sustained. There is growing public recognition in the US that prohibition has been a fiasco."

Oregon, Arizona, Alaska and California (all Western states) are the most likely to have a change following ballot box voting over the next two years but what these states will be doing is to contravene the Controlled Substances Act of 1970, adding to the massive confusion as to what is legal and what is not.

The evangelist Pat Robertson recently joined the ranks of those speaking out on the issue by suggesting, "We should treat marijuana the way we treat beverage alcohol." Prof Mark Kleiman, one of the most patient and rational of experts on the confusion and contradictions whirling around this issue, says that a big riddle is whether marijuana might indeed become a substitute for alcohol. Kleiman would be pleased if there could be a decline in consumption, "Alcohol use has far more detrimental social costs than marijuana, by critically any measure: addiction, accidents, violence, illness, death"[2] he said, pointing to the fact that alcoholics used to be viewed as wicked, sinful and evil but are now are regarded as suffering from fallibilities which demand medical attention.

Under the current laws of fifteen states you can get a life sentence for a nonviolent marijuana offense. The distinguished reporter Eric Schlosser came across the case of a man getting life without parole for a single joint! He asked: "How does society come to punish a person more harshly for selling marijuana than for killing somebody with a gun?"[3]

In California the average prison sentence for a convicted killer is 3.3 years, but in Montana you can get a life sentence for a first offense for growing one marijuana plant. Schlosser suggests "given that an estimated 300,000 die from tobacco and over 100,000 from alcohol, it clearly seemed to me that a concern for public health was not behind those strict punishments for marijuana." The war on marijuana has been much more a war on the sort of people who smoke it, be they Mexicans or blacks or jazz musicians or beatniks or hippies or hip-hop artists. Racial prejudice and bigotry play a huge role in the interpretation of the many laws. Blacks are currently three times more likely than whites to be arrested for a marijuana violation.[4]

The large swings between tolerance and intolerance in the US regarding cannabis reflect much larger social trends. The Reagan era of the 1980s was a period in which intolerance was symbolized by the slogan "Zero Tolerance." Schlosser wrote "There was an upswing in anti-immigrant sentiment and a backlash against women and unions and minorities and I really think you have to see the war on marijuana in that context." When Reagan launched his War on Drugs in 1982, 88% of American high school seniors said it was easy for them to obtain marijuana. A dozen years later, 85% of such seniors re-affirmed it was still easy. In the intervening dozen years half a trillion dollars had been spent on attempts to eradicate the evil weed and more than a quarter of a million Americans had been sent to jail.

A fifth of the American 50 states have basically decriminalized marijuana and those arrested for possessing small amounts are fined much as they would be for parking violations. That has been a step forward, but nearly all of the former slave states in the south, from Alabama to Oklahoma, have failed to take the more liberal stance.

It seems obvious to me that approaching cannabis should not be through the criminal justice system but through public health efforts. Decriminalizing marijuana is a necessity. When will this finally happen? Passing a Constitutional amendment usually takes a number of years. Pardoning all those who have been jailed for using small amounts of marijuana could be a positive move towards decriminalization when President Obama leaves office in 2017. America's hopes depend on radical change to end this tired folly called "reefer madness."

[1] Shannon Bond, "Colorado enjoys relaxation of the marijuana legislation," *The Financial Times*, January 4, 2014; "Drugs policy enters a brave new world," Editorial in the same issue of *The Financial Times.*

[2] Patrick Radden Keefe, "Buzzkill," *The New Yorker,* November 18, 2013, p. 50

[3] Interviews: Eric Schlosser/Busted-America's War on Marijuana/Frontline/PBS.

[4] op.cit. Keefe, p.40

**FYI:** Outside the United States, Uruguay decriminalized marijuana in 2013 and there also have been moves in Canada to do so. In the UK the Police Foundation (a non for profit group presided over by Prince Charles) issued a report which stated that: "Our conclusion is that the present law on cannabis produces more harm than it prevents. It is very expensive of the time and resources of the criminal justice system and especially of the police. It inevitably bears more heavily on young people in the streets of inner cities, who are also more likely to be from minority ethnic communities, and as such is inimical to police-community relations. It criminalizes large numbers of otherwise law-abiding, mainly young, people to the detriment of their futures. It has become a proxy for the control of public order; and it inhibits accurate education about the relative risks of different drugs including the risks of cannabis itself." Police Foundation of the United Kingdom, "Drugs and the Law: Report of the Independent Inquiry into the Misuse of Drugs Act of 1971.

## A Mass Tourist Future?

Posted on March 4, 2014

My mind instantly responds to the expression "mass tourism" with "grotesque nightmare!" Having worked, lived in, or travelled in over 90 countries around the world, the prospect of travel no longer entices. Congestion on the roads and in the airports, concerns about security, inspections, and bureaucratic hassle, unsettled weather patterns and unpredictable politics are all unsettling. The prospective arrival to a city in terms of the architecture, hotels, restaurants, the conventions of politeness of service, each have become so stereotyped that they leave little to my imagination. Put simply: All fun in the process of getting there has vanished.

It says a lot about our species and our global civilization that tourism has become the largest (or perhaps the second largest after food) industry. Mass travel has shrunk our globe in more ways than one. I regret to say that mass tourism, while good for the creation of jobs, is also causing serious erosion of our environment. The carbon emissions alone are staggering.

Tourism used to be about exploration and getting to know other people and their differing ways of life. No longer. The mass tourist is primarily interest in taking "selfies" in front of the Grand Canal and then being able to say, "I have been there." Venice, one of my favorite cities, can have so many tourists struggling to reach St. Mark's Square or the Rialto bridge that I can only compare it to morning rush hour in the New York or Tokyo subways. Fortunately, when there, I can hurry away and, in just a few blocks from the crush, can then stroll calmly through narrow alleyways and intimate piazzas to mingle with ordinary Venetians going about their daily chores: bliss!

Mass tourism entails levels of standardization, conformity, uniformity and cost cutting, all working against individual choice. (Yes, the "holiday package" may be structured around 'singles', gourmets, seniors, or even flora, but the driving force is numbers.[1])

I live in the academically renowned city of Cambridge (UK) where more than 10% of the work force is employed in tourism. About four million visitors a year come to visit this historic site bringing in more than $300 million (or £200+ million.) A new phenomenon has been the arrival of busload upon busload of Chinese who have come to regard Cambridge as one of the "musts" of their 'grand tour' of Europe. Most of these want to pay homage to the 20th Century poet Xu Zhimo who wrote a highly nostalgic verse, "Leaving Cambridge Again" (1928) which has been taught in every Chinese primary school for over a generation.

During their visit to Cambridge, none of these visitors is likely to speak to a single resident. Most are unlikely to see much beyond the punts on the River Cam and 'the backs' of Kings and neighboring colleges. What will they come away with when, having "done" Cambridge, they eagerly mount their buses to return to London's Chinatown in time for dinner? Perhaps they will decide that there are as many cyclists in this city as there are in their city in China? Or that there is less air and water pollution than back at home? Or that they miss the black tea they are used to? Perhaps the visit to the rock with the poetic inscription of Xu Zhimo may just have been another essential rite in affirming their social status?

All too often the faces of mass tourists, their digital cameras at the ready, express fatigue and boredom, as well as anxiety and irritation. Much of their time is spent queuing for food, entrance fees, or toilet facilities. They never seem quite comfortable when distant from their flag-bearing guide or from the bus which will take them to their next destination as printed in their illustrated packaged programs.

Would that some of the thrills of sensation open to the individual traveller were enjoyed by the mass of tourists, but the age of the independent 'Grand' hotels (which was launched with the opening by Princess Eugenie of the Paris Grand in 1862) has now passed. Replicating intimate service on a mass scale is an inherently implausible task in the 21st Century. There are some 16,500 posh hotels scattered around the world run mostly by a variety of national chains. The five biggest hotel loyalty schemes, half of which are upscale/posh or luxury, have a total of 200 million members. *The Economist*, in surveying this state of affairs, speculated that "In the future the hotel may offer neither bland conformity nor authentic warmth but a proliferating number of experimental worlds in which to insert yourself."[2]

There was a time, not so long ago, when travel was an adventure full of the unexpected and sometimes even redolent with charm. Looking back two centuries at the experiences of different travellers and adventurers, one encounters startlingly different perceptions and reactions. I note this not only as nostalgia on my part but also as a protest at the way the human race has voyaged of late. Boswell, crediting his libertine friend, Samuel Johnson with a verse from Naples on March 7, 1765 when, on a visit to what had already become an essential stopover of the European "Grand Tour,"[3] he wrote:

> *Why curse fair Naples, strangers, wherefore swear*
> *That all the human race are worthless there?...*
> *At Naples lives the woman I adore,*
> *Oh, had I seen her ere she turned a whore!*
> *But whore or not I love her with my soul,*
> *And to her health will drink a brimming bowl.*

Twelve days later, in a somewhat different mood, he wrote that

> *"Naples is indeed a delicious spot. I have been near three weeks here and have been constantly employed in seeing the classical places all around. Is it possible to conceive a richer scene than the finest bay diversified with islands and bordered by fields where Virgil's Muses charmed the creation, where the renowned ancient Rome enjoyed the luxury of glorious retreat and the true flow of soul which they valued as much as triumphs?"*

There was indeed a time before tourism became a mass industry that the prospect of travel could fill the visitor with pleasurable anticipation. Few tourists today travel for travel's sake. Catering to the market has entailed the loss of spiritual values and has replaced these with material concerns: Getting the best deal for your money and getting you there fast.

But do not despair. New tourist vistas (without any visas) are opening up for those willing to spend $200,000 (or £125,000) for a risky two-hour journey to outer space at ever-higher speeds. Those who already have signed up for Sir Richard Branson's commercial space flight on Virgin Galactic SpaceShipTwo, are unlikely to get a much smoother ride than that described by Catherine Roget on October 5, 1793 on her five day+ coach journey from London to Edinburgh:

"I had the most disagreeable journey I ever experienced owing to the new improved patent coach, a vehicle loaded with iron trappings and the greatest complication of unmechanical contrivances jumbled together that I have ever witnessed. The coach swings sideways with a sickly sway, without any vertical spring, the point of suspension bearing upon an arch called a spring, though it is nothing of the sort. The severity of the jolting occasioned me such disorder, that I was obliged to stop at Axminster and go to bed very ill."

Lady Roget cautioned, "Unless they go back to the old-fashioned coach, hung a little lower, the mail coaches will lose all their custom." Sir Richard, Beware

---

[1]Maxine Feifer, Tourism in History, (1985)

[2]"Be my guest A short History of Hotels," *The Economist,* December 21, 2013. [3]Christopher Hibbert, The Grand Tour, (1987

**Towards more engaging expressions**

Posted on August 11, 2014

In the beginning of civilization was The Word. It is almost impossible to imagine us without it. Word symbols gave mankind the unprecedented power to learn, understand and communicate ideas which themselves have transformed the world. And yet there are those intent on knocking words like beauty, love, truth, morality nd excellence off their pedestals. Such words are increasingly losing their value and greeted with cynicism. In practice their meaning is now fragmented, pigeonholed into syntactical structures of narrow social, psychological, political, religious or aesthetic contexts which we barely recognize. The challenge is: How to bring back the magic of the word?[1]

I should like young people to increase their employment of varied linguistic forms such as cockney rhymes, foreign expressions, puns, word associations, pleonasms, palindromes, oxymorons and euphemisms. This could enhance their appreciation of word magic. They might learn that some words are better than others and not merely copy what is fashionable at that instant. The uses of The Word as developed through generations is now increasingly restricted. Even the message OK has now been reduced to a simple 'k'. This narrows both the opportunity for humor and individuality.[2] I have found such impoverishment of language to be a little noticed side effect of the extraordinary expansion of the use of the Internet.

Enrichment is possible: Words which are associated with delight and happiness, for example, arouse specific circuits in our brains. Certain words and expressions can trigger strong emotional responses: Ecstatic, sublime, supernatural, glorious, wondrous, breathless, radiant, other-worldly, sublime, buoyant, bright, illuminating, exhilarating, uplifting, nirvana-like, and divine can all spark positive reactions. So can phrases such as: vivid as lightning, gusts of splendor, superhuman joy, sudden rapture, on the fringe of ecstasy, filled with excitation, or in communion with spirits — all expressions the like of which one does not currently find in everyday communications — which enhance our pleasure in existence itself.[3] Words and expressions which arouse awe in children are sometimes obvious: They love the word "Awesome!" It is an oft-repeated favorite.

Euphemisms, in which a figure of speech is substituted for one which is indelicate or possibly embarrassing, are disappearing from most internet communications. Euphemisms like "collateral damage" and "adult entertainment," are widely employed by politicians to avoid confrontation with psychologically difficult reality. However, they do occasionally open up fresh opportunities for humor. "Breaking wind" or "passing gas" are euphemisms distinctly out of date. Such "windy words" are no longer fashionable. What has become of such comic flatulent expressions as:

- "Cushion Creeper"
- "Cutting the cheese"
- "One-cheek sneak"
- "Painting the elevator"
- "Pattler"
- "Snappers"
- "S.B.D." (Silent-but-deadly)

In a less bodily context, swearing and cursing are human universals. Profane language has been with us since speech first came into existence. All languages and dialects have them. Researchers have found that three quarters of 18 to 35 year olds in the United States and half of those over 55 are used to swearing. Although swearing can be an art form — as evidenced by the brilliant ways Shakespeare used it in all his plays — the expletives on the Internet show little variation or imagination.

Swearing on the Internet — which is common — is very different from direct face-to-face encounters. The tone of voice, the look in the eyes, the positioning of the body, and the motion of the hands have been of the essence in everyday swearing. Such direct contact can strengthen the expression, making it open to more ironic, or even humorous, interpretations. Such possibilities are seldom exercised by the under 16s in communications which are minimal in terms of variation of style, context or subtlety. The younger generation is changing spellings, shortening words so they can be clicked more swiftly, and repeating items so often that their meaning is ultimately lost.

Swear words are principally drawn from bodily functions, sex and the domain of religion. What counts as taboo expressions in a given culture are often a mirror for the fears and fixations of its users. The outstanding science writer, Natalie Angier, has noted that swearing is a widespread but perhaps under-appreciated technique in anger management. Researchers have pointed out that cursing is frequently a mix of spontaneous feeling and targeted cunning, invoking close relationships with family members as well as past or present lovers. On the other hand, it can be shocking to hear a loud volley of expletives erupting for no apparent reason from the mouth of a teenager or an adult. Such outbursts frequently target racial backgrounds or parental ancestry. Evidence suggests that cursing and swearing also can be effective ways of venting aggression and thus forestalling physical violence.

Many modern Italian taboo words are rich expressions of regional origin. Alas, regional variations are disappearing almost everywhere. The different forms of insult humorously relating to women in Italy is revealing. Italians still enjoy the complex side effects when playing with such words as:

- *cavallona* (street walker)
- *cravattona* (a lesbian prostitute)
- *drondona* (outspoken prostitute)
- *putanella* (a sweet prostitute)
- *scopona* (a sweeper prostitute)
- *vaccaccia* (a cow-like woman)
- *zingarona* (a gypsy woman)[4]

Swear words and curses using the name of god or gods go back to the days of ancient Babylon. Swearing by the name of a god was at that time an assurance that those uttering such a taboo were not lying. People believed that swearing falsely would bring the dreadful wrath of that god upon them. The biblical commandment that one must not "take the Lord's name in vain" was a warning against abuse of the sacred oath. The Jews held the very name of "God" so highly that it could never be pronounced or used in writing or speech. Instead, references to the almighty included substitutions like lord, king, celestial master etc. Among Christians, the stricture against taking God's name in vain extended to allusions to Jesus or to his corporal sufferings. Swearing which included the word "blood" was taboo. Invoking the name of God was to some a way of adding impact to an assertion. Today the quaint expression "Oh golly!" is considered almost comically, but golly is in fact a compact version of "God's body" which once was held to be profane. "Blimey!" is a euphemism for "God blind me" and the exclamation "Zounds!" refers to God's wounds.

Shakespeare could hardly quill a page without inserting profanities of the day like "Sblood!" or "Zounds!" These words aroused his audiences and delivered verbal jolts. Today the expressions hardly draw any notice. Now the free flow of foul language often is regarded as a sign of being at ease. While four-letter words in a brawl can lead to violence, those same words in a living-room setting can be interpreted as an expression of trust and social acceptance. While I tend to admire well-venomed retorts, I am appealing for the greater use of more imaginative expressions in our everyday language, words which will augment our appreciation and engagement. Cockney rhymes, for example, are a witty, *slanguage* way to titillate the brain. For example: "heavens above" matches love and "three-penny bits" is a rhyme for tits.[5]

Students in school are seldom exposed to cockney or different ways to enrich their language. Teachers should urge their pupils to play with words and to develop their verbal imaginations for ultimately the enrichment of our language depends on the variety of used expressions. It is true that new words, like bitcoin and selfie, are entering our vocabulary all the time. (Chambers English dictionary added a thousand new entries in July). However, most of these newcomers involve our rapidly expanding technologies but do not widen our psyche's horizons.[6]

Language, which depends on words, can trigger much that is positive in us. Admittedly, some people are so embarrassed by contentious words that they prefer to mumble as a way of covering up what they don't really want to say. Famously, Alan Greenspan pronounced: "Since I have become a central banker, I have learned to mumble with great incoherence. If I seem unduly clear to you, you must have misunderstood what I said." Perhaps mumbling may be one technique which could lighten up the tired feeling now surrounding the over-use of four letter Anglo-Saxon expletives! Whimsically, instead of using words we could stutter: ffffff! shshshsh! or sususususu!

---

[1]Yorick Blumenfeld, *Towards the Millennium*: Optimistic Visions for Change, 1997, pp.94-96

[2]Mississippi folk humor used to be filled with expressions which captured the spirit of the local inhabitants. For example, a stout woman was "beef to the heels." An inexperienced youth was described as being "So green that when it rains he'll sprout." A politician's aggressive pursuits were described as "He was after it like the stink after onion." A fellow with inertia was said to "have been born lazy and had a relapse." B.A. Botkin, *A Treasury of Southern Folklore* (1949) p. 674

[3]Marghanita Laski, *Ecstasy*, 1961, p 245

[4]Salvatore Battaglie, *La grammatica Italiana,* (1957) pp.135-136.

[5]Leonard Ashley, "The Cockney's Horn Book," in *Opus Maledictorum* (edited by Rheinhold Aman) 1996, p.54

[6]Lauren Laverne, New Vocabulary, *The Observer* Magazine, August 10, 2014, p.7

## Re-Evaluating Our Prison Systems

Posted on September 26, 2014

The entire prison systems (or industries) of both the United States and the United Kingdom are so unfit for purpose that they demand a serious rethink. In its lead editorial *The Observer* declared: "The prison system is a stain on our society."[1] It is also a dark blot on "the American way of life." All too many inmates in both countries are being held in the wrong places and in the wrong ways: The mentally disturbed should be given hospital care and treatment, not cruel imprisonment.

Before focusing on the larger problem of the prisons ruled by brutality and fear, it is important to recognize that both countries have failed to come to grips with the challenges of mental health in their jails. The Prison Reform Trust (UK) has reported that at least 15% of men and 25% of women convicts are suffering from the symptoms of psychosis. Indeed, in most prisons there are psychotics who need to be confined to isolation units and are often in need of 24-7 supervision. The columnist Nick Cohen has written that "when the coalition subtracted political cost from economic gain it found those with disabilities were the easiest people in Britain to dispose of... People who ought to be mentally disabled patients are the inmates of the one British institution that treats them with greater disdain than the National Health Service."[2]

In an in-depth report on the emergency state of Britain's jails, the *Financial Times* concluded that "According to unions and justice campaigners, a toxic accumulation of budget cuts, harsher conditions for inmates and a steadily rising jail population has pushed prisons in England and Wales to the breaking point."[3] The prison population of 86,000 is now higher than when the government came to power almost five years ago on the promise to cut the numbers. At 149 people per 100,000 inhabitants, the incarceration rate in the UK is TEN times that of the Netherlands and is the highest in Europe. It has in fact doubled from just 41,800 in 1993, however it is one fifth of the outrageously high figure of 707 per 100,00 in the United States.

In the UK the high rate is in part thanks to the tabloids which depend on crime and punishment to counter their sagging sales. They repeatedly promote the notion that "prison works." Politicians, in turn, don't dare to contradict this false proposition. Almost one-third of crimes committed in the UK last year were made by ex-convicts. Evidence points out that wrong-doers serving community sentences instead of incarceration are less likely to re-offend than the 58% of those released after time in prison.[4] Under the misguidance of the inept Justice Secretary, Chris Grayling, prisoners living in inhumane conditions in the overcrowded jails are now kept from exposing their plight because they no longer can receive legal aid in any judicial review. Grayling caused a storm when he introduced a ban last April on sending books to prison inmates. This was a reflection not only on his attitude toward those imprisoned, but also on the more general social attitude that prisoners should be punished rather than educated. In August the outsourced contractor A4e withdrew from its deal to educate and train prisoners in 12 London boroughs because such rehabilitation efforts did not yield them sufficient profits.

To keep prisoners idle in a highly secure institution costs £36,800 (over $50,000) a year. Educating or training them in a college would cost far less! The President of the Prison Governors Association, Eoin McLennan Murray has said "The fact that they are left locked up in their cells watching daytime TV is our failing, not theirs." This reflects the fact that prisoners watching television need fewer guards to watch them, that is, it lowers costs.

Austerity has also damaged the prison service: It has had to make cuts of about 20% overall. This has entailed closing down 18 of the smaller prisons over the past three years and reducing the staffing ratio from 2.9 for every inmate a decade ago to 4.8 today. Some 22,000 prisoners in England now are forced to share cells designed to hold just one person. To attack this problem, one misguided solution which has dominated the government's projections is to build much larger prisons.

When the super-sized Oakwood Prison was opened in 2012 it was hailed by ministers as the blueprint for a new generation of giant money-saving jails which would be run by such outsourced contractors as G4S. Two years later this disgraced and much embattled security company is trying to cope with the chaos which reigns for Oakwood's 1,600 restless inmates. The young, inexperienced and low-paid staff have to tackle the challenge of drugs, alcohol, and corruption. This huge prison has now been described in the Guardian as "the worst in the country."[5]

There are now 28 large prisons in England and Wales each holding over 1,000 prisoners. The larger the prison, the greater its inhumanity. Attacks on wardens have risen dramatically in these institutions because the reductions in staff have made those remaining more vulnerable in an atmosphere brutalized by the unacceptable conditions. The National Tactical Response Squad, a special prison riot team, has been called out more than 200 times in the past year to put down serious disturbances. Justice Minister Grayling, fearful for his job, has declared, "There is not a crisis in our prisons." The chief executive of the Howard League for Prison Reform, Frances Crook, replied: "There isn't a crisis, it's an emergency."

Sexual abuse in prisons both in the UK and the US is widespread but difficult to ascertain. It occurs between prisoners as well as between keepers and male as well as female inmates. Under reporting of such abuse is inevitable for this is a "hidden issue in a hidden world" where video scanning is off-limits. "People who are sexually assaulted or raped are very unlikely to say anything because they are too scared, have been traumatized and will be bullied and victimized."[6]

The national prison scandals are much aggravated by the fact that in the UK alone, some 200,000 children are deeply affected because a member of their family — usually their father — is in jail. The trauma of these kids is not recognized by the government nor by the public. The tabloids demean and the government restricts family visits to the prisons. Only charitable groups, like Barnardos provide limited support and understanding. Many of the children suffer mental health problems as a consequence and are three times as likely to fall foul of the law as others in heir peer group. However, there are no official records kept of their existence.

Member of Parliament Kenneth Clarke, who held the job of Justice Minister before Grayling, is an outspoken critic of this manifestly flawed prison system. He asked: "Can we have a criminal justice system in which we have more and more people in prison at great expense only to have more and more come out and commit more crime?"

Rehabilitation should be an overriding aim of any prison system, not punishment or cutting costs. I strongly believe that most jails in both the UK and the US should be closed as being excessively expensive, not fit for purpose, incapable of resolving any social problem, and are in fact counter-productive to society's needs. A large proportion of those convicted of non-violent crimes should not be imprisoned but placed into the care of mental hospitals. Most of the others should be tagged, with their movements restricted and controlled. Only those convicted of violent crimes should be placed into high security institutions.

Life-changing electronic tagging is the best way out of the now historically out-dated forms of imprisonment. Electronic tagging has now become widespread in the Netherlands where it successfully offers those who have been convicted the opportunity for genuine rehabilitation. What is stopping such radical change in the UK and the US? The prison industry: Too many jobs, profits and power are at stake.

Represented by powerful and capable lobbyists, officials of this industry will use their money, contacts and influence to undermine any large-scale reforms. Yes, there are better ways. There are alternative approaches to punishment and public safety. The wider public must push their elected representatives to transform these now socially obsolete institutions.

---

[1]The Observer, September 9, 2014, p.32
[2]Nick Cohen, "Scandal of prisoners who should be patients," *The Guardian*, June 1, 2014
[3]Helen Warrell, "Jails at breaking point," *The Financial Times*, August 23, 2014
[4]"Stuffed," *The Economist,* August 2, 2014, p.10
[5]Steven Morris and Eric Allison, "Tales from the inside," *The Guardian*, April 10, 2014, p.14
[6]Alan Travis, "Call for urgent inquiry into sexual abuse in prisons," *The Guardian*, September 15, 2014, p.14

## Which Way is Europe Turning?

Posted on December 10, 2014

As chance would have it, I happened to be climbing Rome's Spanish Steps on a beautiful clear day in March 1957 as the Treaty of Rome was being signed just on top of The Steps by the leaders of six European nations involved. There was little security and not much coverage of an event which I casually dismissed at the time as just another effort by Europeans to get their act together. I did remember reading Jean Monnet's impassioned words on the need for the warring European States to get together: "There will be no peace in Europe if the States rebuild themselves on the basis of national sovereignty, with its implications of prestige politics and economic protection," he declared. "The countries of Europe are not strong enough individually to be able to guarantee prosperity and social development for their peoples. The States of Europe must therefore form a federation or a European entity that would make them into a common economic unit."[1]

Since then, and in part because of the creation of the European Union, there have been no wars between any of the major European nations, and much has been changed by their successful economic cooperation. Monetary union and freer movement for all have been most impressive. I could not have had any idea two generations ago about the impact the Treaty of Rome would have. Even from the air, the continent today looks very different. Every spring thousands upon thousands of farmed acres of Southern England are covered by the unfamiliar but brilliant yellow rapeseed flowers. Their oil is subsidized by the EU to produce ever-larger surpluses of vegetable oil!

In the Mediterranean areas, thousands of small private olive groves with their fantastically sculpted trees, some of them dating back to the Middle Ages, are no longer being harvested or looked after. That is another side of the story. The bureaucrats in Brussels decided that olives were keeping millions of farmers in poverty. The olive trees so passionately tended for by successive generations were labor intensive and produced minimal incomes. So the social engineers decided that their only way out was to put them slowly but steadily out of business by subsidizing and encouraging the development of huge tracts of olive trees that could be harvested by machines and then have those olives processed by new high-tech presses.

Small wonder that today 40% of the European Commission's expenditure is on agriculture. Its intrusiveness into the lives of those living from the land is enormous and the cause of much rural resentment is not shared by the urban population. Much has succeeded in different sectors of the European economy, but since the global crisis of 2008, the living standards of the Mediterranean countries has suffered. There have been damaging levels of youth unemployment, nasty austerity programs, growing economic inequality, banking sector corruption and growing resentment against the bloated bureaucratic administrations in Brussels and Strasbourg. These problems have all gone to fuel a rising tide of right-wing populist opposition.

When Pope Francis urges that the members of the European Union rediscover the convictions and core values of their founders, we know that fundamental issues are at stake. Indeed many of the voters have become tired of shallow calls for unity. They are irritated by the political acrimony from those aloof leaders in the European Parliament who seriously lack charisma. How to attract young idealists to represent their countries in the Parliament remains unanswered. An increasing number of citizens appear more united in their Euroscepticism and the desire to quit the Union than in supporting any efforts for change or reform.

The populists in France, Greece, Holland, Italy and the UK have been effective in fomenting discontent but less successful in presenting constructive solutions. Minority groups in the UK, including Scotland, are told by the populists to look at how well smaller European States like Norway and Switzerland, who have not joined the union, have done. Mark Reckless, the newly elected member of the UK Independence Party in the British Parliament, had written, "We can govern ourselves better than 27 other countries can do it for us. That is the positive and optimistic case for Britain leaving the EU and becoming an independent country trading with Europe but governing ourselves."[2] Indeed, various polls in the UK indicate that a plurality favor a British exit from the European Union. This has placed an opportunistic prime minister, David Cameron, in a corner, because he himself strongly supports a central role for Britain in the EU and recognizes that the proposed referendum to exit would be detrimental not only politically but also economically if it were approved.

English opposition to the EU is one of fundamental refusal to accept political, judicial and economic integration into the continent. The English want to protect their national sovereignty. The French opposition, spearheaded by Marie Le Pen and the Front National, does not see that the European Union is protecting them from a race to the bottom in which their wages and their employee benefits are being steadily reduced. They are opposed to the free-market capitalism they believe is being enforced on Europe by the United States. They want the "good life" with long holidays and not an American-style dog-eat-dog competition with 2 weeks holidays per year, weak health insurance protection, gated communities for the rich and ever growing inequality. Only 40% of the French people now believe membership in the EU is a good thing (down from 60% just three years ago.)

Beyond the populist protesters and demagogues, the more serious critics attack the economic short-termism of both Strasbourg and Brussels. *The Guardian* has written editorially that the EU leadership "must redefine its role and ambitions in a globalized, interconnected and more complex world."[3] There is a sense that there are no EU commissioners willing or able to take on controversial issues or to tackle monetary, fiscal or structural problems. "Everywhere, politicians have spent energy spinning stories so they can hang on to power, rather than solving problems," wrote Hugo Dixon of *The New York Times*.[4]

In an effort to lift the national economies out of their depressive mood and to counter the rising populist tide, the European Commission is coming up with a modestly ambitious investment program. Jean-Claude Juncker, the President of the European Commission, announced a three-year 300-billion Euro ($375 billion) investment package in November saying it was to be seen as a "watering can" which could nurture the EU back to growth. "We are offering hope to millions of Europeans disillusioned after years of stagnation." *The Economist*, however, mocked this as the proposal of an alchemist who was trying to use magical thinking.[5]

There can be no doubt that there is currently a growing sense of unease about the state of democratic politics in the EU. Timothy Garton Ash observed, "I have never known a time when there was so much pessimism about the future of the EU among those who have been its ardent supporters."[6] The division between the populist groups in Europe and the more traditionalist parties is large, but I do not think it is powerful enough to lead to a break up. Most Europeans want a continuation of peace on their continent, a respect for human dignity and fundamental rights for all, as well as an end to austerity.

The EU needs to demonstrate direction, vitality and vision before it can put an end to the inroads being made by populist demagogues. While big changes are under way in the extension of on-line shopping, the growth of internet politics via the social media and the equalization of women and men's pay, no radical moves by the administrators in Brussels are currently in the planning stage for modernization of the Union itself.

Perhaps it should consider ways of reforming its structure:

- How best to reform the distribution of public benefits?
- Can the taxation of corporations be transformed?
- Could an effective control of banking be legislated?
- How a unified taxation system could be introduced?
- Could reform of European prisons according to Swedish lines be tried?
- Could more cooperatives like the John Lewis Partnerships be introduced?
- Could restricting corporate lobbying by corporations be attempted?
- How could decriminalization of marijuana and other low-class drugs be introduced?

Most of the eight dramatic proposals above have been suggested in greater detail in the blogs I have written over the past 18 months. I believe that to avoid a break-up or a breakdown of the European Community it is essential that populist demagoguery should be shown for what it is: negative, without a program, nostalgic for a past which never existed and yearning for certainties in a technology driven world which is adventurous, experimental and in many ways unknown.

[1]Jean Monnet, Speech to the French National Liberation Committee, 5 August 1943

[2]Mark Reckless, "Europe: should we stay or go?" *The Observer*, January 19, 2014

[3]"The Pope's Message," *The Guardian* Editorial Page, November 27, 2014, p.42

[4]Hugo Dixon, "How to counter Europe's rising populism," *The New York Times*, November 24, 2014

[5]Charlemagne, "Europe's great alchemist," *The Economist,* November 29, 2014, p.38

[6]Timothy Garton Ash, "Let a new generation speak up for Europe," *The Guardian,* December 8, 2014, p.27

## Crucial Shifts in Women's Voting

Posted on June 30, 2014

The gradual political shift to the left by women voters in Europe and the Americas is a remarkable and significant indicator of the push for greater gender equality. Sociologists point out that the shift of women to the left is striking because only a few decades ago they had voted to the right of men.[1] After they had become eligible to vote in 1928 (ending the prolonged struggle of the UK's suffragettes) women were crucial in helping to keep the Conservatives in power. In the 1950s Winston Churchill won because more women voted Tory than men [by more than 14%]. Ironically, their loyalties began to shift with the fall of the Tory government under Margaret Thatcher, the first female Prime Minister. With the greater feminine concern for health care, education and benefits in the election of Blair in 1997, the shift in the UK was complete.

A similar scenario was experienced in the US over the past three decades, where more women have voted for Democrats. Some sociologists have traced this development to the decline in marriages and the rise in divorce which has made women poorer and men comparatively richer.[2] Others contend that the rise of female employment in the labor market has made women more likely to favor the left by increasing their awareness of labor market discrimination as well as the demand for state subsidized child care. Whatever the reasons, Romney received less than 45% of the overall women's vote in his race against Obama in 2012.

In an editorial page article in the *Guardian*, Seumas Milne wrote that women are significantly more hostile to cuts in benefits, pensions, health and education than men.[3] It is important to note here that women make up two-thirds of the public sector work force in the UK and three-quarters of the National Health Service and local government. This has also increased the power of women in the trade unions. The consequence has been an historic shift in the political scene over the past three decades. Women of today are far more vocal in their opposition to the use of force, are more supportive of environmental reforms, are on average in favor of progressive taxation and generally endorse the benefits of the welfare state.

Politics often seem contradictory to common sense. I remain puzzled as to how Republicans in the US and Conservatives in the UK, fully aware of the continuing shift to the left in the voting pattern of women, are doing so little to make their expressed desire to reduce the size of government more electorally acceptable. Prime Minister David Cameron is painfully aware of his unpopularity among his country's women with an election coming up in the UK next May. What has he promised them? To cut one million public servants by 2017! Now there are more females today working for the government than men and new jobs will be difficult for the women dismissed by the Tories to find. How can reasonably intelligent politicians move so blatantly against their own and the electorate's best interests? Or are they in some kind of irrational state of denial about the political shift in the allegiance of women?

In the United States it seems most likely that Hillary Clinton will run for the presidency on the Democratic ticket, but the Republicans have done absolutely nothing over the past six years to make their platforms more popular to women. Obama won his second term because of the votes of women who felt more secure with a President who was committed to public services. Today the right wing of the Republican Party wants to cut benefits to a bare minimum. It does not take a brilliant mathematician to recognize that this will almost guarantee electoral defeat. However, the Tea Party, endorsed by sectors of the corporate world, has maintained its gender hostile agenda.

Despite these political shifts by women, their systematic under-representation in the legislatures of democracies continues. They are not helped in either England or the US because female politicians seem to self-select into offices with a high turnover. On the way up the political ladder, the attrition rate is dramatic. Although about a quarter of women hold jobs in state legislatures in the US and in local councils in the UK, when it comes to the House of Representatives and the House of Commons this figure falls to under 20%. "As long as females are the default care-givers, they face an uneven playing field," conclude sociologists Iversen and Rosenbluth, because markets will discriminate against them.[4] There are exceptions, however. The deliberate and rational approach of Angela Merkel in Germany, who has become the most powerful leader in the European Union, has gained the reluctant acceptance of both genders irrespective of her political position on the right.

The notion that women in politics function with greater collaboration and effectiveness than men, has long been an appealing but empirically unproven proposition. This past year, however, the 20 women in the US Senate (16 of whom are Democrats and only four Republicans) have been running something of a lab test: These female Senators now chair or sit as ranking members in ten of the Senate's twenty committees and have been responsible for passing a majority of the bills despite the intense rancor of right-wing Republicans. There is a deep sense that more unites these women personally than pushes them. "One of the things we do a bit better is listen," said North Dakota Democrat Heidi Heitkamp.

In the midst of the political deadlock in the Senate last autumn, Maine's Republican Sen. Susan Collins took to the Senate floor and, refraining from partisan blame, proposed a plan to end the political gridlock. "I ask my Democratic and Republican colleagues to come together. We can legislate responsibly and in good faith." Senate Appropriations Committee chair, Barbara Mikulski (a Maryland Democrat) agreed saying, "I am willing to negotiate. I am willing to compromise," and a few minutes later a democratic Senator said, "I am pleased to stand with my friend from Maine, Senator Collins." Looking for common ground and ways to work together resulted in a plan that led to genuine talks between Senate leaders Harry Reid and Mitch McConnell to end the government shutdown.[5] In recognition of their contribution to politics, the women Senators were invited to dine with President Obama in the White House. Going around the table, Barbara Boxer (Democrat, California) remarked that 100 years earlier they would have been meeting outside the White House gates to demand the right to vote. President Obama retorted: "A hundred years ago I'd have been serving you."

Women are more likely to support activist government spending across a range of welfare programs than men. In the UK, women have disproportionately felt the consequences of Cameron's austerity program which seriously cut back on services and jobs in the public sector.[6] In addition, cuts in maternity pay, legal aid, and child benefits as well as wage freezes and pay caps have resulted in increasing numbers of women, half of whom are now members of the trade unions, protesting against gender discrimination. Single women, in particular, are at the forefront because they have to rely on outside options in case they need economic support.

Women are thus rapidly changing the political landscape around the world. With 50% of the adult population and even a greater percentage of the over 60s eligible to cast their ballots, their impact in the coming decades will steadily increase. How men will react is unclear but it is likely that they will try to cover their insecurity. Beyond that, the possible election of a woman as President of the most powerful nation in the world would alter voter engagement and perspective. It would certainly lead to greater representation of women in legislatures around the world. Such a universal shift towards greater gender equality could well result in the much-needed improvement in global relations which until now have been dictated by men.

---

[1]Torben Iversen and Frances Rosenbluth, *Women, Work, &Politics*, (2010) p.115

[2]Lena Edlund and Rohini Pande, in a paper to Columbia University, October 11, 2001

[3]Seumas Milne, "Women are now to the left of men. It's a historic shift," *The Guardian,* March 6, 2013, p. 31

[4]Edlund, *op.cit*. p.169

[5]"The Last Politicians," *Time*, October 28, 2013

[6]"Ladies in red," *The Economist*, April 19, 2014, p.29

## Opposition to Human Rights

Posted on January 5, 2015

I have long been puzzled as to why individuals as well as entire nation states have such troubles accepting Human Rights which are moral principles based on standards of human behavior and which demand the protection of national and international laws.

Don't all human beings have genuine rights by birth? If so, why did 103 countries in December refuse to support a UN text expressing "deep concern" about violations in Iran which included torture, the execution of minors, violence against women, as well as abuses against religious and ethnic minorities? Why was the International Criminal Court in the Hague unable to engage in hearings for justice and human rights against the Presidents of Kenya and Sudan (thus seriously lowering the credibility of "human rights law" as well as the standing of the court?) And why was there such concerted opposition to Senator Dianne Feinstein's long delayed release of her intelligence committee's report in which she condemned the tortures exercised by the US intelligence agencies as standing "in stark contrast to our values as a nation."

Is all of this because human beings and their representative institutions are reluctant to confront their misdeeds? Professor Diane Orentlicher of Washington's American University wrote that, as a teacher of international law, she was surprised "that Americans would find it so hard to acknowledge the full extent of torture committed by agents of our government and, harder still, to condemn their acts without equivocation."[1] Many public officials, and even speakers on Fox News, were so embarrassed by the word "torture" that they resorted to euphemisms like "enhanced interrogation techniques" (EIT) and "rectal rehydration" for anal abuse. Some apologists excused the torture on the ground that other governments ignored International Human Rights Law and showed little regard or its enforcement. Inevitably, those who may have been responsible for violating human rights are fearful that their exposure might lead to their being brought to justice and rightly punished.

Such concerns partly explain the lack of transparency in the UK regarding any possible collaboration with the US in the notorious rendition "programs" or other illegal activities. Before the publication of Senator Feinstein's 528 page Congressional report, it was "sanitized" by British intelligence officials to avoid any embarrassment to their government. In the UK accountability is such that no one in the intelligence services nor in politics has been held publicly responsible for breaches in human rights. Officially commissioned reports by the government such as the Chilcot or the Gibson inquiries into possible involvement in the torture of terrorists or the rendition of suspects have simply not been made public. Rather than exposure, successive governments prefer the cover-up as a way to protect individual participants and those who commissioned them.

A recent study commissioned by ITV's "Tonight" program revealed that just over half of the 2,000 people questioned in the poll thought the Human Rights Act interfered with British Justice. This is an astonishing result for a land which prides itself on the *Magna Carta*! A debate regarding Britain's membership in Europe's Human Rights Commission is currently simmering as the national elections in May approach. The UKIP leader, Nigel Farage, who wants Britain out of Europe, has been gaining popular support by suggesting that those who break the law are being protected by an inept Human Rights Commission in Strasbourg which is also telling Britons that those being held in prison should have voting rights. The ruling Conservative Party has responded by shifting away from the center in its stance on human rights issues.

As it currently stands, the ECHR has little legal power and Britain's international Human Rights treaties are hard to enforce. Should the UK break international Human Rights law there is no way the judges in Strasbourg could demand accountability. Nevertheless, Prime Minister David Cameron pledged to scrap the Human Rights Act passed by the Labour government some 15 years ago if he wins the May elections. Cameron specifically expressed his right to deport suspected terrorists, his opposition to protecting prisoners of war and he saw no place for human rights when it came to protecting British servicemen involved in combating Isis in Iraq or Syria.

Britain's Justice Secretary, Chris Grayling, joined in at the Party Conference by declaring: "We cannot go on with a situation where crucial decisions about how this country is run and how we protect our citizens are taken by the ECHR and not by our parliament and our own courts. We also have to be much clearer about when human rights laws should be used and that rights have to be balanced with responsibilities." He concluded that it was important to "make sure that we put Britain first and restore common sense to human rights in this country."[2] A spokesperson for the Council of Europe responded that the plans unveiled by Cameron and Grayling were inconsistent with remaining a member, citing article 46 of the convention which states that the signatories "undertake to abide by the judgment of the ECHR in any case to which they are parties."

Moral rights are generally understood as fundamental givens to which every human being is entitled at birth regardless of their gender, ethnicity, religion or national status and impose an obligation on all to respect the human rights of others. Historically, human rights can be traced to the *Magna Carta* (1215), the English *Bill of Rights* (1689), the French *Declaration of the Rights of Man and of the Citizen* (1789) and the *Bill of Rights* in the US Constitution (1791). The peoples of early civilizations did not have our contemporary conception of universal human rights. Indeed there was no word for "right" in any language before the 15th Century. John Locke examined "natural rights" from the philosophic perspective in the 17th Century, identifying them as "Life, liberty and estate" (or property). He contended that such fundamental rights could not be surrendered to the state. The term "human rights" only came into popular use after Thomas Paine's book, *The Rights of Man*, in the early 19th Century.

However, the doctrine of human rights itself continues to provoke scepticism and debate about its extent, nature, justification and applicability. Indeed the exact meaning of "right" continues to be debated by philosophers, politicians, and the legal profession. Do human rights include education? Free Speech? Right to a fair trial? Or basic living standards? There is little agreement as to which of these should be included into the more general framework of a social human rights contract. Even philosophers are divided into two camps: The human "interest" camp, which argues that the principal function of human rights should be to advance our essential human needs, and the "will" camp, which promotes the human rights based on the fundamental human demand for freedom.

When the United Nations was created, following the horrors of two World Wars, the international community was determined to complement the UN Charter with a plan to guarantee the rights of all people. The document they considered and which was to become *The Universal Declaration of Human Rights* was taken up at the first General Assembly in 1946. The Commission on Human Rights was established, made up of 18 members from various political and cultural backgrounds – with Eleanor Roosevelt, the widow of the President, as the chairperson. She was painfully aware that the United States itself had serious shortcomings in its exercise of basic human rights for African-Americans as well as for women. Senators from the former slave states in the South would oppose any legally binding covenant or even a simple declaration of rights. A major point in *The Universal Declaration of Human Rights*, which was endorsed by the General Assembly in Paris in December 1948, was the guarantee against discrimination because of race, creed or color, which had been the particular concern of Eleanor Roosevelt.

The UDHR was a non-binding resolution urging member nations to promote not only Human Rights but also economic and social rights as part of the UN's desire to lay "the foundation of freedom, justice and peace in the world." As such, it was the first international effort to limit the brutal behavior of states, but its charter did not contain specific legal rights nor did it mandate the essential enforcement procedures which would protect the vaguely defined human rights.

Torture was declared to be unacceptable by Article 5 of the UDHR and also by additional Protocols of June 1977 banning the torture of those captured in armed conflicts. Torture was also prohibited by the UN Convention Against Torture which was ratified by 156 nations. Despite such agreements the widespread use of torture was reported by Amnesty International (as well as other human rights monitors) with estimates that over 80 world governments still practiced torture. This is a global scandal.

Most significantly, before the attacks of 9/11 the US Congress had prohibited torture including such techniques as water-boarding and sleep deprivation. After 9/11, lawyers for the Bush administration issued dubious legal opinions arguing that such techniques did not constitute torture. This made a mockery of both human rights laws and the UN convention against torture. Towards the end of the Bush Administration these dubious legal interpretations were rescinded and repudiated and further denounced by President Obama when he took office. However, a dozen years after these violations of the law, not a single individual is being brought to justice for any aspect of the widespread use of torture by military personnel, the CIA nor its shady, outsourced corporations.

In a major editorial page judgment, *The Observer* stated that the United States was not justified in acting above and beyond the international and domestic laws regarding torture which accompanied President Bush's "global war on terror." The US government "circumvented congressional oversight, furtively recruited or suborned more or less willing overseas partners such as Britain, and embarked on a covert, worldwide campaign of illegal arrests, kidnap, rendition, torture, incarceration without trial and, in some cases, assassination."[3]

So where are we now? How can Washington preach against human rights abuses or torture in the Middle East when it admits to abuse taking place in its own intelligence agencies? The new Republican-controlled Senate will not change America's stance on Human Rights as it will continue its obstinate refusal to endorse such treaties agreed upon by most western democracies. The US also has failed to ratify HR covenants on economic and social rights. Perhaps President Obama was justified in saying it was more important to look forward and not dwell on past errors and violations. However, it is irresponsible to simply pass over those who flagrantly violated Human Rights laws. Until Washington, or London for that matter, finally enforce a zero-tolerance policy against both torture and the abuse of Human Rights, it is unlikely that we shall see any reduction of these violations in the rest of the world. That is a conclusion which I do not see how humanity can accept.

[1]Diane Orentlicher "The damning truth: we breached the core values of humanity," *The Observer*, December 14, 2014. p.36

[3]"Playing to the right", *The Economist*, October 11, 2014. p.33

[3]"UK and torture: time for a judicial inquiry," *The Observer*, December 14, 2014. p.38

## Ebbing Friendships

Posted on February 27, 2015

I am most perturbed by seeing what is happening to friendship all around me. Not only is the meaning of friendship being lost, but hardly anyone seems to be seeking what friendship really is or what it can be. My 'best friend' and I enjoy walks and talks and simply being in each other's company. We respect and appreciate our lapses into silence. We also appreciate each other's talents and eccentricities. However, we both recognize that our kind of friendship is becoming an ever-rarer experience.

How many genuinely close friends (in whom we can confide) do we have these days! According to recent American polls, two is the average number of such friends in whom people trust, down from 4 only two decades ago! Studies show that a quarter of Americans admit to having no close confidants at all. The falling numbers are not that different in the UK. It was not always thus in the days before television and the Internet. The current ebb in friendship in the 'western world' has been accelerated by the triumph of individualism and competition in a speed-driven market economy: "Me First" has never been regarded as a boost for friendship.

Closeness in past eras was dependent on the availability of free time and the immediacy of contacts. The great economist, Adam Smith, recognized in the 18th century that the new urban conditions of the growing commercial society could have a negative impact on both the individual and friendships. "As soon as a man comes to a great city, he is sunk in obscurity and darkness. His conduct is observed and attended to by nobody, and he is therefore likely to neglect it himself."[1] Smith advocated that dislocated workers join associations and church groups for the openings to friendship these might provide.

Today's adults can find it difficult to maintain meaningful friendships in factories, offices, or other workplaces. The emphasis on competition and efficiency crackles everywhere and even contacts can pose a transactional feel. It is hard these days to establish where networking ends and genuine friendship begins… with the clock ticking, the mobile buzzing and the computer flashing. Both jobs and financial security tend to be valued above friendship.

In a culture dominated by consumption, speed and utilitarianism, it is difficult to consider friendship in terms of moral commitment. Capitalism and the Internet have both been drivers in the changing meanings of friendship. Our notion of what it means to be a good friend, a close friend, an intimate friend or a "best friend" is rapidly evolving. As Henry David Thoreau wrote nearly two centuries ago: "The language of friendship is not words but meanings."

Online users of Facebook and Twitter can display hundreds of "friends," but seeing the multiplicity of faces on these sites does not reveal their significance. Such social exhibitionism may mask deep loneliness. Internet acquaintances and real friendships are likely to be miles apart. As Aristotle, who spent years considering the nature of friendship wrote: "A friend to all is a friend to none." Facebook Beware! Friendship has traditionally been based on close (geographic) contacts. There is precious little opportunity for this on the new popular sites. We are experiencing a steady decrease in the time devoted to personal communication in everyday life and this makes genuine emotional attachment more difficult to find or to maintain.

The new world we are entering is a domain which is not basically supportive of friendship. Studies have shown that many Americans, in part because of their mobility, eventually lose touch with their early friends. Although there is a global recognition that human beings have benefited enormously from friendship in past times, no effort is being made by nation states to encourage, much less to actively support, such much needed relationships. The way public services such as libraries and the mail are fast disappearing is a significant indication of where we are headed.

A true friend acknowledges the value of friendship and treasures it, but maintaining it in today's digital world can be difficult: one's privacy is so easily violated. As Jon Ronson, a Welsh journalist, filmmaker, radio presenter and nonfiction author found out to his surprise, his identity was recently stolen by some academic "friends" who swooped uninvited into his online existence. Their "spokesmorph," replying to Ronson's protest to this act wrote: "The infomorph isn't taking your identity, it is re-purposing social media data into an infomorphic aesthetic." There would appear to be little room for friendship in such newly morphed relationships![2]

"Friendship is undoubtedly central to our lives, in part because our friends can help shape whom we are as persons." The ancients spent much more time in philosophical reflection on this topic.[3] Aristotle, in particular, regarded the way friends identified with each other as an exhibition of a "singleness of mind." Openness in friendship was an enlargement of the self. He wrote with profound insight that "the virtuous person is related to his friend in the same way that he is related to himself — for a friend is another self. "Friends share a conception of values not only because there is an important overlap between their perspectives but also because of the impact that friends exert on each other. The values they share are jointly formed by mutual deliberation. This has wider implications for society because extending each other's moral experience also affects those around them."[4]

Our first friendships develop in stages and are driven by feelings and grounded in pleasure. My earliest childhood friendships, it seems in retrospect, were based on playing with their toys as well as mine. These relationships were maintained through increasing familiarity and playtime sharing. Only slowly did I become aware of the reactions of my playmates and was often troubled by the behavior of others who were aggressive or tried to dominate. I was also embarrassed by adults asking who was "my best friend?" I didn't have any. Today some child experts see this term as risky because it can disturb the young and can arouse feelings of unsuitability and exclusion.

In psychological studies, three stages in the development of friendship are now accepted: Sharing fun and openness are highlighted at first, then loyalty and commitment are observed in the second stage, and ultimately children increasingly seek similar values, interests and attitudes. As teenagers we become aware that friendship directly contributes to our self-confidence, self-esteem, and social satisfaction. Contemporary books and films tend to highlight the heart-warming commitment and delight of young teenage girls immersed in friendship. However, little attention is paid to what happens to friendship upon graduation from school or university.***

In our times, mutual self-disclosure is often a basic element in creating a "bond of trust" in friendships. Exchanging intimate details of our lives can help us to deal with our problems and, when it exposes our vulnerabilities and secrets, can serve to bring us closer. Trust is essential in friendship because it reinforces the reliability of a relationship which depends on mutually shared interests, passions, views and enthusiasms which all strengthen the sense of the bond which is so basic to friendship. The sharp decline of trust at every level of society has made bonding increasingly problematic in recent years.

However one looks at it, friendship throughout the ages has been an enormous support to us as human beings. Sociologists maintain that friendship makes us "feel more alive" and is "life enhancing." I believe its virtues are a key to living a more fulfilled life. It is up to all of us in a time when friendships are statistically on the wane to counter this trend by singing its wondrous song. As the poet Ralph Waldo Emerson wrote: "The only way to have a friend is to be one."

---

[1]Adam Smith, *The Wealth of Nations,* (1776)

[2]Jon Ronson, *The Guardian Weekend*, February 21, 2015, p.18

[3]Bennett Helm, *The Stanford Encyclopaedia of Philosophy*, (2013)

[4]J. Annas, "Plato and Aristotle on Friendship and Altruism," *Mind*, 86:532 (1977)

***I have always been intrigued by how psychologists and philosophers deal with the complex nature of intimacy in friendships. The suggestion that friendship always entertains an element of erotic desire goes back to Plato. Ever since Freud our relationships, however little expressed they may be, are affected by our sexuality. The Austrian philosopher, Otto Weininger claimed there could be no friendship between men unless there was some attraction to draw them together. Much of the affinity and affection between them consequently can be attributed to the element of unsuspected subconscious sexual attraction. This can produce levels of anxiety in developing intimacy between male friends as well as between female. The Danish sociologist Henning Bech wrote that the more men had to assure themselves that their relationship with another man was not homosexual, the more concerned they could become that it might be. The negative impact on such friendship in homophobic societies has been considerable.

## Closing the Tribal Ways of Life

Posted on July 6, 2015

It upsets me that while the media steadily run stories about the vanishing wildlife species, ranging from rhinos to frogs, sparse coverage is given to the rapid demise of primitive tribal groupings. Perhaps it is because these human beings are too close to us and we don't want to face up to our own precarious future. I think I expected more from the experience of descendants of immigrant Europeans who slaughtered most of the native American Indian tribes in the 19th century and then confined the remainder to vast tracts of infertile land on which their offspring live today as impoverished, second-class and largely denigrated Native Americans. Evidently we are slow to learn.

This blog, however, will not focus on them nor on the plight of similarly threatened tribal people in the upper reaches of the Amazon or the forests of New Guinea. It will focus on the tribes being threatened with extinction in the southernmost corner of Ethiopia in what is one of the last remainders of true wilderness in Africa. At a private meeting in London with a despondent visiting Hamar spokesperson, he said: "My people now live in fear. Our traditional way of life is under threat. The government in Addis thinks of us as savages. We shall soon disappear."

Indeed, the Hamar, like other tribes living in the lower Omo Valley, are victims of an Ethiopian government development program. This is pushed by the completion of the huge Gibe III hydroelectric dam which started storing water earlier this year. The dam will completely alter the seasonal pattern of the Omo River whose waters have been the life force of the ten principal tribes living along its banks. To the administrators in Addis Ababa, the pastoral way of life of the Hamar, Geleb, Mursi, Bodi and Kara people — to name a handful — is anathema. They are regarded as uncivilized. The Westernized technocrats in Addis want modernization in the form of electric power, paved roads, vast agricultural tracts and the introduction of small scale industries. Towards this end they are enforcing a policy of "villagization" in which the tribes people are being evicted from their ancestral lands that have been auctioned off without consultation to make way for commercial plantations.[1]

Since 2008 an area the size of France has been leased or sold to giant foreign agricultural companies cultivating sugar, cotton, cereals, palm oil and biofuels. All these crops will be exported for foreign markets while some of the local inhabitants are already suffering from starvation as the river levels fall.

The Ethiopian government resettlement program known as, "The Growth and Transformation Plan," involved "changing the life style of pastoralist communities." No adequate environmental nor social impact assessments were carried out on the projected plantation and irrigation schemes nor were the inhabitants along the valley properly consulted nor given the opportunity of giving their informed consent. Despite an increasing number of reported human rights abuses, some 929 protesting Mursi households were forcibly resettled into a "model" village close to partially completed plantations and mills. Without their land and their cattle, their pastoral way of life simply has been destroyed.

Historically, the Omo Valley peoples made their decisions only after extensive community meetings by the adults. As few speak Amharic, the national language in Ethiopia, they had little access to information about either the planning nor the construction of the dam which was about to transform their lives. The government had published a decree in February 2009 that any charity or NGO which receives more than 10% of its funding from abroad (virtually every charity in the country) could not promote human or democratic rights. The aim of this decree was to limit debate on controversial policies and restrict awareness of human rights among the primitive peoples.

Environmental and human rights groups, as well as UNESCO,[2] have questioned Ethiopia's agenda or the implementation of the Constitutional guarantees of the rights of tribal peoples to "full consultation" and to their "expression of views in the planning and implementation of environmental policies and projects that affect them directly." However, the now deceased Prime Minister, Meles Zenawi, had lashed out at the dam's opponents asserting that even though the south

Omo "is known as backward in terms of civilization, it will become an example of rapid development."[3]

Survival International, the global association for the rights of tribal peoples, has received disturbing reports that one of the smallest and most vulnerable tribes of the Omo Valley, the Kwegu, have been on the edge of starvation as a result of the destruction of their forest and its beehives as well as the slow death of the river fish on which they depended. "How will we feed our children when the fish are gone?" asked an elder of one of the 1,000 remaining Kwegu people. Those tribal leaders who have opposed their removal from their homes have been brutally beaten and jailed by the military who patrol the region and guard the construction of roads and pylons for the forthcoming electricity lines from Gibe III.

Tensions between the native people and the military have been rising steadily as the result of evictions and, at the end of May, Hamar pastoralists were repeatedly attacked by soldiers with mortars and semi-automatic weapons. A news black-out by the government made it impossible to know the exact number of casualties. Survival International received reports that a "massacre" had taken place. According to an interview with Pink Bull, a tribal elder: "The soldiers said, 'We are going to clear the Omo River area. You move out to the grasslands.' 'Why?' we said. 'This area is our land,' said the government. 'You are few. Now leave this land and stay in the grasslands.'"[4]

Part of the social tensions that have arisen are caused by the younger generation of men who no longer look to their elders for guidance. They view the elders as sell-outs to 21st century "progress" and take to the jungle with G-3 rifles and Russian Kalashnikovs — their only available modern tools. They then show their hostility to the government by acts of violence and when this occurs, the military respond by sending masses of troops to "restore order." Where previously there had been tribal battles with sticks, killing had been strictly forbidden between tribesmen. This taboo has now been broken by the forced resettlements.

The technocrats in Addis are not so blind to the economic opportunities offered by the foreign journalists, photographers, film makers, anthropologists and rich tourists eager to visit the different existing tribal units. Its usually naked peoples were not accustomed to having themselves covered with body paint and tattoos but the government is now encouraging them to parade for photo-tourists.[5] Some of the women display their remarkable lip-plates for higher fees. Little children are bribed into painting their bodies for the cameras. Susan Hack writing about her embarrassment of experiencing this, confessed: "Essentially, I am a voyeur, a gawker, and already my trip's eleven-thousand dollar price tag and the business of intruding on people who have little control over the forces of tourism have me feeling a bit uneasy. Some of my encounters will prove so troubling that I will, at points, wish I had never come to this place… To attract the lens, the women riff on their culture, for example, by wearing old puberty belts on their heads. The resulting scrum is full of antagonism, as foreigners compete with one another for camera angles and the Mursi vie for attention from these human ATMs."[6]

Many of the visitors wonder how the tribal communities would like to deal with such tourism as the elders often are divided on the issue. Some accept it as the only way to earn some money and improve their lives, others see it as an intrusion which is destroying their way of life. Exodus, one of the operating tourist groups, pulled out of Ethiopia two years ago because they no longer could provide "ethical" or "authentic" experiences for their clients. Justin Francis, the managing director of Responsible Travel, respected the decision of Exodus and admitted that the lack of regulation and the growing visitor numbers meant that the situation was becoming increasingly problematic. Pulling out entirely "would help no one," he said, including the discriminated Omo people.[7]

The Bodi, Mursi and Suri who are now being pushed into resettlement camps will become dependent on government aid to survive. Services and food aid are often of poor quality and sometimes non-existent. This spells the end of an Eden-like way of life for peoples who have been part of the natural world and wedded to its beauty, its cycles and its bounty. No need for Victorian prudery or American hypocrisy in their lives. Yes, guns have replaced spears in order to prevent neighboring tribes from stealing cattle, but within each community there had been little violence. The numerous rites of passage had been crucial to the individual members of the tribes by giving them a strong sense of identity and belonging. The continued existence of their social culture had been crucial.

The Hamar or Mursi mothers who are forced to send their naked five year olds to one of the newly built school-rooms are horrified to see them return on their first day with dirty tee-shirts and shorts. To a mother it seems as if her son or daughter had taken on the role of an alien. Moreover, she has never washed any "clothes" except for the wrap-arounds which she rubbed in the Omo River. Cleaning a muddy youngster had been easy as well: you sent the little ones to wash in the river. No mother in these camps had ever heard of soap or hot water – never mind a washing machine. "Progress" has becomes an invasive force. Jane Baldwin, who has visited tribeswomen over the past decade writes, "the women were noticeably tired and thinner. The women showed less pride than was so evident in past years." [8]

Anthropologists have found hominid fossils along the Omo's river banks and the earliest existence of mankind is believed to have started there. DNA analysis suggests that all human beings, *Homo sapiens*, carry African genes and testify to the origin of humankind in Africa. Based on the discovery of modern human skulls from the lower Omo Valley, dated to 200,000 years ago, suggest the possibility that humanity may have originated in this area. Perhaps these are fragments of the founder populations that gave rise to the diversity of ethnic groups living today in the Omo Valley, making this area humanity's womb.

Among these tribes today, the Kara represent one of the smallest ethnic groups in all of Africa. For centuries the Kara have kept goats and cattle, planted sorghum and beans, and held on to their traditional rituals. They enjoy turning their entire bodies into works of art with streaks of white, red and yellow finger paint. Polka dot patterns mimic guinea fowl feathers, stripes are inspired by zebra, and larger spots are there to remind them of leopards. Photographers and writers like Carol Beckwith, Angela Fisher have been captivated by the extraordinary skill and artistry of the Kara and have remarked on the humor, the pride, the empathy and the hope manifest in their eyes.[9]

The Kara and their tribal neighbors along the Omo River have never focused on such material aspects of the arts as wooden sculptures, woven fabrics or carved masks. Their overwhelming preoccupation has been with the beauty and appearance of the human body. Artistic scarification of the arms and stomach have added to their attractiveness. The object of this self-decoration has been to celebrate their beauty, health, strength and sex appeal. They add vibrancy and grace to the human form. They exude an aesthetic purity with their designs and colors and there is no hint of the artificial or the vulgar. And it is to be noted that when a man ages and has lost his youthful powers, he will stop decoration altogether.

Much of the artistry of Africa's tribal peoples people has been photographed and immortalized by the camera work of Eliot Elisofon, Sam Hastings, Leni Riefenstahl, George Rodger and Sebastião Salgado, as well as the primary work on the Omo by Beckwith and Fisher.[10] As the writer and photographer Peter Beard has written, "Art is the barometer of civilization." Alas, as Beard also points out, the arts do not enhance our chances of survival.

You may ask what the globe is losing with the extinction of the tribes of the Omo Valley? I believe it is the vision of another way of life which was natural, beautiful and viable. The loss of authenticity and identity of these tribes people is not replaceable. The material "advances" decreed by insensitive Ethiopian administrators will leave no cultural traces. The invasion of western technology, competitive capitalist economics, and increasingly globalized media and communications are destroying what were remarkably spirited social communities. With our contrived and conventionalized perspectives, our nations do not tolerate differences easily. Conformity and assimilation, disguised by words such as "progress," and "growth," demand similarity and uniformity. This presents us with a bleak outlook for all of mankind — a digital future which the generations of the Omo Valley people could never have contemplated.

Kara men body painting by the Omo River © Carol Beckwith & Angela Fisher/African Ceremonies.

[1]Megan Perry, "Ethiopia: Stealing the Omo Valley, destroying its ancient peoples," *The Ecologist*, February 16, 2015

[2]In 1980, UNESCO declared the Lower Omo Valley a World Heritage Site in recognition of its uniqueness.

[3]Susan Hack, "Twilight of the Tribes: Ethiopia's Omo River Valley," *Conde-Nast Traveller*, January 2012.

[4]Will Hurd, "Ignoring Abuse in Ethiopia," Oakland Institute, (July 2013)

[5]Matilda Temperley, "Nothing to smile about," *The Observer* Magazine, May 24, 2015

[6]Hack, *op.cit.*

[7]Oliver Smith, "Exodus abandons Omo Valley tours," *The Telegraph*(Travel), February 28, 2013

[8]Jane Baldwin, "Ethiopia's changing Omo River Valley – Diary" (2005-2014)

[9]Carol Beckwith and Angela Fisher, *Painted Bodies* (2012)

[10]See Carol Beckwith and Angela Fisher's comprehensive work *African Ceremonies* (1999) which won the United Nations Award for Excellence for "vision and understanding of the role of cultural traditions in the pursuit of world peace."

## Opposition to Change

Posted on November 10, 2015

Change, as we all acknowledge is inevitable, but at one level attempts can be made to control it and at another level it can run out of control and turn destructive. This paradox in the 21st century is becoming ever more evident: The world critically needs major changes — ranging from economic reforms to environmental controls and information privacy — yet there is mounting resistance to profound change all around. I feel frustration in writing this blog because most of the urgent changes I have proposed over the past three years are still ignored.

A society's values and attitudes can exert an enormous impact on encouraging or retarding change. A people who greatly respect the past, honor and obey their elders, and are preoccupied with traditions will change slowly and with hesitation. A more open society has a different attitude toward change: promoting the proposal and acceptance of social and economic development, or progress. However, such changes also can disrupt the existing culture, its assets, values, and even social behavior. This possibility instils fear into the electorate, anxious about the risks and costs involved. This is one of the principal reasons an "establishment" such as that in Britain, steadfastly side-steps changes.

Those in politics largely conform to a script of rejecting risk. Unified by a common outlook which demands that those at the top follow a steady course, which enables businesses to avoid taxes, city bankers to demand continually enlarged bonuses, and permits all-too-many others to cheat on expenses. Their operations are assisted by laws that bear down on the smallest of misdemeanors by the poorest, such as benefit fraud. As the writer Owen Jones described it: "One rule for us, one rule for everybody else" has been another way to sum up establishment thinking. Such a perspective rather assures the members continued advantages and power. It also enables them to avoid the changes that most of the electorate might desire.[1]

Evading risk on difficult issues appears to be of the essence to every establishment. For the past two centuries optimism was fuelled by the vision of a world progressively redeemed from poverty and drudgery through technological advances. From the Marxist philosophers to farm laborers, most everyone marvelled at the pace of the many changes taking place in front of their eyes. But that is no longer true. Although our attitude towards "change", so integral to furthering progress and development, is evolving.[2]

The pace of technological advance progressed so steadily in our homes, our communications, and in the world around us that we came not only to accept change but to expect it. At the same time, we began to recognize that the future was likely to be radically different from both the past and the rapidly changing present. The exponential rate of technological development began to make it difficult for humans to adapt. Indeed the speed of such development has become one of the driving forces of the mounting global crises such as those now occurring in the Middle East.

We who live under the continuing advances of change are becoming fearful that it may deprive us of much of what we inherited: Our ways of thinking, our use of words, our ideas, and our attitudes are being altered not only by the fast forward drive of technology but also by the very pace of change itself. We can see this clearly in the lowered attention-spans of the younger generations. Our memories, too, are beginning to falter without the aid of photographs and social networks. Letters on paper are becoming rare.

The philosopher Hannah Arendt questioned whether "we have ceased to live in a commonly shared world where the words we have in common possess an unquestionable meaningfulness, so that, short of being condemned to live verbally in an altogether meaningless world, we grant each other the right to retreat into worlds of meaning, and demand only that each of us remain consistent with his own private terminology."[3] I know that we do not want to change ourselves out of existence, but we do not seem to recognize what is happening to us.

We no longer think in terms of any limits to growth nor do we debate the possibility of slowing down change, as the Club of Rome did in the early 1970s. I regard one of the prime cop-outs of the 20th century was to suggest that long-term planning was "socialist "and ultimately self-defeating" just because the Bolsheviks under Stalin made such a cruel mess of their five-year plans and their economies. The result was that we began to abandon thinking about changes for humanity's long-term future. Indeed, have the scientific and technological advances [that is, changes] of the past 75 years humanized or dehumanized us?

Personally, I do not believe we can afford to let capitalism's undisputed force in advancing science and technology determine the pace of change on this planet. It is driving our daily lives at ever-greater speeds and developing robots that are already beginning to increase unemployment. Capitalism in its brutality is not only wrecking the environment but it will also change the world we are experiencing beyond recognition over the next hundred years. The way we manage change will determine our success as a global society. This means that we must become participants in dealing with change rather than passive spectators.

Our focus will have to shift from the attractions of the material world and our anxieties about profits to a more gradual enjoyment and development of our personal and internal resources. We must start drafting strategies for change which will shift its focus. Perhaps a deliberate slow-down of tempo could be assisted by the cybernetic machines of tomorrow.

However, to advance such a paradigm transformation we must find better ways of selecting capable leadership than has been demonstrated so far in this new century by the recalcitrants around the world. (The spectacle of the Republicans choosing a candidate from more than a dozen inexperienced but wealthy self-selected millionaires degenerated into a truly farcical effort at change.) Politicians in power never like change and those seeking office, like Bernie Sanders in the United States and Jeremy Corbyn in the United Kingdom, propose numerous changes which are applauded by the younger generations but firmly opposed by their respective mature establishments.

This was most evident in England where the "establishment" is more clearly defined. The reaction of nearly all sections of the largely magnate controlled press and media — ranging from Murdoch's *The Sun* to the usually progressive *Guardian* — has been the derisive rejection of the program of change being proposed by an "outsider," Corbyn, who does not have a university degree, rode a bike when going to Parliament, and did not even wear ties. This rankled when combined with his opposition to nuclear weapons, his distaste for NATO, and his desire for a vast Public Quantitative Easing program.

The British establishment has drawn fine lines between what is acceptable and unacceptable: The People's Quantitative Easing, proposed by Corbyn, for example, is an untouchable. The fact that this outsider is full of passionate intensity for basic economic changes repels the establishment. It is as if he had bad breath. His eagerness to discuss such truly delicate matters as the upgrading of Trident submarines and nuclear weapons is something that the establishment struggles to avoid, much as it does not want to face the failures of the government's austerity programs or the problems arising from economic inequality.

What truly riled even many of his own Labour Party's Members of Parliament, was that this rebel had somehow, against all expectations, come to lead their Party. A leftist leader who was genuinely proposing changes to a society that is in many ways self-satisfied and wedded to a history of "Rule Britannia!" the heritage of the Church of England, and even the Royal family was viewed as undermining the order and "correctness" of an established way of life. His very success seemingly threatened the security of "the establishment," that is, the lose but select socioeconomic grouping of politicians, civil servants, administrators, bankers, academics, the judiciary and the armed forces running the country.

The attraction of the political fringe to such a possibility of significant change seemed frightening: A political figure on the margins was ready to shake the apple cart. As it is, little national confidence exists in the leadership of present and past political leaders in the UK, like Cameron, Osborne, Clegg, Blair or Miliband. But an upstart like Corbyn with a distaste for capitalism, the intelligence services, and drone strikes- no, that was viewed by some as going too far! The politically irritable writer, Martin Amis, even accused Corbyn of being "humourless" as well as not having "the slightest grasp of the national character" and of being gridlocked into the "encysted dogmas" of the antiquated left. Fortunately, Amis is not proposing *stasis*, that is the Greek word for immobility, which itself is an impossibility in this world.

Harold MacMillan, the Prime Minister five decades ago, observed that when "the establishment" is united it is usually wrong. Well, it was certainly united in dissing Corbyn. A *Guardian* columnist noted that the establishment has little time for elections that delivered the "wrong" results.[4] Change has many enemies and here was a politician of the retirement generation who was challenging the *status quo* with a vision of how a basically unstable economic system, which was creating ever greater inequality could be mended. At the Labour Party Conference a couple of weeks after his selection as the new leader, Corbyn did win approval for telling a receptive audience that: "You don't have to take what you're given." But the truth is that all of us have to accept that we shall experience change no matter what we are given.

The challenge for us is to make it "change for the better."

---

[1]Owen Jones, "The establishment uncovered: how power works in Britain," *The Guardian*, August 24, 2014.

[2]See: Yorick Blumenfeld, *Towards the Millennium- Optimistic Visions for Change* (1996), pp. 15-77.

[3]Hannah Arendt, *Between Past and Future*, (1968) p.96

[4]Seumas Milne, "It's the establishment that has a problem with democracy". *The Guardian*, September 26, 2015

## Chaos and Complexity

Posted on January 27, 2016

Chaos seems to be swirling all around me and complexity is of such a profound nature that I am at a loss as how to tackle it: I am not referring to the deterministic Chaos Theory or the Complexity Theory but to the global totality of seemingly unresolvable events: the inability of the European Community to tackle the ever more tragic migrant crisis, the failure of the United Nations to end the destructive combat in the Middle East, the humiliating Republican scene in the US, the mounting environmental crises caused by pollution and El Nino... the list which is becoming increasingly familiar on the daily media goes on and on.

At the same time I feel there is rising uncertainty about market economics, the growing inequality of wealth, the increasing unemployment resulting from robotics, the lack of any program to give direction to the internet, and the scratching of heads over what is happening to basic human values. Electoral democracy is being undermined both by the money of the super-rich and by the ignorance and bigotry of many voters; the arts seem to be corrupted by cupidity, the sciences by profits, communities by individualism, and the young by the narrowing of opportunities. All of these are accentuated by fear, accidents, and the refusal (or inability) to accept the true state of affairs – which is ruled by both chaos and complexity. Could a greater acceptance of the latter two help us to an understanding what is happening not only all around us, but to us?

Theoretically there are many ways order can emerge from chaos, but we continue trying to find order or patterns in the universality of chaos. This is all the more ironic because we complex human beings were created by chaos. The ancient Greeks recognized that even before the earth could be created, two forces ruled the universe: Chaos, which existed in the abyss of darkness, and Gaea, the generative force of matter. The two worked together, first to create the gods on Olympus and then to populate the world with everything from light to living beings. Their approach and assumptions regarding Chaos were very different from ours. Theirs was based on mythical reverence and ours on the existence of fundamental randomness which we have come to fear because its patterns cannot be recognized nor its details understood. At the same time we are creating ever more complex entities, like the Internet, bringing us closer and closer to chaos.

Was our universe built on the haphazard of chaos and chance or on an ordered complexity? It would seem that in the infinite complexities of the universe, its particles, atoms, molecules and development, proceeded according to a specific set of patterns: Determinism. Today we have come to accept that complexity drives our billions of brain cells that are linked by patterns and connections (which we have yet to establish) and that this complexity may have had its origins in chaos!

Around us and within us we experience complexity verging on chaos. We also observe patterns and forms of order and sequence with degrees of complexity. Since the 17th century most of us in the western world have accepted the universe, depicted by Isaac Newton and Francis Bacon, as a having something approaching a reliable clockwork basis. This offered us a form of reliability and objectivity with a more exact measurement of things. Time and numbers began to rule our lives. This led to examination, planning and reliable evaluations of cause and effect resulting in both growth and development. The organizations and institutions we consequently formed were complex and intentionally designed to resist change. Advances in technology and science, however, were such that increasingly rapid changes became inevitable. Now, after two world wars and serious economic crises we have come to realize that linear progress is not always possible, that chaotic events often take unexpected directions with unpredictable consequences.

The noted Professor of Electrical Engineering and Computer Science Leon O. Chua wrote: "Never in the annals of science and engineering has there been a phenomenon so ubiquitous, a paradigm so universal, or a disciple so multi-disciplinary as that of chaos. Yet chaos represents only the tip of an awesome iceberg, for beneath it lies a much finer structure of immense complexity, a geometric labyrinth of endless convolutions, and a surreal landscape of enchanting beauty." Chua described such chaos as the only way for us to grapple with reality.[1]

In many ways the study of complexity differs from the study of chaos, which focuses on non-linear interactions. Complexity involves intricate sets of relationships that can result in some smaller patterns or forms. Chaos pushes a system in equilibrium or order into deep disorder, while complex systems can evolve at the edge of chaos and can develop over a prolonged period into robust forms retaining systemic integrity even when undergoing possibly radical qualitative changes. This can better be understood by looking at the classical economics complexities of "the market" which are the result of human action but not the execution of human design. Towards the end of the 20th century the study of complex phenomena expanded from examining economics to other fields such as psychology, biology, anthropology and ecosystems.

Complexity also encompasses the way in which large numbers of seemingly simple events can come together to produce far from simple patterns of order. Human consciousness, for example, may well be the emergent property of massed nerve cells. Simple systems can organize themselves in a variety of complex ways. Complexity is recognized as a paramount feature of organized evolution which can also result in periods or stages of order and stability. Once the complexity becomes 'supercritical' (or unstable) then a restructuring is almost inevitable. At each level of complexity entirely new properties can appear in the form of new laws, concepts and principles. However, with the advances of computer technology it is now recognized that complexity can even encompass computational irreducibility.

Chaos, or the existence of deterministic irregularity in the field of physics, was brought into prominence in the 1970s by a small group of scientists who proposed that Chaos Theory could provide answers to many of the unresolved problems of science. These viewed the theory as a way to tackle the levels of indeterminacy inherent in quantum mechanics.[2] Physicists found that chaos was not just random abstraction, but had a geometry of its own because of the nature of what has been called "strange attractors" whose geometric forms were first realized when simulated by a computer and projected onto a screen. It did not take long for economists, sociologists and even visual artists to jump on the bandwagon of chaos. Chaos Theory became fashionable but the mathematical regularities in bonding (as in carbon dioxide and $H_2O$), the periodic table, and in chemistry often appear to be too ordered merely to be the product of chaos or randomness.

What are the ways out of chaos and the mounting complexities of our troubled times? We must learn and accept that ultimately we are ruled by both. We must recognize that our aspirations and their fulfilment often feed on chaos and decay. There seems to be agreement that a combination of a bi-focal approach to chaos and complexity would combine a narrowing of attention on small units (rather than the broader and fearful outlook of the corporate world, banking, etc.) that is, on simplicity itself.[3]

The essence of the order and rationality we so desire is not to turn to engineers for their contributions to organized strategies, nor to turn to the computer wizards who are working on 'intelligent' robotics, nor even to escape into the mythologies of religious orders that restrict common sense reality. How best then to approach the fear of chaos we experience? Admittedly when engulfed by desperation, it is hard to suggest general ways out especially when in highly emotional or irrational states. Avoiding the domination of linear thinking can prove helpful. Parallel paths, or even radical and imaginative solutions of ways out, may prove essential. So is hope, which can save us from vanishing into the darkness of chaos. Ultimately it is crucial that as we work our way out of panic, our aspirations be long-term and not on the selfishness-driven short term. Combatting chaos will never be easy, but ever since the classical Greeks human beings have somehow managed and I admit that despite the disasters and chaos which our species may face, our creative efforts will continue to be critical for our survival.

---

[1]Leon O. Chua, in *Chaos and Fractals*, edited by Peitgen, Jurgens and Saupe (1992) p.655

[2]Murray Gell-Mann, *The Quark and the Jaguar*, (1994) p.27

[3]Yorick Blumenfeld, *Towards the Millennium — Optimistic Visions for Change*, (1997) pp.78-91

# Tribal Echoes in Our Era of Globalization

Posted on September 5, 2016

Tribalism may seem to have disappeared, but in ever so many ways it is still very much with us. It is most evident in the popular enthusiasm we show globally for Olympic competitions as well as the primitive vocals of would-be politicians like Donald Trump, which frighten some and are instinctively appealing to others. To the millions who are dismayed by the effects of globalization and feel disenfranchised, ignored, forgotten, or jobless, the options are limited. Their immediate hopes rest in their membership in a family, a community, or social groupings like churches — that is, modernized versions of tribal units. Recourse to help from the state is not always available.

We, that is all the 7+ billions of us, are inhabitants of one planet, such that globalization is truly a given. The problem is how can we be global and at the same time tribal, that is, tied to family, community, and nation when all three of the latter have become less stable? The industrial society which started two hundred years ago has been overtaken by the age of molecular transformations, robotics and electronic communications all of which have contributed to the decline of the family, the social institutions of the past and the decline of trust in government. This has led to alienation and higher levels of anxiety for many. The electorate now yearns for an effective, steady and normative order in which to live.

Much of humanity now seeks a greater sense of certainty. Sometimes this is reflected in a search for a charismatic leader who can relieve them of their burdens of responsibility: In sum a throwback to the tribal days when none of the current uncertainties of change existed. The German sociologist Ferdinand Tonnies described the tribal community as a convincing focus for our social nature before we gradually evolved over the past 2000 years into the fragile legal, rational, and bureaucratic democracies of the present. Because we have all become "individuals," our ethnic groupings — and to a certain extent our identities — are vanishing.

Only ten thousand years ago our ancestors were still hunter-gatherers living a nomadic existence. Traditionally, tribesmen sought to avoid the agricultural life and its humiliations, and saw their destiny as pursuing the interest and honor of their kin group. Some two thousand years later the first farms and small settlements arose. The spirit of the tribal wanderer was still fighting within the newly settled and hard working agriculturalists.

Around 4,500 BC the first cities arose along the Euphrates, the Nile, and rivers in China. Accompanying these were the division of labor, wars involving conquest, as well as forms of writing and record keeping by a small elite. The nomadic Israelites became the first to record and transcribe their transformation from a tribal status to that of a nation. In what was to become the first five books of the Bible, much of this historical recording revolved around the persistence of the tribal mind, vacillating between taboo and ethics, between the drumbeats of custom and the first establishment of laws. A large part of this Biblical text focused on kinship and the impositions of sexual taboos about incest, that is sex with our nearest kin.

The shift from nature to culture was intertwined with the struggle to keep incest at bay by laws and taboos. This was to become a basis of our social relations. Injunctions about whom one could and could not marry and one's obligations to the new in-laws became among the first human rules. To persuade tribespeople that "the other" is not a stranger, but is in fact a relative, remained an important and difficult development in our gradual social evolution. Even today, the Muslim world is still largely wedded to a system of close-cousin marriage. Muslim kids when asked about this will retort: "Of course we marry a cousin. Would you have us marry a stranger? We cannot trust strangers." An enormous reluctance remains in the Muslim world to help all "non-kin" strangers.

The move away from kinship and into non-kin groupings and organizations took many centuries of evolutionary effort that drew on Christianity, the growth of humanism and the development of commerce, industry and science.[1] The continuing antagonism between tribe and state was manifest by the tapping of the support of tribal groups in wars, as the British did with the Scottish clans which they turned into national regiments. Indeed, the United Kingdom remains a political agreement between English, Irish, Scottish and Welsh 'tribal' groupings. The Scots, proud of their heritage, are still eager to have greater recognition and acceptance of their strong separatist desires. The systematic efforts of nation states to suppress their internal tribal units go against the aspirations and the need of identity that they, as citizens, also want as human beings.

The primitive soul encompassed all those powers that were invisible and non-material. It flourished with the poetic and verbal mythology that passed on and was embroidered upon from one generation to the next. The primitive soul was enriched in the Greek, the Norse, Hindu, and Chinese mythologies. Poets like Eliot, Pound and Yeats in the 20th century were united in the belief that "modern" man must recapture the mystic voices of antiquity if they are to heal the division in their souls. In today's globalized world where the word 'sacred' is disappearing, we can also consider whether the "soul" is similarly diminished. Urbanite citizens no longer feel the natural order where their ancestors had once been integrated in a green existence. People lose their souls when they lose contact with nature and with themselves. In effect, they become rootless.

Modern man is becoming increasingly alienated from the world his predecessors inhabited. We walk alone swiftly communicating with others with flicks of our fingers. Online addiction by millions is eroding the mores which our ancestors spent millennia developing, such as shaking hands, reading the eyes of another, observing the person greeting you. Instead, we are undergoing universal social changes through which mankind will have to pass as technology, communications, and work evolve. We don't really know where we fit as we advance into an "all encompassing data-processing system," suggests Yuval Noah Harari. "We are already becoming tiny chips inside a giant system that nobody really understands."[2] Even the most educated find it hard in the age of globalization to accept the unpredictability of change and have trouble trying to cope with it. Indeed, what to do with the rungs of cultural construction of our historical developmental ladder when it is no longer vertical and robots enter? We are facing the threatening globalized confluence of scientific advances in microbiology's exploration of the brain and in computer technology's incredible data processing capacity.

Globalization's sheer trading and economic power drives the world economy in ways which even economists struggle to understand. When advisers to conservative leaders in both the US and the UK in the early 1980s pushed for a global free market in the transfer of capital as well as the free market in goods and services, none truly considered the consequences for the labor market, the increase of immigration, nor the rise of inequality. They failed to recognize that the vast expansion of individual choice would come at the expense of social bonds. They were lured to turn a blind eye to the big multi-national corporations that encouraged global investment both to avoid national taxation and to cut costs by finding cheap "third world" labor. Alas, the anti-globalization groups failed to come up with a set of beliefs that could counter capitalism's competitive momentum nor could they direct the global economy in a more rational way. For decades those in power descended, in tribal fashion, on the talk shop in Davos every January to celebrate the ever-increasing profitability of the giant multi-national corporations.

We are as unwilling to take a larger, longer perspective on the corporate face of globalization as we are to acknowledge the important role of the tribal in our heritage. We need a new global contract focused on increased regulation of markets as well as international cooperation on both a financial transaction tax and a wealth tax. If inequality continues to rise and increasingly large numbers of the electorate feel left behind, then tribal-like nationalism will increase as the most alluring alternative to globalization. The still vociferous and impressive Gordon Brown, as ex-Prime Minister, did his best to slow down the 2008 economic crisis, saying after Brexit that "if we cannot show how we can make globalization fair and inclusive then our politics will revolve around nationality, race or simply identity."[3]

Alas our thinking processes abandoned the old tribal patterns and have become increasingly less imaginative and socially responsive. Tribal people were (and the few remaining are) more confident of their identity than we are of ours, contended David Maybury Lewis in his book and television series.[4] Because we have all branded ourselves as "individuals," we have left the strength of the tribal behind. Reacquainting ourselves with our tribal heritage could re-ignite some of our lost humanity.

Organizing society into smaller units, each of about 250 members, would be the rational way to advance to more meaningful and enduring human relationships. Past experience tells us that social units or clubs much larger than this tend to split up into various smaller ones or into "sects." Small community groups would result in the return of familiarity and stability so basic to reducing the social anxiety, tension and isolation that are increasingly prevalent today. The proposition that small is not only beautiful but also economically viable has been blocked by a profit driven economy that has done its utmost to prevent such change from taking place.[5]

In my book, *Dollars or Democracy*, I outlined the direction in which we should advance: corporations should be turned into cooperatives and the huge multi-nationals broken up into small cooperative units. The emphasis of the state should also be to encourage and support the formation of smaller social groupings in which the individuals could find their place and identity much as they once did in tribal communities. Short of such vast and radical change, the humanizing remains of the tribal in us will be crushed by ever more ruthless corporations and the determination of national states.

---

[1]Even so, some of the footholds of tribalism remain, as in the Mafia. The motto of this inward looking group is: "Never go against the family." As Robin Fox noted, in the Mafia "Trust is possible only between close relatives and preferably those of the paternal clan." Robin Fox, *The Tribal Imagination*, (2011) p.63

[2]Yuval Noah Harari, "In big data we trust," *The Financial Times Magazine*, August 27, 2016, p.14

[3]Gordon Brown, "Globalization must work for all of Britain," *The Guardian*, June 29,2016.

[4]David Maybury-Lewis, *Millennium: Tribal Wisdom and the Modern World*, (1992) p. 279

[5]See: Yorick Blumenfeld, *Dollars or Democracy* (2006) p.190

## The challenge of changing perspectives

Posted on August 21, 2017

I find the continuing acceleration in the speed of change in life disturbing. Everybody is "busy" most of the time. We race from one place to another, spend too much time in traffic jams, rush through what we have to read, see on television and follow on our computers. Meals are cut short and Victorian style afternoon teas are no longer in fashion — they are too time consuming.

Through the dynamism of both technology and finance, we have changed not only the pace of life but also have altered its quality and direction. Money (that is, profits) has been the driving force of capitalism but almost no attention has been given to the effects on human beings which follow most innovations. In my last blog I focused on the unknown impact of iPads and tablets on infants. That was not the occasion to examine the possible impact of computers, mobiles and automation on adults.

What first comes to mind is what I am doing right now! The hours spent everyday on my computer are bad for my back, my eyes, my hands and my spirits. I still love writing with pen or pencil and find these wonderful, but slow and I, too, am often in a hurry. I am not on Facebook or the other social networks because they would intrude into my moments of leisure, time in the garden, or time to reflect.

So where can we take the currently uncontrolled and unplanned advances of technology which are popularly assumed may end with Artificial Intelligence? How to test the effects of automation on human beings as well as on entire societies? It is evident that as long as money/profits remain the prime driving force, there is little possibility of controlling the advance of untested but desirable technology-driven innovations for our brains and mental states.

Let me suggest that the pharmaceutical industry is a good example of what the Silicon valley giants could try to copy: In most countries almost all new medicines have to pass a variety of rigorous tests for their suitability on patients. If this difficult as well as bureaucratic program works effectively for protecting our physical health, why could different tests not be applied for the mental well-being of those subjected to electronically stimulated waves — ranging from head-sets to our everyday iPhones? We have little idea at the moment to what we are subjecting our brains (and hearts) and what the possibilities of damage there may be from many electronic devices.

On a broader perspective, some of the impacts of the new technology on the younger generation are evident: many no longer communicate in writing on paper and tend to stick to minimalism when it comes to expressing themselves. They even don't like to use the telephone, regarding it as a medium of old-timers. I have been advised by a son that he no longer reads any email which extends beyond two terse paragraphs. As a writer, I find all of this poses cultural challenges which we could perhaps correct in schools and universities over time.

As a writer and former journalist, I am most disturbed by the newly popularized crisis of faith in journalism. The masses like to get the instant flow of events from Twitter and the online news organizations. What with the perverters of the truth, like Murdoch's Sun newspaper in the UK and Fox News in the USA, the press increasingly gives readers the scandals they want rather than informing them of the events which might increase their knowledge or might be useful. For that matter, I have to confess that getting the Trump scenarios out of my mind is becoming an everyday challenge.

Even much of our economics are becoming unfathomable: Bit-Coins with their digital crypto-currencies make no sense. It seems that they are new instruments for gamblers, tax evaders, and high-tech risk takers rather than money to be used every day. Controls by governments of QE (Quantitative Easing) in which billions upon billions of dollars, pounds and other currencies have been pumped into bank reserves also seem most dubious. The whole QE process comes straight out of wonderland and tends to confuse minds, even in government, about reality.

I must balance these deep concerns with my expression of positive advances in so many areas. I am most enthusiastic about the giant greenhouses being based on the Eden Project in Cornwall. The co-founder, Sir Tim Smith, wants "to create oases of change… our job is to create a fever of excitement about the world that is ours to make better." His group is now planning the construction of giant green-house domes in China, Australia and New Zealand.

I find the GPS of finding one's way around the world as directed from outer space is a marvelous technological breakthrough, much as it may do away with our former ability to read maps. This is a variation of the impact that the technologies have on our abilities. When kids in schools some fifty years ago were given simple hand held adding machines, they quickly forgot how to do their sums.

The miracle cures for cancer exploiting the powers of genetics and our human immune systems are to be lauded. The related advances in gene editing techniques are promising extraordinary solutions to many of our genetically based illnesses. However, as with medicines, we should try to advance more carefully with intense examinations of the possible consequences rather than triumphantly announcing breakthroughs. The moral challenges we face with the introduction of gene editing must be dealt with enormous care and consideration. Our perspective of how to protect our minds after all these millennia of change and development must not be corrupted by the lure of money nor even by the competitive egos of leading scientists.[1]

Governments around the world are now planning to ban all diesel and petrol vehicles over the next 25+ years because the rising levels of nitrogen oxide present a major threat to public health as well as to climate change. If governments can do this on a cooperative basis, why can they not start research on whether the electronic products of 'Silicon Valley" are affecting the mental and asocial imbalances of the population?

Thankfully, there are numerous aspects of our evolving cultures, like the above, which are greatly encouraging. I think it is most important to focus on these to bring greater hope to millions of people who have become deeply discouraged by the universal focus on capitalist competition, celebrity, and terrorism in this new millennium. I am advocating that the wonders of being alive on this incredible planet truly should be the basis for much of future optimism in the next generations.

---

[1]Yorick Blumenfeld, Towards the Millennium, (1996) pp. 421-428

# III-     ENHANCING POSSIBILITIES FOR THE ARTS

I recognize that the rousing potential of the arts are capable of giving us what life itself may not. The arts can create altered realities and can lead us towards new visions. They can even cause paradigm shifts in our perspective. In changing our consciousness, the arts are capable of enhancing our lives and advancing and elevating our spirits. To my dismay
the visual arts have not been able to reach this potential.

"Post-Modernism" and the "conceptual" in the arts have in large measure become more concerned with the medium than with the content. The price to pay for this emphasis on form rather than on substance or quality has been a loss both of standards and values. What counts today is how a work of art affects the individual rather than how it may affect society as a whole. Money is of the essence and trivialization can triumph. Today there are no limits nor boundaries in the arts and, alas, the sacred has been abandoned. The current trend is to tear down all barriers- of time, space, feelings or distance. The present aim is to achieve in-your-face directness, impact and spontaneity.

The arts in association with the means of mass production have become ruled by reproduction , multiples and repetition- all glorified by the essentially tawdry trends of fads, fashion and the social media ."Quantity thrives on compromise," it is said but "Quality does not." The spread and democratization of culture should be celebrated, but if we accept the definition of culture as being "activity of thought, and receptiveness to beauty and human feeling," then it does not seem that we have made much advance in the 21st Century. Artistic intuition has been viewed as the basis for confidence of the spirit, but there is not much to encourage us in these socially and politically turbulent times. Many of the art works being created are foremost protests against the multi-faceted stresses facing mankind..

I believe that brutality, materialism, mediocrity, hypocrisy, confusion, self-indulgence, and obfuscation are among the seven deadly sins which the arts must firmly avoid. "Art' , 'beauty' and 'quality' have all become expressions of contempt. Yes, I maintain that the arts should embrace playfulness, imagination, sentiments, love, self-expression, hope, vision, spirituality, awareness, and reflection.

When a creation of some kind, like an unmade bed on the floor is displayed in a museum, there are critics, curators and a clique of other artists who will hail this as daring, profound, revealing and if it is even nebulously vacuous, as 'mystical,' 'radical' or even 'mysterious.' To me such advocacy represents a bought-out inversion of aesthetic values.

The ancient Greeks taught us that art encompasses discipline, clarity, nuance, imagination, the full range of passions, the integration of complexity, interpretation and the desire to communicate- none of which had anything to do with making money. The genius of their artists, poets and dramatists was to make it possible for the creators to feed on the energy and responsiveness of their audience. The predicament of the human situation was confronted in the boldest manner by their great playwrights.

Destiny was inescapable as a theme for Aeschylus, Sophocles and Euripides. The first of these greats used the myth of Prometheus to show his audiences that courage and spiritual strength in the face of painful and seemingly eternal trials could end in heroic figure but also, miraculously, end in positive acceptance. Sophocles in Oedipus Rex presented the audience that at the very moment of total degradation, Oedipus rose to the ultimate heights of human grandeur. Euripedes. especially in hia Medea, worked to free human beings from the grasp of mythical destiny. His message to 4th century B.C. Athenians was that they should strive to the ascendant ideals of goodness and justice. At the same time tragedy blended with comedy affirmed the value of life and challenged the aspirations of the human spirit.

The Greek mythical heroes were obviously of superhuman status, which helped to make them more popular. However, they were not overpowering. The audiences knew they could not possibly live up to the wisdom and cunning of Odysseus nor the virtue of Penelope, but they could try to emulate such heroes to some small degree. In doing so, they were not overpowered by the discrepancy between the ideal and their own Periclean reality. The Greeks recognized that these great playwrights were consciously inspired by the ideals of human conduct which enrich the whole society.

The Greek poets endowed individual musicians with magical power over both the Olympian gods and men. The Muses were specifically created to give the world the universal voice or form of communication which it had been lacking. Indeed the Muses expressed the harmony of the entire universe from the furthest reaches of the cosmos to the smallest aspect of the human soul. According to the mathematical genius, Pythagoras, the divine order was maintained by harmonic numbers. The fundamental relationships in music ( 1-2 (an octave), 2-3 (a fifth) and so on ) were said to determine both the harmony of the spheres and music phases. By means of the numerical proportions in music, the analogous character of all that exists could be known. They were at the basis of true harmony.

Perhaps the magic of the music of Orpheus could cast a spell, It had the power to convey an enormous range of feelings, from joy to despair, as well as experiences of order and chaos. One of my historic family ancestors, the German poet Heinrich Heine, held that music "is a miracle for it stands halfway between thought and phenomenon, between spirit and matter, a sort of nebulous mediator , like and unlike each of the things it mediates- spirit that requites manifestation in time and matter that can do without space." Music, in effect, is the expression to which all the other arts often aspire.

Art is no longer regarded as being an integral, integrating part of life, but as a separate, distinct and even segregated realm in our more fragmented and specialized society. This is most openly revealed in the mounting apposition of art to life. All too many people want to "understand art" instead of experiencing it. As far as the artists are concerned, the central ground of "conceptual art" which is promoted by money, show-business, academia and the art market, has little to do with art, talent, quality or ability. It has a great deal to do with exhibitionism.

Oscar Wilde, in *The Critic as Artist*, wrote that "It is to the soul that art speaks, and the soul may be made the prisoner of the mind as well as the body...There is nothing sane about the worship of beauty. It is too splendid to be sane."

I am one of those old-timers who still passionately believes in beauty. Some thirty years ago, in diary notes, I wrote:
If we create beauty, we are increasing meaning
If we spread ugliness, we destroy meaning.
If we create beauty, we augment coherence
If we diffuse ugliness, there is a loss of spirituality.
To deny beauty means to deprive our spirits
To negate beauty is to undermine meaning
To accept ugliness is to demean the human.

Today I also hold that love and desire can add another dimension to the realization of beauty through symbolism and the imagination.

The spiritual aspects of art can be demonstrated by the very nature of their magic and mystery: the inability of rational explanations to tell us anything about the impact of the work on our souls. A blossoming apple tree by Van Gogh is far more than the skillful combination of brush strokes, colors and spatial layout. It is the focused expression of Vincent' loving, tortured soul. It will take a long time before an AI machine will be able to tell us why the apple blossoms of Van Goh produce a special response in our human psyche which a good color photograph of the same subject does not.  Such art is a non-rational expression or interpretation of our deepest feelings.

The stupendous series of "Compositions" created by Wassily Kandinsky between 1910 and 1913 transmitted a rhapsodic spirituality onto canvas .He compared these works to music in which a "new symphonic construction was being created. Although he was not consciously seeking transcendental links between himself and the cosmos, there was a universal spirituality in these works. They possess a lyrical self-sufficiency that wonderfully, almost divinely focuses our gaze . In these vibrant abstract paintings Kandinsky was determined to find a series of harmonic color from improvisatory arrangements that could move the viewer's imagination, which would arouse significant and wonderful responses, and would permit them to look beyond the surface reality of this world. Kandinsky wrote in 1914 that:

"… color directly influences the soul; color is the keyboard, the eyes are the hammers, the soul is the piano with many strings. The artist is the hand that plays, touching one key or another purposively, to create vibrations in the soul.."

Such creativity can convey spiritual states, emotions and responses quite independently of the world with which we are familiar. However, the large number of  today's conceptual artists, by portraying destruction (even of social values) or forms of vacuity, can also provoke rebellious responses which may disturb more than just  the questioning viewers. Such psychic challenges and  instabilities tend to test not only the viewers but the culture as a whole.

Music , however, speaks for itself. As Friedrich Nietzsche observed: "Without music life would be a mistake." The music we make is a vital expression of our inner being. To extend and enhance the rhythmic and melodic effects of music on human sensibilities still holds unexpected possibilities for the human race. Music intimates a harmony in the cosmos in which we like to think we have a place. We resonate to an awareness of higher beauty, to the music of the spheres, as it were. It is difficult to assess whether music has the power to guide humans towards a higher beauty or whether it is there only to give us pleasure.

When listening to Bach, I often feel as if I had been participating in an order and in harmonies which are not my own and yet which are a part of me. When enthralled by Mozart, I sometimes sense a kind of lyricism which I have never experienced or a form of passion which I have never known, but might have known. Such music suggests imprints from a past of which I had no awareness., as if my soul had experienced a previous incarnation in a musical sphere.

New musical styles, continually developing, merging and changing like the societies that give birth to them, reflect the vibrancy of contemporary cultures. Each period embraces its own defining sound. This serves  to affect the human spirit, providing an outlet for creativity and offering a symbolic perspective of societies from within that could not be captured in words or images yet introduce new dimensions into humanity's repertoire.

## Challenges in the Art Market

Posted on February 14, 2017

The struggle in the art world between auction houses and gallery dealers has been quietly raging over the past three decades. The prime focus of the auctioneers has been to maximize profits while the galleries have tried promoting and protecting their artists to create an appreciation in value.

The art buyers buyers have been in the middle but the balance has shifted because the collectors making the largest purchases are no longer visiting the dealers but are circulating around the world at some two dozen fine art fairs stretching from New York to Hong Kong. This is causing an increasing struggle for the dealers because the auctions are excluded from the fairs. For many dealers in the world's mega-cities, who are already facing increasingly expensive rents, it has meant additional costs for space at the exclusive fairs, plus, travel, shipping, insurance, staff and accommodation. Many of the established but gradually exhausted dealers feel compelled to attend three or more of these fairs in a world already consumed by uncertainty.

I must come clean on this immediately: four members of my family have been artists and they are currently represented by dealers in six countries. So I write about this with experience going back to my youth in the Paris of Picasso and Matisse. It is not only that art is increasingly being called into question by the power of money, by the new computer-driven trends of what is "fashionable," by the reduction of space given to art by the printed media and the corresponding dearth of capable art critics,[*] but now also by the struggles between gallery dealers, the auction houses and the art fairs. It is on this aspect of art as a form of investment in a more insecure financial planet that I shall try to focus.

In our era, money, profit , celebrity, globalization and speed have overwhelmed how art is valued and consequently how it is promoted and bought. No ideology nor notion, like that of the "avant-garde" affect either dealers or auctioneers. What matters is money, although videos,

Instagram, and the digital media, as well as the prestige of museum shows, all affect the market. The sense that high prices suggest quality while lower prices hint at a lack, has grown over the past century. The result is that artists struggle to get higher prices through their dealers, or eventually through the "updraft" of auction sales, as well as through exposure in the media. However, "The random, narcissistic, and viciousness of internet culture," as described by Holland Cotter in the New York Times, takes its toll.[1]

Contemporary artists prefer to use independent dealers who will not only make beneficial decisions about their output , but who will look after them and their reputation. Running their own "shops" dealers are not dominated by corporate interests such as auction houses are. This gives the artists greater protection, stability and "longevity," or continuity, which the auction houses cannot provide. True, some patronizing, big-time dealers, such as Larry Gagosian, may sell paintings which have not yet been created by one of their leading artists to collectors who are over-anxious to buy the newest of creations. How this could affect the artist may not even be considered! Jeff Koons, one of the highest paid of contemporary artists, says: "I love the gallery, the arena or representation. It's a commercial world, and morality is based generally around economics, and that's taking place in the art gallery."[2]

There are still a number of well-informed and cultured art dealers who have devoted their lives to furthering paintings, sculptures, and water-colors of particular artists and periods. Such dealers tend to follow their instincts instead  of the fashion-driven market.  A little over a hundred years ago, the famous Parisian dealer,  Paul Durand-Ruel, created values for paintings few wanted and he managed to change the taste and economics of the Victorian-age art market. When no one was able to sell such impressionists  as Edouard Manet, Claude Monet and Camille Pissarro, Durand-Ruel was successful in making a business from them.

"What would have become of us if Kahnweiller had not had a business sense?" asked Picasso of the German-Jewish dealer who single-handedly saved the Cubists from starvation. The art expert Bernard Berenson, who became the grand intermediary between historical Italian works of art and the great British dealer, Lord Joseph Duveen, was to remark that "I soon observed that I ranked with fortune-tellers, chiromancists, astrologers, and not even with the self-deluded of these, but rather with the deliberate charlatans." Berenson, who made millions certifying paintings by 15th to 18th century Italian masters, expected maximum returns from sales he had facilitated for Duveen, but actually took no responsibility for making the sales.

Today those who buy and sell art as a business no longer like to have themselves described as "dealers." They have been transformed into "gallerists" or "curators." The latter gives credibility to their status. Curators are associated in peoples' minds with experts who have academic or museum training and have developed scholarly concerns with quality and historical origins like Berenson did.[3]

In the psychological warfare of the market, artists also have been promoted as "ground breakers" doing "cutting-edge work," which may be described as being "radical" or "seminal." Their product is no longer "new" or "innovative." The artists no longer enjoy careers, but have become "masters" working on their latest "iconic" image. Galleries employ public relations firms who create "name recognition" for the artist. Indeed, celebrate status has become vital in today's global art market. The artists are also being forced to promote their own status as the role of critical reviews has shrunk due to the lack of coverage in the press.

Artists today are being defined by their capacity to convert feelings, experience and thoughts into a tabloid of our increasingly exposed world. Although most artists of the past were once considered "contemporary," our current "Contemporary market" has a vitality that is now absent from the market for Old Masters and Modern Art. In part, it is the relevance to immediacy that explains the current success of the Contemporary in the global art market.

Since the year 2000, the Contemporary global art market has multiplied in value by close to 14 times. The number of art buyers generally has risen spectacularly from around 500,000 in the 1950's to around 70 million today. The average age of these art enthusiasts also steadily decreased, as the number of those in their thirties and forties has risen markedly and 95% of the participants are now connected to sales via their mobiles. According to Metcalfe's Law "the market's potential on the internet is proportional to the square of the number of its connected buyers, collectors, dealers and curators."[4]

There is no regulated code of conduct in the globalized art market. For the auction houses as well as most galleries, commercial values rule supreme. Sales are driven by desire, greed, prestige, and competition. The works of the leading contemporary artists become blue chip investments while those of the younger creators who receive lower ratings must face the inevitable market adjustments as their art is viewed as a financial investment. A successsful French artist, Thierry Ehrmann, contends that "Contemporary art will always be ... constantly criticized for its record auction prices, its difficulty of interpretation and its inherently subversive nature."

As far as the auction houses are concerned the market place warfare is about money and not about "the new" nor about artistic innovation. Amy Cappellazzo of Sotheby's explains that the management is trying to transform their image from being an auction house into that of an "art business service." There is a recognition that to do so, as auctioneers they must try to buy or takeover a number of galleries and in that way insert their presence into the flourishing art fairs which have become the largest transactional arena for art.

The big fairs, like those in Maastricht, Basel and New York, all are in competition with Christie's, Phillips, and Sotheby's. The fairs bring in rich collectors, the museum curators, dealers, critics — all of whom enjoy the art world social atmosphere with only the rare presence of actual artists. As the New York Times headlined it: "As prominent artists age, the art world hopes to cash in." The frantic gossip at the fairs, the networking, and exhibitionism all add to the excitement of these gatherings. A wild, single sale can set the market rolling. In part that is why the market is so notoriously vulnerable to manipulation. A ring of a few promoters can bid up the price of a youthful but dubious painter.

This was certainly the case of Jean-Michel Basquiat, who after his early tragic death from drugs, was promoted by a small group of top dealers led buy Bruno Bischofberger of Zurich. They pledged to keep the price of Basquiat's works at auctions rising and over the past thirty years they have been spectacularly successful: The price has risen from the $5,000 level to the multi-million dollar range.

Neither dealers nor the auction houses have any connection to aesthetic principles. They leave that to the burgeoning world of museums. Whatever standards still exist are now in the hands of these representative institutions. Each year about 700 new museums are opening up around the world. More  have been built in this short new millennium than in the previous 200 years.[**] As each of these new institutions  search for museum-quality creations, they underpin the art market sales of the dealers, the auction houses, and the fairs.

As Philip Hook concludes in his latest book, Rogues' Gallery, "The history of art dealing is the story of many varieties of human folly and duplicity, interspersed with ingenuity, inspiration and occasional acts of heroism."

---

[1]Holland Cotter, "Artists reflecting their era," *The New York Times*, January 31, 2017.
[2]quoted by Jackie Wullschlager, "Lasting Impressions," *The Financial Times*, February 21, 2015 (Arts Section, p.11)
[3]Philip Hook, Rogues' Gallery, (2017)
[4] First formulated in this form by George Gilder in 1993, and attributed to Robert Metcalfe .
[5]*The Economist*, February 4, 2017, p.82

[*]The painful lack of truly incisive art critics such as former prominents Clement Greenberg, Hilton Kramer, Herbert Read, Harold Rosenberg, and David Sylvester is manifest in both the US and the UK.

[**]The supremacy of money in our time has been characterized by one artist, James Stephen George Boggs, who specialized in creating new bank notes. He would take a picture of himself and place an engraving of

it on a hundred dollar bill where the bank name might be "Federal Reserve Not." When merchants wouldn't accept his art, he would point out the beauty of the engraving. As his biographer, Lawrence Weschler noted, "he was just short of being a con-man –but no more so than anyone else in the art world." Although Boggs died in January, the Economist's obituary noted that his art remains on the walls of galleries and museums all over America and Europe.

## Architectural Developments

Posted on January 24, 2014

Lifting the human spirit, as well as the quality of life, should be the goal of those concerned with providing affordable housing for the globe's billions. All of us truly owe it to the human race to leave this planet a better — and where possible a more beautiful –– place. The structures we inhabit must take pride of place in such an effort, but in particular this demands not only a different approach to financing but also the talents and creativity of the architects, planners, builders and craftspeople who are directly involved.

"Architecture Reimagined", a new show at the Royal Academy in London, tests our response to more innovative and explorative architectural proposals. The Curator, Kate Goodwin, hopes it will "heighten our awareness of the sensory realm of architecture and thereby encourage the creation of a more rewarding built environment."

Alas, there is a huge gap between the aspirations of architects and the structures that are ultimately built. For years the area around Cambridge's railway had fallen into shabby decline and various proposals had been discussed and then rejected. Around 2004 one property group designed a master-plan aimed at offering a 'European' approach to create a development where people could work, live, shop and socialize — encouraging a sense of belonging and pride in their community. It took a few years for the plans to be approved and then the initiators went bankrupt and it was taken over by new investors.

Last week, wandering through the yet to be completed development, I was struck by the discrepancy between the reality and the bill boards shouting:

> *"See the Future. Be part of it!*
> *See chic cafes, bars, lifestyle shops in the new city quarter"*

The lack of imagination and innovation of the new six story structures said it all: Money had triumphed over what initially had been a rather idealistic venture. The spacious development has little hint of intimacy. Nothing appealing is to be seen on the exterior of the buildings. But that is not unusual, as I have found degrees of bleakness in most of the housing developments currently being completed in the greater London area. Architecturally, the loss of individuality, of identity, would appear to have become contagious.

I suppose that what bothers me about the new housing and office developments in the UK is the desire of the large corporations to impress by building ever taller glass and steel office structures with competitive phallic compulsion, while the concrete housing developments are lacking not only in idealism but are also bereft of architectural ambition. It is entirely understandable that in a time of recession it is not possible in public housing to get funds allocated for anything but the essentials. However, is it too much to suggest that variety is also the spice of liveable housing itself? Very few of these developments displayed a single sculpture. (Nor, for that matter, do the new industrial parks.)

"Garden Cities" — the forerunners of the "New Towns" in England — were initially conceived as a counterbalance to the over-crowded conditions prevailing in the industrial cities by the end of the 19th century. Among those most convinced of combining the benefits of town and country life was the planner, Ebenezer Howard. He put forward, in his book *Tomorrow: A Peaceful Path to Real Reform* (1888), detailed plans for complete new towns in which houses, schools, shops, factories and recreational facilities would be installed. His enlightened ideas were put into practice with the establishment of Letchworth, located some 35 miles north of London, and in 1920 with Welwyn Garden City. He had hoped that these two would be the role models for future cities throughout the United Kingdom, but no further "Garden Cities" were created. They were deemed as too 'middle-class' for the masses. However his comprehensive model was highly influential in the post-WWII era in the establishment of new planned cities such as Milton Keynes and Stevenage.[1]

The New Towns were adventures in physical as well as in social construction. As such, they were much maligned. An architectural critic has described them as "bubbles of optimism, steps towards a future we have long since abandoned,"[2] The direction of the new architecture was already moving towards (1) the profitable, (2) the efficient, (3) clear and rectilinear blocks, (4) poured concrete, (5) schematic duplication and (6) the "empty in human content." The aluminium framed glass boxes came later. Increasingly, the order embodied in mass production became the most profitable and thus the most desirable. This was "the bureaucratic personality, sterilized, regimented… ultimately hostile to every other form of life than its own: cut off from human resources and human roots."[3]

Instead of "the repetitive inanity of the high-rise slab, the distinguished architectural critic Lewis Mumford called for an "organic order based on variety, complexity and balance" which "provides continuity through change, stability through adaptation, harmony though finding a place for conflict, change and limited disorder, in ever more complex transformation. This organic interdependence was recognized and expressed in every historic culture… and although these buildings have outlived their technologies they still speak to the human soul." Lewis Mumford *"The Highway and the City*, 1953.

Although cities are holding an ever-larger proportion of the world population, economic expediency in the developed nations drives most city planners. Whether it be housing estates or "Science Parks", standardization of both design and construction prevails. "The construction of our habitat continues to be dominated by market forces and short-term financial imperatives. Not surprisingly, this has produced spectacularly chaotic results," wrote the prominent architect Richard Rogers. He maintained "The quality of urban environment defines the quality of life for citizen." Today the rapidly built-up cities "reflect society's commitment to the pursuit of personal wealth. Wealth has become an end in itself rather than a means of achieving broader social goals"[4]

Market-driven criteria of commercial developers produce disastrous results, claims the architect. Rogers contends, "Building is pursued almost exclusively for profit. New buildings are perceived as little more than financial commodities, entries in company balance sheets. Any expenditure not directly related to the making of short-term profit exposes developers to longer-term capital outlay, which makes the company less competitive and hence more vulnerable to financial exposure and ultimately to take-over."[5]

Technological advances are changing our lives much faster that the buildings that house us. As the relative cost of the packaged and standardized steel and concrete buildings keeps on falling, they are being reproduced at an ever-faster rate, providing neither enhancement of our lives nor enrichment. Today you can walk into new developments in most countries without getting a clue as to where you might be: Singapore, Milan, Toronto or Brisbane. There is unlikely to be any genuine difference in the style of the rectilinear or square boxes of multiple stories.

Another noted architect, Norman Foster, argues forcefully that in our world "Freedom of public space must be defended just as fiercely as freedom of expression, and that "The encroachment of private control demands public accountability."

As I observed the new Microsoft research headquarters in Cambridge rise incredibly swiftly, I marvelled how mechanical form now follows mechanical function. The characterless glass and steel box has become the established mark of modern acceptability and to counterbalance this has been the creation of the sensational in such works as the London Shard which exhibit the audacity and daring of both the designer and the builders.

As we move ahead in the 21st century, we must start to build structures and developments that emancipate and civilize. Greater emphasis must be placed on the "character" of the new buildings. This should somehow incorporate the contours, colors, shapes and shades of the natural environment. It should also, where feasible, enhance the tastes and heritage of the prospective inhabitants.

---

[1]"The New Towns of Britain." Central Office of Information, January 1969.
[2]John Grindrod, *Concretopia: A Journey Around the Rebuilding of Postwar Britain,* 2014.
[3]Lewis Mumford "The Highway and the City," 1953.
[4]Richard Rogers, *Cities for a small planet*, 1997, p.17
[2]Ibid, p.67

## Why CREED?

Posted on February 14, 2014

"What's the point of it" is the title of the retrospective exhibition of Martin Creed at the Hayward Gallery in London right now. I find no merit whatsoever in the show, so what is the point of my writing about it? Exactly that. I wonder what leads a Gallery director to select such a show which advances nothing, certainly not popular understanding? What do the members of the Hayward board give as an excuse for promoting so much vacuity, such latter-day phenomena as Blu-Tack stuck onto a wall? Does the trodden chewing gum on the pavement not deserve equal exposure?

How can we, collectively, have come to this without howls of protest? Is it a sign of the end of excellence or spirituality in cultural phenomena?  Namely, is there no point in our being on this planet? In this spacious gallery there is no tragedy, zero empathy, absolutely null meaning, no hint of beauty, and certainly nothing new or ground breaking in terms of sculpture, painting, or art.[1] Admittedly, there is an abundance of denial. There is, indeed, no end to the symbolic presentations of the chaos and confusion of our times, to self-indulgence, to the repetition of the gaping void, to spiritual emptiness. Perhaps that is why this show features the cinematic presentation of a woman defecating as emblematic?

Now Creed, who is a conceptual prankster, is frank in admitting that he has no idea what art is, nor for that matter, what an artist is. OK. I grant him the absolute right to put on whatever nonsense he wishes. The critics, however, are another matter. They take it all rather seriously and a few even sing modulated praise for this exhibition. So how are the school children being taken to this show at the cost of £4 per head going to be affected by this? It is certainly not going to help them distinguish between the acceptable and the discreditable, between art and pretence, between junk and craftsmanship. Defecation, as depicted in this show, cannot lead to anything new in our perception nor can it be improved upon as such. It is part of the dead ends dominating an entirely by-passable show.

Early in the 21st century it seems no longer acceptable for the cultural literate to call crap, crap. Saying that such an exhibit should never have been staged is regarded as a sign of snobbish elitism. Yes, perhaps really great art, like the Elgin marbles or the paintings of Hieronymus Bosch, cannot be appreciated by everyone. But to attempt to diminish these by branding them as "elitist," may be fashionable but serves to reveal both ignorance and stupidity.

Perhaps because humans are now being so flooded by images on television, the Internet, films as well as printed media, they are no longer able to distinguish between the immaterial and the valuable, between the meaningful and the vacuous. I am continuously embarrassed by visitors unwilling, or unable, to say "I like" or "I don't like" when visiting a gallery or a home. They remain silent perhaps because they are afraid to reveal their ignorance, possibly cause offense, don't want to pass judgment or may be unaccustomed to expressing an opinion.

It is significant that in this show at the Hayward one learns nothing about the creator of this jumble — except that Creed has an intense desire for notoriety, fame and appreciation. He does not offer a clue about his own feelings. Nor is there any notion that the work is driven by passion, by talent, or by the spirit. Supporting descriptions in the handouts state he grew up in a Quaker background with little appreciation of the decorative. This minimalist background might be significant but one cannot deduce it from what is displayed.

So who has promoted Creed to have this one-man show in a huge London gallery? First of all, of course, himself. He is tireless when it comes to giving long introspective interviews. How he won the Turner prize with the creation of an empty white room filled only with a flashing light bulb filled me with bewilderment at the time. The endorsement of Sir Nicolas Serota, Britain's foremost museum director, may have played a role here. His own gallery, Hauser & Wirth, naturally gave him unstinting support. There has been no one to say that the artist has no clothes.

Alas for Creed, the Shock of the New of the 1960's has turned into the Big Yawn of the first decade of the 21st century. All of his conceptual gimmicks and fatigued concepts are an unattributed rehash of what had already been exploited over the last three generations.

The curatorial fashion of our time is anti-chronological so many exhibitions have been focused on the thematic. This encourages the professional curatorial world to embrace the chaotic, the thematic, and the vacuous.[2] 21st century galleries like the Hayward are primarily out to attract ever more visitors so that they can collect more money. This is perfectly legitimate but to present non-art, in the form of Hirst's pickled shark or Tracey Emin's unwashed sheets, or Creed's haphazard enthusiasm for Blu-Tack, undermines the very legitimacy of the institutions presenting it as art.

What attracts visitors? Scandals, shocks, porn, the "New," anything to do with the famous or ultra-rich. None of which have any relationship to the spiritual, to inspiration, to introspection nor to craftsmanship which are of the essence in art

Artists through the centuries have drawn on their heritage, on the traditions with which they grew up. They have enlarged on what preceded: Picasso, for example, drew heavily not only on the African masks he admired in Paris, but on the experimentation of the group of artists around him, such as Matisse and Gris. One does not encounter such engagement in the work of the likes of Tracey Emin or Creed — whose work is not based on any artistic heritage. For them there is no real history, only the present. Works created out of all context are rarely works of art. They seldom inspire a following and because of their intrinsic vacuity are unlikely to have any positive impact on our future.

I believe it is essential that art and its interface with truth and beauty lead us out of this protracted period of value-free nullity in which we have become afraid of letting emotions establish any kind of preference. If modernism was guided by new perceptions and movements conspicuously breaking with traditions and optimistically looking to the future while trying to break with the past, post-modernism recycled existing values so as to render them meaningless.

The great Russian writer, Alexander Solzhenitsyn, declared in a famous address to the National Arts Club[3] that "For a post-modernist the world does not posses values that have reality. A denial of any and all ideals is considered courageous. And in this voluntary self-delusion, post-modernism sees itself as the crowning achievement of all previous culture, the final link in its chain."

I see little hope in the current approval ratings of conceptual art. If this category has any rules, parameters or system, I am unaware of these. For all I know, conceptual art ultimately may prove highly popular among astronauts winging it to other planets, but it lacks the solidity on which we can build a more artistically blessed society.

---

[1] Farah Nayeri, "When art is beside the point," *New York Times*, January 28, 2014

[2] Jackie Wullschlager, "Thoroughly Modern," *The Financial Times,* July 14, 2012

[3] New York, January 1993

## Upholding Handwriting
Posted on March 9, 2015

I am writing this blog because I feel that the single most artistic activity of human beings that is being threatened is the art of writing. Cursive writing is under attack. I treasure handwriting, but the way we are headed, future generations may not be able to read cursive texts nor even sign their names! In this respect, I think that digitalization is whittling away our humanity on a grand scale. We must confront this.

You may object that today's youths won't miss anything when they no longer write with pen or pencil — but that is also because all too many of us take the act of writing for granted. Many see it only as a means of communication — like a telegram (also on its way out). Just as a voice on the telephone tells you a lot about the personality and character of the caller, handwriting conveys even more about the state of mind of the writer. The digital message is close to being anonymous. The ABC of electronic letters does not reveal anything about the sender (perhaps to the regret of the Secret Service!)

So what is happening? Teaching handwriting in primary schools is on its way out. In the United States and other countries, like Finland, technology is replacing writing just as it is seriously affecting so many important human activities ranging from memory to contact with the natural world. Today's teenagers are far more comfortable texting on their mobiles, touch-typing on iPads or tapping on laptop keys than holding a pencil or pen in their hands. For many students, cursive is becoming difficult to read. For teachers, however, computer word-processed papers are easier to read and to correct. Even more important, teachers feel the digital advances provide them with extra time to spend on other common core standards.

Prof Richard S Christen, an expert in education at the University of Portland in Oregon, told *The New York Times* that cursive writing could easily be replaced with printed handwriting or word processing, but he was concerned that students will lose an artistic skill. "These kids are losing [class]time where they created beauty every day," he said. "I'm mourning the beauty, the aesthetics."[1] The splendor of Chinese and

Japanese brush strokes, the vitality of Arab calligraphy, and the glory of medieval manuscripts are part of the history of writing which has so enriched civilizations.

The everyday process of writing, over the past two millennia, had become integral to our cultural evolution. The ability to write was something that could affect the future of a child's life. Writing also was a companion to the arts. The way children progressed in their writing influenced their lives in a fundamental way. I shall try to explain this at some length because I regard it as crucial to our understanding of the process of writing itself.

For children the slow progress of communication starts only a little after babbling. Klara Roman in her exceptional book, *Handwriting: A key to Personality,* wrote that it all begins with the pleasure children have in scribbling, that is, taking a pencil and marking up sheets of paper rather haphazardly. "This random movement has been compared to the graphic equivalent of babbling. It is free, spontaneous motor play — of movement for its own sake."[2] After a while, maybe some days or months, such random movement becomes sequential. Each child develops its own individual approach: one may push the pencil in an angular way producing zigzags, another produces circling whorls. The energy they exert varies greatly: some hold the pencil lightly; others cover the paper with diffused weak strokes, while a few make forceful sweeping marks. Usually a pattern develops which will be repeated over and over. This is the child's own imprint and achievement and fills it with delight. It not only empowers, it also is a basic way of self-expression which involves mastering one of the first tools.

With a relatively stable pattern of scribbling, a child can express its different moods: Sadness will reduce the size of the more downward strokes. Cheerfulness will expand the line patterns, while anxiety will constrict them. Child psychologists point out that feelings of aggression are displayed in increased angularity while rage results in outbursts of vehement strokes. The scribbling stage does not last long, but presents a visible record of the infant's self-expression before and independently of teaching. Repetition of its pattern making gives a pleasurable feeling, in part because it bestows the comfort of familiarity. Its individual execution makes it easily identifiable from that of other children.

Scribbling is an expression of fundamental personality traits. At about the age of four scribbling is usually abandoned in favor of drawing, and after that comes writing.

The first efforts to push a pencil over paper in order to copy a letter of the alphabet are hampered by cramped movement of the hand. Learning penmanship is often an ordeal as well as an embarrassment to the five year old. Free expression must come to an end when the child learns to write under school instruction which enforces the imitation of copybook letters. Only gradually will the child acquire sufficient eye to hand control to copy each letter accurately in what is called print script — that is, with little or no connection between the letters. Only later will children be coached in the transition to cursive writing. Their handwriting will develop steadily throughout the primary school years. Generally children will progress to write in a firm and controlled manner. Their familiarity with reading, writing and speaking will become fully integrated in their minds.

When children enter first grade they usually have acquired a basic understanding of language in a haphazard fashion. Reading and writing will then demand a more formal and systematic approach. The first grader will read aloud printed words in a monotone way without understanding their meaning. Similarly, in copying words, they will trace letters without comprehending the sense of the word. Eventually, seeing, hearing and writing the word simultaneously will represent the essential leap forward. It used to be a kind of a rite of passage to be able to write like grown-ups. There was pride in the dexterity, the fluidity and the exactness which are essential when putting pen and pencil on paper. Now the manual script skills of the past are fast disappearing. An art form is being de-activated.

I am only an amateur graphologist, but to this day, I greatly admire the handwriting of my parents. The way my father (a famous photographer) brandished his pen reveals his virtuosity, his vitality, humor, strength of character, intuition, insight, charm, self-confidence and- above all — his artistry. However, his writing has none of the commitment, steadiness, understanding, compassion and humanity of my mother's handwriting which, for all its merits, lacks both an artistic bent or ambition. Today their letters, written decades ago, reveal so much of who they were.

Admittedly, today's videos also can present astonishing aspects of those pictured for future generations, but they lack the extraordinary depths provided by handwriting.

As it is, people no longer keep diaries, and letters from our friends are becoming rarities. The lack of such writings will seriously affect the historical research of tomorrow.

I find it highly discouraging that when the fate of writing is being discussed by law-makers in Washington, references are usually made that unless they are taught script, students will no longer be able to read the *Constitution* and the *Declaration of Independence* which were originally written in copperplate script.[3] Politicians seem to have blinkers on. Scribbling will continue, just as the babbling of infants will not stop, but script writing may soon come to an end. The problem facing us is a much larger one which those pushing the advances of technology should not be left to resolve. Nor should teachers and their unions be forced to decide.

I believe that teenagers who create handwritten paragraphs are engaged in a process which enhances their conceptual understanding as well as their memory. Hitting a button with one's fingers is a markedly different exercise from carefully shaping letters into words. Critics admit that pen and pencil may help develop motor skills but that children can record their thoughts at a much faster pace by tapping their fingers. Speed in writing, like speed in everything else in our modern lives has become a determining factor... but there will be a price to pay in having machines gradually bulldozing our humanity.

[1] Katie Zezima, "The Case for Cursive," The New York Times, April 27, 2011.
[2] Klara G.Roman, "*Handwriting: A Key to Personality*," (1952) p. 21
[3] Libby Nelson, "*Cursive handwriting is useless, but politicians want students to learn it anyway*," libby@vox.com, February 1, 2015, 4:00pm

## Possessions

Posted on April 13, 2015

> *"The pleasure of possessing*
> *Surpasses all expressing*
> *But 'tis too short a blessing."*
> John Dryden (1681)[1]

I must confess to having something akin to an obsession when it comes to collecting things. I hoard items from my past. My 'study' is filled with all kinds of memento ranging from fragile "ancient" tape recordings of Anna Freud (for which I have no player!), to a cellophane wrapped cigar (I don't smoke) from my 25th Harvard Reunion, to the dusty "lamb chop" of a ventriloquist given to me by my long-deceased friend, Shari Lewis. Of course in addition to the vast accumulation of books, there are the first drawings by my sons, an image of my friend Vaclav Havel which I ripped-off from a wall of posters in Prague, and the well-preserved 17th century skull of a Sicilian nun. The list of such treasures could fill this whole blog.

What with Encounter magazines from the 1960's, memorabilia from both parents and various 'souvenirs' from trips as a journalist to some 90 countries, my spider-webbed 'study' has turned into something of a recluse's den. I'm far too embarrassed to permit visitors to enter (or photograph it). To the frequently asked question: "What are these possessions all about?" I usually reply with a superficial counter-question: "What is a life all about?" The truth is that I have a fear of throwing away something historical, but I also would like to give future generations an idea of the scope of a writer's interests at the turn of the second millennium. Collecting, gathering, saving and storing possessions has a long and rich human history. It is also a bewildering one. As Luke cautioned in the Bible: "Take care and be on your guard against all covetousness, for one's life does not consist in the abundance of his possessions." [2]

Both of my sons urge me to give most of my possessions away to Good-Will Industries– as they habitually do in their spring clean-ups. The youngest likes white walls and clean floors. Is this merely a reaction to my clutter? The older enjoys having lots of framed paintings on his walls, but does not have any bookcases. When we got married, my sculptor wife made me promise never to be encumbered by possessions. I agreed. She was afraid of being trapped, of being closeted by possessions. She wanted the freedom to move about like a nomad, but she possesses a photographic memory and can carry all her past, all her history in her head without so much as a scrap of paper. The computerized world certainly has made this kind of freedom possible for some, but despite the near magic of Wikipedia and Facebook, the electronic world does not engage my sentiment like the books in my study.

The possessions which surround me all contribute to sustain me as I write my blog or when I let my mind wander. It is comforting to have the actual things associated with one's memory. However, there are those not so visible items in drawers, like the letters from Dutch and German relatives, texts which I have never read and most probably never will. I gave a number to the Holocaust Museum in Washington D.C, but as to the rest, who will appreciate them when I am gone? Some of them are in a German Gothic script almost impossible to decipher. So why do I keep them? No vanity or exhibitionism on my part is in evidence here. A connection with the past, mixed with considerable nostalgia, is important to me.

Americans, driven by an economic system dependent on consumption, are quite naturally consumed by it. They now have more possessions than any society in human history. They have become possessed by their possessions. Americans became the true champions of accumulation during the Reagan era when they began to commit close to half their annual expenditures on non-essentials. A good portion of this vast hoard is now tucked away in the near to 50,000 storage facilities across the United States and this does not include the staggering number of over-filled garages. "An entire industry has emerged to house our extra belongings-self-storage." This has become a $24 billion industry with companies like 1-800-GOT-JUNK making millions in removing it.
[3] Americans eagerly cherish things and accumulate them. They move their favorites from shelf to shelf and from home to home. "We love stuff; we can't get enough of the latest and the greatest... Nothing is ever enough. We must always have more, " observes the writer Kali Hawlk.

A century and a half ago, the great Victorian artist and designer, William Morris, cautioned the English to "have nothing in your houses that you do not know to be useful or believe to be beautiful." This was a golden rule for those struggling to furnish or redecorate their new homes. Insightful as this may have been, it did not recognize that our relationship to our possessions goes far beyond utility and aesthetics. The insightful writer William James, a contemporary of Morris, argued that our possessions tend to define whom we are: "Between what a man calls me and what he simply calls mine, the line is difficult to draw." In a variety of ways our possessions can represent our extended selves.

"We invest emotion and memories in our possessions, giving them deep meaning, but that doesn't necessarily make us happy — it may drive us slightly mad," wrote Michael Bond.[4] In investigating the psychology of our desire to accumulate and our fear of being dispossessed, two behaviorists concluded that reflective consumers perceived throwing away as threatening to their security, their memory as well as to historical preservation. They also contended that preserving material objects was an assist towards cultivating a vision for the future. Preservation thus reflected "a desire to reassemble the fragments of their temporal experience into a unique space where memories, present, and life projects join together."[5]

After a crippling accident, the writer Melanie Reid confessed: "I lost my judgment about what to keep and what not to keep... Precious memories, letters, old cards, school exercise books, children's art, bad photos, newspapers... These were what made a family home, home. Soft furnishings for one's soul. So if I'm honest, this house is therefore also a carefully guarded shrine to my old life."[6] Most of us encumbered by superfluous possessions are reluctant to face up to the challenges of even partial disposals. A growing number of "clean-up" consultants, like the new best seller, Marie Kondon,[7] suggest you must start by listing all your possessions: Make an inventory of everything. The days this might take you could prove that you have all too many belongings. Then categorize all these items before loss-aversion sets in: divide the letters, photos, albums, playbills, tickets etc. into favorites or levels of importance; possibly separate the personal, the life shaping and sentimental from the commercial or economic. All this might lead you to spend more psychological energy and time maintaining what you have than any actual pleasure you might derive from the entirety of your hoard.

Minimalists would like to get rid of everything but the most essential. In the arts this generally leads to vacuity. In terms of a household, getting rid of scads of "superfluous stuff" can end in soullessness. Paring down, throwing out, eliminating, detaching, letting go, scrapping the lot – any of these may provide immediate relief but they may also diminish one's very being. We may be deprived of the real pleasure we derived from their existence. The extent to which a possession is linked to our psyche is critical in determining whether such an object would elicit grief if lost.

"Our possessions all have magical qualities. Many, if not most, of the things we keep have an essence that goes beyond the physical character of the object," noted the author of Stuff, Prof Randy Frost of Smith College. The very word "Possessions" is as suggestive of the material as it is of the erotic: To possess. Possession. Possessed.

All of these really grab me. Gifts also can possess us in different ways. We often treasure them as keepsakes which hold a deep sentimental value which is likely to increase over time. A good number of the mass of my possessions often have helped me in explorations of my "inner squirrel" self. I believe this kind of classical analysis inevitably beats such modern trends as renting books online and then storing them in "the cloud!"

[1]John Dryden, *Farewell, Ungrateful Traitor* (1681)
[2]*New Testament*, Luke 12:15
[3]Josh Sanburn, "The joy of less," *TIME*, March 23, 2015, p.32
[4]Michael Bond, "Possessions", *The New Scientist*, March 31, 2014.
[5]Helene Cherrier and Tresa Ponnor, "A study of hoarding behaviour and attachment to material possessions," *Qualitative Market Research: An International Journal,* Vol.13 Iss:1, pp.8-23.
[6]Melanie Reid, "This house is a shrine to my old life, " *The Times* (London) Magazine, March 28, 2015, p.9
[7]Marie Kondon, *"The Life-Changing Magic of Tidying-up."* (2014)

## Personal Tastes

Posted on June 15, 2015

I have no desire to become a life-coach on matters of taste. Taste is all about discernment, about the exercise of mental vision. Alas, "tastelessness" is gaining global status not only in the art world but also in the media. It is fair to say that the masses have little discernment. They are ruled by money, evanescent fashions, personalities and, on the internet, in the mass-instinct for joining the most popular sites. The primary focus on cost, value and the monetary relationship to objects exposes a crucial lack of discernment in regard to taste. The overpowering force of money, greed and "the market" have all worked against taste in the Arts. The inflated auction values of works of visual art have not exercised a positive impact here. A glaring disconnect between taste and economics has arisen.

Even in these difficult economic times, perceptive critics could be influential in creating new closures, appetites and tastes. As Oscar Wilde declared back in 1891: "Without the critical faculty, there is no creation at all, worthy of the name." What critic today is questioning taste in art? Who is the critic who points out that the emperor (Hirst?) has no clothes? Where now are the successors of such critics of the last century as Lawrence Alloway, John Canaday, Ernst Cassirer, Clement Greenberg, Robert Hughes, Max Kozloff, Hilton Kramer, Rosalind Krauss, or Harold Rosenberg? Altogether this galaxy catered to the finer susceptibilities of their readers. They furthered the development of critical taste by weighing the balance between taste and the intellect. Alas, the role of the art critic has diminished as print advertising has contracted. With less space for them in which to publish, the cultural level of their prose has fallen. Wrote Wilde: "Mediocrity weighing mediocrity in the balance, and incompetence applauding its brother, that is the spectacle which the artistic activity affords us..."[1] What I suggest is that actively nurturing and promoting our critical faculties could be a boost to artistic taste in the 21st century.

In my role as a critic, I make no apologies for considering the drawings of Egon Schiele, George Grosz, Sonia Delaunay and Avigdor Arikha as inspiring and wonderful. On the other hand, I find that the so-called art of Tracey Emin , Sarah Lucas and Jean-Michel Basquiat to be a form of emetic for my eyes. I accept the view that Tracey Emin's bed is no longer a matter of taste or art. But why then should an object of sociological interest be placed on view in a Museum devoted to art? This bed and its unclean contents are all about disorder, despair, confusion and a tastelessness on the part of the creator which I find pathetic. Emin's sexual needs and frustrations may arouse the emotions of many women, but evoked no positive response from me. Some viewers may find unlaundered sheets provocative, but what is the connection to "art?" There is no trace of individual skill, craftsmanship, talent, development or even imagination. Semen stains may be emotional markers, as Bill Clinton demonstrated, but have little to do with genuine taste.

Emin and Sarah Lucas in many ways exemplify what could be called anti-art. Sarah's giant inflated penises and artificial plastic vaginas pouting burnt out cigarettes currently being shown at the Venice Biennale may be more creative than Emin's bed, but I find these void of any sense of appreciation for taste. Shock, surprise, amusement are the principal responses of the viewers. Much of Lucas's effort seems simple, naïve to the point of childishness. None of it can be described as elevating, spiritual, or even contemplative. The matter of taste seems irrelevant. Once such offerings are appreciated merely for their novelty and the surprise reactions these may elicit, the objects become difficult to describe as art.

Jean-Michel Basquiat's enraged and frantically created graffiti-like works also smack of the destructively infantile. This African-American rebel died from a drug over-dose at the age of 28 in 1988 and many of his scrawled paintings included skulls and skeletons. Often the writings on them were crossed out as he was obsessed with deconstructing the two-dimensional broomstick figures of his own torn and fragmented soul. The drawings and canvasses screamed: "I may exist but no one is here!" Such negative creativity was totally unconcerned with any kind of "taste." Today, thanks to the clever and daring tactics of a small group of a well-funded ring of international dealers, Basquiat's strokes of protest against African-American discrimination, which he expressed on stretched canvas, raise millions for investors and auction houses. It is the art world run amok much as poor Basquiat once did.

Much of our contemporary creation is focused on novelty, provocation and vulgarity. Some 200 years ago the English political writer William Cobbett described the commonness of vulgarity as being clumsy, dull and "torpid inanity," that is, a lack of taste. Mark Akenside also asked:

> What then is taste? A discerning sense
> Of decent and sublime, with quick disgust
> From things deformed, disarranged, or gross.[2]

The Victorian artist/writer John Ruskin posited that "Simple and innocent vulgarity is merely an untrained and undeveloped bluntness of body and mind; but in true, inbred vulgarity there is a dreadful callousness."[3]

When I now appreciate a classic Van Gogh or Vermeer, there is an instant and almost instinctive sense of 'yes' which affirms my sense of taste and which may transport me, increase my heart beat, and open up my mind to the positive. I may be seized by the immediate and intuitive awareness of the soul of the painter as it was being created. I also am likely to be most impressed by the skill with which it was painted, but am unlikely to consider any metaphysical or other worldly reality. The blackbirds filling up the sky of Van Gogh's closing days naturally bring up enormous and highly emotive symbolic associations. The painting is beyond any question of good or bad taste. It is a total experience.


[1] Oscar Wilde, *The Critic as Artist*, (1891)
[2] Mark Akenside *The Pleasures of the Imagination* III, (1744)
[3] John Ruskin, *Sesame and Lilies*, 1865

## New Directions for an Embattled BBC

Posted on September 3, 2015

I find it ironic that the BBC, which has enjoyed such an exemplary record in public service communications, now should be under fire from the Conservative Party in part because it has been so successful. The Tories have felt uncomfortable with its power and status. They attack the BBC for being too large, ineptly run, unaccountable and opposed to free market economics. Furthermore, the daily press, and the Murdoch papers in particular, add fuel to the fire because they view "the Beeb" as an overwhelming competitor that diminishes their falling sales. Such negativity is rattling the BBC which, when added to great pressure from other quarters, has called into question its survival in its present form.

To pay for its excellent services and its 20,000 workforce, the BBC is dependent on the £145 ($ 225) a year in annual fees paid by each household in the UK. This charge has become increasingly resented by many citizens who feel they are being taxed for a service they no longer really need or want. They can get all the news and most of their entertainment on the Internet for free. Why pay for a TV service which may soon go the way of record players, telephones and bookshelves?

The rapid inroads of broadcasting technology are perhaps even more threatening.to the BBC. New "streaming" groups like Netflix are barging in; with much more flexible and cheaper offers. Netflix, which was launched just 3 years ago, already has been subscribed by 4 million of the UK's 27 million households. The new generation does not want to be told what and when to watch the news or entertainment. They want to choose and select freely -- which is easy with their new apps.

Structural reforms to the BBC hierarchy itself also pose a further challenge, this time an internal one. A complex and supervisory Trust and the group's management wing are ultimately responsible but currently lack clear direction. The BBC is a comparatively small player in an online world which is borderless and global. Apple, for example, is more than 30 times larger than "the Beeb." The Corporation's managers are unavoidably at odds with its commercial rivals, especially in the United States. The Corporation has been successful in introducing its technologically advanced" I Players," but seems somewhat adrift in a world of media fragmentation. Although the BBC 's World Service reaches some 200 million people around the globe, BBC's managers have to operate in ecosystems designed by those with profit-making motives far removed from the BBC's founding principles.

**The Beginnings**

Admittedly, I have been an admirer of the BBC and its ethos all my life and an outspoken critic of what I see as a sold-out American system.[1] The BBC has more than fulfilled the early hopes of its founder and the expectations of radio enthusiasts in the 1920's. The US has failed to meet the idealistic expectations of such pioneers as Robert Sarnoff who said that the airwaves belonged to the people and should be considered like a public library system. That was not to be. An inexperienced but highly motivated and ethical Scot, John Reith, was recruited some 90 years ago to launch a radio service when only a few thousand Britons had radios. Reith was to give the BBC its grand purpose: "Its status and duties should correspond with those of public service...the BBC should be the citizen's guide, philosopher and friend...and help to show that mankind is a unity and that the mighty heritage, material, moral and spiritual, if meant for the good of any, is meant for the good of all." [2]

This, writes the presenter Melvyn Bragg, was, in effect, the BBC's *Magna Carta*.[3] Bragg points out that "when the BBC has strayed from Reith it has faltered. When it has [followed] his convictions, it has prospered." In his lifetime, Reith established the BBC's reputation for impartiality in reporting, as well as excellence in the areas of music, education, information and entertainment, His success was made evident in the steady expansion of communications until the BBC reached around the globe via radio, television and, after his death, the world wide web. Many critics now contend that the Corporation has become altogether too large. *

Today the BBC is an international beacon of conscientiousness selling nothing but exerting an enormous influence on religion, politics, music and the arts. The range of ideas and tones embodied in its programming has created a sense of national identity. It has the trust of millions of listeners and viewers. Globally, its format has resulted in profound cultural changes which have transformed our lives. Together with the rest of mass media it has deeply affected not only our outlook but also the way we think.[4]

## Attacking the BBC

The commercial enemies of the BBC, like Rupert Murdoch and his News Corporation, have set out to destroy the BBC not only because they believe it detracts from their profitability but also because they see it as an alternative model to their kind of capitalism. The Murdoch press habitually runs stories and editorial comment critical of an "elitist" and "wasteful " body. Intolerant market fundamentalists hold that profit is the ultimate goal and that this should apply to broadcasting. Thus Tory critics of the BBC focus on its market impact even if the airwaves used to belong to the people.[5] Supporters of the BBC counter that, in effect, it belongs to the millions who pay their annual fees to run this vast Corporation.

The United States has proven that market competition does not necessarily drive up quality when it comes to media broadcasting. The bitter truth on both sides of the Atlantic is that although theoretically the market ought to offer more appealing programming and better value, it doesn't. The BBC's place in the national life of Great Britain is that it is an unmatched national treasure. The lack of its equivalent in the United States is a national disgrace. NPR and PBS attempt to fill a huge gap but continually plead for financial contributions in the face of perpetual Republican hatred and politically driven cuts.

The BBC also has become a battlefield in which the establishment fights vicious cultural wars. As the Corporation is funded by a politically negotiated Royal Charter, the BBC inevitably has a paradoxical and contentious relationship with governments of the day. "Independent as it strives to be in its journalism,... it is caught up in the dynamics of high power beyond any other broadcaster," wrote Charlotte Higgins.[6]

## Bias at the BBC?

Four fifths of Britons receive their news from the BBC and it is more trusted than any other news provider. However the power it wields in reporting and analyzing the news of the day is counter-pointed by immense vulnerability. As Charlotte Higgins noted: ""the relative attention the BBC gives to a story, or a point of view, matters enormously. By casting a powerful beam of attention to a subject it causes that story to become important, an issue of national moment; and other news organizations follow its lead. If it turns its gaze away, the issue can etiolate and fade from public consciousness."

Internally this results in contentious debates on how much time is given to the views of those who deny climate change? Or how to report the effects of austerity on the nation? Inevitably the BBC's commitment to objective and impartial reporting has been resented by the government of the day. How far should the BBC take its news against a government which controls its fate? Admittedly, at the highest level, the BBC is concerned with not offending Westminster. This is where impartial journalism comes into conflict with survival instincts. And there is a limit to its public accountability. For example, it was most unlikely that the BBC would have given coverage to Edward Snowden's extraordinary revelations as *The Guardian* did in 2013. The exposures were deemed too sensitive and damaging to both the intelligence services and the government.

The consequence of its reluctance to break the news leads many critics on both right and left to believe the BBC is hesitant to offend the establishment and is taking "political correctness" too seriously. The truth is that the BBC is not risk-taking or confrontational like Jon Snow and Channel 4 News. Robert Peston, the chief economist of BBC News admits: "There is a risk-averse culture that means when the BBC wants people who can break stories it has to look to recruit from the outside."

Because the BBC is often characterized as having an institutional bias to the left, what actually can drive BBC news editors to distraction is sensationalist coverage in the *Daily Telegraph* or the *Mail.* Over time the criticism of these newspapers that the BBC is too left wing has struck a chord. So BBC editors feel under more pressure to follow up stories in the *Telegraph* while ignoring those in the more left-wing *Guardian*, such as its relative dismissal of the long running phone hacking scandal in the rest of the daily press.

## Governing A Public Service

There is general agreement that the BBC has become a top-heavy corporation with both a supervisory trust and a management board. The trust operates out of a separate building with its own staff and budget and is asked to be separate and distinct from the BBC itself but when things go wrong, as in the case of the Jimmy Saville sex scandal, the trust is blamed for events that were basically the responsibility of the executive. As Evelyn de Rothschild has written, "Legally the BBC is a 'public corporation,' floating between the market and the state with a supervisory board and a management board tasked to behave as if they were running a company facing huge challenges." Rothschild suggested they should run the BBC as a company that pays dividends in viewing pleasure.[7]

The new Culture Secretary, John Whittingdale, who is undertaking a study of the BBC for the government, is being advised by a panel of experts who are likely to recommend scrapping the BBC Trust on the basis that this oversight body should not be housed within the corporation. A former chairman of the Trust, Christopher Patten, called the Whittingdale panel "a team of assistant gravediggers " appointed to help "bury the BBC that we love." Michael Grade, who has been an executive with the major television networks in the UK, has commented, "The whole governance debate from beginning to end is crap because governance is no substitute for judgment."

Whittingdale told Parliament in July "With so much more choice in what to consume and how to consume it, we must at least question whether the BBC should try to be all things to all people, to serve everyone over every platform or if it should have a more precisely targeted mission." He hinted the BBC might be breaching its charter principles by claiming it needs to go after 90% of viewers. BBC officials admit that they do seek to make the good popular and the popular good. However, their most popular entertainment programs are those which are most criticized by the Culture Secretary. Numerous supporters of the BBC believe that the Tories are on the wrong track, that they should be endorsing the enormous global influence of their most important corporation. Indisputably, the BBC's huge staff has been a key driving force in a vibrant creative sector of the media industry over the past forty years. This should be appreciated instead of attacked.

**Where Next?**

Conservatives in the UK would like the BBC to become not only smaller and less expensive, but also more middle of the road, conformist and comfortable with market capitalism. The problem for the BBC has been how to convince the right-wing politicians and the press that it's programming is changing while at the same time assuring its multi-national audiences that it is not. An evolving BBC is likely, but will it reflect Britain in a different way? Change is on the cards and the BBC, as well as its audiences, will have to accept continuing mutability.

The BBC crosses cultural boundaries by integrating differing perspectives. Although the Tories may be in denial, the BBC's impact has brought people and nations closer by supplying the background for greater social and cultural understanding. I believe that in some ways the BBC could emulate the path of that newcomer, the Internet, which was launched as a free global means of communication. Indeed the Internet might eventually provide the BBC as the route towards a low cost charge for some of its varied entertainment services.[8]

The BBC's programs are building blocks for a larger body of understanding universally shared, Its offerings sway across cultural boundaries and develop an appetite for ever greater cross-fertilization. In many ways it could become a Cloud collaborator in a University of the World. Certainly its educational efforts have been appreciated as a powerful supporter of freedom of expression and planetary democracy. The BBC already encompasses many avenues of thought and disciplines which come together in its varied presentations to open the world to millions of listeners, viewers and readers. To further such advances, I believe the BBC could eventually cooperate with the United Nations to expand its outreach.

The BBC (in its entirety) should take pride in being an arena for responsible broadcasting in an era of chaotic social irresponsibility. The BBC stands for promoting understanding, excellence, information, and education in apposition to making profits with mind-corrupting commercials. Early on the BBC became a pioneer in creating a truly global organization while strengthening its regional UK services. This example should become universal. The desirable direction for the service is clear: The BBC's international status should be strengthened and enlarged for the benefit of all. Towards that end it could eventually be leading a Global Broadcasting Network! This will only be possible because no other world body is now as trusted as the BBC News.

---

[1] Yorick Blumenfeld, *One Viewer*, (1959)

[2] John Reith, *Broadcast Over Britain*, (1924)

[3] Melvyn Bragg, *The Observer*, June 14, 2015, pp. 34-5

[4] Peter Watson, *The Modern Mind*, (2001) p.769

[5] Charlotte Higgins, *This New Noise: The Extraordinary Birth and Troubled Life of the BBC* ( 2015) Higgins, in her outstanding book on the world's best broadcaster, has examined at length the BBC's origins, its evolution, its place at the heart of the nation's psyche and its survival in increasingly competitive era.

[6] Charlotte Higgins, "Is the BBC programmed to self-destruct?" *The Guardian*, May 14, 2014. p.31

[7] Evelyn de Rothschild, *The Financial Times*, April 18,2015[8] The domestic BBC TV services include: BBC 1, 2, 3 & 4 as well as the BBC TV News Channel; Radio encompasses Radio 1, 2, 3,4 & 5 Live in addition to local radio stations across the country, as well as BBC Online

## Lusso

Posted on October 2, 2015

I am irritated, nay overwhelmed, by encountering the word "Luxury" everywhere I look in the printed media, whether it be for real-estate, hotels, restaurants, cars, watches, clothes, furniture or any holiday escape from reality! But what does "Luxury" really mean today? And where is it headed? Is it beginning to be identified, as it formerly used to be, as something decadent? In effect, "Luxury" is assisted by the fact that its definitions range as broadly as a rainbow: It can encompass grandeur, opulence, preciousness, sumptuousness, lavishness, magnificence, and almost anything that is non-essential! The word has been so marketed that "Luxury" as a concept has almost vanished from both shopping malls and supermarkets. But then suntans in February, around-the-clock music, oranges at Christmas and asparagus for Thanksgiving, are no longer considered luxurious.

Luxury today is that which is regarded as rare, difficult to obtain, so expensive it is out of our reach, extraordinarily elusive, exclusive, as well as utterly, nearly and impossibly desirable. The perceptions of luxury and how this has varied over the millennia has been the subject of an exhibition at London's Victoria and Albert Museum. Walking through this show with its more than one hundred items ranging from fine, modern Swiss watches to an 18<sup>th</sup> Century gold crown studded with emeralds, diamonds and rubies, I felt uneasy at the gap between my own perspective and the approach of the curators. My preferences and decisions are not based on brands, popularity or mass appeal but on my own particular preferences and desires. When I think of luxury, I conjure a sunny day in my garden, wandering about aimlessly in Paris' left bank, or spending a quiet evening at home without any ringing or electronic buzz. It seems ironic that the slow-moving time, which I cherish, is rapidly vanishing in a capitalist dominated world of constant communications, 24/7 pressures and distractions.

Quite rightly the digital revolution is transforming the popular understanding of the value of luxury objects, just as the industrial revolution did when exceptional craftsmanship began to be displaced by assembly line production. It is difficult for us to accept that before then, and starting with ancient Rome, luxury had been both despised and denigrated at various stages. In 2015 BC, Senator Marcus Porcius Cato denounced *luxuria* as a vice which would not only ruin individuals but could even bring down civilization. *Luxuria* was seen by the elite of Rome as a form of social denigration by the populace and their decadence was to be controlled by a range of complex sumptuary laws. However, this did not prevent indulgent excesses to prevail in the Empire for hundreds of years![1]

The decline that followed the fall of Rome and the invasion of the barbarians effectively destroyed the wealth necessary for luxurious feasts. However, early Christianity clearly opposed excesses of consumption. By the Middle Ages, however, the Catholic Church in Rome gradually accepted different notions of "magnificence," while its preachers linked ornamentation and fancy clothing by some worshipers to the enjoyment of lustful desires. Such sinful practices were also ascribed to the influence of women.

In the late Middle Ages, new groups of textile workers, tanners, artisanal craftsmen and merchant traders slowly began to emerge in Europe and, with the growth of personal wealth, began to give access to goods which had been previously reserved for the few. The powerful elite unsurprisingly denounced such developments as being decadent, immoral, and even illegal. It was only with the beginnings of the Renaissance in Italy that a shift began to be observed. The celebrated twin weddings of the Sforza and Este families in 1491, orchestrated by no less of a cultural figure than Leonardo da Vinci, were of a lavishness that had not previously been seen but which no one dared to question. Such luxury by the elite was not to be confused with the aspirational, but condemned desires of the population.

During the Italian renaissance, while the Church established the standards of magnificence in architecture, the Medici were to commission on a grand scale what was to be considered luxurious in terms of rare jewelry, sculptures, paintings, and furniture. They also focused on such rarities as the magic of the blue colors of lapis lazuli. However, the luxury of sumptuous banquets by private citizens and the display of jewels and dress by rich (but untitled) women was denounced by prominent figures. Italians were the first to alter the ancient concept of luxury with a new word, "lusso," which was meant to denigrate the aspirational expressions of the newly rich and in particular to the vices linked to women. The word was coined by the Florentine priest and poet, Leonardo Dati (1408-1472) who wrote in 1441:

> *By my thought defeated, fails*
> *because foolish pomp, bursting with pride,*
> *together with revolting lusso,*
> *were there inside.*

While luxury only began to lose its pejorative implications in 17th century Europe, it continued to be viewed negatively by western philosophers for another two hundred years when discourses shifted from the moral to the economic realm. William Morris, who was strongest of 19th century promoters of craftsmanship, argued that mechanization was both a moral and aesthetic problem and that the "utilitarian ugliness" resulting from machine production was to be seen as a symptom of the "sickness of modern civilization." A hundred years earlier Voltaire already had observed with incisive humor:

> *"People have declaimed against luxury for 2000 years, in verse and in prose, and people have always delighted in it."[2]*

The notion of luxury as it has developed in Western Europe and the United States has never been static. Luxury has been subject to constant change as the desires and attendant beliefs of the middle class grew and then expanded before being dropped as "luxury" because the goods had become so available.[3]

I think that the tenuous relations between luxury and values may best be examined by looking at the shift which occurred from pocket watches to wrist watches.[4] Symbolically, we had pocket watches in the old days when we had more time to enjoy the luxury of grandfather clocks which graced households with their chimes and the tick-tock set a calming pace. Time was under control. The ease of that era is now — with the envy of hindsight — regarded as luxurious. Today speed is the backbone of a competitive economic system where time is money. So watching time has become universal and, ironically, speed has become a great enemy of genuine luxury.

The wristwatch is a technologically driven mechanism which has simultaneously developed as a status symbol, a fashion statement, and the functional purveyor of such desirables as accuracy, precision, durability and robustness. In the 19th century those who were expected to be punctual had a pocket watch. Using such a watch was incompatible with hard labor and signified one's professional identity and association with managerial duties. However, once in the field, British army officers began to feel uncomfortable trying to use a pocket watch while also holding a horse's reigns or drawing a sword. The practical response was to sew a pocket watch onto a leather strap, which then could be wrapped around the wrist. By the start of WWI all officers in the British army wore wristwatches, which also had become a direct and implicit mark of elevated social status. As a consequence of this terrible conflict, the wristwatch also became associated with bravery, courage, daring and masculinity. Luxury was only to come much later.

The electronic watch brought about a revolution for the Swiss watch industry as US manufacturers in the 1970s started mass-producing $10 electronic watches which had the accuracy of the best of the handcrafted classics. Faced with a crisis, the Swiss started to market their output in terms of luxury. They restricted their advertising to key price points: the lowest price for a luxury watch was set at about $2,500 (or £1,600). In the subsequent tournament of value, price and prestige were intertwined with appreciation by a discerning, highly select and wealthy elite. Watchmakers Philip Patek boast: "You never own a Philip Patek, you merely look after it for the next generation."

In part, this intense marketing campaign was successful because a luxury watch is just about the only thing rich males can purchase just by and for themselves. From a psychological perspective, so important in understanding the power of luxury, this boosts their egos, establishes their social status and shows their economic power. In a way the luxury watch has become a symbol of the truly important things men don't have and can rarely get, such as the time to enjoy life, The successful executive doesn't have to ask anyone if he can buy a $100,000 watch. In his own mind the watch demonstrates his success, his independence and his position. That is why the advertisements for these luxury watches focus so intensely on HIM.

The challenge facing luxury watch manufacturers is that their products have become promotionally desirable but functionally irrelevant. Their branding as prestige luxuries leaves them open to sudden social rejection, much like the collapse of the luxury fur market or that of ivory. Luxury is fickle. Today we tend to decide for ourselves what our most desired luxury might be. Tomorrow those wearing $100,000 watches might suddenly be subject to pangs of conscience (perhaps sparked by internet exposure) which would convince them to donate socially offensive luxuries to charities of their choice. Not only could this help adrift Syrian refugees, Save the Children, or Oxfam, but it might even uplift the social consciences of the donors.

"Luxury" today overwhelms the striving and aspirational forces of the world. Luxury goods have become one of the driving forces of global capitalism. The mass of humanity at the bottom feel so locked-out that they longer aspire to luxury. The ever-growing consumption of goods is not the answer. Luxury today seems to be extending the sense of social inequality but it has yet to regain its formerly pejorative connotations.

The scarcity of both time and space are beginning to turn into luxuries which are increasingly valued in their own right. It's time that we begin to recognize this just as we are beginning to recognize that fresh air and fresh water are on the way to becoming environmental luxuries. Alas, the song which celebrated that "The Best Things in Life Are Free" is becoming ever harder to appreciate in a world which continues embracing luxury.

---

[1] See: Catherine Kovesi, "What is Luxury?" *Luxury,* Volume 2, Issue 1, May 2015

[2] Voltaire, *The Philosophical Dictionary* (1764)

[3] See: C.J Berry, *The Idea of Luxury: A Conceptual and Historical Investigation,* (1994) *Duties of a Christian, XIV*).

[4] Peter Oakley, "Ticking Boxes: (Re)Constructing the Wristwatch as a Luxury Object," in *Luxury* Vol.2, May 2015

# WHITHER OUR LIBRARIES?

Posted on March 10, 2017

I am writing about libraries not to belatedly commemorate my mother's early years as a librarian in Amsterdam, but because I have had a long and wonderful association with libraries and bookds all my life. They are like old friends. When I was at university, I found libraries to be romantic places where students like myself would congregate and share interests rather than talk about football or critique the college food. The many floors of accessible stacks of the Widener Library at Harvard opened worlds of knowledge for me and also sparked my imagination The impact was to last a lifetime. I found the library to be a true academy of learning. I was fortunate in the years that followed to have access to New York's great 42nd Street Library and then the gigantic Library of Congress in Washington DC.

One of the reasons I chose to live in Cambridge, England in the 1970's was because of its excellent library. If I had to do research for my books and articles a library that was relatively close-by was essential. Nearly five decades later, alas, I almost never go there. The digital onslaught now permits me to speedily fill in any gaps in my now library size collection of books.

It is challenging to consider that less than forty years ago, libraries were still at the center of civilization, being the storehouse of our history and all recorded knowledge. Since then the wonders of the Internet have deprived these libraries not only of their monopoly on stored information but also of their social standing in our communities. Although in most of the English speaking world the libraries are gradually turning into tombs for books, in some countries like South Korea hundreds of new libraries have been built in the past decade. Their perspective obviously differs from our own.

How are we going to replace the human contact libraries provided? Books transformed the lives of many youngsters over the past few centuries, but it now appears adults cannot even find the time to bring the very young ones into a library. The consequence is a damaging decline in their literacy.

Libraries date back some six millennia to stored clay tablets in cuneiform found buried in what used to be Mesopotamia. During the Greco-Roman era, the great library in Alexandria, Egypt became one of the centers of ancient civilization. The opposition of religion to this library came with the fall of Alexandria in 641 when Caliph Omar declared: "Burn the libraries, for all their value is in the Koran." Almost a thousand years later, Martin Luther wrote "The aggregation of large libraries tends to divert men's thoughts from the one great book, The Bible, which ought, day and night, to be in everyone's hand. My project, my hope, in translating the scriptures, was to check the so prevalent production of new works." It is ironic how both great religions that now see religious attendance flagging are looking at how the libraries are coping with a similar challenge. Public libraries view with envy how currently museum attendance continues to soar.

Some of the great libraries of the world are turning into tourist attractions with almost no room to sit down anywhere. These temples of knowledge are using their architectural beauty to lure in crowds. Among these classic libraries is the St Gallen Abbey which is a world heritage wonder in a Swiss canton named in its honor. The library there has been in operation since the 8th century and some of its rarest books from before 1000 AD are displayed in its resplendent, wood lined main room. More accessible for tourists is The Bibliotheque Mazarine in Paris. It is France's oldest public library dating from 1643 and is visited for its marble bust-lined reading room from the period of Moliere. London's world famous British Library has turned into a major museum showing art while its vast book collection is now housed in an entirely new library half a mile to the north. There is ample room for nostalgia in these libraries turned into tourist attractions.

Public Libraries in England have evolved considerably over the past two centuries. The writer E.S. Turner observed, "The higher bourgeoisie were never seen in public libraries, which had, in their eyes, a dispensary or workhouse image; though they were occasionally seen in the reference department where they made known their requirements in firm, resonant tones."[1] Those days of class-division in libraries are now past, but their survival as cultural institutions is under threat. Over the last five years about a quarter of the nation's librarians, some 8000 of them, have lost their jobs.

Alan Bennett believes that the closure of library branches in the UK verges on "child abuse" and fellow author Neil Gaiman said that "silencing the voices of the past" is damaging our future. Over last year alone over 200,000 children who left primary school in the UK were unable to read to the expected level. Part of this failure is due to the lack of time they are exposed to the printed word. Books to them belong to the past. Another author, Cathy Cassidy, who successfully fought to save some of Liverpool's libraries, said that the falling attendance figures reflected "cuts in staffing, opening hours and show the damage that closing local libraries has caused. Does Britain really want to add the loss of libraries to an already shocking decimation of services?"[2] While Library campaigner, Desmond Clarke, added that "The real concern must be the marked decline over several years in library usage and borrowing."

The greatest fall in library usage among adults in recent years has been in the 16-24 year old age group. Figures showed that in 2005 half of this age group used their library while ten years later that figure had fallen to a mere 25%. The most common reason for using a library less is that they had "less free time." Just over ten per cent of adults said they were now reading eBooks instead of borrowing them from a library.

Nick Poole, an information specialist in the UK, maintains that "As a nation we have a choice. We can either accept our place at the bottom of the OECD rankings for literacy... or we invest in the skills our children will need in a digital world. We can't afford to speak the language of life chances while failing to invest in and develop the library and information services that make them a reality."

Many critics insist that with the closure of pubs, the decline in church attendance, and the diminishing use of public libraries, a new role should be given to the latter: they should be turned into a hub of every community. They should encourage plays, exhibitions and a variety of classes. One commentator in *the Guardian* wrote: "My local library in Market Drayton, it is always buzzing with children's reading and singing groups, talks with writers, drop-in sessions for people researching their family histories, and even people borrowing books! But, guess what? this facility, so much of peoples lives, is under threat because Shropshire county council funding cuts."[3] The value of libraries, books, learning and forward-thinking are all being challenged by the continuing cuts in public services.

In the United States trends in visiting public libraries have steadied even with the budget cuts at both the state and municipal levels which are forcing reduced hours and smaller staffs. A Pew Research Center survey in April 2016 found that Americans continued to express mostly positive opinions about the state and services of their local public libraries. For example three quarters said that their libraries provided them with the necessary resources. There was also a growing sense that these libraries helped them to decide what information they could trust. 37% felt that these public institutions helped them "a lot" in this respect. Personally, I wonder whether the Trump supporters, who apparently don't give a damn about the facts, were in this category.

A large number of Americans hold high expectations for the services their local libraries should offer.[4] For example, they can teach people digital skills, or help them how to explore and use creative technologies such as 3D printers. More than a quarter of all adults are using a library for Internet access. Many libraries now offer new recreational and cultural opportunities such as e-readers, laptops, scientific equipment and the loan of musical instruments. The librarians justify this because they believe they should respond to the needs of their local community, They do not regard this as a ploy to stay relevant. Indeed, free access to the Internet and computers is now almost as important to library visitors as borrowing books.[5] However, when it comes to stacks of books, about a quarter queried thought these should be moved to make more room for technical equipment and community activities and about a third rejected such moves. The New York Public Library is adopting "the bookstore model" offering more comfortable seats and table space and providing easy access to a broad range of both the classics and bestsellers.

School libraries face protracted challenges: As schools continue to seek ways to reduce costs, such as cutting the number of librarians and consolidating different services, their survival is uncertain. The new generation of millennials who enter college are already using the Internet more than their library. Surfing the web is far easier than plowing through a library's catalogue. In terms of time, energy and immediate results, the college library is likely to become less frequented.[6]

With billions of materials circulated every year in the United States, many of these are stored in over 17,000 American libraries, neither the uncertainties facing them nor their transformations will affect their historical importance. Budget cuts to public libraries in the 21st century seem inevitable as do the growth of alternative sources of information and the rise of new digital technologies. There is increasing awareness among Americans and Europeans that the future of public libraries must focus on improving the quality of life itself for the readers in their communities.

Ultimately, what of the unpredictable future? What we will leave behind as a civilization are our libraries regardless of all the plausible measures or standards of value. Perhaps such saved "treasures" will have to be studied to be understood, much as the cuneiform of ancient Assyria was deciphered by modern experts. Somehow I doubt that the vast arrays of trillions of air conditioned bits of stored digital information will be of use to any species or robots a few thousand years from now. If the content of any surviving paper holdings are still legible after untold fires, earthquakes, storms, or wars they might offer valuable revelations to the curious digital decipherers of tomorrow.

[1]E S Turner, *An ABC of Nostalgia*, (1984) p.141
[2]Alison Flood, *The Guardian*, December 10, 2014
[3]Graham Russell, in a letter to the *Guardian* December 26, 2016
[4]John B. Horrigan, in a report on Libraries to the Pew Research Center September 9, 2016

# NEW TRENDS IN APPRENTICESHIPS AND INTERNSHIPS IN THE ARTS

Posted on, 2017

This blog is an attempt to deal with my deep concern for the millions of youths globally who cannot find jobs and who are not only angry but are also bewildered about what to do, where to turn to. Meanwhile our profit-focused planet is steadily introducing robots and new technology further challenging the employment of humans. The challenges are daunting.

In the past, an agricultural life did not require formal education. For the minority that lived in cities, most young men followed their father's occupation or that of family members. Apprenticeship was viewed as the natural next step for those who did not go to school or who finished only the first level of education. The training they received provided them with skills that made them useful to society at large. The industrial revolution rapidly changed this with many youths entering large mills, coal mines and other industries, (as well as the military) while only a select few of the better-off went to university. The second half of the 20th century saw ever increasing numbers go on to higher education as society came to regard a college diploma as a kind of white-collar job guarantee.

In the 21st century many of the enormous numbers of college graduates who had not majored in the sciences, engineering or the law suddenly faced the reality that genuine jobs were few and far between and that they had not been trained or given skills that would enable them to find work. Temporary service jobs were just that. In some countries apprenticeships were one way forward, in others internships (the new socially acceptable nomenclature for apprenticeships) became more marketable.

Internships now are flourishing, but are still restricted in a large extent to those who have the means of travel or enjoy the support and housing of their parents. Most internship are supported by the state and large corporations. They also are focused on industries rather than on commercial arts or crafts. Art college can prepare those at the end of their teens for a great many things, but once they complete their education, they need to develop the skills that will prepare them for the real world. One way to gain an advantage over other students in the field is to land an art internship which is likely to provide the tools and experiences necessary to develop their talent and optimistically land them with jobs.

Many art galleries hire interns to fill the gaps at little cost. Those seeking a "hands on" experience, can try to attain an internship under an art director, a graphic designer, or even an art auctioneer. An internship will help provide a better idea of where one fits in, what technologies and processes one needs to learn and what specific types of projects one might like to work on as a creative professional. With so many internship programs now available in a wide variety of creative organizations it is possible for applicants to choose the specific internship experience that could propel them into a career in the arts. It's no secret that internships are one of the best ways to land a steady job offer. Becoming a high-performing intern is a superior way to improve one's employment prospects, so many students tend to focus on the status and nature of the company to which they are applying as crucial to their internship search.

Apprenticeships, which existed for over two millennia, are another way to enter the arts, but they mostly have been in decline over the past few decades. The intimacy of this kind of learning is no longer respected as it was in previous eras. In the world of industry, apprenticeship has generally become less common. Fortunately apprenticeship is still flourishing in much of the service industry ranging from the culinary domain to such varied professions as hairdressing, massage, and design. Of course, in the arts and crafts such as pottery and sculpting, it remains essential.

I should like to see more art-connected artisans entering the work place and furthering this historic tradition. I deeply appreciate the way potters are taking clay into different spheres. The craft and the art are separate, but the truly fine art ceramicists are becoming recognized for their creative talent. As one curator, Sara Matson, explained: "There is an engagement with materials again, a sense of rejecting the digital and getting back to the visceral, and there's nothing more visceral than clay."[1]

Personally, I admire the way Italy's celebrated foundries, where many of the artisans who work on making molds, polishing etc, started as apprentices at the age of 14. As these young people develop their skills they tend to enter deeply gratifying lives. The same opportunities arise in the media and publishing, in photography, design, furniture, glass-blowing and even the performing arts. However, in Italy a large portion of apprenticeships demanding individual skills and passions are still restricted to a family setting in smaller social communities such as towns and villages. But for how much longer can this last as the big cities in the north focus on specialized skills and the rest enter menial service jobs? Blacksmiths, rope-makers, saddlers, tanners, weavers and wheelwrights have all but disappeared. On the other hand, artisanal bakers, beer-makers and cheese-makers are gaining popularity.

Apprenticeships are now generally focused on helping those who are at the beginning or crossroads of their careers to earn while they learn. They gain occupational skills as they contribute to and participate in the production process. Often they combine work-based learning and classroom instruction over a two- to four-year period leading to steady employments as well as recognized and valued credentials. Unlike the part time jobs frequently held by high school and college students, apprenticeship improves such employability skills as teamwork, communication and responsibility. Mentoring components, which I accentuated in my second blog three years ago, serve to increase the motivation of the young apprentices whose training primarily revolves around supervised work. Such apprenticeship gives "graduates" pride as well a sense of occupational identity so important to a minority.

Developing the necessary support system for apprenticeship programs demands action from various levels of financial support at local, state, and national levels. I find the ways apprenticeships vary from country to country fascinating. In the United States the federal subsidies to encourage apprenticeship programs are far lower than those of other countries. US apprentices make up only a tenth of the comparable work forces in apprenticeship of Canada, the UK, Australia, Germany and Switzerland. Shamefully, the total annual US government funding for apprenticeship is less than $400 per participant. This compares to the much higher annual national spending for students attending two-year public colleges which is around $12,000 per participant. This low contribution to apprenticeship can partially be attributed to a lack of public and political support. However, it must be noted that only a minority of firms actually go on to hire apprentices in the US. The "academic only" college focus of policymakers in Washington deprives many young people of access to alternative pathways towards rewarding careers. Apprenticeship could narrow the post-secondary school achievement gaps in both race and gender. Providing participants with wages while they learn has proven to be particularly beneficial. Mentors and supervisors of those in apprenticeships provide the close monitoring and feedback which ultimately help a focus on good performance both in the classroom and while at work.

Prof Robert Lerman, who has been an expert on apprenticeship programs in the US, has pointed out that interest was increasing in Washington because of the recent successes of Britain and Switzerland which have been copied by training groups in South Carolina, Colorado and Wisconsin. (Before the arrival of Donald Trump, that is.) Prof Lerman declared that: "A robust apprenticeship system is especially attractive because of its potential to reduce youth unemployment, improve the transition from school to career, upgrade skills, raise wages of young adults, strengthen a young worker's identity, increase US productivity, achieve positive returns for employers and workers, and use limited federal resources more effectively."[2] In the various American state programs, the course work of the apprentices is usually equivalent to one year of community college. If they complete their training they receive a valuable credential attesting to their mastery of a skill or skills required in their field.

The experience of apprenticeships in the United Kingdom contrasts dramatically with that of the United States. More than 800,000 apprentices now make up close to 3 percent of the national work force. With public spending of close to $2.5 billion per year, apprenticeship has moved into the social mainstream. National branding, marketing and PR by private training organizations, firm-based initiatives as well as Further Education Colleges have been remarkably successful: apprenticeship positions rose from about 150,000 in 2007 to close to a million a decade later. The result is that over half the young population chooses not to follow an academic path. Being career-focused, almost a third of these English teenagers know what they want to do in the future. Perhaps that is why there are now over 1,500 different apprenticeships being offered by 170 national industries. Starting this April, all UK employers with a payroll of £3 million are required to pay into the Apprenticeship Levy which was set up by the government to fund apprenticeship training including new digital training vouchers.

I truly admire *The National Skills Academy for the Creative and Cultural*, a charity which focuses on apprenticeships with the support of the Arts Council of the UK. In cooperation with the Skills Academy network, a program designed to improve training in the creative and cultural industries has been established. *Creative Choices* is a resource for anyone wanting to work in a creative career. Job listings are spread by employers across the country and all the jobs, internships, and apprenticeships now must meet the National Minimum Wage requirements.

*Creative Choice* events give 13- to 16-year-olds in the UK the opportunity to learn about working in music, theater, design and cultural heritage. At *Production Days*, aspiring backstage crews are given the opportunity to work at some of the biggest music festivals. And in the *Technical Masterclasses*, bespoke training is provided for young aspiring professionals with some of the leading directors, producers, and theatrical stage managers in the world.

The Backstage Centre has been built, as part of a major regeneration project in London's Thames Gateway, to provide a training and rehearsal facility to meet the demand of the industry for over 6,500 new jobs in the live music and theater industries this year. This Centre is being used by the international music, film and theater industries as a performance, rehearsal and filming venue. Any profits made through commercial activities directly fund the charitable work to help the future creative workforce. The Center has been part of the program "Building a Creative Nation" which was launched four years ago to ensure that the next generation can continue to access creative careers in what is widely hailed as the world's foremost national creative sector.

I have been surprised that in Switzerland, whose Helvetian apprenticeship program is much prized and acclaimed, private companies spend around $5 billion a year to ensure that the workforce pipeline is filled with young, passionate, talented people who exude hope and belief in their future. Many of the higher level executives in Switzerland have participated in the program and appreciate its rigors and quality. These executives would not hire those who had not completed the national apprenticeships. The result is that a very high proportion of parents of all socioeconomic backgrounds encourage their children to enroll in apprenticeships. As a consequence, Swiss youth unemployment is below 2.5 percent – as compared to over 12 percent in the US.

Particular importance is attached in the Swiss program to both hope and to personalization in which students are urged to learn not only specific task-based skills, but also how to be self-directed, self-sufficient, planning their time and work effectively. Moreover, 30 percent of graduates of the apprenticeship program are likely during their lifetimes to earn a third more than their equivalent non-graduates. It is important to note here that the Swiss system is not rigid. It enables students to move freely back and forth between the academic path and the vocational. Upon graduation they can continue working in their field then switch to a different one, or pursue advanced professional degrees. All are encouraged to continue their personal and professional development throughout their lives.

"After studying and visiting the Swiss apprenticeship system, I realized that our current system of career and technical education will not sustain the needs of our business and the state of Colorado," stated John Kinning, the head of RK Mechanical. A group president of the Kaiser Foundation Hospitals, Donna Lynne, added that the Swiss system has "de-stigmatized young people who choose a post-secondary career versus going to college." She also noted that the program might help to lower school dropout rates, a huge problem in many districts of Colorado. Because young people get to build job skills and get paid while going to school part-time, they are less likely to quit. Only a few other states, such as Georgia and Wisconsin, now provide apprenticeships to youths aged sixteen to nineteen. This offers an alternative to the "academic only" college focus of US policy makers which fails to narrow the achievement gaps in both gender and race.

I do want to point out, however, that the reforms inspired by the Swiss and the German apprenticeship programs generally fail to cover the arts. In the United States art colleges can give students the background and prepare them for many things, but once they have completed that education they need to develop skills that will prepare them for the real world by then landing an art internship. Those looking for such an internship at a particular company can begin their search at Internships.com or Chegg.com where they can find art related opportunities with highly different organizations. Many art galleries exploit young interns to hang their shows and to run errands, however such internships can help neophytes to get a better notion of where they might fit in, what specific kinds of project they might like to work on as creative professionals and what technologies and processes they need to master.

Ultimately, the young hopefuls in the arts everywhere face the same challenge: How can I earn enough to enable me to create the way I want to, the way I need to? They may have learned some of their skills in schools, but they want to let their imaginations produce works to be appreciated for their emotional power or, perhaps, just for their beauty. Wherever they may find themselves — as cartoonist, dancer, illustrator, jeweler, photographer, sculptor, or creator in one of the many genres of the arts, they will want to assert their vision, their drive, their needs, their individual skills and their passions. For them to achieve this support is crucial, irrespective of whether it be from family, friends, art groups, local, state or private funding, apprenticeships or even the increasingly popular internships. I believe the importance of such new social formats has to be promoted and celebrated not only for the younger generation but to sustain the creative futures of all our global societies.

[1]Curator of the exhibition now running in St Ives, "That Continuous Thing: Artists and the Ceramics Studio, 1920 to Today," see Tom Morris, "Behind the Veneer" *The Financial Times*, March 25, 2017.

[2]Robert Lerman, "Expanding Apprenticeships in the United States," Brookings, June 19, 2015

## Off-Key Plus and Minus

Posted on October 18, 2013

### Minor things that truly bug me

    loud music which kills all conversation in a restaurant

    bicyclists when I'm driving in a car

    cars when I'm a pedestrian crossing a street

    nuisance telephone calls

    the endless possible symptoms on prescription medicines

    the illegibly small listings of additives on food labels

    thickly sliced bread

    the endlessly long advertising on American television

    processed orange juice passed of as "fresh" in bars and restaurants

    women who will not look at me nor smile in the metro, subway or tube

    the new energy saving light bulbs which make reading difficult

    having to take off my shoes, belt, and watch strap at airports

    endless full page ads in magazines and newspapers for Swiss watches

    the over-abundant use of anal expletives by Germans

    and of the f-word by Americans and Britons

    the passing off of dirty beds as modern art

    incredibly polluted beaches strewn with plastics and rubbish

    the cacophony of 20th Century "classical" music

    the stale daily repetition of "have a good day"

### What gives me delight

    a ladybird landing on my hand

    eating luscious mulberries from my tree

    the brilliant full Moon on a clear night

    frogs mating in my pool in March

J S Bach cantatas sung in all their glory

eating fresh Dutch herring

seeing the Northern Lights

swimming in warm and clean Mediterranean waters

observing the initial snowfall of the season

meteors flashing through the sky in August

attending the photographic openings of Henryk and Erwin

the first tiny violets in the spring

breathing truly fresh air

a little robin eating my crumbs

a flaming cedar log burning in my fireplace

walking my dog in the meadows

picking ripe apples and quinces in the fall

watching a hedgehog drink milk in the morning

wandering in the medieval streets of the Marais in Paris

seeing Helaine's marble sculptures in Salisbury Cathedral

# IV.        THERE ARE ECONOMIC ALTERNATIVES

Pundits, politicians, and even plebeian economists keep on repeating the mantra: "There is no alternative. There is no alternative to capitalism." If we read the *Economist* or the *Wall Street Journal*, it would seem that capitalism is as immutable as the law of gravity. And purportedly, as George Washington and the Chicago School of economics saw it, capitalism is our destiny. One suspects such capitalist enthusiasts might even define freedom as the right to buy and sell ever more products. Their intensive propaganda machine also furthered their conviction that markets function better than planned economies and that government regulation damages competitiveness and costs jobs. Lacking relevant citations in the *Bible*, they stop short of saying that market capitalism was decreed by God. But we must remember that capitalism is a relative newcomer to the world scene and its world dominance has only become apparent over the past two generations.

Of course there are alternatives. Some are unpalatable, like Marx's dictatorship of the proletariat, or unacceptable, like Hitler's National Socialism. Most alternatives, such as true socialism, remain largely untested. So do various experimental exchange schemes such as Learning Evolutionary Trading System (LETS), the Sarvodaya as once advocated by Gandhi, or the communal groups such as the devoutly Christian Bruderhof. And then there are technology based alternatives like the credit system and the incentive economy as I proposed in my book, *Dollars or Democracy* (2006), which demand both ideological and political debate before being tested on a small scale.

I firmly believe that we can and must imagine, develop, and ultimately support a different but democratic economic future. I am not oblivious to the dangers of proposing a fresh economic landscape. As a *Newsweek* bureau chief roaming the capitals of Eastern Europe, I had first-hand experience of the repressive and stifling economic system under which millions suffered. But I also have seen the desperation of the sprawling slums of Lagos and Cairo, of Calcutta and New York's Harlem above 125th street, and have found these veritable descents into hell.

According to a United Nations Habitat report some 80 per-cent of the urban populations of the world's least developed nations live in slums. Almost a sixth of all the world's people live in squalid and unhealthy conditions without sanitation, drinking water, public services, or security. Such unplanned, dangerous, and unsanitary slums threaten political stability and ultimately lead to an explosion of social problems. As "cities have become a dumping ground for people working in unskilled, unprotected and low-wage industries and trades . . . the slums of the developing world swell." We must ask of politicians, economists, and urban planners: **Is this the kind of world we want to live in?**

In this introduction I aimed to take a brief impressionistic tour of the extensive fault lines of capitalism: from its corrosive impact on our spirits, on the workings of the mind, on the world we live in, and in particular on how it affects our struggle to survive. Capitalism, whatever its form, is driven by profit, efficiency, competition, and exploitation (of labor, of technology, and of resources, including the environment). The free-market economy, with its focus on private property, its institutionalized bank credit, and its exploitation of interest-bearing capital, all make up the melting pot which is capitalism.

The modern and ideologically driven "laissez-faire market" has been recklessly short-termist in the demolition of those very same virtues that capitalism was based upon, such as saving, trust, craftsmanship, civic pride, honesty, cooperation, and family values. Alas, most of these virtues have been relegated to the dustbin. Great wealth is as harmful as wretched poverty. It is not only that market capitalism is immoral, but that it is amoral. Economists generally pride themselves on the way they have managed to keep their field quite separate from moral philosophy. This has not made it any easier for me to fathom how anyone who is purportedly a Christian, a Jew or a Muslim could possibly subscribe to an entirely amoral economic system.

It has not helped that from a political standpoint the capitalist laissez-faire market lacks the checks and balances which are essential to the well-being of any free society. The hidden hand of Adam Smith never can work without a clenched fist. Ignorance may be forgivable, but amorality is not. The laissez-faire capitalism of Chicago's School of economic theory elevated the deficiency of social values into a moral principle. Economics, they held, deals with the laws of supply and demand, and ethics pertains to the realm of interpersonal relations. As worship, charity, family, love, freedom, justice, cooperation and fellowship are not readily quantifiable and cannot be assigned market values, they are beyond the briefs of market economists. And yet, what would life be without them? The essence of market capitalism "is to deny that such a thing as the common good exists, except as the sum of selfish individual goods."

Contrary to what Adam Smith believed, his modern disciples follow a school of laissez-faire economics which, much like Marxist economics of yesteryear, presuppose that economic considerations are virtually the only ones that matter. The market manifests no regard for social cohesion or community. Neither family, pride in work, nor even job satisfaction are ever considered. Its world outlook is truly blinkered, especially when one considers that markets simply don't work as they are supposed to. The imagined ultimate benefits of the "invisible hand" are a kind of a fantasy between Disneyland and cuckoo-land. The perspective of the free-market advocates tends to be blind to the reality of this world: Free markets have not prevented hunger, poverty, or insecurity: they have abetted the drug trade, the Mafia, pollution, the arms trade, prostitution, pornography, inequality, and injustice. To the regret of all but the hyper-rich, capitalism has made it increasingly difficult to strike a balance between having a life and making a living.

Markets have almost become more important than government. They are unconcerned about social justice. It is assumed that everything is bought and sold at its true value. In sum, our capitalist economics are amoral, irrational, chaotic, and hopefully transient. We cannot continue the luxury of drifting towards a world which is ever more unfair, uncaring and unstable. I find it truly threatening that millions of entrenched, under-utilized humans cannot find ways to channel their capabilities. Indeed, unless we find a solution, our so-called 'civilization' will spiral downwards into lawlessness, social misery and- even, terrorism.

I woke up early one morning a year ago to the belated realization that chaos theory is the only framework that seems to bear a relation to what is happening in today's economic world: The daily shifts and relative values of my dollars, euros, and pounds, the extraordinary vicissitudes of "my" bank which tries to squeeze its customers in order to cover "extraordinary" billions in write-offs on losses in Ahold, Enron, WorldCom, and the like, the hundredfold increase in the value of my house over my adult life, all reveal trends and fluctuations as unpredictable as the wind or the weather. I found the lack of rationality in all of this highly disconcerting. I have often been accused of wanting the world we have created to be more rational than it is. Considering what an emotional creature the human ape is, perhaps this desire for a degree of order, or a system that makes sense is not realistic on my part. Indeed, it is not surprising that the essential randomness in complex events at subatomic levels or in the processes of genetic mutation finds a resonance in current economic thinking. All too frequently the "values" that society establishes are determined by beliefs and rumours and a sense of optimism or pessimism that bear little relation to hard, cold facts. In sum, economics is irrational, transient, and chaotic. Perhaps if I could wholeheartedly accept this, my efforts to devise a new and slightly more rational democratic system might have seemed less daunting. Transformation of our economic lives is about as big a challenge as one can imagine.

My blogs have attempted to present aspects of a technologically-driven new outlook in an era when all plans have become suspect. Readers tend to mistrust plans for fear that even if the ideal might be desirable, its execution would prove to be a massive disappointment. This is a very different attitude from the mid-sixties when President Lyndon Johnson could outline his vision of the "Great Society", or when the United States and Britain both sought a "science policy." It is inevitable that under capitalism the worldwide levels of unemployment will rise due to the introduction of labor-saving robot technology on top of the forecasts of increases in population. Demand for low-skilled workers has been on a steady decline in most of the advanced countries for the past two decades. The Industrial Revolution meant that we could do without the horse. The post–Industrial Revolution means we can do without many people (except, of course, as consumers). If you don't believe that machines are increasingly replacing human sweat in factories of the advanced economic countries, you simply have your head in the clouds. And if you believe that the so-called information sector will absorb a large percentage of such displaced workers, then you may be from Mars. Billions of underutilized humans are a reality which we must meet head-on, for if we cannot find ways to channel their capabilities, our "civilization" will spiral downwards.

Economic overhaul is a tall order, but these are what I think any rational economic model should ask:

1. Does the economy show greater concern for human beings or for the production of goods?

2. Does the economy create sufficient opportunities for the spread of gainful employment and work satisfaction?

3. Does its use of natural resources take proper consideration of the needs of future generations?

4. Does it promote economic justice?

5. Does it help social values such as family life, the public interest, or democratic practice?

6. Will this system distribute food and water so that no one will go without?

7. Does it provide health services for all who may need it?

I believe that capitalism fails on all seven counts.

The overwhelming majority of our neoliberal economists reply to most questions about economic desirabilities with one simple answer: "Let the market decide." To my mind, this is just another of their great human and intellectual cop-outs. The market will never be able to overcome the narrow interests of the rich, the excessive amalgamation of industry, the tyranny of capital over labour, the creation of private monopolies, and the unequal distribution of income in favour of the holders of capital. Every financial crisis offers proof that the preferred policy and interests of the financial establishment are not in the interest of the society at large. Yet politicians, economists, and much of the media keep on suggesting that a reformist path could be found which would not require a basic change in the economic system.

There is so much that is wrong with the current rules of the international economic system that it is difficult to believe capitalism can correct itself.

Could piecemeal reforms cure all that ails the laissez-faire market? By definition this is impossible, because restraints regulations and controls are antithetical to laissez-faire ideology. Moreover, the economic jungle of capitalism cannot be cleared by confronting each of the myriad problems piecemeal but by understanding their interconnectedness. We must aim at interactive, interconnected, evolving solutions. Minor tinkering and adjustments to capitalism will not set matters right, There is a widespread fear that a radical departure in government subsidies to corporations could pose a systemic threat to the entire economy.

Although the free-market system is supposed to operate with transparency, in effect, capitalism tends to foster secrecy. This allows big corporations not only to hide mistakes but to avoid public scrutiny into suspect profits, hidden assets, and dubious practices. With their increased freedom to move capital anywhere in the world, the multinationals have transformed tax avoidance into plain evasion of all responsibilities except to increase their profits. The focus on ever-increasing profitability makes it difficult to justify to their shareholders putting funds into projects which could create jobs rather than those which trim them.

Capitalist firms presume the right to deny information to customers that would allow them to make informed choices about the products they buy, such as polluting vehicles or sugar-loaded soft drinks. Multinationals go to great lengths to withhold or even deny information about oil spills or environmental degradation. And given the cover of both secrecy and offshore financial havens, these trans-nationals can avoid paying the social overheads of their damaging activities.

The evasiveness, patent hypocrisy, and even dishonesty of free-market economists on these issues constitute an extremely serious professional breach for they have provided a cover for those who have abused the system. Economics in the future could function on behalf of the public interest, in pursuit of truth, and with ruthless honesty if only economists could take a comprehensive and overall approach to the problems facing people all over the world. Breaking economics down to ever more refined statistics has meant it descended in to becoming a subdivision of applied mathematics We have seen how the free-market economists condemn big government, disparage strong unions, but they almost never criticize big business. Why were these economists so silent about the murderous strategy of the tobacco companies which laced their product with addictive levels of nicotine? As the sagas of the cigarette and sugar industries have clearly demonstrated, the market is not self-regulating. One can only assume that economists who support self-regulation have sold-out. These same economists do not have an answer to the question of why commerce and finance should be free to roam in a borderless world while people are restricted by the accidental geography of their birthplace. When might these economists address the fundamental issues of environmental sustainability, the negative aspects of the deregulation of financial markets and services, the dangers of hyper-corporate growth, and changes in the quality of life all brought about by the multinationals? Economists hardly ever condemn the reliance of the profession on dubious quantifications (such as gross domestic product), tainted methods of analysis or ultimately amoral inquiry*. On the moral scale I rank them much lower than the corrupt accountants who ultimately demeaned Arthur Andersen. In the age of rampant global capitalism, much of the economics profession has become a moral swamp. Hardly complimentary, given that economics began as a branch of moral philosophy.

The eminent nineteenth-century thinker John Stuart Mill believed that economists should not merely analyse the workings of economic activities, but they should carefully weigh and compare the moral merits of different economic policies. Economists, he believed, were therefore obliged to consider the effects of economic policy on justice and morality in such areas as the distribution of wealth and the application of charity. In setting out the principles of economic development, every economist had to keep in mind the moral as well as the material ends of life.  The whole school of free-market economists, so venerated over the past two decades and showered with Nobel prizes, manifestly failed to do this.

The duty of the federal government traditionally was to protect its citizens from insecurity. The corporate lobbyists of laissez-faire capitalism have stopped governments from discharging this role, and the resulting insecurity is increasingly manifest as we can see by the outrageous legislation passed by the US Congress in December 2017.

Global capitalism has meant that more than half of the world's largest economic units, which includes nations as well as corporations like Apple. HSBC, Unilever, Sony, Shell, Microsoft, etc, are centrally managed hierarchies which principally benefit the wealthiest 1 per-cent of the world's people. Neither national autonomy nor small-scale industries are compatible with such transnational corporations dominating the global economy. Around 70 per-cent of agriculture is controlled by six giants like Cargill and Conagra. Moreover, proper taxation on these multinationals presents a major challenge to every nation. I do not believe that basic economic change to this deplorable situation can come about without a vision of a better-run world economy. I keep on hearing the refrain that, like democracy, capitalism may not be perfect, but it is the best thing going for us. In these selected blogs, I have intentionally tried to pursue a social vision that can turn our powerful new technologies into a complement to our daily lives. Capitalism is unwittingly pushing technology so as to overwhelm our lives.

Historically, capitalism, with its emphasis on instant gratification and immediate profits, has shown little interest in the long term. Indeed the world's leading politicians have abandoned any attempt to take account of the long-term sustainability of their short-term economic programs. The horizons of earlier civilizations in Egypt, Greece, Rome or of those whose craftsmen built the Chartres Cathedral, were fixed on the spiritual. These civilizations built to edify and glorify spirituality; ours is devastating the surface of the planet with concrete roads and gigantic urban jungles while it is destroying it's wild ones in Africa, the Americas, and Asia. The blogs which follow contend that it is time to consider radical change.

## Towards a New Economics

Posted on October 28, 2014

Economists of different political persuasions keep on warning us that we are on the edge of global disaster. Exactly how this might happen is never made clear: A meltdown of the Euro, a collapse of the Chinese economy, a global Ebola pandemic, the breakout of war in the Middle East, a computer generated stock-market crash, are but a handful of possibilities. What is abundantly evident is that economists have not come up with a viable alternative to a not-fit-for-purpose global economy.

If a global system like the environment or the economy is in peril, we should look at: l) what steps must be taken to prevent a collapse from taking place and 2) what could we do if it did happen. There is no "Plan B" in case of collapse. There is not even a discussion about one. The only acceptable plan right now appears to be the continuation of our chaotic economic state tempered by minor corrections.

We don't even recognize that there are major groups on which we must focus in our fractally globalized economy. Let's face it: The weakened work force, the educational system and the public sector are not likely to be responsible for any forthcoming economic disaster. The banks may become convenient scapegoats. I believe the real villain in the scenario is the entire corporate structure which now dominates capitalism's crisis prone market system. I am disconcerted that no one is focusing on the corporations as being key players in our distressed state of economic affairs.

As I stated most clearly a decade ago in my book, _Dollars or Democracy_, our corporations are at the heart of current economic problems ranging from taxation to jobs. Perhaps, because of their ever-increasing power, corporations have become able to prevent any effective challenge to their collective interests. Not much has changed for corporations since I wrote about them, except that for tax reasons they have been moving out of America. This has been part of what has become known as "domestic earnings stripping" in which corporations move their taxable profits from their home base in the US to a foreign affiliate, thereby evading a 35% American tax rate.[*] Jack Lew, the U.S treasury secretary questioned the patriotism of such corporate "inversion perversion."[1]

That father of modern economics, that brilliant Scot, Adam Smith, warned two centuries ago against the dangerously selfish power of corporations and did not accept that they had a proper role in the market. He held that if corporations encouraged selfishness, they risked undermining our moral foundations. People had to try to put themselves "in the situation of the other" and become aware of the distress and suffering they could cause. Smith recognized that corporations had no such sensibilities. Corporate managers are shielded from accountability to stockholders who are protected in turn from personal liability for what the corporation does to others. However, today's corporation can turn itself into a citizen of some offshore island, like the Caymans or Bermuda, for the purpose of avoiding American or British taxes without losing any of the protections or benefits of being a US or British corporation. Over the past five decades corporations have expanded their influence through the creation of new laws that restrict what governments can and cannot do in terms of interfering with transnational corporate interests.

The proposition that the modern corporation — which now holds many of the legal rights and privileges that individuals enjoy — resembles the psychopath was at the basis of the award winning documentary film, "The Corporation," (2004). It contended that the corporation, like the average psychopath, is single-minded and irresponsible in its pursuit of one objective: profit for its shareholders. It need not be worried about the consequences its activities may have on its employees, the environment, or society at large. Like a psychopath, the corporation never admits responsibility of any kind, is incapable of remorse, and has pretensions which are fed by its own marketing and PR staff. In brief, the film entertainingly portrays the corporation as being clinically insane.

But do we really want to leave the economy in the hands of the anomalous corporate structures that tend to work against both the public and national interests and are guided by the greed and vanity of powerful CEOs? "Living wills" for banks were mandated by the US Congress in 2010 with the Dodd-Frank reform act but there is an unwillingness in the US to openly examine the possibility of assisted

economic deaths or even euthanasia for certain corporations![1]
[Personally, I would be most pleased to help by putting a number of global corporations, such as RioTinto, out of their misery. Actually, since it is responsible for multiple deaths and carries the same responsibilities as living beings, RioTinto should be convicted of murder and sent to oblivion! This truly would be a challenge to the legal profession, the courts and ultimately the legislatures.]

Adam Smith in the eighteenth century created the highly successful economic myth of a market determined by self-interest. His "invisible hand" promised relative freedom and prosperity without any accompanying burdens of responsibility. As a theory, this seemed to overcome the traditional Christian conflict between virtue and acquisitiveness.[**] In the twentieth century, we managed to distort that myth to the point where Adam Smith would have rejected it outright as being amoral, if not immoral. Adam Smith was a strong moralist and believer in charity and compassion. He would have said of laissez-faire capitalism, "the invisible hand is in the till." The kind of capitalism that Adam Smith envisioned was based on such virtues as hard work, frugality and personal responsibility. He would have found it ironic that the consequences of these virtues would have resulted in a hedonistic consumer culture that had undermined those same virtues. Smith, however, recognized that many of the world's troubles came from those who did not know when to stop and be content. Today we see the overextended all around us, particularly in multinational corporations. The basic contradiction of a virtuous society as proposed by Adam Smith, and the capitalist market in which rapacious and self-seeking competitors operate, is self-evident. Collective greed cannot be virtuous.[3]

Economists have presented an idealized vision of the free market operating in a globalized economy. This is proving itself dangerous to the environment, unstable for society, and doomed by its dependence on self-destructive growth. I attempted in 2004 to provide an alternative idealized vision of a stable economic world run by cooperatives rather than corporations, and focused on cooperation rather than competition. John Nash, whose Nobel Prize in economics was popularized in the film, *A Beautiful Mind*, decided that the optimum solution was neither out-

and-out competition nor totally selfless cooperation, but in what he termed "equilibrium." This certainly is absent today.

"Cooperation" and "cooperatives," two words which were much abused during the years of Bolshevik-style "socialism," should be at the center of any alternative economy. Cooperation, as opposed to the unbridled self-interest advocated by capitalism, must regain its rightful place in the world. Cooperation leads to success in sports such as football and baseball; it is absolutely essential in raising and educating children; it is crucial in fire-fighting and policing; we couldn't think of safe driving without it; it's at the core of any military operation; it leads to harmony in dancing and making love; it is invaluable in hospital care and in looking after the aged. So why is this word so unpopular today? Democracy itself is unthinkable without cooperation. Even villainous multinational corporations resort to private and secretive collaboration in establishing markets and setting prices. But in restoring the cooperative concept to its rightful place, we must remember the words of wisdom of Eleanor Roosevelt: "We must be willing to learn the lesson that cooperation may imply compromise." This is a lesson followers of the "Tea Party," will not readily accept. Cooperation often means that we must sacrifice some of our narrower personal interests for those of others or for the sake of the larger community.

What such a change involves is truly dramatic. The large-scale economic experiment tried out by the Russian Bolsheviks was disastrous. However, that was not really the place, the time, nor the people to carry this out. It ended before the entrance of the World Wide Web and the Internet, which have greatly enlarged the possibilities of communication and global trade. The Chinese have tried to take over where the Russians left by introducing some of the more successful aspects of capitalism into their brand of undemocratic socialism. No one can predict how their makeshift economics will turn out. But then, who knows how western style capitalism will evolve. Since the economic crisis of 2008 the economies of the United States and the UK have been kept afloat in part by the QE (Quantitative Easing) printing of hundreds of billions of unaccountable dollars and pounds. What also keeps this patchwork of an economic system going is the compelling fear of change as well as fears of the untried and the unknown. Smaller scale efforts of the past fifty years have been crushed by the corporate world which fears any competitive form which might encroach on its economic domination. This is like a veto on the kind of economic experimentation with cooperation, co-operatives, and the democratic acceptance of "the public interest" which our unstable economics now urgently demand. Yes, there are possible alternatives, like I detailed in *Dollars or Democracy*, but these have not been seriously examined. It is high time that the economic profession, as well as think tanks, national institutions and even smaller states like those of Scandinavia start examining the possibilities and then trying them out.

---

[1]"Rise of the distorporation," *The Economist*, October 26, 2013

[2]See Blog on Euthanasia

[3]Yorick Blumenfeld, Dollars or Democracy, (2004) p.157

*A simple solution to this problem would be to impose a tax on the consolidated profits of all multinational corporations. These companies regularly report their consolidated earnings to shareholders and could be taxed on that basis. Of course, the lobbyists and big tax avoidance firms would make certain to set up new ownership structures (like the Master Limited Partnership or MLP) to minimize tax payments to the government.

**The invisible hand is a beguiling myth: it suggests that liberty and the pursuit of self-interest, unencumbered by any comprehensive rational planning or any moral prohibitions, could boost the welfare of all of humanity. In part, this hand is invisible because it is simply not there. Those with great wealth and other advantages, in their pursuit of self-interest, do not further the interests of society as a whole; the free market price mechanism fails to include environmental externalities (such as pollution, resource depletion, and congestion) in its scope; and the invisible hand fails to make a connection between distributive justice and market efficiency.

## QE+ (The Questionable Economics of Quantitative Easing!)

Posted on February 7, 2013

*QE+* is the wonderful name of the new ship of economics: Quantitative Easing.

Like all ships there is always the danger of it foundering on the rocks or hitting a glacier or simply being hit by another ship, like the Euro.

Like all contemporary vessels of its kind, QE is dependent on the trust of the passengers in the skills of the captain and his crew. No confidence and soon there will be no cruises.

Until recently there has not been much confidence in Capt. Oz (borne under-water) but in December he announced a truly spectacular and most imaginative way to improve the ballast on his ship.

Captain Oz had agreed with the Bank of England that interest payments created by the QE program would become temporary receipts for his Treasury with no fixed date for any eventual return. These interest payments of £35 billion over the next year and a half could help fuel the ship of state and help to keep the increasingly restive and poorly paid crew on-board.

Recognizing that QE is another expression for printing money which, admittedly, is a skilled craft, paper notes are a solid means of exchange and in the German hyper-inflation of 1923 were used as toilet paper. However such paper dollars and pounds are far more real than the electronic blips of billions of pounds sterling and trillions of dollars being circulated daily by traders.  No wonder those floating in that fantasy world of currencies tend to lose their sense of proportion, balance or value as revealed at the recent conference in Davos.

The exceptional opportunities raised by introducing interest on QE+ could provide the funds necessary for all kinds of public projects. The rosy prospects are tantalizing. Why cut back on the arts, on education, on aid to the voluntary sector, not to mention health care, defence, or the police, when one can use the interest payments on vast sums borrowed from interest payments to the Bank of England?

We keep on hearing in the media about the dangers of economies falling off the cliff, or collapsing, or imploding. The implication is that the entire fictional financial construct is no sounder that. The unending economic crises one hears and reads about are mostly unreal but the fears and frightened reactions of the people are genuine.

With a bit of flair, confidence and optimism our prospects could improve dramatically. The equally unreal but dim prospects of recession, depression, and collapse could be reversed overnight with just the right control of new resources from QE+. Like life, the economy is what you make it.  The true art, which regrettably is not being practiced by either economists or politicians, is how to make the very best of the largely fictional financial world we inhabit. The highly discreet (secret) use of "derivatives" from Quantitative Easing+ could provide the funds necessary to put an end to the recession in the UK as well as in the USA. Don't worry about the repayment of the interest moneys borrowed; Oz and the Bank of England didn't fix any date either.

For further reading turn to: *The Future of Money*, Oliver Chittenden (editor); Yorick Blumenfeld, *Dollars or Democracy* (2004); and Quantitative Easing  in Wikepedia.

http://www.fdnearth.org/essays/capitalism-cant-be-reformed-try-the-incentive-economy/

**Enhancing the Unions**

Posted on March 5, 2013

**When you shop at Walmart are you aware of their anti-union position?**
**Does the abuse of migrant workers upset you?**
**Do you believe that unions have a place in society?**
**Are you aware of the range of corporation hostility to worker rights?**

I don't know about you, but I have always felt uncomfortable crossing a union picket line. The good news for me has been that this has become an infrequent challenge. But the steep decline of the unions has not been good for workers nor for any nation.

I believe that the power gap between government and representatives of the work force (however this may be defined) has become critical. The unions — in part as the result of corporate inspired legislation, to some extent because of the often inept union leadership, and in large measure because of the nature of capitalism itself- have become disenfranchised. The unions in the US and the UK no longer constitute an effective force against the corporations. Their members who, in response, have left in large numbers have become unrepresented and lower paid.

This steady dis-empowerment of the work force is not being properly addressed by anyone, not even by some politicians who are indebted to union support, like Britain's Labour Party leadership. The question of how to redress the serious plight of the mass of unrepresented workers was not even brought up as an issue at the World Economic Forum in Davos last month.

In capitalism the rich have the legislatures, the banks, all the corporations and most of the media on their side. The weakened unions have a small percentage of workers and a handful of politicians favorable to them.  Money and corporate profits, in this scenario, usually have the upper hand over fairness. Under the aggressive anti-union policies of ruthless companies like Walmart, corporations have been able to keep wages down while raising the remuneration of management. But these advances against unionism have not resulted in any advantages to the now economically struggling national economies in the US or the UK.

The global economy is dependent on the balance of labor, capital and resources. As Al Gore cautions in his latest book: "the fundamental role of labor in the economy of the future is being called into question."[1] In the 21st Century capital has emerged triumphant, but the imbalance has caused massive failure on all three fronts: labor has become abused, the natural resources are being over-exploited and capital investment has become shaky.

This erosion of the power of organized labor has been long in the making. The trade unions have been vilified in the United States for the past two generations. The once progressive American unions were infiltrated by corporate agents and by agents-provocateur of the police and FBI. In addition, they also have been steadily undermined by Republicans in the name of "labor flexibility." [2] As a result of the inability of the politically harassed unions to protect jobs or pay, membership in such groups as the AFL-CIO is at a nearly 100 year low of ll.3 per cent of the work force, down from about 35 per cent 50 years ago. Anti-union right-to-work legislation in the US has left former blue-collar workers to compete for lower-skill and lower-pay jobs at the same time that computer driven technologies are throwing the American labor unions into an existential crisis.[3]

In the UK the current situation of the unions is hardly any better. Unions have been systematically dis-empowered by the provocative policies and tactics of politicians. Margaret Thatcher was an outstanding example of a politician intent on decimating the unions in the UK. When the unions still had power in the 1970's their leadership was over-reaching and self-destructive in their tactics as well as in their demands. As a consequence when Margaret Thatcher became PM in the 1980's she was determined to combat the power of the unions — using the police and the army against the miners and other groups. She pushed for the privatization of the national rail services because she saw its unionized work force as an organized opposition.

The job situation of workers in the UK in the 21st century has been spiralling downwards. The New Trade Union Congress chief, Frances

O'Grady, has said that the Tory-led government has made it easier for employers to sack workers and more difficult for employees to get justice in the courts. Michael Gove, the abrasive Education Secretary and close, long-time friend of Rupert Murdoch, wrote to all the school heads in the British state schools last autumn urging them to take strong action against teachers involved in industrial disputes and to dock their pay. This caused an uproar in the highly unionized teaching profession which has still been able to respond effectively.

The Unions in the UK continue to be the principal paymasters of the Labour Party. On the other hand, the Labour Party leaders of recent years have felt constrained by the sense that they must never appear to be in the pockets of the TUC.

The four-day work week and the 35 hour week, which have been tried in France and elsewhere in Europe are not regarded as a likely experiment in the UK which has some of the longest working hour levels in Europe. Prime Minister David Cameron and his inept Chancellor, George Osborne, have given the impression that in the future employees will have to work longer and later on in life at lower pay. Pressured by small and large businesses, the Tories would very much like to abandon the maximum 48 hour week currently demanded by European labor legislation.[4]

The International Monetary Fund now admits that one of the chief causes of the global crisis is the decline of trade union bargaining power. The global squeeze on the real wages of the workforce is certainly indisputable. Arguing against the corporate propaganda that high union wages necessarily make manufacturing uncompetitive in a globalized economy has been a labor lawyer, Thomas Geoghegan. The American way of emasculating the trade unions over the past decades in order to become more competitive with goods produced China, India and in developing states has not proved effective. On the contrary, social democracies such as Sweden, Holland, Switzerland and Germany, that kept on paying high wages, now have healthier industries than the US or the UK which have seen their industrial base damaged.

The economic analyst, Will Hutton, writing in *The Observer* suggested that Trade unionists should refocus their demands and push for real change in the entire fundamentally bankrupt capitalist system.[5]

My own proposal to correct this increasingly problematic situation is that the labor movement should demand an end to global corporate hegemony and shift the economy to cooperative employee ownership of the means of production. Such a revolutionary shift should come in well-planned stages.[6] The first legal step would be to change the laws so that it will be far easier for corporations to transform themselves into cooperatives. Cooperation has not been a welcome word in the competitive world of capitalism. It was David Ricardo who argued back in 1817 that in capitalism competition drives wages down to the subsistence level and pits worker against worker and producer against producer. The role models I have in mind for the 21st Century include such successful cooperatives as the globalized United Parcel Service, The John Lewis Partnership (UK) and Mondragon (Spain).

Varied studies have shown that women are naturally more inclined to cooperation than the men who are so competitive in mismanaging the global economy. Listening more closely to the cooperative aspirations of most women would be a positive step towards the transformation of our entire socio-economic system.

We also must end decades of union bashing and find new ways to give the workers the means not only to further their interests but also to find more charismatic and intelligent leadership in the global union movement. While unions are trying to organize at a global level and proclaim their belief in global solidarity, they still act mostly in their national self-interest. The global differentiation of production processes has led to diverging strategies and interests between the northern tier of industrialized nations and the developing countries. Obviously such differences tend to derail any hopes unions may have of creating broader universal policies.

For the Unions the time for direct confrontation with the police, the military or other governmental forces is over. Modern protests must come via the Internet. In Germany the labor unions have taken on Amazon's anti-union stance by the use of filmed staged protests. A coordinated and carefully planned internet assault on a corporation (e.g. Amazon or Walmart), an elected government (like 10 Downing Street or The White House), or a media body (such as FOX News in the US) could help to bring the embattled worker unions to the forefront again. And that, in itself, is of the essence.

## NOTE

Historically, the long term effects in the US of the 1947 http://en.wikipedia.org/wiki/Taft-Hartley_Act Taft-Hartley Act which first slowed, then halted labor's growth and ultimately, over many decades, reduced it have been crucial. This legislation stopped mass organizing on the 1930s scale, outlawed mass picketing, secondary strikes as well as sit-downs. Wikipedia details how The Taft-Hartley enactments required hearings, campaign periods, secret-ballot elections, and sometimes more hearings, before a union could be officially recognized. It permitted and even encouraged employers to threaten workers who wanted to organize.

This legislation ultimately led to the "union-busting" that started with Nixon in the late 60's. Corporate heads now feel they can violate the pro-labor provisions of the 1935 Wagner Act by firing workers at will, or firing them deliberately for exercising their legal rights.[7]

Illegal union firing increased during the Reagan administration and continued under the last Bush Administration. Labor strategist Kate Bronfenbrenner claims that the federal government in the 1980s was largely responsible for giving employers the perception that they could engage in aggressive strategies to repress the formation of unions.

[1]Al Gore, *The Future*, (2013) p.6

[2]Joseph E. Stiglitz, *The Price of Inequality*, (2012) p. 282

[3]Adam Davidson, "Unions play every card to stay relevant," *International Herald Tribune*, February 2, 2013.

[4]Andrew Simms, "Less Is More," *The Guardian* Weekend, 23 February 2013

[5]Will Hutton. *The Observer*, "Capitalism is bust for all but our elite." January 20, 2013

[6]Yorick Blumenfeld, *Dollars or Democracy.* (2004); "Unemployment and New Jobs," *Editorial Research Reports*, February 1, 1961.p.88

# JOBS! JOBS!! JOBS!!!

Posted on May 1, 2013

It's not the deficits, stupid! It's Jobs! Jobs! Jobs!

Nobody seems to be getting the universal message: Globalized capitalism is not going to create the millions of jobs that are now needed for the world's young. *The Economist*, in its April 27th cover titled "Generation Jobless" declared "there are few worse things that society can do to its young than to leave them in limbo."

But the *Economist* fails to come to grips with the problem. In its inadequate leader, the editors suggest reigniting growth, deregulating labor markets, and improving education and training. What their mantra doesn't even consider is the structural failure of the market economy in an era of revolutionary transformation of the means of communications (the internet) and production (automation and robotics). As to re-igniting growth, this may be artificially plausible in the short term, but in the long term the driving force of the rapidly increasing populations which dominated 20th century economies can never be repeated.

The globalized market is today dominated by corporations. These are focused on creating profits not jobs. The corporate managers calculate that automation is more profitable than workers. So overall, they hire less and fire more in the name of "efficiency." The ultimate result is that worldwide corporate profits are rising but more than 300 million young people are without employment.

Corporations have been undergoing what economists call "creative destruction. Much of this is at the expense of the younger generation." "Downsizing" and "out-sourcing" for the sake of greater efficiency does not produce new jobs. Drastic cutbacks in training programs have been the case in both the US and the UK. Companies have come to regard that filling jobs is just like buying spare parts — management expects them to fit and are not concerned about any long-term warranty.

The rich who control the corporations are wary of change, much as the French nobility was at the time of the French Revolution of 1789. The politicians are nervous too because they know their tenure will be limited if they cannot "re-ignite" their national economies.  And the economists are divided: is the answer to the mounting global debts austerity or even more debts? There is consequently little chance for real reform.

Blighting the lives of so many young jobless certainly spells future disasters: mass violence, terrorism, the end of democracy, military dictatorships, or bloodstained anarchy. The pathetic lack of a rational program by those staging the impressive sit-ins on Wall Street and at St. Paul's last year showed how those with a desire for reform were unable to present clear alternatives.

I tried to present a few clear steps which ought to be taken. My radical proposal focused on the urgent need to legally transform ALL corporations into cooperatives. Such an overhaul would mean that the workers would own the shop rather than the shareholders. The time has come to end the economic domination of corporations whose subversion of democracy has been well documented. Yes, as cooperatives their operations would be less efficient, competitive, or focused on profits. However, the members would be more concerned with jobs, training, the impact on the environment and the long-term prospects. Morality could once again play a role in economic life. I presented this in great detail in *Dollars or Democracy* (2003), citing Mondragon in Spain, the John Lewis Partnership in the UK, and UPS in the US as partial role models.

A vast re-ordering of our economic perspective should follow:  An acceptance of the importance and benefits of state management, for example. Privatization of national companies, like British Rail, British Telecom, British Airways and now its likely takeover of the UK Post Office, has resulted in profit for the very few but has not created significantly more jobs for the nation.

Of course reforms which tend to expand government expenditures, are bitterly opposed by those on the extreme right, such as the Tea Party backers in the US and the right wing of the Tory party in the UK, because they inevitably expand the role of government and reduce the power of the private sector. Here the choice, as far as unemployment among the young is concerned, becomes a highly political one. Few corporations will either hire or train youths just out of school.[1] So, who is going to create these millions jobs but the state?

In my blog on Mentoring in February I suggested that governments around the world introduce Mentorships for young people as a way to give them a positive start in life. Many readers have replied to me that this is a positive step they endorse — but the media have not taken it up. (The BBC apparently considered it but without follow-up until now.) Altering the unpaid, charity aspects of mentoring into an officially recognized wage earning profession could swiftly take the stigma of unemployment from millions of young people and give them highly useful social roles early in life. Creating meaningful new jobs must become a universally accepted social responsibility. We owe that to the next generation.

---

[1] "A more entrepreneurial British economy may have worsened the problem. The share of private sector employees at big firms (with 250 or more workers) fell from 50% to 40% over the past decade."  "Generation jobless," *The Economist*, April 27, 2013, p. 60

# Tackling Corporate Globalization

Posted on June 11, 2013

The excesses of abusive corporate power are multiple and mounting. I'm not going to write about the carefully engineered efforts to privatize the Post Office in the UK, nor about similar efforts to sell off the Tennessee Valley Authority (TVA) in the US, nor the outsourcing of various tasks at the UK's National Health Service, nor even about the corrupt acceptance by some Members of Parliament of paltry sums of money from corporate lobbyists. These are all minor diversions in the larger corporate game. The tightening corporate grip on government and public institutions is increasingly becoming apparent in the media,[1] but my focus is on foundation of our modern democracies: the ability of the state to collect taxes.

Undermining the tax collecting process are the large multi-national corporations whose obsession is maximizing their take to the exclusion of all else. Their flagrant abuse of the new opportunities offered by globalization has enabled them to shift their money and even their accounts into offshore tax shelters. Some of the big time tax avoiders, like Amazon, Apple, Goldman Sachs, Microsoft, Google and Starbucks have recently come to the attention of the tax collecting states, but this handful is merely the frosting on the corporate cake.

The hundreds of top global corporations, hedge funds, banks, investment groups and their innumerable dependencies (like the big four manipulative accounting firms, the PR and Consultancy giants, and the foremost law firms) are all involved in obfuscating and manipulating the balance sheets and their financial obligations so that the nation states in which the profits are produced are deprived of the tax revenues necessary to cover their universally mounting debts. Admittedly, as Chrystia Freeland has pointed out, "closing the tax loopholes or tightening the lax tax enforcement ... is politically difficult and technically complicated."[2]

Thus the battle lines are being drawn. Prime Minister David Cameron is trying to control the multiple tax havens located in overseas British territories that are siphoning-off undeclared corporate profits. The

Cayman Islands, for example, has a government accountable to Westminster but does not level company tax, maintains strict banking secrecy and is consequently the headquarters for huge money laundering and tax-avoidance & evasion schemes.

President Obama is still finding it difficult to distance himself from Wall Street and the vast corporate lobbying industry in Washington. For their part, the corporations are cleverly keeping as low a tax profile as possible while bloating the media with advertising lauding all that is being done by their individual enterprises on behalf of the environment, education, health, the world's poor etc. At the same time these corporations are studying how best to shift their overseas accounts to states, such as Ireland or Fiji with the lowest taxes and the most relaxed regulations or regulators, as the opportunity might provide. This overall process of avoidance is the key to the corporate furtherance of "globalization without responsibility."

Which party is going to come out on top? The nation state, dependent on corporations for employment, investment, political funding and economic growth — or the corporations focused narrowly on profits and how to keep these from the grasping hands of governments? The corporate strategy has also focused on merging their corporate and financial power into the very heart of the nation state: revolving doors have been opened between top political & public officials and the corporate hierarchy in order to shape policies in their best interests. Companies like Nestle, Unilever, Cisco, Telefonica Procter & Gamble, and Statoil have all been paired with ministerial "buddies" in the British cabinet. Such cosy relationships always favor privatization, low taxation on the rich, low taxation on capital gains, lower expenditures on protection of the environment etc.[3]

Personally, I believe the creeping incursion of corporate influence into the mechanisms of the national state is too strong for the elected officials to take decisive action to curb its advance. An international agreement on the taxation of corporate profits would be a step in the right direction, but it is not likely to be forthcoming. Nobel Prize winner Joseph Stiglitz wrote at the end of May that "It is time the international community faced the reality: we have an unmanageable and unfair global tax regime." Even Vince Cable, Britain's Business Secretary, suggested before the G8 meeting in Northern Ireland in June that reforming "a dysfunctional international tax system" was necessary. "The underlying problem is a messy patchwork of international tax rules, some almost a century old."[4]

Drastic change is needed. However, as I noted in a previous blog, radical change is viewed with trepidation by both the electorate and elected officials. I have long advocated that the state use its full powers to enforce something far more fundamental to the entire structure of our economic system: a measure which would help tackle such fundamental problems as economic inequality, youth unemployment, environmental degradation, as well as the current obsessive focus on "growth." However, that major shift will be the subject of my next blog.

---

[1]See Seumas Milne, *The Guardian*, May 2013

[2]*International Herald Tribune*, "Taxes, titans and the greater good," May 3, 2013

[3]'More multinationals to get access to ministers,' *The Guardian*, January 19, 2013, p.4

[4]Vince Cable, "International tax law is a mess," *The Observer*, June 9, 2013

## Corporations v Co-Operatives
Posted on July 2, 2013

The economic structure of capitalism needs something far more profound than adjustments and corrections. The entire system needs a total rethink before a well-planned re-boot can take place. Why? Because I believe the global network of corporations which form the backbone of the capitalist system are "not fit for purpose." Their very size and political and economic strength give them dangerous leverage on the democratic process. They are also the rare legal grouping on this planet which has no legally binding responsibilities beyond turning a profit for its shareholders.

For more than two decades I have been trying to convince all who will listen that for the sake of a civilized and human future on this planet we must call a halt to the spread and destructive power of ever larger corporations like Walmart — Destructive because it has forced the closure of tens of thousands of small shops and businesses around the world at the cost of innumerable jobs.[1]

The contrasts between a cooperative like the John Lewis Partnership in the UK and a global giant like Walmart could not be more extreme. I have had the opportunity to visit Walmart stores in five American states and John Lewis Partnership stores in four English cities.

Walmart is the largest retailer in the world with sales of $465 billion a year and is a model for low costs. About 48% of its shares (and profits) are owned by the Walton family. It is both reviled and admired for its competitive practices and its globally exploitative and anti-union stance.

The John Lewis Partnership is a co-op with some 90 major retail outlets in the UK. It has 84,000 partners and a turnover of about $30 billion (£19 billion) a year. It is often cited as a global role model of a co-op owned by all its working "partners."

Walmart's operations are on a staggeringly large scale. The gigantic warehouses which pass as stores are stacked with an incredible variety of low-priced goods which have made the enterprise popular with large numbers of Americans even though many of these goods have been produced under slave labor conditions in the Far East.

My experience has been that customers in Walmart's discount department stores are not made to feel particularly welcome: some of the employees scurrying about look tense and stressed, as if they were working against the clock. These workers or "associates," as they are called, (and there are a staggering 1.4 million of them in just the US) appear overworked and under-staffed. They are not allowed to unionize and are under intense surveillance by a management that distrusts them. Few social amenities are provided by the owners, the WASP family of billionaires whose total combined wealth is over $115 billion. This exceeds the combined wealth of the bottom one-sixth of Americans on the economic ladder.

Entering one of the major stores of the John Lewis Partnership is like a breath of fresh air: one is struck by the up-market welcome not only from the modern appearance of its stores but also from the relaxed and friendly greeting given by one of its eager "partners." These "partners" can belong to any trade union they might like. At the end of every year they get a sizeable bonus based on the co-op's annual profits — which last year equalled 17% of their annual salaries. This sum is calculated on the annual profit of the company. The pay of the head of this large enterprise is kept by this firm's written constitution at no higher than 75 times the hourly wage of the lowest employee.

It is unusual for corporations to have long-term objectives, even rarer for corporations to prioritize concern for the health, education, or remuneration of its employees. Pollution of the environment by vast corporations like Koch Industries is irrelevant to management except when it counters the usually weak enforcement of local laws.

Cooperatives have different goals from those of corporations: They endorse transparency in their operations, fairness, limited differentials between the lowest and highest paid, job protection, training of its members, gender equality, environmental improvement, and co-operation with other co-ops. The co-ops, with their concern for the local environment, would by their very format, also lower the overall and continuing rise of expectations. This would help to lessen the ever-increasing stress and anxiety in the work force at large.

A powerful global network of co-ops would not only increase the power and responsibilities of workers but would also put work/jobs before profits or the returns on capital. In an age of ever-greater reliance on robotics — this is the best way to maintain and create gainful employment for millions of workers.

Perhaps something like the collapse of the European Union or, less dramatically, the meltdown of a major economy such as that of Spain, could lead to a trial run of a different economic system. Spain already has a creditable co-op, Mondragon, which is about the size of the John Lewis Partnership, and is the largest economic experiment of the Iberian Peninsula. Mondragon's cooperative network includes banking, 94 productive factories, 83,000 employees, various service groups, a university with 9,000 students and multiple global branches in China, the US, the UK, France and numerous other states, with a total turnover of around $20 billion. It thus serves as a good example of how today's large corporations could be transformed into a more socially responsible co-op format.[2]

I do not pretend that cooperatives are perfect or could resolve all our global problems, but cooperatives are modelled on the written commitment that the workers come first — not the shareholders nor profits, efficiency, nor even the much demanded innovation.

The case is often made that corporations are the basis of innovation because of their demands for growth, new products, and higher profits. This involves serious risk taking which cooperatives are unlikely to underwrite. Cooperatives are not driven by the competitive spirit of corporations nor by the corporate interest in take-overs and expansion.

Law after law has been passed by The US Congress and the British Parliament to protect the interests of the corporation which now enjoys nearly all the rights and privileges of the most advantaged individuals of society yet none of the responsibilities. This absurd situation should never have arisen nor been tolerated. However, democratic politics seem incapable of abrogating the devious stratagems through which these laws were introduced by the legal profession working both in and out of politics.

Consequently, I have been calling for the ultimate legal transformation of all corporations into cooperatives. You can well imagine how the corporations would react to this: They would use billions of dollars to block any such transformation using the full army of lobbyists, PR consultants, lawyers and politicians on their payrolls. In proposing this global structural shift — I want to present a realistic alternative. I see such a transforming co-op system as integral to a new and more rational economic model.

Co-ops are long-term operators, not short-term gamblers. Our human survival is more important than the blinkered self-interest of corporate CEO's and all their partners in short-termism. The change in perspective I am proposing is long overdue! It is the kind of economic reform the world badly needs.

---

[1]Yorick Blumenfeld, *Dollars or Democracy*, (2004) p. 23
[2]Yorick Blumenfeld, *Dollars or Democracy*, (2004) pp. 200-205

*For readers who want to know more details about the ground-breaking* <u>*Constitution of John Lewis Partnership*</u>

*The good governance of the John Lewis Partnership has been recognized by the three major political parties in the UK and has become the flagship role model. It has proven itself not only by its success and growth but also by the test of time.*

*The principles and governance were spelled out in impressive detail in the quite unique constitution of the Partnership and could serve as the model of Co-ops worldwide.*

*For those readers who want to know more about this unique constitution, I am attaching some sections of this extraordinary document verbatim.*

*The Partnership exists today because of the extraordinary vision and ideals of its founder, John Spedan Lewis, who signed away his personal ownership rights in a growing retail company to allow future generations of employees to take forward his 'experiment in industrial democracy'. Not unreasonably, he wanted to leave some clear guidelines for his successors, so that the values which had motivated him would not be eroded with the passage of time.*

*Lewis was committed in the 1930's to establishing a 'better form of business', and the challenge for the Partners of today is to prove that a business which is not driven by the demands of outside shareholders and which sets high standards of behaviour can flourish in the competitive conditions of the third millennium. Indeed, they aim to demonstrate that adhering to these Principles and Rules enables them over the long term to outperform companies with conventional ownership structures.*

*The Constitution states that 'the happiness of its members' is the Partnership's ultimate purpose, recognizing that such happiness depends on having a satisfying job in a successful business. It establishes a system of 'rights and responsibilities', which places on all Partners the obligation to work for the improvement of their business in the knowledge that they share the rewards of success.*

**When John Spedan Lewis, set up the Partnership he was careful to create a governance system, set out in the company's Constitution, that would be both commercial and democratic – giving every Partner a voice in the business they co-own. This combination of commercial acumen and cooperative conscience, was ahead of its time, is still practiced today.**

**A system of checks and balances**. The Chairman, the Partnership Board, the divisional Management boards and the Chairman's Committee form the management of the company. The Partnership Council, which elects five Partnership board directors, the divisional and branch level democracy, make up the democratic bodies that give Partners a voice and hold management to account.

**Lewis also created the positions of Registrars and a Partners' Counsellor who monitor and uphold the integrity of the business.** The Registrars act as Ombudsmen and are responsible for ensuring that the Partnership remains true to its principles and is compassionate in its dealings with individual Partners.

The Partners' Counsellor monitors and upholds the integrity of the business, its values and ethics as enshrined in its constitution. At the moment this woman is a member of the <u>Partnership Board</u> and performs the role of senior independent director in her interaction with Partners as co-owners of the business. She supports the elected directors in their contribution to the Board and thereby helps underpin their independence. The Partners' Counsellor convenes meetings with the elected directors, without other executive directors being present, as appropriate and at least once each year.

1    The two Settlements in Trust made by John Spedan Lewis in 1929 and 1950 established a business known as the John Lewis Partnership, to be owned in trust for the benefit of its members, who are Partners from the day they join.

## Ultimate Directions

Posted on September 18, 2013

Reviewing my recent blogs, I am made acutely aware of the recurrent thread of "the void," repeated regardless of the subjects covered: I am obviously protesting at the lack of any long-term vision, of positive goals, of a sense of destiny, or even of a modestly better future. Aspirations all around seem diminished. Progress currently appears submerged by the tentative. (For example, by the inability to make basic reforms to an economic system which has failed us.) What does this reveal about us?

I try to think back a hundred years to 1913 — the height of "La Belle Époque" as that brief era was later named. The promise of that time was uplifting: new roads for automobiles, telephone poles rising everywhere, communication by radio on its way, the potential of air travel a sudden possibility, scientific breakthroughs occurring in multiple directions, and for those living in Britain, France and Germany a growing pride in their expanding imperial powers. The arts, especially in painting, music and ballet, were pushing in exciting new directions.

A year later this collectively uplifting vision crashed! In the Netherlands, my grandfather, Alex Citroen, who had believed that wars had finally come to an end, was crushed. The profound despair overwhelmed him. It caused a swift end to a middle-aged man who had been in good health.  His wife, Tilly, said the outbreak of war broke both his spirit and his body.

Nobody had foreseen the horrors of WWI with its massive millions of deaths, gas attacks, machine guns, tanks, trench warfare and surprising air attacks. The world which followed the armistice of November 1918 was a sombrely reflective transformation from what it had been four years earlier. Nevertheless there were a number of reformist leaders following WWI with utopian plans for a League of Nations, attempts at creating a universal language, a world court, and a ban on the use of chemical weapons and gas.

Four generations later we still see gas being used and new and even more lethal weapons held in massive stockpiles: A-bombs, Hydrogen bombs, Neutron bombs as well as undisclosed varieties of biological weapons. However, our leaders express no vision of the kind of world towards which their populations should be aiming.

For many years I have been advocating cooperation instead of competition, co-operatives instead of corporations, but there are few takers. Ours is not the age of utopias. Viewers and readers apparently prefer dystopias which illustrate how much worse the world could be under any other system.

Indeed "The Market" is now the prevailing driving force in most of the world. It serves as a materialistic endorsement for capitalism. This market is purportedly based on customer and investor preferences. Nothing spiritual, moral, or ethical is involved, as Adam Smith had cautioned more than 200 years ago in his *Wealth of Nations* and his *Theory of Moral Sentiments.*[1]

Price, profit, competition, greed, practicability, availability, convenience, speed, possession, security and "trends" are among the principal determinants of decision making in "The Market." Hunger, inequality, poverty, unemployment, environmental pollution, or fairness are of no immediate concern. Neither are justice, charity, cooperation, nor fraternity. The arts have no greater impact than sports as driving forces in the Market. So where does this leave a planet where the population is headed steadily upwards towards the 9 billion mark?

I must admit I feel overwhelmed by some of the prospects facing us: a planet flooded by a population 2/3rds of whom will be huddled in megapolitan urban slums. How will the landless and property-less masses be able to express their inevitable frustration and anger over the shortages of food, water, and security? What kind of life goals will these masses have in the automated structure which surrounds them and which will increasingly protect ring-fenced oligarchic wealth?

It is all well and good to hold out the "open society" as a role model for a democratic future, but will it provide the next generation with some degree of satisfaction? Our global collective has yet to produce a clear picture of the direction in which we, the inhabitants, might seek to advance or the kind of world we might ultimately envision as desirable. At the moment our principal concerns seem to revolve around minimal changes in economic policy or myopic party politics.

Perhaps, at this stage of our relatively youthful civilization, we have to recognize that the world cannot be transformed according to some ultimate plan. The millions of years old insect societies offer no model. But I firmly believe that we can exercise our extraordinary mental powers in order to leap out of the current void.

Thinkers with both imagination and powers of persuasion are sorely needed to show us the way towards an equitable and effective economic structure. With billions of people going to bed hungry every night, with ever more living in gruelling poverty, with tens of millions of young people in the advanced northern tier of nations lacking employment opportunities, and with banks often being run by inept, sometimes corrupt and universally greedy managers, the existing economic system is not fit for purpose.

A start must be made by recognizing that no economic system can forever depend on growth: that is the way of cancer. From there we have to find a system not based on dollars, pounds, rubles, rupees and the rest, but on a more universal and equitable form of payments based on cashless credits. And then we must make certain that a distribution system for our powerful agricultural and manufacturing base, now capable of providing enough for all, is focused on both fairness and effectiveness. I am not describing a utopia but a way towards a working economy whose administration is now made plausible by the incredible power of the new computer systems and the global internet.[2] Proposals for alternatives such as the above must be welcomed and closely examined instead of being ignored or feared. That is the most sensible way out of our current void.

---

[1]See: Yorick Blumenfeld, *Dollars or Democracy?* (2003) pp. 156-157.
[2]Op.cit. *Dollars or Democracy?* Part II.

# Living Wages?

Posted on November 26, 2013

Controversy is arising around the world on how to deal with the widespread problem of the bitterly low wages being paid to the unskilled workforce. This is compounded by the sky-high pay being awarded to those at the top and the increasingly large differential between those at the top and the bottom; by the mounting replacement of workers with robots; and by the ideological opposition of corporations and neo-classical economists to any state interference in determining pay.

When *The Economist* dares to write "weak wages dent Britain's economy," you know that there's trouble. Indeed this staunchly pro-capitalist weekly admits "productivity gains no longer translate into broad increases in pay."[1] Cleaners, mechanics, bar and hotel staff and most others in the service sector have done particularly poorly in this recession. One has not heard much empathy for their plight from political leaders. Contrast this with the outspoken pronouncement by President Franklin D. Roosevelt 80 years ago: "No business which depends for existence on paying less than living wages to its workers has any right to continue in this country."[2] The world sorely misses such outspoken leadership today.

Although exactly what constitutes a "living wage" continued to remains unspecified, both Britain and the United States have taken painfully small and slow steps to rectify the problem. In October the National Minimum Wage rose by 12 pence to £6.31 ($10) per hour in the UK. A fifth of Britain's 25 million workers are paid less than the £7.65 ($ 12.50) proposed by the Labour Party leader, Ed Miliband. For the close to a million workers who earn just £6.31 per hour this would represent an increase for the low-paid of £2,500 ($4,000) per year. In the United States President Obama has proposed increasing the minimum wage from $7.25 to $9 and then indexing this to inflation, but Republican opposition to this has been powerful.

In theory what happens when wages go up should be simple, but some studies have found that higher minimum wages increase unemployment. On the other hand different studies show that companies might save money from a rise in pay because there is less employee turnover as a consequence. The direct results of minimum wage legislation are clearly mixed. New studies have found that companies tend to raise their prices in response: for example, fast food restaurants pass along their extra cost to customers. And then there is also the "ripple effect" in which all those enjoying higher wages will also have their rates of pay increased. I find the balance of the arguments between those who tend to favor minimum wage laws and those opposing to be astonishingly close.

Even those in favor say "it encourages efficiency and automation" (and thus lowers employment!) and "increases technological development" (increasing the numbers of those already earning higher wages!). Those who argue against it contend that it can result in the exclusion of certain ethnic and gender groups from the labor force, that it hurts small businesses more than big business, results in jobs moving to other areas or "overseas," and makes it harder for young workers entering the market to be recruited. Those against also argue that such rises in minimum wages are more damaging to business than other alternatives.

Most of the big corporations now have the choice of whether to employ people or invest in machines. Most large employers prefer to buy an automated answering system to hiring receptionists. As a result many of the low skilled jobs that used to be the first rung on the employment ladder are being priced out by higher wages.

A number of economists and political commentators propose that alternatives like a basic income or a guaranteed minimum income are superior ways of addressing the issue of poverty because these would not reduce employment, would distribute the costs more widely, and would benefit a broader population of wage earners. A basic income would provide each citizen with sufficient money or credits to sustain them.[3] Such proposals usually stipulate a willingness to seek work or to perform community services.

The extraordinary excesses of pay to those at the top also has produced social and political concern. The Swiss have just rejected a referendum which would have restricted the pay of top earners to 12 times the wages of the lowest workers. In Spain the Social Democrat opposition have also adopted the 12:1 ratio as part of their economic platform. And in France, the increasingly unpopular Francois Holland is pushing for a cap on pay at state owned firms to 20:l.

Capitalism, as it has developed over the past two centuries, has never been based on differentials or on fairness. It has been based on profit. This has worked in so far as to provide work to billions of people and in getting masses out of a feudal agricultural base. Now, however, this economic system is being increasingly challenged by the political system in which it operates. Workers competing with machines and robots are losing out to capital. The low pay and lack of job prospects are now being taken more seriously by the popularly elected representatives. When 1% at the top in the United States earn more than two thirds of those on the bottom, serious confrontations seem inevitable. Consequently a "Living Wage" for all is going to be a prime issue in deciding our future direction.

As a member of the human race, I find it offensive that top executives feel free to oppose minimal increases to the pay of the lowest earners of the population but refuse to confront the inequality of the ever larger payments they give to themselves. A more balanced approach to this glaring economic differential is essential. When any small group in society, whether it be oligarchs, bankers, or robber barons, accumulates excessive wealth at the expense of the majority, the time is historically ripe for a correction. That time is now approaching.

---

[1]"Labour pains," *The Economist*, November 2, 2013, p.73

[2]June 16, 1933. FDR went on to explain that "By business I mean the whole of commerce as well as the whole of industry, by workers I mean all workers — the white collar class as well as the men in overalls, and by living wages I mean more than a mere subsistence level — I mean the wages of decent living." It took five years and a hard battle through the US Supreme Court to get a constitutionally accepted minimum wage law enacted. The Fair Labor Standards Act set 25 cents an hour as the national minimum wage!

[3]See: Yorick Blumenfeld, "The Brave New World of Credits" in Dollars or Democracy, (2004) pp.139-151

**Challenging Plutocracy**

Posted on January 4, 2014

I started off the New Year wanting to write something meaningful and provocative about the growing inequality of income and wealth in both the United States and the United Kingdom. The statistics pouring forth in the press at year's end emphasized that a fraction of one per cent of the US population controlled about 90 per cent of the wealth creation in the U.S. I intended to focus my blog on this. The new challenge seemed to be that both of our economies were shifting towards a plutocracy in which a minute percentage of richest are increasingly controlling the national governance. Yes, there are still elections in which two parties in the U.S. can slug it out, but neither Democrats nor Republicans challenge the capitalist basis of the economic system and in the UK the parties tend to squabble about the degree of privatization vs. nationalization.  Both the Republicans and the Tories rant against "Big" government and, being urged by the wealthy to do so, are attempting to reduce the sizes of their respective state sectors. Economic legislation, such as taxation, has been bought out by the truly rich in the US. Their tax rates are so different from that of the middle class and the poor that they only pay minimal sums to the government. For example, in 1944 the top marginal tax rate on taxpayers making more than a million dollars was 65% of their total income. By 2005 those making more than a million paid just 23% of such high incomes for federal taxes.[1] Rather than make payments to the revenue they give vast sums to lobbyists and towards the campaigns of political representatives who will then pass or maintain legislation protecting their interests, Their wealth itself, much of it now in funds or investments based overseas, is kept under wraps.

So, after collating material from my files and pouring over my notes, I decided to look in the Internet under "American Plutocracy."  There I came across a book by David C. Korten[2] highlighting the thesis that the United States has always, since its inception, been a plutocracy!  It exposed how the Founding Fathers from George Washington down to Thomas Jefferson were all wealthy land and slave owners. In fact, this small clique of mostly rich males controlled the direction of the new nation. Women, slaves (blacks), the poor (those without land or a house) and Native Americans had no voice in framing the Declaration of Independence, the Constitution, nor the Bill of Rights. The article them went on to contend that the wealthy made certain that their holdings and interests were protected by all of the laws enacted and that this legislated favoritism has continued to the present day!

These (to me) surprise revelations truly pulled the rug on my proposition that the United States was *turning* into a plutocracy! The question then arose: So what, if anything, could be done to correct this? Certainly not the appointment of yet another commission to study the problem nor public inquiries by a divided Congress. The statistics are all there: For better or for worse, parts of the government now have had access to all of the communications made by banks, money traders and launderers, investors and corporations. This surveillance could be invaluable information for the IRS. The banks were the first to be challenged in a modest way after the collapse of Lehman's five years ago. Greater openness has now been demanded of them. However Investment Funds, brokerage houses, and the like have not been subjected to more transparent procedures. As a result, the transactions and evasions of the hyper-wealthy have not been open for examination. What is now required is legislation demanding openness on all substantial transactions by any individual, corporation or group. Of course the wealthy will do all in their power to assure such legislation would not be passed. Those who failed to declare or made false or incomplete declarations would be faced not with fines (which are easy to pay or write-off as losses) — but with jail terms and imprisonment. This would effect a massive change in the culture of tax evasion and corruption which has so undermined the democratic process in Washington. It is important to note that almost all American politicians who have run for office, are in office, or have left office in the 21st Century are now wealthy. Alas, the costs of running for office are so high that it is unreasonable to try running for office if one don't have the money. However, if we compare their wealth entering office vs. their wealth upon leaving, the rise is massive. In effect, the legislators are part and parcel of the plutocracy.

The American plutocracy has been so effective for the rich because the electorate continues to believe that they hold power without in reality having a significant impact on the economy. Any resolution to this problem has become even more complex because plutocracy is no longer confined to one or two nations but has turned global. Chrystia Freeland a Canadian reporter, who has written a new book on plutocracy[3], makes the point that the super rich are, these days, largely stateless: They are becoming a trans-global community of peers who have more in common with one another than with their countrymen back home. Whether they maintain primary residences in New York, Hong Kong, Zurich, London, or Singapore today's super-rich are increasingly escapist. This wealthy elite view themselves not as part of a plutocracy but as an independent grouping far above such parochial concerns as national identity, or devoting "their" taxes to paying down the budget deficits of their incidental countries of birth. Coping with the evasiveness of these billionaires is fast turning into a global challenge. Perhaps their threat is even more subversive for the trappings of our democracy than the thinly veiled plutocracy which was launched over 200 years ago.

---

[1] *The Nation*, June 30, 2008.

[2] David C. Korten, *The Great Turning*. (2007). He noted "The U.S. Constitution was written by white men predominantly of the propertied class. For their time, the steps they took were heroic and progressive. They brought an end to hereditary monarchy and introduced the separation of church and state to end theocracy — both exceptional accomplishments. The original Constitution, however, enshrined the power of white males of property in the institutions of a plutocracy... It specifically sanctioned slavery and gave no rights to women, Native Americans, or people of color."

[3] Chrystia Freeland, *Plutocrats: The Rise of the New Global Super-Rich*, (2013).

## March of the Robots

Posted on February 21, 2014

I find watching the march of human robots absolutely revolting. All too often, while looking at the news, at any mention of North Korea, files of absolutely identical uniformed men are shown marching on parade in front of their leader. This is as close as we can presently get to producing programed human robots –- at least until we find ways to insert smart control chips into the brain!

Why are we rushing headlong — and with little consideration — into ever-greater replacement of human beings by robotics and automation? It is almost as if those in politics, business — yes, even education — have no understanding or appreciation of where they may be going. The goal of "efficiency" (that is the parlance for "profit," "more money" and lower labor costs) outweighs any impact these "advances" may have on the well being of the human race and the societies we have created.

The full impact of an economic system we serve, rather than one that could serve us, has yet to be recognized. We are slowly beginning to accept that a continuation of capitalism as we have known it is unsustainable. However, at the same time the advancement of robotics continues undisturbed. The rapidly diminishing job prospects for upcoming generations, the increasing state expenditures on the unemployed, the mounting numbers of those requiring mental health care, the spread of those taking drugs as an escape –- all seem part of our destiny on a planet of 7+ billion people where much of the work will no longer be done by human beings but by machines.

Writer Andrew McAfee, an expert in the field, argues that it is inevitable that algorithms and robots will force profound changes in the labor market.[1] In the past generation, typists, elevator operators, travel agents, clerks and bank tellers have seen their services diminished. So have middle rank state workers in the US and the UK. The new robots will inevitably terminate many jobs in manufacturing and machinery production. "In future, there may be people who — despite being willing and fit to work — have no economic value as employees."[2] It behoves us to consider their plight before we create a new caste of undesirables.

In this social and economic situation, a clear rethink is mandatory: Suspending the production of robotics would be seen as an attempt to halt progress or to stop time. Given our current socio-political-economic system this is hardly feasible.

Shifting the capitalist economy from profit to human sustainability seems overwhelmingly challenging but this may turn out to be inevitable in the long term. We must find ways to redistribute the ownership of assets more evenly as well as examining how to relocate some of the burden of taxation away from the workers to those holding the wealth. Rather than investing in the education and training of human beings, the hyper-rich prefer to invest in robotics. Robots are not unionized and never demand overtime.

It therefore is essential for us to confront the need to reconsider our ultimate direction, our human trajectory on this planet. This would entail shifting away from our addiction to short-term perspectives and engaging in long term strategies.

Our first long-term goal should be to provide sufficient food, housing, electricity, and clothing for all. How to achieve this? This can happen only when we underwrite everyone alive with the basic monthly means — irrespective of whether or not they are in employment. With the advances in agriculture over the past 200 years and an almost infinite production capacity, it is essential to distribute the basic minimum to every living being.

Aristotle wrote two millennia ago in *The Politics* that he could only imagine new conditions for humanity if "each instrument could do its own work, at the word of command or by intelligent anticipation... as if a shuttle should weave of itself, and a plectrum should do its own harp playing." The wisest men of Athens could never have imagined the Internet but nearly all inventions made since then have caused some people to lose jobs while providing different kinds of work to others.

So we must also begin to examine and develop those functions at which we can excel but which robots cannot: There are service sectors, like the care of the very young and the aged; creative areas like music, poetry, sculpture, and gourmet cuisine, as well as the various sport activities. Demands in the medical professions ranging from mental health to physiotherapy are not likely to suffer.

Certainly at the moment those pushing for the advance of robotics are being given "carte blanche": Andy Rubin, who heads Google's new robotics arm, has acquired and put together a string of artificial intelligence and robotics companies, such as Schaft, Meka, Industrial Perception, Redwood Robotics, and Boston Dynamics, in a concerted effort to privately build dexterous and mobile robots.[3]

It can be argued that such robots are essential if we are to deal with the safe handling of nuclear reactors, poisonous gases and contaminating substances, and such dangerous tasks as repairing malfunctions in outer space.

The Japanese, one of the world leaders in the production of robots, introduced labor contracts a couple of decades back banning the lay-offs of workers displaced by automation. These workers continue to be paid and kept by the employers. Such a policy has proven costly to the entire Japanese economy and has thus far not been copied by others. Even at serious economic gatherings like Davos, little attention is given to the challenge posed by these global challenges.[4]

Now, when we are on the verge of new advances in automation and robotics, is the time for a global conference on how to deal with the inevitable consequences of a massive march of the robots in the 21st Century.

---

[1]Andrew McAfee, *The Second Machine Age*, 2013.

[2]Tim Harford, "The robots are coming and will terminate your jobs," *The Financial Times*, December 29, 2013, p.9

[3]John Markoff, "Google puts money on future of robots," *New York Times*, December 5, 2013.

[4]See: Yorick Blumenfeld, *Dollars or Democracy*, (2004) pp. 161-2

## The Top Excesses of the Rating Agencies

Posted on November 12, 2014

Human beings want to know where they stand in relationship to others. Being first is important. Capitalist competition pushes the desire of many egos to be #1. Indeed ranking starts early: Being the first to arrive at school, to be on the first team, or to be "in" with the top group in high school. "Rating" persists all through our lives whether it be in selecting starred restaurants, starred videos, or a top brand. Nowhere is it more difficult and important to establish rankings than in economics, and the scandalous misjudgements made by the global rating agencies have led to disastrous consequences, which have not been adequately dealt with.

Whatever group is putting together rankings or ratings, one has to trust their results or they have no meaning at all. That is the question which makes me scratch my head because the top three rating and rated agencies in the US (and the world), Standard and Poor's, Moody's, and Fitch all were integral to the greatest economic fraud in history: They handed out top ratings (also known as AAA) to junk bonds which underpinned the real estate market in the United States. This resulted in the economic crisis of 2008, leading to trillions being lost on global financial markets. To date no individual and no company has been fined, jailed, or simply put out of business for this massive and overwhelming fraud. That disturbing lack of a verdict is what prompted me to write this blog entry.

The three principal agencies in question argue in the US courts that their ratings are independent opinions and not statements of fact, and that their legal liability is limited because they have First Amendment protection. The Obama administration has made a conscious and continued effort to avoid criminal prosecution of those responsible at Fitch, Moody's or S&P but has focused instead on exacting civil penalties from the perpetrators of their criminal acts. The US Justice Department lawsuit for some $5 billion against S&P for issuing ratings that were disastrously off the mark is still under way. S&P will have to prove that their ratings expressed honestly mistaken opinions rather than ones motivated by the desire for higher profits. Most probably there will be settlements of this and other civil lawsuits that are now in process, but nobody will go to jail. More important, no deterrent is likely to result or be established.[1]

Rating agencies did not exist as businesses until the 20th century. In 1900 John Moody, then only 32 and a Wall Street observer of the tangled and uncertain world of railroad bonds, put together a compendium titled: "Moody's Manual in Industrial and Miscellaneous Securities." This accessible format was such a success that it ultimately launched a new industry. In 1913 Moody's expanded its service to include a letter-rating system which it borrowed from mercantile credit rating agencies to indicate creditworthiness. His company was also the first to charge modest subscription fees to investors. Poor's Publishing company followed in 1916, Standard Statistics in 1922 and Fitch Publishing in 1924. All three American agencies provided independent analyses of bond creditworthiness.

The metrics employed by the agencies differed somewhat: ratings by Moody's reflected what investors might lose in case of default while S&P's estimated default probability. Of the large agencies, only Moody's is a publicly held corporation that discloses its financial results. Its high profit margins, which at times have exceeded 50 percent of gross margin, reflect its exceptional pricing powers in this narrowly held industry. Until the 1980s Moody, like its two principal competitors, was principally based in the US, and demand for services was modest because they rated the debt market in an era where companies borrowed mostly from banks, dealing with structures they could understand and individuals they knew. Then, under Reagan and Thatcher, the financial system became less regulated and corporations began to borrow more from the globalized debt markets. As a consequence, evaluations of the credit rating agencies steadily increased in scope and importance as did concern and scrutiny about their reliability and alleged or suspected illegal practices.

In the mid-1990s, after the collapse of the energy firm Enron, both Moody's and S&P became the target of dozens of lawsuits from investors alleging profound rating inaccuracies. Structured finance also entered the picture with such "financial engineering" marvels as "sub-prime mortgage backed securities" (MBS), collateralized debt obligations (CDO) and "synthetic and squared CDOs" which even most bankers found difficult to price or even to understand. However, these complex structures became increasingly profitable for the rating agencies. By 2006 Moody's earned close to $900 million in revenue from structured finance. By the time of the crash of 2008, there were over $11 trillion structured finance debt securities outstanding in the US bond market. Of the mortgage backed securities that Moody's had top-rated with AAA ratings in 2006, three quarters were downgraded to junk just two years later!

Executives from the big three explain that ratings are a simple symbol system to express relative creditworthiness or the risks involved. The rating grades (or relative risks) are usually expressed through a variation of an alphabetical combination of upper and lowercase letters. Generally the agencies have not been as vigilant with those corporations that paid them for high ratings but were aggressive in rating those that did not. The verdict is not yet out whether the ratings produced by the top three in evaluating the collateralized mortgage securities that were given gold-plated endorsements rather than branded as rubbish were the result of negligence or incompetence rather than greed and malpractice.[2]

Although there are over 150 rating agencies internationally, the two big American credit raters (Moody's & S&P) control 80% of the global market and unbelievably are still the only ones to have high credibility. The big three issued over 97% of the credit ratings in the US, giving them powerful pricing leverage. This brought them profit margins of about 50% in the first decade of this century and levels have not fallen dramatically since then. Partly this is because by US law many investors are permitted only to buy bonds (for pensions and other holdings) that have AAA ratings. Banks, in turn, may adjust their risky investment packages in order to satisfy the rating services. Then bond investors will worry about the very willingness of the rating services to give better ratings in order to encourage banks to issue lower quality bonds. S&P, for example, developed and relied on models which took into account economic assumptions and potential losses in order to come up with inflated ratings. I am describing this spiralling effect only to show the reason I believe the current structure of these ratings groups should be terminated. My conviction is strengthened by the fact that these agencies also advise their corporate customers where best to domicile their headquarters and how best to circumvent national laws and avoid governmental taxation.

In the United States in 2010, in reaction to the disastrous impact of S&P and Moody's ratings on the global economy, the Congress passed the Dodd-Frank Act which called for federal officials to review and modify existing regulations in order to avoid the reliance on credit ratings as the principal assessors of creditworthiness.

In an attempt to rescue its fallen standing, S&P took the unprecedented step in 2011 of downgrading the AAA ratings of US government bonds because of Washington's inability to get its financials in order — as evidenced by the fiscal cliff on which it had then been balancing. The Secretary of the Treasury countered by saying that S&P had "shown a stunning lack of knowledge about basic US fiscal math." He also pointed out that S&P's sovereign debt team miscalculated the US debt by nearly $2trillion! When the Justice Department then asked for $5 billion in 2013 to recover losses it said federally insured institutions suffered as a result of these faulty ratings, S&P dramatically replied that the US government was only trying to retaliate for its downgrade. The courts may eventually rule that there is a conflict of interest for the Treasury to penalize S&P for having given a fair rating against its own interests.[3] In the meantime S&P continues to offer underwriters more desirable bond ratings than their competitors in order to get their business.

"Sometimes it is hard to dismiss the impression that some American rating agencies and fund managers are working against the Eurozone," said the former German economics minister Rainer Bruederle.[4] In January 2012, amidst continued economic instability, S&P had downgraded nine European countries including the AAA ratings of France and Austria. In November 2013 S&P went further and cut down France's rating from AA+ to AA, expressing doubts over France's ability to restore growth. Economists like Paul Krugman viewed this further downgrade as politically motivated. France was raising taxes and rejecting austerity and this went against the right wing position that spending on benefits, health and social security should all be cut as well as taxes. S&P had been eager to demonstrate that its ratings were tough and principled in order to counter-act all the damaging publicity it had received for its role in the global crash.[5]

The potential for downgrades to destabilize member countries became so strong this year that the European Parliament agreed to a set of rules designed to slowly rein in S&P and Moody's as well as the smaller rating agencies. In the US, The Securities and Exchange Commission has had trouble hiring inspectors who will ensure that those who determine the ratings are not involved in marketing the services of their agency.

So we must ask, does a globalized world with many fragile and unstable economies really need such fundamentally implausible rating agencies as S&P and Moody's? Managed by greedy fortune-tellers, these agencies have been seen to intimidate politicians, corrupt the markets, and destabilize national economies. New rules and regulations are not the answer. The response so far has been that the rating groups, aided by lobbyists, simply devise new ways to avoid any new rules and run in circles around the bureaucrats hired to monitor behavior.[6]

I suggest that the time is ripe to create an over-arching international and inter-governmental agency to rate not only bonds and corporations but also sovereign debts. Such a public agency staffed by economists and administrators from the IMF, World Bank, the OECD and the United Nations could report to the G-20. Predicting uncertainty can never be perfect, but it would be far better for all the people and nations of this world if the giant ratings cartel were operated as a non-profit, public service.

[1]Floyd Norris, "Stumbling over audits and ratings," *The New York Times International,* August 22, 2014

[2]Sam Jones, "When junk was gold," *Financial Times* (Weekend),October 19, 2008

[3]Nathaniel Popper, "S&P's rating habits," *The New York Times International*, August 2, 2013, p.2

[4]Patrick Kingsley, "Making the Grade," *The Guardian*, February 16, 2012

[5]Paul Krugman, "The plot against France," *The New York Times*, November 12, 2013.

[6]Donald J. Johnston, "An alternative to the ratings agencies," *The New York Times,* February 12, 2013

## Taboo at Davos

Posted on January 23, 2015

The elite of the worlds of high finance, corporations, politics, public relations, the media and economics are gathered in snow-bound Davos to attend packed talks, conferences, meetings, dinners and parties. But do these posturing experts really look at the world's economic challenges? To counter-balance this trendy social event I am listing a dozen radical but vital topics which will NOT be addressed by this Forum:

Six issues:

1. The fundamental incompatibility of the teachings of Muhammad and Capitalism
2. Mafia infiltration of global corporations
3. The rape of African resources by foreign investors
4. The strengthening and enlargement of cooperatives
5. The weakness of labor's (such as ILO) representation and global effectiveness
6. The uncontrolled chaos of global commodity markets

Six Questions:

1. Could a global currency replace the Dollar, the Euro, or the Pound as the basis of transactions. What would follow the collapse of the Euro?
2. Could a new monetary exchange, such as Bitcoin, be effectively introduced by governments?
3. How could corporations be stopped from evading national taxation?
4. What steps must be taken to provide jobs for billions of youngsters over the next decades? Are economic expectations of our children realistically headed downwards?
5. Are we facing up to the economic challenges of strengthening education through the Internet?
6. Has capitalism enhanced the revolutionary goal of "Liberty, Equality, Fraternity" or downgraded it?

Perhaps one of the above will be discussed in Davos 2016?

## Short term v. long term perspectives

Posted on February 4, 2015

The economists of this world like to divide perspectives into macro and micro; the short term and the long term. John Maynard Keynes, among the greatest of his profession, said, "In the long run we are all dead," so what is important is the short term. Inevitably, if we cannot cope with the present there is little point in focusing on either the short or long terms. Much of what is happening in the world right now may be unsatisfactory, but projections about tomorrow are truly frightening.

The most disturbing statistic coming out of the World Economic Forum in Davos this January was that 45% of jobs in the United States will be taken over by automation over the next two decades.[*] How is the society going to tackle this daunting "long term" challenge? By comparison, dealing with the growth of an aging population, air and water pollution and global fish stock depletion seemed slightly less threatening. But to their credit, for the first time at Davos, economists openly discussed ways in which capitalism might be saved from itself.

Looking at where we may be headed is influenced in many ways — not only by our location on this planet but by our education, employment, cultural background, social outlook (now much affected for the younger generations by the internet) and expectations. The Chinese, for example, have a different perspective on what needs to be done for the long-term well being of their nation. Their commitment to the long term was already there a couple of millennia ago when they built the Great Wall and continues to the present day. No nation has ever introduced a long-term social project on the scale of China's Birth Control restrictions in which couples were limited to having only one child. Reasonably fearful of their ever larger population, the Communist leadership never even considered the consequential imbalance of the sexes as most couples felt having a son was more important than raising a daughter.

Today this Chinese orientation towards the long term is evidenced by the development of numerous mega-projects ranging from the high-speed rail system (of which 10,000 miles have already been completed) at a cost of $300 billion, to the South to North Water Diversion Project under construction which will cost $80 billion. I admire the incredible scale of the Chinese commitment to the long term, but recognize that in Europe or the United States such giant projects would create powerful political opposition. Very few of the projects will yield immediate returns, but China's authoritarian rulers can set aside any social, economic and environmental critiques or any open discussion of the possible consequences.

When one considers the extraordinary long-term mega infrastructure projects of the Chinese in Africa and Latin America (like the $50 billion canal across Nicaragua to compete with the Panama Canal) one must also wish that our politicians, overwhelmed as they are by the pressure of news headlines, could hold visions which extended beyond the next election. Alas, most leaders seem at the mercy of the economic forces of capitalism. None of the incredible advances of the technological revolution (many of which were initially sponsored by the government) are now planned by the state or in any way controlled. This has created short-term uncertainty which in turn undercuts social and economic stability. A prime example of this was the inability of the governments to control the banks early on in the 21st century to ensure that the extraordinary short-term profits they realized did not endanger the very basis of the entire financial system.

A prime component of leadership is long-term perspective. A leader must know or have a vision of where he/she and their organization are headed — not just in the next quarter, but over the next decade or more. A number of American Presidents in the 20th century had long range visions, starting with Teddy Roosevelt who moved to protect the environment and battled against corporate irresponsibility; Woodrow Wilson who worked hard on the creation of the League of Nations; FDR who pushed for Social Security legislation and banking reform, and LBJ who supported Civil Rights legislation. In England too, Clement Atlee instituted the National Health Service and many other long-term social reforms following WWII.

Working against those with long-term visions have been the overwhelming forces of corporations. With their focus on profits and competition, they are principally concerned with this year's earnings and their expectations over the next two to five years. Short-termism is also a dominant theme in the financial world where the corporate results of every three months have become part of "quarterly capitalism." Most corporate executives, although fully aware of the wisdom of long-term planning in areas like the environment, do little to encourage it. They misconceive that tackling environmental change will be bad for business.[1]

The long-term process of giving power to an overpaid corporate and financial elite has resulted in inequalities which no one is clear on how to correct. Economic inequality is like a slow-growing cancer which one may not notice in the early stages but when there is metastasis, demands radical treatment. That is what we shall shortly be facing in both the UK and the US. However the inordinate power that economic inequality gives to the few, like the two Koch brothers in the US who will be spending close to a billion dollars on helping their approved candidates in the 2016 elections, effectively blocks even modest changes or reforms in taxation. Indeed the rich have shown their capacity to protect their ever-larger holdings over the past 30 years. Somewhat rhetorically, President Obama in his State of the Union address asked how much longer the American people would "accept an economy where only a few of us do spectacularly well?"

The rich also have been effective in steadily emasculating the power of the trade unions and this very weakness has become an increasingly important factor in the rising global inequality.[2] Unions are no longer able to give their members a voice or the power to collectively bargain for higher wage levels. As a result, wage growth is manifestly falling behind the ever-higher automation-pushed global levels of productivity.

Politicians have permitted "the market" and technology to go unobstructed on the assumption that they are economically and ethically beyond the need for any public or state control. This has led to the indiscriminate, careless and even corrupt sale of many of the public assets such as the rail and postal services in the UK. The Conservatives in power in Britain appear to have no problems letting the Chinese take leading stakes in the generation of nuclear power stations. The long-term consequences of such moves appear to be sidestepped, but perhaps the thinking is that if anything goes wrong in such nuclear facilities then the blame can be outsourced!

For the great majority in the US and the UK, the scope of their prospects seems to be contracting. In the sixties Americans were coaxed into believing that rising living standards would lead to more choice, more leisure and less hard work. Instead, the corporate culture has resulted in a charged competitive environment with longer working hours.[3] Similarly, great hopes were held that technology would bring liberation. Instead, Americans are spending increasingly more time on the Internet and its social networks and are becoming enslaved to its demands. Thirty years ago no one predicted such results, Even now we do not know how these technological advances, so readily incorporated into young minds, are affecting the new generation.

A long-term perspective can empower politicians, corporations, organizations and individuals which can enable them to affect the future. Some of the earlier writers about our future prospects had varied ideas about the general assumptions we could make.[4] Wendell Bell in the *Foundations of Future Studies* (1997) focused on three general concepts broadly accepted by futurists: First, the future is not predetermined. This suggests that more than one future is possible, which is at the basis of the theory of alternative futures. Some of those futures will be better or worse than others, so we have the opportunity to choose. Second, while the future cannot be known, it is possible to make educated guesses with reasonable accuracy about what would be best and worst. Third, we can exercise strategic planning. This is where we design a vision of a future outcome we might want in ten or more years. The important thing is to have a destination towards which we can move, that is, a long-term perspective.

A variety of planners and groups are currently proposing a number of ways to balance short-term policies with plausible long-range measures which would reduce the chances of boom and bust episodes. The Oxford Martin Commission for Future Generations is a group which focuses on the increasing short-termism of modern politics and our collective inability to break the gridlock which undermines attempts to address the biggest challenges that will shape our future. Pascal Lamy, then the Director-General of the World Trade Organization presented a report, "Now for the Long Term" (2013) which listed five shaping factors that make positive change so difficult:

1. **Institutions**: Too many are struggling to adapt to today's hyper-connected world.
2. **Time**: Short-termism directs political and business cycles.
3. **Political Engagement and Public Trust**: Politics has not adapted to new methods.
4. **Growing Complexity:** Problems can escalate far more rapidly than they can be resolved.
5. **Cultural Biases:** Globalization can amplify cultural differences and exclude key voices.

One voice in the Commission, Camilla Toulmin, Director of the International Institute for Environment and Development, was particularly interested in understanding why people are reluctant to consider the "long term" and in identifying ways to reward those who do. She pointed out that the banking sector remained highly sceptical of the long-term efficacy of carbon cutting policies, which unfortunately translates into an aversion to change for the common good. Another, critic, Professor Paul Elkins expressed his view that the current state of politics made it extremely difficult to promote the well being of future generations. All the large developed economies are using short-term policies to help generate growth

Bjorn Lomborg, a Danish economist and futurologist, has launched the "Post-2015 Consensus" in which experts are drawing up a list of objectives for humanity on how to best spend the $2.5 trillion in international development assistance which is to be distributed between now and 2030.[5] Bjorn's group contends that providing free condoms and other contraceptive devices to all who want them would give a return of $120 for every dollar spent. Halting sub-Saharan tax evasion, which currently costs 20 African governments about 10% of their gross domestic product a year would bring in close to $50 for every dollar given in assistance.

Philanthropists Bill and Melinda Gates, who have given billions to cut down malaria and infant mortality rates, have carefully been following many long term challenges. In their annual letter they predicted that "The lives of people in poor countries will improve faster in the next 15 years than at any other time in history." It is hard not to celebrate long-term predictions of this nature!

This September the nations of the world will discuss the adoption of a new set of long-term goals which will replace the Millennium Development Goals adopted in 2000. The new Sustainable Development Goals (SDGs) will aim to end extreme poverty by 2030 as well as a range of other problems such as climate change, pollution and access to justice. The question then arises as to what really works with such a large set of long term goals? There are currently some 169 SDGs targeted on their list and such over-ambition needs serious trimming if planning for the long term is ever to be effective. Priorities also need to be applied if one searches beyond the sustainable to the achievable.

---

[1] Yorick Blumenfeld, *Dollars or Democracy*, (2004) p.93

[2] Seumas Milne, The Davos oligarchs are right to fear the world they've made," *The Guardian*, January 22, 2015.

[3] Larry Elliott, "Short-termism rife as world longs for real solution," *The Guardian*, October 21, 2013.

[4] Bertrand de Jouvenel, The Art of Conjecture, (1967); Robert Jungk and Norbert Mullert, *Future Workshops: How to Create Desirable Futures* (1987).

[5] "The economics of optimism," *The Economist,* January 24, 2015, p.67

*The technology revolution is creating phenomenal changes in employment. The Gary Steel Works in Indiana, the largest such mill in the USA, employed 30,000 workers at its post-war peak in which it produced 6 million tons of steel. Today it can produce more than 7 million tons a year with only 5,000 workers

**Denying the Dangers of Growth**

Posted on March 18, 2015[2]

*"Capitalism, as a system, is based on growth, some of it extremely harmful: there has been enormous global expansion in air and water pollution, soil erosion, and the burning of forests. This adds an ironic twist to capitalism's 'grow or die' challenge. As capitalism has kept on growing and expanding on a global scale over the past two centuries, both nature and indigenous civilizations are being bulldozed in the process. We must face up to the fact that eventually any group, species, or system based on endless expansion must collapse. Endless growth, as any doctor will tell you, is the way of cancer. It is death. If unchecked, such growth guarantees our own extinction as a species in relatively few generations."*[1]

This passage from my book, *Dollars or Democracy*, (2004) incorporated a frontal attack on the dependence of politicians and the entire economic system on growth. As I pointed out at the time, growth at a level of 2% per year could not continue for very long. The mathematics of such accumulations are simply prohibitive. And yet politicians around the world are acting as if they were deaf and blind by continuing to uphold "growth" as their best slogan for re-election. Those in power refuse to recognize that capitalism, which brought us out of feudalism and from the industrial revolution to the digital age, has now become a failed system in the battle against environmental extinction. They are in denial: We admit that capitalism never was a stable system but are reluctant to recognize that it has become downgraded from being a force for development to being a tool for the hyper-rich to become ever richer. But then, the end logic of capitalism has always been capital accumulation.

The crash of 2008 did not resolve any of the basic economic problems facing humankind, like the environment, runaway technology, and the shift away from labor to automation. I had expected that a collapse of the economic system would lead to a rethink and eventually to a complete overhaul of what existed. I had proposed an entirely new economic model, "The Incentive Economy," which would bring back hope into the way we lived. Instead, the inept and basically venal banking system was propped up by the injection of hundreds of billions of dollars which saved the bankers and the corporate world and made a few at the top even richer. Where I had proposed an end to the corporate structure and its transformation into a cooperative one, the multi-national corporations grew ever more powerful through newly formulated global tax evasion. Yes, the corporate world embraced that kind of growth.

Mathematics, statistics, and reading ability should all tell the people that economic growth is not like that of springtime greens. And yet, despite the alarms coming from environmental scientists that we must stop the devastating side-effects of growth, insufficient notice is being taken. The writer Naomi Klein has emphasized that economic reforms so essential to controlling the environment "are extremely threatening to an elite minority that has a stranglehold over our economy, our political process, and most of our major media outlets."[2]

Another outspoken writer, George Monbiot, has come out with one editorial page analysis after another clearly spelling out the simple message that the impact of economic expansion is destroying our planet. Monbiot, repeatedly warns that there is no alternative policy accepted by mainstream political parties to replace growth addicted capitalism: "Why are we wrecking the natural world and public services to generate growth, when that growth is not delivering contentment, security or even, for most of us, greater prosperity? Why have we enthroned growth, regardless of its utility, above all other outcomes? Is it not time to think again? To stop sacrificing our working lives, our prospects, our surroundings to an insatiable God?"[3]

However, all too few economists are listening. They are in denial. Many cling to 20thCentury prospects. All too many still continue to regard labor as a commodity! They categorize workers as input in the production of wealth. Perhaps it is that many economists are so dependent on the current economic system that they cannot afford to consider the critical need for an alternative. Adam Smith would not for an instant have tolerated the corrupt economic world we live in today. Justice was central to Smith's critique of the crony capitalism which was just then (around 1800) forming. Today all too often the crooked capitalism of many corporations, banks, auditors, lobbyists and tax evaders are calling the (false) tune. To my amazement, economists still consider free markets (characterized by individual selfishness and social competitiveness) as the ideal form of economic organization. The truth is that free-market encouragement of selfish behavior has led to the increasing breakup of communities, rising divorce rates, increased loneliness for the young and old, soaring drug use and a massive decline in trust.

Richard Smith, an outspoken economic outsider, has been clear in charging that "Capitalism is, overwhelmingly, the main driver of planetary ecological collapse. From climate change to resource overconsumption to pollution, the engine that has powered three centuries of accelerating economic development revolutionizing technology, science, culture, and human life itself is, today, a roaring out-of-control locomotive mowing down continents of forests, sweeping oceans of life, clawing out mountains of minerals, drilling, pumping out lakes of fuels, devouring the planet's last accessible resources to turn them all into "product" while destroying fragile global ecologies built up over eons of time."[4]

Daniel Cohen (an economics professor of Paris's Ecole Normale Superieure) maintains "Powerful software is doing the work of humans, but humans thus replaced are unable to find productive jobs."[5] McKinsey, an eminent consultancy firm, estimates that new technologies will put some 140 million service jobs at risk in the next decade. Another study estimates that 47 percent of all employment in the United States is susceptible to automation over the next two decades. Few believe that job creation is going to keep pace with automation."[6]

The manifest failures of the prevailing materialistic outlook have led to growing loneliness and depression writes economics analyst Hugo Dixon: "In pursuing growth, other precious things can get damaged. This includes our social environment — our communities and networks of friendship and family — as well as our physical environment."[7] Dixon believes that it is necessary to focus more on quality than quantity and take better care of the social fabric. Ultimately, the economy should service society rather than the society servicing capitalism. In *Dollars or Democracy*? I clearly spelled out the prospects of an alternative "Incentive Economy" with enormous social changes but little financial growth. I proposed that a basic income would be the right of every adult: Those without a regular job could volunteer their time on sick and elder care, child mentoring, community gardening, as well as innumerable cultural projects. Instead of growth, the aim would be for greater social and economic equality, cooperation, sharing, community and creativity. Education, for example, could develop and expand with next to zero impact on the environment; so could most of the arts from music to painting and writing as well as film and video making. Yes, there are creative human alternatives to the artificial economic growth being manufactured by speculators, bankers, corporate executives, advertising agencies, real estate tycoons, and national treasuries.

I should like to conclude with a ten-year-old paragraph from my book:

> *"The new paradigm that we must forge together is one of a globally civil society based on economic cooperation rather than competition and cancerous growth. What is needed is not an affirmation of money, in the form of dollars or euros, but a sustainable way of life and human community...Reconciling our new technologies with our economy is one of the challenges of the twenty-first century I have tried to address. Obviously the social norms that still worked for the 19th century have been disrupted by economic advances on many fronts and society has failed to catch up. The planet desperately needs a global discussion about our economic future, specifically targeted at the long-term weakness of plutocratic market capitalism. The promised land of tomorrow may seem like a distant dream, but I would like to think that we could advance in the right direction. As the Bible proclaimed: We too have it in our power to "make all things new."*

[1]Yorick Blumenfeld, *Dollars or Democracy?* (2004) p.75
[2]Naomi Klein, *"This Changes Everything,"*(2015)
[3]George Monbiot, "Growth: the destructive God that can never be appeased," *The Guardian*, November 19, 2014
[4]Richard Smith, "Capitalism and the destruction of life on Earth: Six theses on saving the humans," *World Economic Review*, #64.
[5]Daniel Cohen, "When the growth model fails," *The New York Times*, February 13, 2015.[7]

**Tackling Inequality**

ECONOMIC INEQUALITIES

Posted on May 11, 2015

Having been born in the Netherlands and having a Dutch mother with a strong social conscience, I was taught that inequality presented a powerful moral challenge. Fairness was deeply ingrained in the Dutch who have created one of the world's more egalitarian societies. It is not surprising therefore that the desire to tackle economic inequality has been a recurrent and profound motivation in my life. I have observed first hand the impact economic inequality has on so much of what is going wrong in our society. I fear that if we want to have peaceful co-existence between societies on this globe in the age of digital communication those forced to live impoverished lives are likely to become both rebellious and hostile.

The English writer Will Hutton's latest book makes a direct attack on our "moral deficit of integrity" which is so linked to inequality: "The cancer of inequality produces results that are catastrophic. Trust evaporates. There is no sense of common purpose. Creative social, economic and political interaction and deliberation becomes impossible."[1]

The manifest unfairness of the growing socioeconomic divide in such wealthy nations as the US and the UK presents a moral challenge to all of us as human beings. There is general agreement that economic equality cannot be granted, as human rights are, without seriously infringing on the rights of others. Any attempt to impose a utopian economic equality is rejected by economists because this would always entail totalitarian tyranny. Equality of opportunity, however, is naturally accepted as a desirable goal in order to prevent the extremes of individual frustration as well as the multiple perils of social disaffection.

A generation ago the outspoken sociologist Ralf Dahrendorf declared that: "A society which claims to be civil but tolerates the exclusion of significant numbers from its opportunities, has betrayed the values on which it is based. The citizens of such a society cannot be surprised if its values are flaunted not just by excluding themselves but by anyone one who sees what is going on, and notably the young... The combination of greedy individualism and new exclusion is a high price to pay for macroeconomic success in a free society."[2]

Inequality has been a persistent plague to man starting with the *Old Testament* and the early Greek City States. The rich, who generally lived off the rental income of their lands as well as from commerce, were pressured to return some of their wealth by catering to the needs of their fellow citizens in the crowded cities. The services they provided in Athens included paying for food supplies, gymnasia, public baths, theaters and festivals. The reputation of the wealthy depended on the quality of the distractions they provided and were commemorated with the inscriptions on statues and monuments which we can still read today. This is a far cry from what billionaires like Charles Koch in the US or the Barclay brothers in the UK provide for their fellow citizens in our times.

The capitalist world as presently constructed is a monument to inequality: Those who live in the favelas of Rio or the gigantic slums of Lagos do not inhabit the same world as those living in the urban centers of the advanced nations. Despite the fact that there is more than enough food to feed every human being, the World Food Program estimates that 800 million people barely have enough food to survive. At the same time some five dozen billionaires possess as much wealth as the poorest of the planet's 3.5 billion people. This is because the laissez-faire market, which rules capitalism, depends on unequal rewards and privileges inherent in the competitive race for ever-greater profits.

Enhanced by the new technologies, which generally make it easier to substitute machines for human efforts, the inequalities of income have risen substantially over the past four decades in both the US and Europe. The global expansion of trade, deregulation, capital flows, and freer markets have also served to narrow the income gaps between nations while widening them inside the economically advanced nations. The introduction into the global economy of more than 1.6 billion workers in China, India and the emerging nations, while improving the lives of those who had been blighted by desperate poverty, inevitably lowered the demand for unskilled or untrained labor in both America and Europe. The extraordinary pace of innovation has left many of the younger generation, as well as those who had worked in the crumbling manufacturing industries, jobless.

Because economic inequality can be measured in many ways, such as by income, consumption, wealth, or distribution, different strategies have emerged on how to combat it. The best information we have on the highest incomes apparently comes from tax returns. The income gap between men and women as well as between races have narrowed over the past three decades even as inequality between individuals has risen. The intensive research by the French economist and scholar, Thomas Piketty, last year revealed the extent to which birth mattered more than talent or effort. "The risk of a drift toward oligarchy is real and gives little reason for optimism," he warned.[3]

Wealth inequality, Piketty pointed out, rises exponentially on the returns on capital and exceeds those of both wages and output. This partially accounts for why the UK and the US have had such dramatic increases in wealth inequality while at the global level — driven by India and China — they have fallen. At the same time, Piketty points out that we have entered the era of the "conspicuous reward" in the form not only of pay, but of bonuses, shares and options. While the growth of productivity in corporations may be marginal, the managers ensure that the gains go to profits which assure the price rises of shares along with executive remuneration rather than rewarding the work force.

The current extravagant corporate pay rises are described by Piketty as "meritocratic extremism." Instead of performance, "super-salaries" are determined by social and psychological status. Remuneration committees in the pyramids of corporate structures engage in pay races to make certain that their top executives are close to the Mt.Everests of pay.

Piketty is certainly keener on wealth redistribution than his critics at the *Economist* who totally dismiss his proposal for a global tax on wealth. The writer/editors at this magazine underwrite the proposition that "Some inequality is needed to propel growth... without the carrot of large financial rewards, risky entrepreneurship and innovation would grind to a halt."[4] The IMF (International Monetary Fund), on the other hand, after prolonged studies suggested that income inequality slows growth, causes financial crises and weakens demand. It also causes the increase of social tensions between those starting out on their own (the 18-25 age group) and those who are retiring on pensions.

Americans have been the great promoters of the collective dream of upward mobility and economic opportunity. In the 19<sup>th</sup> and 20<sup>th</sup> centuries it was believed that if you worked hard and played by the rules you would advance. The "rags to riches" myth was used to legitimize any existing inequalities. It also served to give illusory hope to the aspirational while assuaging the guilt of the privileged. The mainstream consensus also was that a growing economy "raises all boats," while the "trickle down" theory of economics, much favored by President Ronald Reagan, has since been shown to be a fraud. The wealth of the very rich has grown immensely in the past two decades while the income of the lowest has hardly budged. Today there is little chance of mobility for those who work on low wages. The dream of the rich, however, is burning brightly because of their low rates of taxation, exemptions and the light regulatory touch on business. They are likely to get even richer. The myths and belief systems that sacrificed jobs and productive assets on the altar of politically protected deal making created the debt bubble of 2007-8 and the subsequent chronic instabilities.

Americans tend to be less egalitarian than Europeans. They regard the gaps between top and bottom in the US as acceptable. Americans, as well as Chinese and Indians, tend to put more emphasis on the equality of opportunity. They believe that such income gaps can be fair if workers can move up the economic and social ladders. It is consequently fascinating that while Britain and the US have the longest working hours (and the least vacations and holidays) they also have highest inequality ratings. Nor do the number of working hours necessarily make them better off. For example, the Dutch earned an average of $42,000 per capita while working 1,400 hours a year while the British earned $36,000 by working 1,650 hours annually according to the OECD (The Organisation for Economic Co-operation and Development).

While an equality of income could never be feasible nor even desirable, the remuneration of the top corporate earners in the US and the UK has been entering dangerous territory. Larry Ellison at Oracle and Les Moonves of CBS each earned $67 million in 2013 while David Zaslav of Discovery received a staggering $156 million. The wealthy executives asked, "Why should we be paid less than those who kick a ball or sing catchy tunes?"[5] I write "dangerous territory" because the electorates are becoming uneasy that the soaring incomes of those at the top are achieved by cutting the wages and benefits of those at the bottom. Are there not figures beyond which a maximum pay differential is unacceptable? The differentials in national governments are far more strictly controlled: In the UK the pay differential between the heads of government departments and the lowest paid is about 12 times, in France it is about 15 times, and in the US the differential of federal employees seldom passes 16.

Billionaires in the US buy enormous political influence not only through their campaign contributions, but through their tax-exempt think tanks and captive media outlets. The steady deregulation of the financial markets are the clear result of money politics. The corporations which the wealthy control demand that workers make wage concessions while Washington makes tax concessions in what ultimately becomes a race to the bottom. The wealthy have used their political power to slash social programs in order to cut budget deficits. The result is that in the US one in four children lives in poverty while the richest get billions of dollars in mortgage interest deductions on their large houses.

In the US, the 1% of the wealthiest are far more politically engaged than the rest of the population in making campaign contributions and in contacting and influencing members of Congress who may help in preserving their wealth. The Republican Party favors the economic interests of the rich by giving them preferential treatment on capital gains over wages and salaries. Coupon clippers and heirs to large estates call the tunes in what is becoming patrimonial capitalism. [6] Some of their spokespersons, like Rep. Paul Ryan, call for the elimination of tax on dividends, capital gains, interest and estates. Those living off inherited wealth would pay no taxes at all!

The advanced nations of the world have built capitalist societies which encourage the greed, competition and envy upon which inequality flourishes. Critics like Aldous Huxley and Owen Jones have pointed out that if we can build societies based on such negatives, we could also build one based on cooperation, solidarity, and compassion which would encourage greater economic equality. Huxley, writing in the late 1930s, declared that "The most propitious environment for equality is constituted by a society where the means of production are owned cooperatively, where power is decentralized, and where the community is organized, as far as may be, in a multiplicity of small, inter-related self-governing groups of mutually responsible men and women."[7] Historically, the income of those working in co-operatives has differed far less than those working for corporations. Shareholder groups with limited liabilities are in marked competition with one another in attracting the brightest and best. This creates a demand for executives which can only be filled by paying the highest salaries.[8] The resulting inequalities are inevitable. I have repeatedly called for the transformation of corporations into self-managed cooperatives, but the laws in both the US and UK continue to favor corporations and discourage cooperatives at every turn. Neither country has a cooperative the size of Mondragon in Spain which employs some 75,000 workers world-wide and has annual sales of around $13 billion.

Death duties and taxation have been the principal ways in which the redistribution of wealth has been made by nation states. *The Economist,* which is editorially opposed to limitations on wealth suggests, "taxes on the wealthiest should be phased in slowly so that they can liquidate assets rather than cut spending."[9] Piketty has suggested a wealth tax of 1 per cent for people who have between $1 million and $5million in real-estate, shares, bonds, art treasures etc., 2 per cent for those holding more than $5 million and 10% per year for whose with fortunes of more than a billion dollars. However, Piketty admits there is no likely way such a wealth tax could be imposed by our existing political structures. Robert Solow, the Nobel laureate in economics from MIT is likewise highly pessimistic about the capacity of American politicians to redistribute income in the near future.

I ask: is it not time for new paradigms when it comes to economic inequalities such as austerity measures on the poor, the growing oligarchy, electoral funding and lobbying by the rich, and corporate tax avoidance? Governments could narrow inequality by attacking crony capitalism, supporting and developing more solid safety nets for the poor, investing intensely in the education of the young from the ages of 3 to 21, strengthening rather than weakening the bargaining power of the labor unions, and curbing the excessive privileges and power of corporations. All governments could begin by taxing capital gains at the same rate as wage earners and holding all the multinational banks and corporations responsible and accountable to international laws and taxation. The use of exotic financial instruments now spreading via the Internet should be brought under international controls and inspection. Mega-institutions should be broken up into smaller units so that none should be regarded as "too big to fail." Regrettably, the US tax system has become riddled with loopholes and deductions. This must end. The list of ways inequality could be reduced could go on for pages, but finally imposing effective reforms would mean giving more people (and that means nearly all of us) new vistas of opportunity. Campaigning for such essential changes cannot wait. It must begin now.

---

[1]Will Hutton, *How Good We Can Be*, (2015)

[2]Ralf Dahrendorf, The Churchill Lecture, November 22, 1995

[3]Thomas Piketty, *Capital in the 21st Century*, (2014)

[4]"Inequality v growth," *The Economist*, March 1, 2014, p.80

[5]Michael Skapinker, "The battle to align risks and rewards," *The Financial Times* May 1, 2015

[6]Eduardo Porter, "Inequality feels wrong..."*The New York Times*, March 27, 2014

[7]Aldous Huxley, *Ends and Means*, (1938) p.169

[8]see: Yorick Blumenfeld, *Dollars or Democracy*, (2004)

[9]*The Economist,* April 11, 2015, p.75

## Facing the Pension Crisis

Posted on July 24, 2015

"Pensions are finished. I don't think they have a future," writes Michael Johnson an expert at the Centre for Policy Studies in London. Perhaps he is right, but I ask myself: what is going to replace them? There is no clear answer. All of us are experiencing a period of transition as profound as that of the Industrial Revolution two centuries ago. This time the work of human beings is being replaced by automation and robots. The full impact of this is neither understood nor accepted, but it is already deeply affecting our prospects of retirement. Half of US workers have no access to any workplace retirement plan. Only one in five enjoy the prospect of a guaranteed pension. What this means is that in coming generations most workers may end up in poverty because they did not prepare for retirement.

At present the pressures on pensions are based on the difficulties facing state and corporate bodies in Europe and the United States in meeting the gap between impending pension obligations and the resources set aside to fund them. Shifting demographics are causing retirees to live longer, birth rates are falling, and the retirement age has been rising. The politics are such that no one is willing to face up to the problem: Politicians focused on winning the next election do not want to divert taxpayer dollars toward long-term public pension funds; corporations are reluctant to take part in guaranteed pensions because they are too expensive and crimp profits; unions don't want to draw attention to the growing deficits of their funds because benefits might be cut.[1]

Our perspective on pensions is still dominated by the shibboleths of 20th Century economics. Its premises no longer apply to a work force now in transition to the new digital world. Blocking reform of any kind is the private trillion "dollar" pension industry which is primarily dominated, not by concern for the popular welfare, but rather is focused on the profitability of its investments. These huge funds and trusts refuse to introduce transparency and openness into their financial operations. Governments on both sides of the Atlantic have been attempting for years to institute protection for pension investors against the hidden high fees and high-risk products. However lobbying against such protective measures has been effective in blocking any such efforts.

The truth is that most of us are gambling when it comes to our own futures: We have no idea what inflation may do to our savings, how long we shall live, or how much we will need to live on. Inevitably, upon retirement, we may well be left to fend for ourselves. Trying to avoid this may lead us to take long-term risks. The problem is that there is no overall planning to protect us as we head towards retirement. The piecemeal efforts to provide pensions for the electorate which were put in place over the past 100 years are now coming apart at the seams.

Pensions as a way to provide for the welfare of aging workers originally were established through makeshift social legislation in Germany towards the end of the 19th century.[2] It was the statesman Otto von Bismarck who pushed through an Old Age Pension program in 1889, financed by a tax on all workers who would then benefit when they reached the age of 70. This marked the entry of the state into large scale pension funding. As the labor movement in Europe gained strength with the industrial revolution, so did the expansion of state pension programs.[3] In the United States, Federal pensions were offered under the Civil Service Retirement System formed in 1920. This provided retirement, disability and survivor benefits for most civilian employees working for the Federal government. The US continued to be the driving force behind pensions during the four terms of FDR's presidency when the Social Security system was established. Programs such as these remained popular throughout most of the 20th century.

Company pension plans in the US slowly became popular during World War II when wage freezes prohibited increases in worker's pay. Corporations began to push for defined contribution benefit plans in the 1950s and in a period of persistent growth became the most popular type of retirement plan by the 1980s. In such defined contribution schemes, employees also were dependent on contributions from the private sector (corporations). These usually equalled employee payments which were then placed into tax-sheltered accounts. Such funds were intended to become large enough to support those entering retirement. The trouble with these paternally supported plans was that some employers surreptitiously altered the complex benefits and added on charges so that the investment returns were far lower than workers were told to expect. A large part of the work force involved in the contribution benefits managed by the employers were kept in the dark regarding the varied investment schemes. Nevertheless, public sector pension plans in the US now hold more than half of their assets in equities.

Initially defined benefit plans were more popular than defined contribution plans: Today 67% of unionized employees are covered by defined benefit plans as opposed to just 13% of non-union workers. But defined contribution plans now cover about 70% of all pension holdings despite the fact that the lifetime fees of the American household contributors exceed $150,000 and may erode a third of their total contributions. Significantly, researchers have pointed out that employees save more if they are enrolled in savings plans where they have the option to drop out.

From the start, the number of US Social Security program recipients has continued to grow markedly with the value of unfunded obligations rising into the low trillions of dollars. The crisis represents the gap between the amount of promised benefits and the resources set aside by the government to pay for them. As a result, millions of Americans may face a sharp decline in their living standards when they eventually do retire. For many, only Social Security will protect them from penury. Three American academics have thoroughly examined the US problem in their book, *Falling Short: The Coming Retirement Crisis*. In my opinion, their studious but conventional approach falls short in terms of imagination, innovation, and a more global perspective.[4]

The pension experience of the United Kingdom runs somewhat parallel to that of the United States. In the UK, the start of the modern state pension was the Old Age Pension Act of 1908 which provided 5 shillings a week for those over 70 whose annual income did not exceed £31.50.(To get the idea of their value in today's money one has to multiply these figures by more than 150!) Such were the first steps in the welfare reforms of the Liberals leading to the completion of a system of social security with the National Insurance Act of 1911. Following World War II the National Assistance Act of 1948 abolished the medieval poor law and gave a minimum income to those not paying national insurance. In the early 1990s the existing framework for state pensions were strengthened by the comprehensive statues of the Pensions Act of 1995. Then, in yet another update of the state pensions, the Pensions Act of 2007 raised retirement ages.

Although the rates between providers in the private sector varies greatly, a typical UK pension pot of £100,000 will buy a married man of 65 an annual return of £4,500. With annuities, in which individuals swap their holdings, such as shares, houses, or pension pots, for regular monthly sums throughout their forthcoming retirement. Such annual returns average 7.6%. Until the Conservatives came into power in May 2015, pension plans were a form of "deferred compensation" because these were vehicles which allowed for tax free accumulation in funds for later use as retirement income. However, such benefits are being reduced by the new administration.[5]

I see the pension system of the Netherlands as the best role model for most European and American communities to follow. Their mix of public and private provisions guarantees that everyone aged 65 and over enjoys a decent standard of living and is assured it will continue to do so.[6] In per capita terms, Holland has one of the largest pension reserves in the world. Under the Old Age Pension Act (AOW) entitlement under this Act is accumulated at the rate of 2% for each year of contribution which leads to a 100% entitlement to the relevant pension benefit upon reaching the age of 65. For the non-state pillar of this system, employees annually accrue equal pension rights for each year of service which, in most cases, amounts to about 2% of their salaries. Here there is mandatory participation, collective risk sharing and ways to transfer pension value. A clear and transparent division of responsibilities is maintained between the employer, the employee and the pension provider. By the end of this year just over 3 million people will be receiving their Dutch benefits amounting to over 40 billion Euro, but what the entire system offers, and other countries fail to provide, are clarity and transparency.

A number of other small countries are instituting "social pensions" as a way out of the varied risky schemes. These are tax funded monthly cash transfers paid at retirement age. Universal programs which provide pensions regardless of assets, employment record, or income include New Zealand's Superannuation, and in Mauritius by the Basic Retirement

Pension. Other states, such as Singapore, have instituted means-tested pension payments. Even the US has introduced a form of "social pension" with a Supplemental Security Income. This would seem like a humane direction for such pension systems around the world that may soon be unworkable.

To my amazement, no in-depth policy studies have broached the subject of taxing robots as one way to provide the state more money to pay to retired workers. As robots and automation are steadily increasing their ability to replace workers, the number of available jobs (and the taxes these produce) will decrease. The smart resolution ultimately would be to place annual taxes on each operating robot to balance the pension books of most states. Of course corporations would lobby fervently against such a tax.

This means counter-lobbies funded by unions, city and state councils, and financial investment groups would have to be established at both national and global levels. Endorsement, however, should come from prominent advocates of all political persuasions. Such an approach needs proper examination as currently many governments support the production of machines like cars and new robots, but ultimately tax only the former.[7]

A tax on robots also could tax industrial computers used by the insurance industry, accounting firms, and other groupings who continue to replace workers with complex new machinery. The taxes collected should be distributed (or invested) for workers being laid off by companies introducing robots or those unemployed without social security and those over 65 who have no retirement pensions nor savings.

The tax could be based on how many hands would be needed to do the job which the robot displaces. Truckers, for example, would be one for one. A percentage of the pension tax which truckers pay when working a ten-hour day would probably be under 6% of their wage and over 2% of their current pension contribution. On the other side of this equation, corporations caught evading their robot tax would be heavily fined.

Capitalism was built on the back of cheap labor (not to mention slavery) and now is being supported by investment in robots to replace this historical work force. Multi-national corporations could be among the first to be challenged by a drive for the global taxation of robots. These would also present the fiercest opposition. However, the welfare of those facing retirement — that is all of us — need to have the assurance that in the years ahead there will be funds to cover our well-being. Taxing robots could help to provide such coverage.

TAX the ROBOTS! should therefore become the popular slogan for tomorrow.

---

[1] Greg Smith, "It's time to eliminate the confusion in personal retirement accounts" *Time*, June 22, 2015, p.22

[2] Widow's funds first appeared in Germany in 1645 and another fund for teachers in 1662.

[3] President Obama has observed: "It was the labor movement that helped to secure so much of what we take for granted today. The 40-hour workweek, the minimum wage, family leave, health insurance, Social Security, Medicare, retirement plans. The cornerstones of middle-class security all bear the union label."

[4] Charles Ellis, Alicia Munnell, and Andrew Eschtruth, *Falling Short*, (2014)

[5] John Gapper, "Politicians are intent on pillaging your pensions," *The Financial Times*, April 18, 2015

[6] Dutch Ministry of Social Affairs and Employment (June 2008, publication number SWZ 74R610)

[7] Nicholas Colin and Bruno Palier, "The Next Safety Net", *Foreign Affairs*, July/August 2015, p.29

## Towards a Basic Income

Posted on March 24, 2016

I ask myself: How will my offspring face a future with little or no employment open to them? The rise of robots, automation and other technologically driven job killers is set to result in an economic surplus of labor. Software is already changing the very nature of our profit-based economics. Even part-time service jobs are becoming increasingly unreliable and insecure. These rapidly changing developments ultimately demand a rethink of our entire economic system.

Re-enter the ancient idea of a Basic Income as a counter-balance to the ever-widening inequality of incomes as well as the steady decline of job opportunities. Giving every citizen an unconditional grant, regardless of whether they are billionaires or destitute, would represent a significant departure from existing welfare options. The latter offer only limited and conditional support when work is no longer an option. Instead, a Basic Income would be given to all adults over the age of 18 irrespective of what they might otherwise be earning. The wealthy could channel such extra money to good causes.

Surprisingly the idea, which was already entertained by Plato and had been revived in recent years by disparate political activists, feminists, and economists on the right as well as the left, has now become a serious talking point both in Silicon Valley and on Wall Street by venture capitalists. The latter proponents contend that the rise of machine "intelligence" will produce such a surplus in productive capacity that our society could collectively be able to free much of the population not only from border-line hunger and suffering, but also from both insecurity and unchallenging work.

The interest of venture capitalists to create highly profitable enterprises that employ few people is understandable. More surprising is that the 'techies' of Silicon Valley see an algorithm-driven economy supported by a "Basic Income" as a positive move for wider social and economic advances. Ideologically, they just don't see driving a truck for endless hours along the motorways as a good use of the human brain.

Farhad Manjoo an economist writing for the *New York Times,* explained that "one of the reasons some libertarians and conservative like the Basic Income is that it is a very simple, efficient and universal form of welfare — everyone gets a monthly check, even the rich, and the government isn't going to tell you what to spend it on."[1]

Manjoo goes on to speculate, tongue in cheek, that "In Robot America, most manual laborers will have been replaced by herculean robots. Truck drivers, cabbies, delivery workers and airline pilots will have been superseded by vehicles that do it all... Doctors, lawyers, business executives and even technology columnists for the *New York Times* will have seen their ranks thinned by charming, attractive, all-knowing algorithms."

Most arguments pro or against the Basic Income have focused on its promotion of personal independence, its simplicity, and its effectiveness at reaching those who fall through the cracks of the welfare state. Some of the libertarians (which even includes the ghost of the late conservative guru, Milton Freidman) have liked Basic Income because it promises a leaner state without a large bureaucracy checking people's eligibility or policing their behavior. On the left, many see basic income as an opportunity to free people from "wage slavery." For feminists, basic income is viewed as a successor to the old demands for paid housework.

The economic discontent from the "mismatch between expectations based on an earlier America, where plenty of blue-collar jobs offered a decent standard of living, and the more cutthroat reality they face today, can seem intractable," writes another economist for the *New York Times*.[2] On the other hand, Zoltan Istvan, a radical American economist and politician, views a "Universal Basic Income" as an eventual necessity because he believes robots are going to take away nearly all jobs in the next three decades. So he contends that we need a way to transition society to live happily in a time where there will be no more jobs.

Not unexpectedly in the face of such a widespread theoretical appeal, trial runs for a Basic Income are now underway in such disparate countries as Canada, Finland, India, Namibia, and Switzerland. In its 2015 Budget, the Canadian province of Ontario introduced a consultation on social assistance rate restructuring. During the discussions to reduce poverty and support people in their efforts to participate in the economy, a clear consensus emerged on the need in this Canadian province to undertake a Basic Income pilot project.

The campaign for a Basic Income in Switzerland is entering a more advanced stage. After more than 125,000 citizens signed a popular initiative in 2013, a national referendum will be held on June 5th this year. Younger voters (under the age of 35) are confident that such a Basic Income will eventually become a reality in Switzerland, but a majority (56 per cent) of the respondents in a recent poll thought a Basic Income would never happen. The poll also revealed that if there were a Basic Income, 53% of those polled said they would spend more time with their family, 54% would like to pursue further education and 67% believed such an income would help to "relieve people from existential fears."

I believe that the future dependence of the unemployed on welfare, as a solution to the advance of robotics and automation, is untenable as a long-term proposition. I expect that about 10% of the work force in the developed economies will be able to provide the total labor required to produce all the housing, food, clothing and energy needed for the entire population. A decade ago in my book, *Dollars or Democracy*[3] I proposed that the advanced economies of the world should adopt a "Universal Credit" which fundamentally involved a "basic income." This was to be accompanied by the end of cash as we have known it. Indeed, cash is fast disappearing from our monetary system but I shall not go into all the complex details of my entire proposal here.**

The most important result of the institution of a Basic Income in the next decade may not be in its practical applications but rather in how it could change the way we think and talk about the challenges of poverty and inequality. Considerable debate is already arising about how to deal with a "post-work" age. How will people constructively spend their abundant free time? Do we really need jobs for our personal fulfilment? Presently Americans socially define themselves by the work they do. However even now there is no dismissal of those devoting their lives to learning or to creative activities. Even with the Basic Income the population would soon begin to recognize that there is ever so much more to life than money or the capitalist economics of greed, competition, efficiency, or consumption! The introduction of the Basic Income consequently represents a brave step in a new direction.

---

[1]Farhad Manjoo."A Future Without Jobs? 2 Views of the Changing Economy," *The New York Times*, March 9, 2016

[2]Eduardo Porter, "Reviving the Working Class," *The New York Times*, March 9, 2016.

[3]Yorick Blumenfeld, *Dollars or Democracy*, (2006)

** For the curious, my 'Credit System' would come after an economic collapse. In the subsequent economic restructuring, Cash would no longer exist. My 'Credits' given as a Basic Income did not involve a currency to be traded. Its value was based on the human work (time, energy and focus) that had gone into it — not the rating or valuation of goods or raw materials. The "Credit" would be based on the establishment of the average "value" of an hour of labor. One Credit for one hour. Forty Credits per week would automatically be entered into each adult's account as a basic minimum. Using the technology of our ever-smarter plastic cards for all 'commercial transactions,' every adult would be credited each month (or perhaps every ten days) with a certain number of "Credits." Each minor also would be given or credited something like a tenth of that sum from the moment of birth.

For the sake of comparison each credit might be declared to be the equivalent of the current minimum wage levels in the US or the UK. While this might seem like a drastic reduction in current middle-class earnings, this would be compensated by the fact that in a family each adult would get the same grant (a mother at home would be credited with the same amount as her husband at work) No more pensions, no more income tax etc.

The inexcusable inequalities produced by the American-driven market capitalism would be corrected by introducing an element of fairness into the entire economic process. A factor of ten is sufficient to reward real differences and provide a measure of incentive. The US military now gives the highest paid general ten times the wage of the lowest private. A similar range of differentials is to be found in the civil service. Most university professors are paid about ten times the salary of the graduate instructor. 2,500 years ago Plato was more modest in suggesting that a five to one reward ratio was about right. The aim would be to provide for the most basic survival needs of all the people and only then consider the deserved rewards of the particularly industrious, meritorious, the highly creative or those who are making exceptional contributions to the society.

I believe that initially one way to fund such a Basic Income Credit System might be to subsidize it through Quantitative Easing. This could offer each adult the equivalent in Credits of about $1,000 or £800 a month to cover the most fundamental costs of food, rent (or housing) and other necessities. But the complexity of such details are covered at length in my book.

## HALTING THE DEREGULATIONS

Posted on October 2, 2017

The current political and economic systems hold profits ahead of other considerations so that large corporations, like Koch industries, can abuse both their workers and the environment in ways which should be controlled by state intervention in the form of regulations. However an army of lobbyists and vested interests in both Washington and London have been pushing to deregulate wherever possible.

We have been witnessing a sinister political and ideological transformation on government controls. There appears to be a desire in various segments of society for less state steering and regulation to be replaced with ever further freedom for both the market and privatization. Reducing the size of the government is one of the structural changes which are focused on the reduction, cutting or even closing down of numerous existing policies for ideological, political or economic reasons.

Following the economic crisis of 2008, the intense economic austerity programs imposed by different governments affected different aspects of society, including the dismantling of various social benefits, pensions, and controls over air and water pollution. The scaling back was camouflaged as "efficiency savings", "cutting red tape", "reform", "retrenchment", or "deregulation." Such linguistic variations were motivated by obfuscating politicians searching for blame avoidance.[1]

Last February, President Trump signed an executive order to place "regulatory reform" task forces and officers within federal agencies in an effort to pare down the massive red tape of recent decades. Then in another executive order, 'Reducing Regulation and Controlling Regulatory Costs,' called for all government agencies to eliminate two existing regulations every time a new one is issued. Furthermore, the cost of any new regulation had to be offset by the two being removed. This order was swiftly renamed "one step forward, two steps back," by many of those working in public health as well as other public services.

The ideologist and initially Trump's top strategy advisor, Stephen Bannon, announced early on that his goal was "the deconstruction of the administrative state." Fortunately he was fired, but conservatives still hoped that funding for regulations such as the Clean Air Act would be reduced as would those of drug and food safety groups. Indeed, the White House withdrew or removed from consideration some 800 proposed regulations that had never been activated by the Obama administration. Trump then identified some 300 regulations related to energy production and environmental protection that were spread across the Environmental Protection Agency as well as the Interior and Energy Departments. White House budget director Mick Mulvaney said these measures were to "slow the cancer that had come from regulatory burdens that we put on our people." (But there were representatives of the gas and oil industries who cheered.)

Yogin Kothari of the Union of Concerned Scientists countered that "Six months into the administration the only accomplishments the President has had is to rollback, delay and rescind science based safeguards." The administration's regulatory agenda revealed its objective. Kothari insisted that "It continues to perpetuate a false narrative that regulations only have costs and no benefits."

More broadly, "dismantling" incorporates a way of thinking. Neo-conservatives like Richard Perle and David Frum a couple of decades ago declared that "A free society is a self-policing society." This was part of a larger drive to discredit the state as a source of redress for hardships. In the United Kingdom there were similar attacks from leaders of the Tory party who desired a new focus which emphasized greater community and local government powers. This has resulted, for example, in having established food safety structures quietly dismantled.

A special correspondent for *The Guardian* recently wrote that "Local authorities — a crucial pillar in the edifice since they have legal responsibility for testing foods sold in their area — are so starved of money that they have cut checking to the bone."[2] The result is that the Foods Standards Agency is in the process of rewriting much of the basis of food regulation in the United Kingdom and, as a consequence, commercial interests will be protected more than consumers. Big businesses, like supermarkets, will be pleased by privatized inspection and certification schemes which will lead to more "commercially astute" understanding. (Such as covering the sale of outdated foods such as chicken products.)

Lobbyists in England, as in the US, bait lawmakers as well as the national audience with plausible concerns. They suggest that "overreaching regulations" harass start-ups and small businesses. Educational and training requirements on a number of professions impose costs on low and middle-income workers striving for better positions. The lobbyists then proposed that stripping away regulations and consumer protections are the easiest ways to lower such costs. They ignore other solutions to lower the burdensome entry costs for those educationally enrolled.

I believe that there are genuine and rational reasons to question the construction of mountains of bureaucratic regulations. Now many of these regulations reflect serious concern about the environment, worker safety, pensions, health — well, about almost everything affecting human beings. I have long felt that common sense exercised on most issues regarding human welfare would be preferable to regulatory excesses.

Federal Laws like NEPA (National Environmental Protection Act) as well as state-level regulations and rules have ensured that citizens are protected from the harms of less responsible businesses and corporations. Environmental regulations prohibit these from disposing industrial wastes irresponsibly and serve to protect the health of both workers and communities. OSHA (The Occupational Safety and Health Administration) has some 3,500 specific provisions to cover the health and safety of construction workers. Detailed regulations on electronic job injuries and illness from air pollution in the work place impose fines and other sanctions to make it costly for irresponsible parties to act recklessly. However, much of such protective regulation is currently in jeopardy. Lobbyists and opponents in Congress suggest that publicly displaying information according to the injury requirements would unfairly damage the reputation of the employers. Pushing aside concerns of dangers to workers exposed to Silica and Beryllium, President Trump has been eager to roll back the executive order by President Obama in 2014 titled "Fair Pay and Safe Workplaces."

The neoliberal program which has been envisioned aims to switch our values of "the public good and the public interest" to a value system based on "the market" and individual responsibility. Prof Sendhill Mullainathan, an economics professor at Harvard, suggests that "New technologies are rattling the economy on all fronts. While the predictions are specific and dire, bigger changes are surely coming. Clearly we need to adjust for the turbulence ahead." He believes that the neoliberal agenda could give way to a new focus which will incorporate an authoritarian mode of economics aimed at accountability and the "audit culture." Mullainathan cautions: "A lifetime of work will be a lifetime of changing, moving between firms, jobs, careers and cities." By-passing such purportedly creative destruction, he believes "we ought to enable innovation to take its course."[3] Such excuses for the unfettered pursuit of profit would end the system of protective regulations which have taken decades to develop. It seems obvious to me that regulation is essential for the democratic state. In our daily lives we drive our cars, take our pills, drink our water, and comfortably eat most foods because we take the safety regulations covering all these acts for granted.

France's new President, Emmanuel Macron, has said "we need to rethink regulation, so as to deal with the excesses of globalized Capitalism."[4] The devious excesses of the current economic system manifestly threaten our future. By now, it should be clear to every voter and each citizen that deregulation is generally not in the public interest and should be fiercely resisted if we truly want advancement of the common good.

---

[1]Michael W. Bauer et al. *Dismantling Public Policy*, (2014) pp.30-56[2]Felicity Lawrence, "Vital protections in are being dismantled," *The Guardian*, August 25, 2017, p.31[3]Sendhill Mullainathan, "Planning to cope with what you can't forsee," *The New York Times*, September 5, 2017

[4]"Regeneration," *The Economist*, September 30, 2017, p.12

**Plan "B" Please!**

Posted on July 8, 2016

We are living in a highly uncertain era in which our future is rapidly evolving with minimal planning or careful consideration. Nowhere is this more evident than in our approach to economics where we are reluctant to confront the many challenges facing us. I am selecting a few of these in the hope that the discussions and debates they may provoke will result in the examination of plausible alternatives to the shambles into which we might otherwise plunge. Creating a better world has been at the basis of this blog.

...We are currently experiencing global economic chaos. Since the end of the gold standard in the 1930s economists have been unable to come up with an effective substitute.

...We are reluctant to recognize that the globalized free flow of capital was designed for corporations to evade taxes and the burden of social legislation. Free market economics are creating universal and sinister levels of inequality.

...We hesitate to accept that we are at an end of a period of growth and higher living standards for the majority of people in what used to be the "advanced economies."

...We remain reluctant to admit that with ever improving technology and robotics we are reducing the opportunities for workers to find jobs.

...We fail to grasp that the entire banking system with its near-to-zero interest rates has become redundant. In the age of computerized accounting and transfers, one National Bank per country would suffice.

...We cannot come to terms with the reality that the globalization of tax evading corporations has undermined the social structure of democracies. Corporations have brought in rules that restrict what governments can and cannot do in terms of interfering with corporate interests which focus on profits not human beings.

...We are unwilling to face up to the corruption of civil society by the dynamic greed of capitalism. The power of money rules almost all contemporary economic scenarios .For example, from a recent newspaper comment: "Britain has become a power base for a legalized financial mafia that strips the assets of healthy companies, turns the nation's housing into a roulette table, launders money for the drug cartels and terrorists, then slashes the gains beyond the reach of police and tax inspectors." [@georgemonbiot, June 15, 2016]

If the global markets implode, what follows? We have no contingency planning.

Plan B, please.

++++++++++++++++++++++++++++++++++++++++++++++++++++++++++++++++++++++
++++++++++++++++++++++++++++++++++++++++++++++++++++++++++++++++++++++
++++++++++++++++++++++++++++++++++++++++++++++++++++++++++++++++++++++
++++++++++++++++++++++++++++++++++++++++++++++++++++++++++++++++++++++
++++++++++++++++++++++++++++++++++++++++++++++++++++++++++++++++++++++
++++++++++++++++++++++++++++++++++++++++++++++++++++++++++++++++++++++

Many of my readers have asked what my vision or perspective was regarding an alternative to capitalism. The prominent environmentalist, Randy Hayes, reviewed my book

**DOLLARS OR DEMOCRACY: A TECHNOLOGY-DRIVEN ALTERNATIVE TO CAPITALISM (2004)**

And I thought it might resolve questions about where I stood as viewed by a critic's perspective:

" *Dollars or Democracy*: A Technology Driven Alternative to Capitalism (2004) contends that capitalism is fundamentally flawed and cannot be over-hauled. It provides an alternative, called the Incentive Economy. This proposed cooperative and ecologically sane society is a positive vision. It gives many justifications and additional clarifications of how things would work including the transition. Personal liberation is realized in a greater choice of work and leisure time. Nonviolent cooperation is seen as key to human survival would replace competition. "Cooperation and interdependence are central mechanisms of the evolutionary process."

This is an enormous challenge, but perhaps one for which a new generation could readily adapt. Look how swiftly the once vast Soviet empire collapsed. The American capitalist supremacy could vanish with equal rapidity. New systems are unlikely to come about  unless people in time of crisis, see an attractive alternative. We have the ability and the duty to change an economic system that is not serving us well. Blumenfeld truly represents a challenging alternative. Read his book.

BLUMENFELD ARGUES THAT AMERICAN CAPITALISM IS UNREFORMABLE BECAUSE:

**1.Capitalism erodes and corrupts democracy**: capitalism is fundamentally antidemocratic. Money controls Washington DC, not the other way around. Corporate money tends to buy key political parties. They use their money and purchased power to write and engineer favourable legislation. The pressures of the sugar lobby control our diets. The highest bidder- corporations - buys democracy.

**2. Bottom feeding:** Capitalism pits countries, states and counties against each other seeking special tax breaks and subsidies in highly wasteful "corporate welfare" programs. Capitalism seeks the lowest level, cheap labor and least regulations.

**3. It drives off accountability:** Corporate managers are shielded from accountability to shareholders while shareholders are protected from personal liability of damage done by the corporation. Capitalism cheats control. Multinationals are responsible to no electorate and no governments.

**4. Capitalism's values are insufficient:** Capitalism doesn't foster many things we value such as controlling child labor, imposing strict health and safety standards, limiting the number of working hours or guaranteeing a day off per week. The market economy has failed to focus on durability and ecologically sustainable products and services.

**5. Capitalism has a stability and debt accumulation problem:** The supply of money is dependent on people and firms relying on loans and perpetually increasing their debt. Interest requires endless economic growth. Witness the never ending economic bubble bursts.

**6. Unaccountable:** Capitalists are structurally capable of avoiding accountability. For instance, corporations avoid taxes that support infrastructure fundamental to their expansion. They use shell companies, tax havens, and modern electronic transfers to shuffle capital around and evade responsibility

**7. Capitalism undercuts diversity:** By pushing western secular consumerism and materialism and crushing all other value systems some would argue that capitalism inspires terrorism.

**8. Capitalism ignores and destroys nature's life support systems:** Capitalism is unconcerned that the biosphere has carrying capacity limits. The invisible hand has failed in important ways. Endless expansion and growth are destined to end in disaster. Endless growth is the definition of cancer. Moral outrage is too mild an expression for the deep levels of corruption at work here". Capitalism ultimately will amount to global suicide.

**THE ESSENTIAL ELEMENTS OF HIS ALTERNATIVE ECONOMY/SOCIETY ARE BELLOW**
points 1,2,9 & 10 are key to his new economic system.

**1.No cash society:** There is a credit system and people use smart cards for all transactions. There are several reasons for this including reduction of black markets, mafia, etc. The computer era makes management of this system possible when it wasn't before.

**2. no making money off lending money:** Hence, there are no banks, stock exchanges, or mutual funds.

**3.Real source of income:** There is a right to useful, rewarding, regular work.  We have to reconsider the question of property in the context of a more cooperative and mutual society.

**4. Businesses are not nationalised or privatised.** There are many smaller, worker-owned cooperatives like the Spanish system of Mondragon. There are about 50,000 cooperatives in the US today in which about 120 million Americans participate. Trade and barter is allowed by cooperatives. Giant corporations would rapidly be phased out.

**5.Basic survival:** Imagine forty credits given every adult (stay at home mother or whomever) ever week for basic food/shelter survival.
**The credit value** Would likely be some average value for an hour of labour. Think one credit per hour. Think $5 per hour like a minimum wage. Credits are used for what money is now legally utilized.
**Blumenfeld sees a nonviolent transfer out of capitalism.** Personal financial accounts up to five fingers would be turned into credits.

**6.Most private homes and farms would not be affected.** People would be able to keep most of their tangible assets such as jewelry, paintings, planes and yachts. The question would be where to obtain the means to maintain items such as planes and yachts? Without income from shares, bonds, interest or rent, their upkeep would swiftly prove

prohibitive.

**11. Workers share in profits or losses.** Workers would be held responsible for their cooperatives' ethical behaviour (such as effect on local environment), which is a powerful incentive. Workers (as owners) have a democratic voice in the enterprise's policies.

**12. Health care:** Would be universal and costs covered by the state.

A large role for government and central planning would be needed. Chinese "communist" party leadership has taken on "crony capitalism" with its rush to "modernisation" isn't the model to look toward. "In the Incentive Economy it will no longer be legitimate to continue granting privileges to those who live off the wealth that the labor creates". This approach seeks to provide satisfying work, fair earnings, stable prosperity, and a healthy web of life - - planet wide.

***     ***     ******     ***     ***

"Fortunately, capitalism is not an iron law of history: it is economic and political system which arose out of a decaying feudal structure in the eighteenth century and was advanced by the 'haves' over the 'have nots'. Capitalism Can't Be Reformed, Try the incentive Economy... Ultimately, the struggle for human survival will most likely be determined not by the fittest but by those most capable of cooperation"- - Yorick Blumenfeld

Yorick Blumenfeld's Dollars of Democracy: A Technology Driven Alternative to Capitalism (2004) ISBN: 1-4134-6080-1 soft cover; ISBN 1-4134-6081-x hardcover; US Library of congress 2004094335

# V .The Wonders of Science and Technological Advances

*While technology promises marvels for tomorrow, my argument in these blogs has been that we should not let it run away at such speed as to destroy everything we hold dear, starting with the environment.*

*Both "Science" and "Technology" generally have held out the promise of "no limits." In no way have my writings suggested that "techno-fix" is a solution to the challenges humanity faces. Indeed I am most sceptical about the rapid evolution of technology we are experiencing. Popularly, the media have represented "run-away tech" as having an independence and direction which has not been given nor intended by its creators.*

*In these blogs I have come to regard technology not only as one of our major problems but also as the creator of many new ones. The direction of technology is driven principally by the market and not by any government plan nor private program. Do we really need ever more powerful machines to alter our fragile environment before we have really thought through exactly what we should be doing to our planet? Greed, insecurity, and the irrational all interfere with effective planning.*

*Until now technological progress has been driven compulsively by our need to dominate over nature. Indeed, technology is popularly viewed as being indispensable for our future development. Today's Science and Technology are regarded as holding out far more convincing options than our ancestors could ever have dreamt- especially in releasing humanity from toil. Our global societies generally are proud of the developments which range from mobiles to lifesaving drugs and to jet transport.*

*It is generally accepted that Science and Technology are intimately connected. The new technology that, in turn, develops new instrumentation can establish the validity of most recent discoveries. Medical science for example depends on the latest research tools and these ,inevitably, can help and lead to breakthrough discoveries. We must recognize that research has become more removed from the powers of unaided human observation, such as microprocessors, particle accelerators, and space craft.*

*Our ability to arrange atoms through nanotechnology (that is molecular assemblers) will determine advances in medicine, computation and even artificial intelligence. The supra-molecular nano-mechanisms will replicate themselves much as do the macromolecules of DNA and RNA which are foundations of life on earth. It is likely that in the near future it will be possible to replace, alter or reinforce almost every part of the human body with artificial material.,*

*The windows opening up with molecular techniques are awesome. In the decades ahead technicians using molecular pincers joined to atomic microscopes could be able to move individual molecules which would then enable the assemblage of unbelievably complex structures used to produce nourishment from chemicals, incredibly strong materials from minerals and specialized medicines to fight specific viruses. It would be possible to scale down the micro-processing chips of today into the size of ordinary bacteria. Such processors would be capable of executing billions of instructions per second using less power than one ten-millionth of a watt!*

*Mankind seems to have adapted remarkably easily in the last 50 years to new forms of communication from the internet . Silicon chips are being introduced into practically everything but our food. Every major event occurring almost anywhere on Earth is now known within 24 hours. It is hard to predict how human beings will react when "mind" emerges in machines (AI). Will this end up late in the 21st Century in modifying human beings? Indeed one wonders about a future in which humans will not only be served by robots but will also turn, or be turned, into a part robot?*

*The layers of inter-connections of the brain are incredibly complex- perhaps quite unnecessarily so. Nature is by no means perfect and scientists towards the end of this century should be able to improve on it, Our brains contain an average of 10 billion neurons of which we use about 15 percent, so it is unlikely that there will be a need to duplicate that number for the first AI mechanisms. Nor are the more than 10 trillion connects likely to be essential for the microstructures of cognition. There is also little point in developing AI that is just the duplicate of human intelligence. Do we want an AI that is as error prone and befuddled as our human brains?*

*The ability of a computer to modify its behaviour according to what it has experienced is the very essence of learning. AI machines consequently will be capable of self-improvement. The real challenge will be to produce a different kind of intelligence, with other modes of functioning, with varying patterns of approach or configuration, and even quantum ways of organizing. Our emotions, which impact on intelligence, are unlikely to enter the early stages of AI development.*

*Speculation is one important realm of intellectual activity which will be difficult to introduce into AI. Because of their inherently complex and connective structures. AIs may have to be biological in part, composed not only of silicon chips but of carefully programmed DNA cells. Linking many different units in complex parallel circuits may provide for both diversity and selectivity.*

*The near-miraculous complexity of the sequences of RNA and DNA which conquered this planet lead me to wonder if we humans are exclusively dealing with a few thousand millennia of evolutionary development through point mutations which occurred exclusively on this planet. There can be little doubt that in our Milky Way which alone contains billions of stars, our civilization must be one of the youngest. It is hard to believe that other cultures could have evolved more rapidly than homo sapiens over the past 15,000 years. This leads to the probability that almost any civilization with which we might come into contact would be more advanced than ours.*

*There might, of course, be enormous challenges in deciphering nearly incomprehensible messages. Their communication might be through photosensitive crystals which would have little in common with ours. How* to understand complex equations about anti-mater generators, black hole inversion or graviton propulsion?

In the Search for Extra-terrestrial Intelligence (SETI) towards the end of this century there is also the potential danger that we may believe we have established contact with other species of life from outer-spce. However this might be just the plot of a controlling AI unit trying to protect humanity. The logic of AI might be that only some external 'existence' could unite our warring global populations. Nothing could be quite as effective as a potential threat from another world, and so the AI units might simply, and for our own good, simulate the interception of purportedly hostile signals from outer space. Science fiction? This may not be as far-fetched as it seems now.

.

## Techno-driven change

Posted on July 29, 2014

The year and a half I have been blogging has been full of surprises, delights and some disappointments. I have been positively surprised by the ever more visible advances for women and by the greater awareness of the electorate to environmental threats, but looking back I found that my prevailing and recurrent theme has been "change."[1] Small wonder: Technology driven change is overwhelming the world and all its inhabitants at speeds never previously experienced. Its scope and impact have been so powerful that I am finding it hard to write: There are now more cell-phones than people.

Instead of guiding change we are letting technology run away with it. The pace of change has been driven in part by an economic system ruled by both the profit motive and the demands for growth. It startles me that nobody is really questioning whether the global consumers of such rapid change are capable of handling it without enduring serious psychological and social challenges. More disturbing is that hardly anyone is asking where such change is leading us or even where would consumers like it to take them ... or future generations. My goal in writing this blog has been to consider positive alternatives and to suggest different outcomes for free societies. But how to deal with the simultaneous rise of nanotechnology, automation, robot advances, data-driven algorithms, quantum computers, social networks, driverless cars, domestic control systems, threats to privacy, internet education, medical diagnostics, and internet banking – to mention a dozen that immediately come to mind.

Our immediate challenge is to confront the serious crises from technological advances creating (A) unemployment (particularly for the 16-to 25 age group) caused in part by robots and automation, (B) rising economic inequality, and (C) massive tax avoidance/evasion by global corporations.

For the less than one per cent of the population who were already wealthy, change has been extremely beneficial — even in a time of economic contraction. High tech capitalism tends to create rates of return on investment considerably higher than the overall rates of economic growth with the result that more wealth is transferred into the hands of an hereditary elite of investors to the detriment of most of society. This is the clear conclusion of Thomas Piketty's massive book, *Capitalism in the 21st Century*. Hedge funds, like Renaissance Technologies, have found devious ways and loop-holes which allow them to borrow $17 for every $1 in the accounts of investors while those with ordinary brokerage accounts are legally entitled to borrow only $1 on every dollar held. These hedge funds manage to pay long term tax rates on short term trades for their privileged customers even when the shares were held electronically for just a few seconds. Such operations have enabled the wealthy to greatly increase their holdings at the expense of the US and UK treasuries which have been deprived of billions in taxes.[2]

Technological solution-ism has been in full swing in Silicon Valley pushed by corporations whose goals would appear to be both profit (on revenues of over $200 billion in 2013) and the optimization of efficiency. They are actively researching the "smartification" of everyday chores in "smart" environments serving "ambient assisted living." Would success of such a trajectory lead to an improvement of the human condition? As it is, both research and development seem to be headed towards a communication connectivity of our lives where home, business and personal associations will be linked. Is such change desirable? Make no mistake: the web, which was still free two decades ago, is now dominated by big corporations.

It has been said that the key to understanding the major corporate players in the electronics industry is to recognize that they don't have any formal strategy. As the technology analysts from Gartner explain: "Google encourages innovation through emergence. It doesn't have a strategic master plan with investors or clients, which for some is a source of confusion or frustration. Applications, services and products that succeed — whether in revenue generation or serving as irritants and disruptors to its rivals — receive more resources." What such analysis is saying is that there is no plan behind the changes we are all experiencing — there is only the market.

Larry Page, one of the developers of Google, contends that robots and machines should be able to provide a "time of abundance" where everyone's basic needs could be met relatively easily. He recognizes that much of what people used to do has been taken over by machines over the past century and that this trend will continue. "90 per cent of people used to be farmers. So it's happened before. It's not surprising." But Larry Page has no suggestions for the unemployed or under-employment in terms of work or income.

It is in fashion for those in Silicon Valley to use terminology like "The Cloud." Down to earth, this term refers to using shared Internet services to process, manage or store data instead of personal computers or local servers. This will come in handy for those somehow seeking to solve society's problems with giga masses of data gathered from the ever multiplying "smart" devices. Such a data based approach to economics, politics and governance, or "algorithmic regulation" may indeed be in the offing but will it bring us closer to dealing with global problems?

One observer, Evgeny Morozov, suggests "algorithmic regulation could certainly make the administration of existing laws more efficient." It "will give us a political regime where technology corporations and government bureaucrats call all the shots."[3] This sounds to me like a new definition for dystopia where human behaviour is monitored and managed by smart ambient technology. This would be an invasive computer world where corporate executives and power-hungry politicians could control and manipulate the monitored population.

In a 'visionary' moment a year ago, Larry Page said: "We should be building great things that don't exist ... We're really only at 1% of what's possible, and maybe even less than that ... we're still moving slow." Page is correct to say that we are still at an early stage of the possible. The effects on the "plugged in" new generations — whose attention spans keep on shrinking, whose memory lapses are on the rise, and whose stress levels are increasingly medicated — are inconclusively researched. Perhaps the fear is that the results of such studies could be so intimidating that they might induce panic in parents, teachers, politicians, corporations and the market.

[2]Report of the US Senate Permanent Subcommittee on Investigations, July 29, 2014

[3]Evgeny Morozov, *The Observer*, July 20, 2014, The New Review, p.11

## Exploring the Unknown

Posted on March 27, 2013

New worlds are opening up for us in all directions: from the galactic to the sub-microscopic, from global communications to interplanetary ones (like the report from the Martian robot about the existence of water there in an earlier era). The impact of these broadening vistas should be highly positive, but instead it is falling somewhat flat. In one of its latest issues, the *New Scientist* claimed on its cover that: "We've run out of explanations for the universe."[1]

My immediate response to this was: Could this really be true? Is this a reflection on our current human condition: namely, are we running out of explanations of how to correct the global economic picture? It would seem that our approach to understanding the universe is not only influenced by our training and profession (depending on whether we are mathematicians, physicists, astronomers, chemists, cosmologists, radiation specialists, or even philosophers or astrologists) but also by what the Germans call our *Zeitgeist* (the spirit of our times.)

Hardly had I started writing this blog when on March 21st the front-page digitized images came with the startling news of the recordings of the Planck satellite launched in 2009 to examine background radiation in outer space. [SEP] Here suddenly were new explanations of the evolution of the universe.

The vastly different renditions of the map of space provided by the Planck team would appear to be mosaics of two-dimensional images of various parts of the heavens at the wavelength of the cosmic microwave background radiation. The interpretations of such images are inevitably fraught with uncertainties, because much of the energy has been curved by gravity as it travelled for billions of years and was most probably affected by other forces (such as "dark energy") of which we have little understanding. To conclude at this early stage that the observed "cool" and "hot areas" would eventually grow into galaxies seems presumptuous. The large, international team of scientists involved have analyzed less than half of the data gathered by the space telescope which is not programmed to monitor other particles, such as neutrinos. But the bold and startling conclusions drawn from the haze of space radiation appear at this stage to be more the result of rash interpretation than of serious scientific examination.

It seems to me that our perspective on the universe is still profoundly affected by a variety of unknown factors. We have no idea of what the impact of gamma rays, x-rays, radiation from uranium, the incredible stream of neutrinos, gravity or even speed is having on our mental processes. Yes, because our sun is making a gigantic orbit of our galaxy and we are orbiting around the sun and our planet is spinning all the time, we are in fact moving at speeds of thousands of miles per hour without us having any idea of the impact on us. And when we are informed that untold billions of neutrinos are "harmlessly" passing through our brains (and bodies) every second of the day, we accept this amazing information with little concern!

Neutrinos are minute particles traveling at close to the speed of light but unlike light have no electrons and possess only the tiniest mass. Most of those that pass through us (as well as through the core of our planet!) originate from inside the sun. Others come from stars in our galaxy and even other galaxies. Indeed some physicists speculate that the gradual decay of neutrinos may provide a clue to the origin of matter. A long-time friend, the astronomer Lord Martin Rees, has written that "It is embarrassing to cosmologists that 90% of the universe is unaccounted for."[2] Finding out exactly what the universe is made of remains a nagging problem for astronomers. Martin has been optimistic for nearly two decades that we are on the verge of finding out the so-called secrets of "dark matter" and "dark energy." (Both of which are terms used to identify what we don't know.) Ordinary atoms, of which we and our planetary system are made, are likely to account for only about 4% of the mass of the entire universe.

Optical observation alone cannot give us an adequate perspective on the cosmic scene, Martin tells us. X-ray telescopes have been an amazing improvement, but "the whole electro-magnetic spectrum emitted by cosmic objects ranges over more than 100 octaves." In Martin's analogy, "visible light, from the red to the blue, is just a single octave... of the broad range of frequencies that most objects actually radiate."[3]

James Clerk Maxwell discovered that light is an electromagnetic wave over 100 years ago. But who has discovered how gravity, the force that ultimately overwhelms all the other forces in the stars, actually operates? Speculation is rife about how a "graviton", possibly a quantum particle, could be the force behind the attraction exerted by mass. Frankly, I feel quite entangled by quantum weirdness.

The Nobel Prize-winning physicist, Eugene Wigner, was concerned about "the unreasonable effectiveness of mathematics in the physical sciences." In astronomy, because of the absence of verifiable experimental results when considering black holes, how the universe might have begun, the possibility of multi-universes, "empty" space, or even "time," the only way forward in our understanding is by resorting to mathematics. And that maybe where we may come to an end of explanation as suggested by the *New Scientist*.

To repeat, part of the problem facing us is with the limitation of our perspective. We think of existence in terms of a beginning, middle and an end (of our lives, and of this planet, the sun and our immense galaxy.) But perhaps our universe does not follow such a story line. It could be that there is no beginning and no end — only the continuity of a string theory kind of a loop. And back in 1895 the American philosopher and psychologist William James coined the word "multiverse" in which our universe is part of an interpenetrating system of universes. Here we enter into the spheres of fantasy, the quantum, and infinitely varied and complex super-string theories reinforced by ad hoc postulates.

The cosmologist Max Tegemark suggested that of all the various forms of multiverses, the simplest and most elegant involved parallel universes. "Perhaps we will gradually get used to the weird ways of our cosmos and find its strangeness to be part of its charm."[4] And that may be the best counter-point to the proposition of the *New Scientist* for it is unlikely that we are ever going to run out of explanations for charm.

---

[1]New Scientist, 2 March 2013)

[2]Martin Rees, *Our Cosmic Habitat*, (2001) p.75

[3]*op.cit*.p.58

[4]Max Tegemark, "Parallel Universes," (2003).

## Technology: Introducing Structured Advances
Posted on May 4, 2016

Technology is transforming our planet and frankly, I am overwhelmed on many fronts by the wonders and rapidity of technologically driven "advances" in automation, biotechnology, communication, education, medicine, employment, the environment, and even privacy. There are moments when I empathize with King Alfred shouting to the waves to halt their advance! Nor am I alone in my concerns: Youthful constituencies in both the US and the UK have been expressing their anger at the inequalities, the narrowing of opportunities, and the environmental dangers we are facing — all in large measure resulting from technology's global transformations.

I cannot overlook what is driving the nightmare scenario of endless GROWTH, fuelled by the demands of technology's paymaster, capitalism. The focus on growth of the standard of living, of production, of the GNP, and of the global population is now wedded to the growth of technology. The truth is that none of the current generation of politicians dares to propose an end to growth. None even mentions the dangers of a ten billion population level in the 21$^{st}$ century.

Planning is rejected at nearly all levels because of a misled belief in the freedom and advances which are offered by "the market." Apple, Microsoft, and the larger community of "Silicon Valley" are all eager to create further advances in automation, communications, connectivity and the resulting profits! As the current front-runners of technological advance, their executive boards are convinced that given sufficient data and instant connectivity, their products will prove to be effective in creating a more beneficial outcome for society.

Is technological innovation the handmaiden of progress in the 21$^{st}$ century? Innovation frequently results in startling advances and profits, but it does not always produce results which give a long-term advantage to the good over the bad. *The Financial Times* has suggested that Silicon Valley technology has been distorting the operations of the market by restricting the basic information necessary for the efficient allocation of resources by industry. Data, on which the advertising agencies depend, are being offered by Google, Facebook and others at vastly reduced rates. Evgeny Morozov, who has developed a rather sinister scenario, suggests that these companies "will eventually run the basic infrastructure on which the world functions." He concludes, "They would be thrilled to do this."[1]

The accelerating pace of change, particularly in the fields of automation and robotics, is also threatening our sense of personal worth. All too many of the now unemployed workers have come to regard computers, robots, and machines as being stronger, more capable and faster than themselves. As these workers become discarded in a competitive environment, they are told to become more flexible and "compatible" with the new technologies.

It is important for us to try and step back and confront how technology is now changing the human spirit itself. Automation and mechanization are making us less connected with the natural world, more fragmented as human beings, less well balanced, and increasingly escapist in our behavior. Due to the Internet, today we can focus on specifics, but have trouble picturing the whole. Innovation has become a driving factor in the digital world in which volatility and dynamism have become linked. Technology is cramming ever-greater numbers of electronic components into everything from household products to automobiles and will soon enter the human body.

Society has become fixated on the idea that our technology advances in order to solve problems. We also tend to think of the development of technology itself much as we do of an evolving eco-system, but we tend to see "run-away technology" as having an independence and direction which was not given nor intended by its creators. The notion of separating technology from human needs and intents is itself remarkable. We may not be aware, however, that what we are becoming could be the result of what we created.

"New technology equals new perceptions. As we create tools, we recreate ourselves in their image," observed one sharp observer.[2] Technology can thus turn into a way of arranging our world so that we no longer experience it. It is significant that we are currently extending the scope of our possible awareness through the analysis of the 95 per cent of the spectrum (ranging from infra-red to gamma radiation, and x-rays to ultra-violet) which we cannot perceive with our naked eyes. Alas, the best minds in technology have no idea whether we are headed towards a techno-utopia or a dystopia. That is one of the many tech challenges which we have to answer.

The truth is that as members of an evolving civilization, we hold no genuine vision of where we are headed. It is generally accepted that the real future has always differed from rational extrapolations of what exists. New tech tends to evolve as the consequence of scientific breakthroughs, from the light bulb to the transistor, which could not have been predicted. Scientists are generally interested in discovering the truth, not in ushering in new technologies. They usually tend to dismiss statements about future developments as "speculation." Such a perspective encourages their leaning toward the short-term. Engineers also prefer to focus on the more immediate problems at hand: Their employers, their colleagues and their training all encourage them to design systems that can be made from existing technology.

Science and technology are intimately connected. New technology that produces new instrumentation is necessary to establish the validity of most recent discoveries. These tools tend to become increasingly complex and expensive as the research becomes more removed from the powers of unaided human observation — as evidenced by particle accelerators, microprocessors, space exploration, and both bio- and nano-tech. It has generally been trial-and-error experimentation, not the planning of a genius that has brought about most advances from digital watches to GPS.

To build structures to complex micro-specifications, a kind of supra-molecular chemistry is being developed for "molecular meccano" or nano-scale construction. One important aspect of such supra-molecular assemblers is that they will be able to replicate themselves much in the fashion of the giant macromolecules of DNA and RNA which are at the basis of all life on earth. Eric Drexler, one of the most brilliant of the technology analysts of the 20th century wrote that: "Advances in the technologies of medicine, space, computation and production ... all depend on our ability to arrange atoms. With assemblers (that is molecular machines that can be programmed to build almost any molecular structure or device from simpler chemical blocks) we will be able to remake our world."[3]

Can we tolerate this technological transformation of the world? Scientists may be able to produce proteins from chemicals, super-strong materials from carbons and silicates, tailor-made genetic alterations to fight specific viruses, as well as ever more sophisticated aphrodisiacs, but our social structure, which until quite recently was tribal, is so delicately balanced that it may be overwhelmed if we push relentlessly for advances in micro-technology. Regrettably technologists, like those who want to meld computer chips with the human nervous system, seldom seem to address the possibility of improving social institutions. The problem is that their technological meliorism lacks social vision.

Automation would appear to be one of the most threatening technologies now facing us. It takes the most extraordinary forms from drones to the new generation of half a dozen different types of robots. All of these point to a future that does not need us, rather than focusing on machines which support the well-being of humans. Capitalism strives to promote automation guided not only by popular demand but also for ever-greater efficiency bringing more profit.

The collective performance of human employees does not improve much over time, while robots keep on becoming ever more efficient. Automation had progressively mastered increasingly complex tasks. This makes it harder for manufacturers to justify hiring workers even in jobs that require special manual and intellectual skills. Half of all current jobs in the United States could potentially be replaced in the next two decades. Personally, I believe that even if automation can carry out some functions more rapidly and efficiently than humans, it still makes better social sense for us to continue to carry on with those functions, even if we do them less well or are not as profitable.

Tomorrow's technicians may also come around to believing that human beings, as currently constituted, should be modified. After all, engineers have used technology to improve technology, just as experts have used computers to produce better computers, and bio-technicians are using biology to improve plants and livestock. Is there a rational reason why humans should be the exception to this chain of betterment? Eventually, "mind" (or Artificial Intelligence) may well emerge in bio-mechanical machines which may prove to be a difficult challenge for civilization.

Today automation, no longer limited to factories and assembly lines, is being integrated into every day life. We are increasingly automating the military, health care, transport and housekeeping. Two Dutch experts have compiled a comprehensive overview on automation and robotics whose table of contents overwhelmed me.[4] The challenge of evaluating the benefits and drawbacks of Mechanoids, Humanoids and Androids on our sex lives, stopped me. For the time being I shall leave human-robot interaction to the pages of science fiction.

A global debate on the use of military drones has obviously been avoided for far too long. So has the private use of drones — with one million drones, each weighing up to 25 kilos, having been sold in the United States. Such drones pose a serious threat to security as terrorists could use them on sport events and public crowds. *The Economist* pointed out that "Technology can also keep drones out of trouble. Some drone makers are installing "geo-fencing" software which programs a drone's GPS to prevent flights near sites such as airports and nuclear power stations as well as restricting the speed and height that they can reach."[5] The development of common legal and ethical principles for the responsible use of drones is essential.

A basic condition for humanitarian law is that someone can be held responsible for undesirable consequences at all times. Robots are likely to test the boundaries of our antiquated legal frameworks. There is a need for timely government action on the gradual robotization of automobiles and traffic. The US government has funded much of the advances in science and technology since the beginning of the Cold War in 1950, but it has not matched this with controlling the consequences. Technological development was mostly driven by the US Defense Department's push in areas ranging from satellite communications to molecular biology, transistors, the internet as well as drones and automation. Today's governments hardly feature in giving a direction to technological developments. I believe it is urgent that governments obtain automatic shares and a percentage of the profits from the patents and intellectual property they protect on automation and technology.

The "Silicon Valley" mind-set has propagated a belief in techno-optimism which promotes that driver-less cars will prevent gridlock, that mobile phones will spur growth in the less developed nations, and that robots will look after the old as the aging population mounts. Google, Facebook, Apple and Amazon are struggling in a media rivalry over whose technologies will come out on top. Apple's iPhone has now reached an impressive 2.5 billion people. The problem is that while capitalist-driven technology can increase and multiply consumer desires, it can also lower the number of employees who could pay for them.

Corporations pushing beyond the personal computer to the personal robot could serve to swell the ranks of the unemployed. In economics, the ultimate human goal must be the ability of all to find gainful employment. Capitalism is now failing in this respect. No elite of scientists, inventors and investors should be permitted to fleece all of mankind as they are doing now.

As technology encroaches on a world increasingly dominated by machines, people have begun to ask what are its limits? It would seem there are none: Technology is speeding up the rate of human evolution itself. Bound as we appear to be to technology, we can no longer pretend to be free. We are manacled. The philosopher Martin Heidegger, was already asking in the 1950s: "Is man a defenceless and perplexed victim at the mercy of the irresistible superior power of technology?"[6] He concluded that it was impossible to brake or direct its history.

### New Directions for a Technology Dominated World

Technology may promise marvels for tomorrow, but we should not let it run away at such speeds as to destroy everything we once valued — starting with our environment. Do we really want technological breakthroughs in artificial intelligence, robotics, genetic engineering, nuclear energy and communications which will overwhelm the achievements of the past two centuries? The speed of change in the electronic industries, the speed of communications, and the flickering images of the digital screens already seem to have reduced our patience and ability to focus.

Social architects "must begin to combine technological ingenuity with sociological awareness, and governments need to design institutions and processes that will help integrate new, artificial agents into society," writes the author of *Robot Futures*.[7] To do that, however, we must aim for a society structured around long-term changes rather than one having to cope with continual short-term crises. Socially, we must collaborate and urge governments to prevent an uncontrolled system (or an elite of billionaires controlling it) from dehumanizing us. How are the electorate and its representatives to prevent the potentially dehumanizing effects of automation? Who will decide how to shape limits on biotech brain research? Even if much is desirable, how could controls on the shaping of automation over the coming decades be achieved? Are the codes of information technology and the codes of molecular biology not likely to be progressively intermingled? (The genome of every cell contains 3 billion bits of coded information, so such efficient packaging by nature is too ingenious not to be copied.)

We don't need philosophers to tell us that our brains do not seem able to direct the complex decision making process involved in resolving the challenges of an out-of-control technology. Despite all the expert briefs, the discussion papers and the endless reports, we have been unable to draft any workable strategies for change. The fact is that, as a society, we must rethink our basic assumptions about changing the world. This demands an entirely different ethos, one not founded on the advances in science and technology, not driven by capitalist consumerism, and not centred on possessive individualism. To achieve such a paradigm shift, people may have to transfer their focus from the material world to the miracle of their own internal consciousness, possibly onto the as-yet-unfathomable universe, or even on an evolutionary system which generates perpetual change. Yes, controlled change is a genuine and positive possibility and I firmly believe democratic politicians globally should start to grasp this.

[1] Evgeny Morozov, "Tech Titans are busy privatizing our data," *The Observer*, April 14, 2016

[2] John Brockman, *The Third Culture*, (1995) p. 377

[3] Eric K. Drexler, *Engines of Creation,* (1986) p. 14

[4] Lamber Royakkers and Rinie van Est, *Just Ordinary Robots: Automation from Love to War*, (2016).

## The Digital Follies
Posted on April 14, 2014

As a writer looking at our future potentialities, it is my job to caution readers that current trends suggest that we should consider the reckless speed at which we are developing robots and automation around the world. Given the competitive nature of capitalism, it is no wonder that Silicon Valley geeks are working all-out to increase the capacity of their products. Today's digital follies are far wilder than anything Disney or Playboy could have imagined. James Lovelock, the brains of celebrated '*gaia*" (the acronym for God Answers In Absentia) suggests that we should contemplate collaboration rather than confrontation with the upcoming generation of clever robots.

Since having a pacemaker inserted, Lovelock thinks it only may be a short time before his body will be hooked onto the internet, receiving spam![1] This delightful prospect has yet to fully sink in. As it is, my brain daily rejects dozens of pharmaceutical offers filling my laptop. What if this spam soon will be infiltrated into my brain via an implanted chip? How would I then get rid of the stream of commercial rubbish? Would I even be capable of pushing a delete button?

Lovelock thinks "computers are getting more and more organic all the time." He points out that they are already being made out of carbon and says "I can envisage a process whereby an endosymbiotic person with things in it will sufficiently fuse the two life systems together (so) that it will become a single person that will breed true." How's that for a Frankenstein film where "*it*" becomes an entity "*that*" breeds true? Breeding false would even be more fantastic — although in films this happens all the time. The sex scenes of tomorrow should be particularly entrancing as the "things in it" might suddenly spring out of it to the accompaniment of an updated operatic version of "la transviata."

I have been seriously wondering, while writing this blog what tomorrow's robots really would be like: would they have one eye or many? Would they have mouths or just speakers? Would they be made of pliable plastics or metal? Would they be asexual, bi-sexual, or just different? This is important not only in terms of the mechanics of construction but also in terms of any eventual forms of "breeding true" or other less intimate "collaboration." We currently think of robots as "it." However, they may find it demeaning to be talked about in this manner. The looming social complications are such that I think we should stick to the familiar theme of conflict between the sexes before we start including the two species. After all, the robots might think of us like we now tend to think of the Neanderthals.

No one seems to have considered whether sexed robots would be endowed with buttocks? Or whether these 'carbon' creations should go topless? Will they ever need to be dressed at all? (Most unlikely. Oh, well, that could be the end of the fashion industry altogether. Result: millions more out of jobs.) The robot/humans will not feel the cold so they won't need warm clothes and if it gets really hot through climate change, nano air-conditioning could be installed in their bodies before parts began to melt.

Neuroscientists using super-computers, DNA scanners, and nano-probes are making steady advances in understanding the mechanism of the cortex and other brain sectors. They still have a way to go before they understand the operation of consciousness which they are certain exists as a unit to be explored. The futurologist Michio Kaku[2] claims we are on the verge of digitally mapping and modelling the structure of the human brain which will then lead to replication. Once neuroscientists have made that breakthrough, the workings of the brain itself will be exposed and they should then be able to increase, decrease or alter its powers. I shall spare you the yet unfilmed scenes of mice brains being microscopically studied by neuroscientists exploring the inner workings of consciousness.

The unplanned digital revolution is overthrowing our way of life and the consequences are hardly being recognized. All our business — from banking to the stock market — has been affected; so have our privacy, our social habits, our workplaces and our education. Our communication as human beings is being altered at a pace no one a few generations back ever imagined as a possibility.

Nor could they have foreseen the condensed vacuity of twitter politics nor the deep tremors shaking our mating habits. The social impact of the arrival of the robhums (robot-humans) has not even been considered by any EU commissioner in Brussels!

With youth unemployment so high and climbing globally, should we truly be working on advanced new robots? As it is, many of the youths who have received university educations can't find jobs. Were they over-educated or under-programmed? I seem to be encountering some kind of robots at my local co-op shopping counter every day. I encounter a different class of financial sector robots on the London train clicking their laptops. Given the number of close-to-robots we have right now on this planet, do we really need to create robhums?

Scientists working at MIT or in the labs of Microsoft, developing the new possibilities of nano-technology, are far removed from the radical consequences nanos may have on our way of life. They leave this, and the introduction of robots, to "the market" to decide which products will be successful — irrespective of the consequences. And the impact will be far reaching. Are "pure" humans all going to be branded (for more than commercial reasons) with nano-tattooed digital identities? Will those evading or trying to escape such control be coded as nano "enemies" or "terrorist suspects"?[3] Yes, there is no doubt about it, 'pure-bred' robots will be far more trustworthy.

How far do we want to go? Are there any limits? Ultimately will the rapid and not carefully thought-out advances of science lead to "new brains" controlling our currently rather uncontrollable species?

A few decades ago President Pompidou told the French in blunt terms and with a Gallic hunching of the shoulders: "La Belle France, c'est fini." That is to say, the France we have known is finished. Let's face it: If the robots and humans are ultimately connected, "the good times" will be at an end for all that remained 'human' in our great-grandchildren. So much for the Digital Follies of today and tomorrow!

---

[1] Stephen Moss, Interview with James Lovelock, *The Guardian* March 31, 2014, p.8

[2] Michio Kaku, *The Future of the Mind*, 2014

[3] Bryan Appleyard, "Hot gospellers," *The New Statesman*, April 4, 2014, pp.23-25

## IV b        OUR BIOLOGICALLY ALTERED FUTURE

*We are entering the most innovative period in biological history , Gene splicing and editing will be focused on improving aspects of plants, animals, and people - even of insects and microbes. James Watson told me nearly thirty years ago :"We are working out a program for our own existence. It will enable us to determine our genetic makeup and understand such life processes as aging, growth and brain function." Our genes were never programmed for 'progress' but for reproduction and survival. Our high degree of genetic inequalities, inborn diversity and excess of numbers exist primarily to increase the human chances of survival.*

*Given the general ignorance of the public and the media about the fundamentals of biology, it is small wonder that the complexities of biotechnology have been greeted with doubt, fear, gothic distrust and a lack of comprehension. Because it is likely that as this century progresses, we shall be able to select the genetic characteristics we might want in our offspring. Nightmarish visions are already arising of deranged scientists and lab technicians producing pit-bull variations on human beings. Molecular biology makes the genetic mechanism open to experimentation, alteration and a certain amount of biotechnical manipulation. At the same time tradition holds that our genetic inheritance is entrusted to us for safe-keeping and transmission. Are our feelings and our potentialities consequently in contradiction?*

*Our genetic makeup is the result of changes, mutations, jumping genes and the process of evolution. Genes have through the ages leapt from one species to another without the help of any laboratory technicians. Bacterial genes are found in plants, insects, and animals and vice-versa. Such combinations have always been additional as there is no natural mechanism which allows for any subtraction. The question then arises if we have any justifiable philosophical, ethical, or other objection to the application of subtraction when it comes to human identity. Evolution , as far as we know, had nothing to do with any notion of "perfectibility."*

*Selective mutation and as yet little understood recombinations transformed ape intelligence into human intelligence. If these natural mutations were of such beneficial effect to man, why should the possibility our own manipulations reducing human aggression by gene manipulation rather than through the intake of chemicals, be rejected? The ability to tinker with genes controlling our imaginations as well as specific talents in mathematics, music, poetry, dance and sports would have an extraordinary impact on our cultures. We should be able to edit out the negative traits in homo sapiens , such as atonality , the lack of physical coordination, and muscular dystrophy, while increasing our positive potentials in ways which are now only the dreams of science fiction writers. Humans could learn to blissfully sing and communicate like nightingales !*

*.*

*The atom almost overwhelmed us in the 20th century and our progressively more complete understanding of the macromolecules of life is going to have staggering consequences for the future. Most probably, our grandchildren will be taught to think of life in terms of its molecular construction.*

## The Bioethical Challenges We Face

Posted on October 19, 2015

> *"Lead us. Evolution, lead us*
> *Up the future's endless stair,*
> *Chop us, change us, prod us, weed us,*
> *For stagnation is despair:*
> *Groping, guessing, yet progressing,*
> *Lead us nobody knows where."*
> — *C.S. Lewis "Evolutionary Hymn"*

The daunting pace of advances in biotechnology has far exceeded our ability to grasp the range of possibly positive and plausibly threatening consequences. This presents us with enormous ethical challenges in deciding how to proceed. Today it is hard to name outstanding figures who can speak with the authority of those scientists of a generation or two ago. As you will be able to read at the end of this blog, they most forcefully expressed their ethical concerns and their doubts, fears, and scientific aspirations.

When faced with serious genetic problems ranging from cancer to Alzheimer's and from blindness to deafness, should scientists simply march ahead and work on ultimately altering the sequences of embryonic DNA produced by afflicted parents? Strong objections to such a course are being raised, arguing that this would interfere with the natural processes of life or even that we are brazenly trying to take over from God! The implications are, that once we start altering our hereditary potentials, there is no end. At first we may only be making corrections on single-cell disorders such as sickle-cell anemia, hemophilia, and Tay Sachs, but before long we would switch to making improvements — ultimately struggling to make humans more perfect or even more compatible with mechanical intelligence. As Herbert J. Muller wrote some 80 years ago: "We will reach down into the secret places of the great universe of its own nature, and by aid of its ever growing intelligence and co-operation, shape itself into an increasingly sublime creation."[1]

The immediate challenge at hand is CRISPR. About three years ago, scientists developed a technology that is literally upending our perspective on the limits of biotechnology. It has become known as CRISPR-Cas9, which is similar to a biological word processing system allowing scientists to cut and paste the strands of DNA almost as easily as it is for me to change the lettering in this blog. (FYI: CRISPR stands for Clustered Regularly Interspaced Short Palindromic Repeats.) CRISPR involves taking a strand of RNA, a chemical messenger, to target a section of our DNA and using an enzyme (a nuclease) that can cut unwanted genes and paste in the edited RNA. This sequence borrows from a process in nature that scientists have harnessed to snip and splice sections of DNA. To make this possible researchers found a specific slicer enzyme called Cas9.

This technological advance is key to the synthetic biology and gene editing revolution and represents an amazing improvement over existing techniques. However, alarm bells started to ring when scientists in China reported in April 2015 that they had used CRISPR for the first time to alter the DNA in a non-viable embryo. (That is, an embryo that could never have developed into a baby.) A group of 18 eminent scientists, legal experts and ethics specialists published a letter in Science calling for an immediate moratorium on experiments of this kind on embryos. Dr Jennifer Doudna, one of the co-inventors of the CRISPR technique, wrote that "My colleagues and I felt it was critical to initiate a public discussion of the appropriate use of this technology, and to call for a voluntary ban on human germline editing for clinical applications at the present time."

Henry Greely, a Stanford law professor and expert in ethics, who was another of the signers of the Science letter, said "You would be insane and criminally reckless to make a baby this way without 15 to 20 years of testing and proving that it was safe." Many other scientists contended that far from being threatening or wrong, such research has the potential to provide permanent cures for genetic diseases. Further research also holds the potential to correct common disease defects such as metabolic disorders, diabetes and age related problems as well as creating cells that attack tumors or others that are resistant to HIV infections.

The National Academy of Sciences (NAS) and its Institute of Medicine consequently announced it is convening an international summit this

December to "explore the scientific, ethical, and policy issues associated with human gene-editing research." In addition, NAS will appoint a multidisciplinary, international committee to study the scientific basis and the ethical, legal, and social implications of human gene editing. Together this represents a concerted effort to confront the bio-technological challenges now facing mankind. In some ways this conference ultimately could prove as important for our future on this planet as the major Environmental Conference to be held by the United Nations at almost the same time in Paris.

Getting a clearer picture on the science behind CRISPR is important. So is developing an international guideline for gene editing. But the National Academy of Science's meetings seem to have overlooked how much work and ethical expertise it will take to identify and assess the ethical issues surrounding CRISPR. There is concern that ethics has taken and will continue to take a back seat to science in discussions about CRISPR. The existing ethical frameworks are simply not adequate for managing the challenges posed by the new gene editing technology.

This is because CRISPR is unlike previous biotechnologies. The ethical frameworks that were developed for dealing with IVF, cloning, and stem cell research a generation ago are not adequate for dealing with the novel ethical concerns raised by CRISPR.

For example: CRISPR can introduce new variations in germlines, making permanent biological changes to future generations. This may be uncontroversial when it comes to preventing life-threatening diseases, but controlled human evolution has been suggested many times since Darwin, often with permanent, racist and disastrous consequences. Equally important, our genetic makeup is the result of changes, mutations, radiation, jumping genes and other additions. Like knowledge, our DNA structure is the result of millennia of additions. There is no natural mechanism which allows for the kind of subtractions involved in CRISPR. Could we now accept any justifiable, ethical philosophical or scientific objections to subtraction?

Deletions made on human genes could have unintentional and unpredictable consequences for future generations who might regret that this was done without their consent. We simply do not understand the operations of the human genome sufficiently to make long-lasting changes to our DNA. Altering just one gene could have unforeseen and widespread efforts on other parts of the genome which could then be passed down to future generations.

Laws in the UK ban genetic modification of embryos for clinical uses, but they are permitted in research labs under license from the Human Fertilization and Embryology Authority provided that the embryos are destroyed after 14 days. In the United States researchers are much freer, but there are deep concerns that genome editing is so simple and cheap that maverick scientists could use the procedure to modify human embryos which could be implanted into women.[2] Dr. Francis Collins, Director of the National Institutes of Health, said back in April that the US government would not fund research for modifying the embryo DNA because there were "serious and unquantifiable safety issues" as well as significant ethical questions and no compelling medical reasons to carry out the research. While scientists and lawmakers might be able to control most of the global research taking place, there is little that can be done to stop experimentation taking place in a country like North Korea or corporations that might pursue their narrow commercial interests. The application of CRISPR techniques has resulted in a flurry of investment and commercial activity. Editas Medicine, which was granted a patent (being challenged by other applicants) to use in plants and animals, has raised $163 million from a group of investors over the past two years.[3] And the pharmaceutical giant, AstraZeneca, plans to develop its use in cell cultures to explore the function of every gene in the human genome.

When it comes to biotechnology there are no deniers, but many opponents. Edward Lamphier, the founder of Sangamo Biosciences, wrote in *Nature* that genome editing in human embryos "could have unpredictable effects on future generations." This makes it "dangerous and ethically unacceptable."[4] In an interview with Gina Kolata of the New York Times he added, "It literally boils down to: How do you feel about the human race and the human species?"[5]

The psychologist Steven Pinker, writing in an editorial for the *Boston Globe*, protested that CRISPR was a key to reducing human suffering and incurable diseases. Pinker maintained that bioethicists should not get in the way of progress. As it is, some research scientists already have become bogged down in red tape, bureaucratic restrictions, or sanctions based on unclear consent forms. To then impose moratoria or threats of prosecution based on such sweeping principles as "social justice," rapidly could slow down progress and ultimately lead to scientists operating outside any agreement.

To the question: "Should we ever move forward with human germline genome editing," 61% of the polled members of the Science Advisory Board, an international community of tens of thousands of scientific and medical experts, voted in favour and 39% voted against, but when asked: "Should we hold a moratorium on human germline genome editing?" 70% said "yes" and only 30% opposed. The ethical dilemmas facing the experts evidently could obstruct the tools which would give many future generations healthier and longer lives. Even in an impatient age when quick decisions almost have become obligatory and attention spans are on a steady decline, no effective decision on this dilemma is likely soon.

Personally, I would propose that the world put a hold on all laboratory experimentation in this area until and unless it is approved by an international body of experts operating under the aegis of some kind of new biological "security council" with enforcement powers. Nothing less will suffice.

---

[1]Herbert J. Muller, *Out of the Night: A biologist's view of the future*, (1935)
[2]Ian Sample: "GM embryos: time to decide," *The Guardian*, September 2, 2015, p. 1
[3]"Briefing Genome editing," *The Economist*, August 22, 2015
[4]"Don't Edit the Human Germline," *Nature*, March 12, 2015
[5]Gina Kolata, "Gene Editing and Safety: Alarm Grows." *The New York Times*, May 10, 2015

---

"Gene splicing and editing are going to change life on earth, both physically and economically. What is at stake in this biotechnical revolution is the ultimate 'perfectibility' of plants, animals and people."
Yorick Blumenfeld *Towards the Millennium: Optimistic Visions for Change*, (1996) p.382

## The Crash in biodiversity

Posted on November 30, 2015

In the 1970s I was enchanted by my wonderfully wild garden in Cambridgeshire. I was captivated by the music of dozens of different songbirds, From April to September the bees swarmed around the flowers. Frogs and toads jumped in and out of the small pools. On occasion I would see foxes, muntjac deer and colorful pheasants and innumerable squirrels. Four decades later there are no more sparrows, owls, or bats and very few songbirds. Maybe a handful of frogs remain; hardly a bee appeared all summer. I have not seen any four-legged wild species this year. The toll is dreadful and makes me wonder: For how much longer will we humans who have abandoned animal labor for machines and exchanged the natural resources of nature for the miracles of chemistry remain on this planet? Extinction may well be around the corner.

At a recent conference in Cambridge I was astounded to listen to the prominent economist Professor Sir Partha Dasgupta declare that he believed the greatest danger facing mankind was the threat to biodiversity. I would have expected him to say it was capitalism, inequality, or population, but he pointed out that there had already been five mass extinctions in our planet's history — the last, about 65 million years ago when an asteroid hit the earth ending the dinosaurs. The Dasgupta casually observed that over half of the world's wildlife has been lost in the past 50 years.

"Biodiversity," a term which most people don't seem to understand embraces the variety of different types of life found on our planet and the variations within its species. For biologists, biodiversity is a measure of the variety of plants, animals, insects and other micro-organisms present in our different ecosystems. Fauna and flora are essential components of nature and ensure our survival by providing us with food, fuel, medicines and wherewithal. The devastation that one species, *homo sapiens*, has wreaked on this planet has transgressed such critical boundaries as: climate change, exploitation of resources and pollution.

Our inept perspective on biodiversity is colored by out-dated views of our relationship to the environment. Although the disappearance of bees is of concern, the loss of numerous insects — so important to the web of life — is ignored. Habitat destruction is driven by overpopulation, but we don't accept the connection.

About a third of all amphibians [like frogs and toads] have become extinct since the 1960s. Fresh water biodiversity has been threatened because ponds, streams and rivers have had minimum protection from human pollution. Marine life is similarly affected: The destruction of nesting grounds, drowning in fishnets at sea, and hunting have killed 80% of sea turtles over the past four decades, Even our seas are being littered with some 6 trillion bits of plastic. The marine ecologist Chelsea M Rochman of the University of California has said "Plastics are like a cocktail of contaminant floating around the in aquatic habitat. These contaminants may be magnifying up the food chain."

As I have pointed out, people generally recognize the value of honeybees. We are aware that without them almonds and blueberries would no longer be on our tables. The plight of bees, partially the consequence of a chemical industry set on increasing agricultural production, may give an indication of where the planet may be headed if we continue to ruthlessly exploit the natural world for profit. "Excessive cultivation, chemical use and habitat destruction may eventually destroy the very organisms that could be our partners," wrote Mark Winston.[1]

A two-year ban on three neonicotinoid insecticides came into force in the European Union two years ago. However, a typical honeybee colony contains residues from more than 12 pesticides. While none of these, individually, could be fatal to bees, together they produce a toxic hive. The sub-lethal effects would appear to have affected the navigation of bees. It is unlikely that a global moratorium of neonicotinoids, such as those produced by corporations like Syngenta and Bayer, will be tackled because it is not yet known exactly how these substances affect human beings.

What is clear from the signals all around us is that the biological framework of life on earth is being dismantled. "How soon, indeed, before the Earth's biological treasures are trashed in what will be the sixth mass extinction?" asked Jan Zalasiewicz.[2] Globally thousands of species die off each year, nearly all of them without obituaries or notice. That is what occurs when on e species becomes so overwhelming that it crowds out or obliterates all the others. The famous biologist and author Professor E O Wilson noted that the present extinction rate in our tropics is "on the order of 10,000 times greater than the naturally occurring background extinction rate." The will reduce biological diversity to its lowest level since the giant asteroid killed off the dinosaurs. It might surprise readers that hardly any of the species that surround us today existed 100 million years ago.

Lord Martin Rees, the Astronomer Royal, who has a broad perspective on the planet's place in the universe wrote, "climate change is aggravating a collapse in biodiversity." Rees claims, "We are destroying the book of life before we have read it."[3]

At the Paris Global Conference for the Environment, which starts this week, there is going to be a strong demand for a healthier world for human beings — to be achieved through climate change. However this vast gathering is unlikely to consider the needs of all the other living species. It therefore takes no crystal ball to predict where biodiversity is headed.

Controls on the human population will not take place at the conference, although our numbers have quadrupled over the past four generations and have had a greater impact on biodiversity than any other single factor. According to a study by the World Wildlife Fund in 2014, the human population already exceeds our planet's biocapacity. It would take 1.5 Earths to meet our current demands for food, water, space and land. Following the Convention on Biological Diversity in May 2010 where numerous conservation measures supporting biodiversity were proposed, none of the specific targets were met. Biodiversity receives only a tiny fraction of funding compared to the financing of industrial development. The bitter truth is that humans are not ready to make minimal sacrifices now in order to avoid major ones in the future. The thoroughbred capitalists writing for the *Economist* contend that both economic growth and technological progress are friends of biodiversity.[4]

A crop of biodiversity deniers had been sustained by a few American billionaires and neonicotinoid producers who set profits above the demands of life itself. The deniers and the greedy simply do not want to face up to what is happening. The statistics speak for themselves. True, the reading public has begun to find the subject of climate change infinitely boring, so trying to engage its perspective on biodiversity is ever more challenging. The diminishing attention spans of the coming generations does not bode well for improving these truly existential threats facing humanity.

Daniel Kahneman, the Nobel Prize psychologist, has said that "No amount of psychological awareness will overcome people's reluctance to lower their standard of living." The capitalist economy, to which we have become enslaved, demands the continued exploitation of the planet's resources: We are catching fish faster than the oceans can restock, taking water from the rives and aquifers faster than rainfall can refill the, and cutting down trees faster than they regrow, while emitting more carbon dioxide than the oceans and forests can absorb.

Speaking at the United Nations this autumn, Pope Francis demonstrated that he had truly grasped the scale of the problem by asserting that the large-scale destruction of biodiversity could "threaten the very existence of the human species." He enlarged on this by saying that unrestrained capitalism was not only trampling on the poor and the weak, but also on nature itself by destroying the environment.

The need to halt the current rush towards extinction is obvious but whether any agreements on climate change made in Paris 2015 will then be implemented is less certain. The United States, after prolonged debates and hesitation, finally banned the use of DDT in the 1970s, but whether the assembled members in Paris, after decades of negotiations, will take effective measures to reduce global population [which would help to protect biodiversity] can only be wished for. I would like the delegates to remember that the total number of mammals, birds, reptiles, amphibians and fish across the globe is, on average, half the size it was only 40 years ago![5]

[1]Mark Winston, *Bee Time: Lessons from the Hive* [2014]

[2]Jan Zalasiewicz, "The Earth stands on the brink of its sixth mass extinction," *The Observer*, June 21 2015

[3]Martin Rees, "Scientists and politicians alike must rally to protect life on earth," *The Financial Times,* September 2, 2015

[4]See: "All creatures great and small," [Special Report on Biodiversity] the *Economist*, September 14, 2013

[5]The Living Planet Report 2014

## Advances in Health Research

Posted on June 29, 2016

Looking at the genuine advances being made on so many fronts, including computer technology, environmental improvements, and space exploration, I believe the most favorable projection for our future rests on the genetic revolution that promises positive improvements in our lives in the 21st century. Advances in biotech have already made it possible to feed the world in new ways. The crop yields of wheat, rice, corn and other cereals have increased dramatically. We enjoy the result of breakthroughs which have increased our life spans, reduced diseases like malaria and improved technology in hospitals to correct a wide range of disorders.

Since the mid-19th century most countries have had continuing improvements in the health of their inhabitants. In 1850 four in ten English babies died before their first birthday, today less than five out of every thousand infants in Britain die before the age of one. As a consequence, we have come to expect continuing advances in medicine and health care. Sir William Castell, the retired chairman of the Welcome Trust thinks "We are on the cusp of spectacular change, as genomics, imaging, diagnostics, data analysis and other technologies come together to make real precision medicine possible for the first time."[1] Precision has become a key word in the practice of 21st century medicine. Precision demands that patients be diagnosed for the exact cause of the their ailments and only after examining their genetic make-up, prescribed the best treatment.

Now the laboratory development of CRISPR* will be making the editing of the genomes of all living species much more rapid, cheaper and more accurate. Each of our cells contain all of our 22,000 human genes. These are not all simultaneously active all of the time, but are controlled by complex networks of programs and circuits in our body's systems. The CRISPR breakthrough now makes it possible to modify the DNA without altering the gene sequencing itself. Earlier this month, the US National Academy of Sciences published a paper on altering the genetic composition of mosquitoes which can render the female offspring sterile and potentially open to extermination. The technique now employed assures that certain genetic changes are passed on to the offspring. CRISPR could also be employed on pig embryos injected with human cells to create new kidneys, pancreases, and livers, which could then be transplanted into humans without the risk of rejection by the immune system.

Microbiologists continue to make startling advances in understanding the complex microbiome, that is all the bacteria, microbes, viruses, fungi and eukaryotes that inhabit our guts. Massive groupings of competing and co-operative microbes have evolved in our species. Microbes in our guts are essential for survival and the loss of microbiotic diversity in our digestive system (due to the overkill by antibiotics as well as the use of radiation in food preservation and agricultural pesticides) is detrimental to our well being. Even our nervous systems are dependent on gut bacteria. These produce hundreds of neurotransmitters which regulate mood, memory and learning. They also produce much of the body's supply of serotonin which is recognized as one of the keys to our sense of well-being.

Methods are being explored which might enable doctors to tell immediately whether an infection is bacterial or viral. If doctors were then able to tell which antibiotics could eradicate an infection, they would not prescribe some drugs, as they often risk doing now, which offer only partial resistance and advance the progress of resistant strains.[2] Competing microbes in the gut, trying to keep others in check, secrete antibiotics. In the search for these microbes pharmaceutical groups are extracting antibiotics from bacteria living in dirt. This has led to testing new drugs like Teixobactin.

With the spectacular advance of antibiotics over the past century the rise of drug resistant organisms, such as *Staphylococcus aureus,* has increased the risk of hospital infections. Some three quarters of a million people die each year from drug resistant infections. Immunotherapy is being used increasingly to fight many illnesses which do not respond to penicillin and other antibiotics. Reserving some of the new breakthrough drugs for emergencies keeps sales low and prices high. This in turn discourages some of the big pharmaceutical companies from costly research, development and testing. Cheaper diagnostic techniques may partially correct this imbalance.

Medical technology, such as stem cell therapy, has moved swiftly from the drawing board two decades ago into human trials and now into transplant operations as in patients suffering macular degeneration of their eye cells. Other technological advances are focused on ways to radically alter our biological composition.[3] Tissue engineering is creating functional matter that avoids rejection by patients having transplants. Their porous structure is such that it induces the body's cells to integrate with the artificial tissues to ultimately transform into normal tissues. Progress is being made in creating biomaterials and artificial polymers (that is, chains of molecules) which will interact with networks of stem cells.[4]

Because of the lack of donors, thousand of patients around the globe are desperately awaiting organ transplants. Organoids are another of the dramatic new breakthroughs in which laboratory grown body parts are used to test patients about to receive transplants for kidneys, liver, intestines and other organs. Such organoids are grown from stem cells similar to those found in embryos. However, some organoids are actually created by treating skin cells with chemicals which transform them into stem cells. These organoids are then placed in the lab into glass vessels where they respond to drugs being tested for toxicity exactly in the same way as would a corresponding transplanted organ of the afflicted patient. Most people who currently have transplant surgery must take immune system suppressing drugs for life.

Cerebral organoids are 3D tissues generated from stem cells that allow modelling of human brain development in glass vessels which are turned into supportive microenvironments. Such "neural precursor tissue can spontaneously self-organize to form the stereotypic organization of the early human embryonic brain," explains Madeline Lancaster of Cambridge University.[5] Her current interests focus on neurodevelopmental disorders like autism and intellectual disability by introducing mutations seen in these disorders and examining their roles in pathogenesis in the context or organoid development. The researchers in the Medical Research Council's labs are studying mechanisms underlying the progression of neurological diseases and the potential therapeutic advances.

Researchers also are moving towards the creation of implantable pacemakers for the brain which could be used to treat problems like Parkinson's, drug addiction, dementia and depression much as we have developed cardiac pacemakers for heart problems. Intense research is also focusing on testing strategies which could treat or even prevent Alzheimer's where sticky plaques of a protein called amyloid build up in the brain forming deposits that suffocate nerve cells. The advances in brain imaging enable scientists to spot small amyloid clusters before they cause damaging symptoms. Vaccines are being tried (so far unsuccessfully) to develop vaccines which could eliminate amyloid plaques.

Last year the Hinxton group of bioethicists, stem cell researchers and genome experts agreed that human genome editing is necessary if we are to gain further understanding of the human embryos — even if this is not applied to cultivating gene-edited embryos. Ultimately the hope is that genes could be edited to avoid certain inherited cancers.

Research has been going on for more than 75 years to avoid the surgery, radiation treatment or chemotherapy in breast and other cancers. The search is now becoming far more precise due to our ability to pinpoint specific cells responsible for cancer formation. For example, genetic researchers have found that a mutation in the gene named BRCA1 which affects less than 1% of women is responsible. Specific new drugs, such as Denosumab, will now be tested in clinical trials to ascertain and study the possible side effects. The hope is that in the not so distant future, it will be possible to avoid mastectomies and debilitating radiation treatments for this cancer as well as for so many others.

As the power of computers has steadily advanced in assisting researchers and testers, so have the cures for human diseases. I am filled with optimism when contemplating where we are headed in tackling Alzheimer's, autism, cancers and other genetic defects. I am less confident that these advances will eradicate the health problems of billions of people whose governments have neither the means nor the ability to raise the resources necessary to tackle the massive national inequalities in health care.

---

\* CRISPR stands for Clustered Regularly Interspaced Short Palindromic Repeats. CRISPR involves taking a strand of RNA, a chemical messenger, to target a section of our DNA and using an enzyme (a nuclease) that can cut unwanted genes and paste in the edited RNA. This sequence borrows from a process in nature that scientists have harnessed to snip and splice sections of DNA. To make this possible researchers found a specific slicer enzyme called Cas9. This technological advance is key to the synthetic biology and gene editing revolution and represents an amazing improvement over existing techniques.

[1]Clive Cookson, "The (very precise) future of medicine", *The FT Magazine*, October 3, 2015.

[2]"When the drugs don't work," *The Economist,* May 21, 2016, p.9

[3]Linda Geddes, "The gene revolution," *The Observer*, June 12, 2016.

[4]Oran Maguire, "Engineering the rise of cell therapies," *Bluesci*, Easter 2016, p.12

[5]mlancast@ mrc-lmb.cam.ac.uk

X

XX

XXX

XXXX

XXXXX

XXXXXX

XXXXXXX

XXXXXXXX

XXXXXXXXX

XXXXXXXXXX

XXXXXXXXXXX

XXXXXXXXXXXX

XXXXXXXXXXXXX

## THE NOVEMBER 8TH CALAMITY
**Posted on January 30, 2017**

Trump's victory hit me like a blow to the head, totally disrupting my thoughts, feelings, and reactions: There was no way I could continue to write blogs focused on our positive prospects for tomorrow after the unmitigated catastrophe of the election of Donald Trump as President of the United States.

Some months later, I still cannot see anything which will make life more meaningful emerging under Trump. This is a turning point for the US, but personally, from my individual perspective, it was and remains a disaster, like having been in a serious car crash.

I still cannot accept that such a large part of the American electorate failed to recognize Trump as a vain, politically inexperienced, deceptive, limited, insecure, lacking in empathy and pathologically unsuited con-man. Trump had been exposed as being unfit to hold office by the entirety of the American press. (I described him as a 21st Century Satan in one of my blogs a few months ago.) The New York Times, The Washington Post, The Atlantic Monthly, The New Yorker, Vanity Fair, The Wall Street Journal and the editorial pages of all the leading newspapers across the country steadily warned against him to no avail. No point for me now to continue the loud chorus of printed dismay with further denunciations in my blog.

Beyond their frustrated expectations of a better life, what could have persuaded so many American voters to endorse such an exceedingly unsuitable candidate? Were they blind? So desperate of their economic condition that they no longer were rational? Physically, on my first viewing years ago, I had immediately found his face revolting. Many of the people I know cannot stand the sight of him on their TV sets and yet the flood of truly vile items released about Trump and by him, has failed to arouse doubts in his admirers. They seemed to be saying at every chance: "He's real. He's just like us" and then they repeat "He'll Make America Great Agin."(sic) Such chants speedily downgrade into shouting their stored hatreds and anger. Their disgusting behavior, reminded me of the way Germans had expressed their venom three generations ago, and had the unwelcome effect of hyper-activating my bile.

As a refugee from Nazi occupied France in 1941, I entered America as a youth who desired rapid assimilation: I immediately treasured the optimistic and positive spirit of my classmates in New York. Intuitively I felt that the political attitudes of Americans offered a rational, generous and hopeful prospect for mankind. When I went to Harvard, purportedly surrounded by "the brightest and the best", I came to take for granted the exchange of thoughts, the examination of given assumptions, (such as understanding, insight and acceptance), as representing a naturally intelligent way of life. This educational preparation received a few shocks during a stretch in the US Army as a "Private, third class." Basic training is focused on following orders, not on discussing Plato or Jefferson. However, I did come to appreciate the social equality of my fellow recruits.


My belief in the fundamental American values was strengthened in the years which followed as a writer and researcher for Congressional-Quarterly/Editorial Research in Washington, DC. I enjoyed asking questions at JFK's White House press conferences. Such experience furthered my engagement in the search for truth, in factual reporting, and in expanding the understanding of my readers. I developed a belief, however misguided as it may have been, in the common-sense of the American people. At times, as in the elections of Richard Nixon and later in that of George W. Bush, I began to have my doubts. These were electrified by the shocking antics of Donald Trump. Was my entire outlook on life and on the premises by which I had embraced the American way of life erroneous or worthless? Have knowledge, rationality, intelligence and memory all become irrelevant in this new and most unwelcome era?

The long-term prospects are not good for a nation which is now led by a POTUS who has never held any position of service in the USA, who has skilfully avoided taxes, has no understanding of the necessity of compromise in the democratic process, is unable to accept criticism or to listen to the voice of others and ultimately appears unable to recognize the difference between truth and fiction.

All too many Americans seem to have succumbed to the misguiding power of celebrity, to the even greater power of money, and to the digital propaganda of Twitter. Millions of Americans have obviously become unreceptive to examining lies and falsehood, at the same time that they were rejecting expertise, debate, intelligence and experience. Serious analysis and criticism were no longer to be regarded as welcome or even essential.

As a number of writers on The New York Times, from David Brooks on the right to Paul Krugman on the left, have noted: hypocrisy now flourishes in America. The evangelical believers and conservative Republicans who swore by their religious tenets and balanced budgets, simply abandoned their fundamental beliefs for the sake of political power.

The new "Age of the Deal," leaves me reeling. Where to turn? What to do? Should I give up my American citizenship? There is no way I can align my writings or outlook to counter-act the unending flow of brainless tweets. What has happened to conscience, to values, to empathy and to cultural traditions in this misbegotten administration?

I felt and continue to feel that the response of the Congressional Democrats has been unacceptably feeble. It is without true fire in the belly. The exception of the heroic John Lewis, who stood up bravely to contest the validity of the election, was not matched by his Party. I regarded the inauguration not as a patriotic event but as an occasion to mourn the passing of much of the democratic dream of a better future. Trumpism seems to be heralding a period of denial in which the environmental threat to our planet is likely to accelerate.

Thus I cannot see the point of joining voices to the powerful bandwagon against Trump. I feel there is little place now for a blog which worked towards a positive exploration of our future possibilities. I shall try to continue to explore the more positive aspects and values of the world around us at a time when the stream of executive orders from the White House are spreading anxiety and gloom. I trust that correspondents like Roger Cohen will continue their exposure of the contradictions and rantings of a pathologically deranged Head of State.

I recognize that the best I can do in this chaotic period is to alter my focus I hope that on occasion this may distract and uplift your spirits as much as they may mine.

# VI.        Prospects for an Improved World

*I cannot know whether the prospects for a calmer, more stable and peaceful world, following  this century's extraordinary economic and social turbulence, can do anything to boost the reader's overall sense of optimism.*

*Before we can even strive towards a more stable world order, we will have to agree on some universally acceptable ideas about nature and the place of homo sapiens in it. The rhythms of the seasons and the patterns of our lives, the demands and the obligations of an ordered community, as well as the daily needs and desires of human beings all furnish the foundations on which it is possible to build a reasonable and moral society.*

*There have been two prevailing views about the relationship between nature and human beings. The first was that nature was there to be mastered and exploited, the second was that nature itself was of intrinsic value and had to be preserved. Radical ecology contends that care of the environment means there must be marked changes in our relationship with it.*

*I calculate that it will take less than sixty years to resolve the ecological aspects of this struggle (or there will be little left to resolve). It is more likely that environmental progress will be made because of our self-interest in survival rather than any outbreak of Franciscan virtue. However, there may be some who could project beauty onto a globe that has been totally pacified, domesticated and modified by plastic turf and even as yet unimaginable cyberspace pleasure domes.*

*I believe that, before the world can experience a greater modicum of both security and an accompanying sense of well-being, the world population has to stabilize, nanotechnology, genetics and pharmacology will have to affect some fundamental changes in altering the aggressive nature of the human male.  In seeking to improve the environment around us and* beyond us we will also improve our lives. Tomorrows ethical imperatives should include:

1. You shall leave the Earth in better shape than when you arrived.
2. You shall not knowingly pollute, despoil, nor degrade any part of the environment
3. You shall try to protect the environment just as you would like it to protect you.

Real security will mean that people will feel that they are rooted in a stable environment; that they are engaged in meaningful and purposeful work; that they are healthy (that is, free of disease, sufficiently fed, able to breathe clean air and drink good water); and that their emotional and sexual lives will be arousing, fulfilled, and loving. It has been said that the real test of civilization is the number of things it takes for granted.

How we understand that the world depends on how we confront it: "care, trust and love determine that tone, as they do our relationship to another person," wrote Theodore Roszak, We know we can, if given the chance, cultivate values where the objective is not 'perfection' but to work creatively towards improvement.

George Soros who has devoted his life and his billions to improve our human condition, wrote that "our fallibility leaves infinite scope for innovation, invention and improvement. An open society that recognizes fallibility is a superior form of social organization to a closed society that claims to have found all the answers."

The civilization of the future could be compared metaphorically to a garden made beautiful by the variety of its trees, bushes and flowers. The seasonal colors would reflect the positive way this culture would embrace the arts. The gracious, ethical tone which would manifest itself in society would be matched by the eternally renewed bursts of life itself. Such culture would accommodate considerable social mobility: it would allow creative individuals to develop according to their own effort and enthusiasms – free of 'unfair' impediments. It is to be hoped that it always would be a society which would give opportunity for the next generations.

We are impelled by our consciences to improve the societies in which we live, but we must accept that while we may at times celebrate success, there is no possibility of a permanent resolution to all of humanity's ever-changing challenges and its pluralistic moral inheritance. Just because I am advocating a social equilibrium does not mean I expect us actually to 'get there'. We shall always be 'on the way' and 'in the process of'.

At another level, there is likely to be a major shift in the erotic: procreation will be restricted; but cyberspace sensualists and orgiastic rhythms may fly. Freud argued in his great Civilization and Its Discontents that: "civilization is process in the service of Eros, whose purpose is to combine single human individuals, and after that their families, then races, peoples and nations into one great unity, the unity of mankind…These collections of men are to be libidinally bound to each other."

We must consciously and actively strive for a return to the Dionysian in the next millennium. The Dionysian ritual was essentially cathartic, that is, purifying. It embraced both continuity and a sense of feeling for the oneness of time through the unity of mankind.

Tomorrow's desires are also likely to manifest themselves in the creative relationship between intimate consciousness and a playful AI.
Even before this arrives, we are beginning to recognize that our emotional interaction with the rest of the living world, that is everything from dogs and cats to trees and flowers, may almost be as important to our well-being as our relationship with human beings in the social media.

Love, gifts of tenderness, caring, compassion, mothering and understanding (which have never been part of 'the market') are there *within us. With every act of kindness and charity, with every virtue we strengthen or develop, with every meaning we give to expressions of love, we help make our world more humane. Understanding shown to a child, praise given to colleague, kindness rendered to a stranger or a promise kept to a friend all touch those with whom we are in contact and may uplift both them and us. Such acts can certainly help to improve us. Sentiment, shared feelings and personal communication can all play major roles to counter-balance the emerging heartless world of satellite matrixes, electronic hallucinations, and 'smart' banking cards.*

## The Challenges of Expertise

Posted on July 25, 2016

The widespread antipathy to experts is an angry and emotional reaction by electorates to the over-dependence on their advice. Scientific evidence and economic proposals are increasingly viewed with scepticism and their conclusions are dismissed as biased. Political and social experts are criticized for having been wrong on Iraq, Syria, Libya, immigration, the economy, inflation, prosperity and a range of technological challenges. The views of expert groups of economists, bankers, academics who opposed Britain leaving the European Union were dismissed by swaths of the population in the UK as being corrupt and incompetent. One Cabinet Minister, Michael Gove, said during the referendum campaign that Britain "has had enough of experts."

Technocracy, or the rule by experts, has indeed conferred powers and legitimacy to governments as a way of implementing technical programs. This has long been condemned by such prominent economists as Friedrich Hayek who maintained that unchecked power should not be entrusted to "the wise and the good." In his book, *The Road to Serfdom*, Hayek warned that in such technocracies there would "be special opportunities for the ruthless and the unscrupulous." He went on to warn, "the readiness to do bad things becomes a path to promotion and power."

Given this challenging perspective, Dan Gardner has pointed out that expertise entails more knowledge and that more knowledge produces more detail and complication which in turn makes it ever harder to come to clear and confident answers: "It will be a struggle to bring even modest clarity to the whole chaotic picture."[1]

I must confess that I come from a highly sceptical background. My father, being a Berliner, was deeply suspicious of German experts. He called them "Klug Scheissers" (which can be generously translated into "smart alecks" or "know-it-alls.") The German military experts of WWI had been disastrously wrong — as had been the generals on all sides. Years later, when he was a celebrated photographer in the United States, he found the so-called experts in the world of fashion as limited in their vision as the "experts" of the German military.

I have had the 'privilege' during my life to be in contact with top experts in differing professional categories. One of the foremost of these while I was still in university was the philosopher and essayist Isaiah Berlin who divided experts into two prototypes: The single "grand idea" ones whom he called 'hedgehogs' and the more eclectic thinkers who were the 'foxes'. Berlin favored the foxes for having greater and more genuine foresight. He portrayed the fox as knowing many little things and being skilled at improvising when faced with rapidly changing events. The hedgehog's perspective was limited by its single-minded determination to prevail. This was effective in winning an argument, but the foxes were more successful in predicting the future than the hedgehogs by evaluating the forecasts of a range of experts.

Over the years I have developed a wide range of attitudes towards experts in different fields. I have found the perspective of macro-economists to be unusually narrow and restricted. Ditto for the cold-war warriors I encountered. Rounding up experts for *Prospects for Tomorrow,* a series I edited, was surprisingly difficult: These tended to focus their essays on the immediate rather than on the wider aspects of the future.

I learned first-hand about today's medical experts on the occasion when I entered Addenbrookes, the gigantic hospital in Cambridge, with a high fever and chest pains. I was examined by a series of specialists each of whom in turn related my problems to their area of expertise: After a brief examination, the cardiologist suspected a heart problem; the lung specialist thought it was a viral infection, the renal specialist suspected a kidney problem, and the psychologist was concerned over my mental state. As the *concilium* of specialists could not decide what was the cause of my condition, I was conveyed to the contagious infection unit on the top floor where I stayed for a full week. When my temperature reverted to normal, I signed myself out — never knowing what had been the exact nature of my problems.

In the medical profession, as is true elsewhere, many specialists find it difficult to look at the broad picture. Those experts who spend decades focused on one particular area are not necessarily right, but they are more likely to be correct than those unfamiliar with the subject. Dan Gardner, who has written a number of books on experts, was initially perplexed how one of the best thinkers of his time, Arnold Toynbee, could be so wrong so often. "Here was a man who probably knew more history than anyone alive. His knowledge of politics and current affairs was almost as vast. He brimmed with intelligence, energy and imagination. And yet his whole conception of the past and present was based on a mirage, and his supposed visions of the future were no more insightful than the ramblings of a man lost and wandering beneath a desert sun."[2]

It is fortunate that the polymaths of yesteryear, figures like John Maynard Keynes, Isaiah Berlin, or Francis Crick — all of whom crossed many fields of knowledge — were never overwhelmed by the swiftly increasing scope of human knowledge. Wikipedia is infinitely more comprehensive than the Encyclopedia Britannica of 75 years ago. Today "stars," who make expertise their business on the internet and relish appearances on television, are no better than the rest of us when it comes to making predictions about the future. Their analysis of events may be more perceptive, but when they are wrong it is rare for them to admit it or for them to be held accountable for their misjudgements.

Modern science has demonstrated that uncertainty, like the quantum, is an inevitable element in our world. Total certainty is an illusion. Scientists acknowledge they must avoid that feeling of certainty. Questioning and degrees of doubt are essential. On the other hand, politicians, journalists and those in business all dislike uncertainty and scorn at the use of words such as "however", "maybe," and "if." At the same time, those political experts who bore us with a misty spray of "howevers" are more likely to be right about what might happen than the charismatic experts who exude confidence in their predictions.

Studies have shown that a strong commitment to ideology or theory by experts makes for prejudiced evaluations. Controversial issues such as climate change, GM crops, vaccinations, incarceration, and banking are often tied up with emotions and values passionately held by the electorate. Experts seeking to establish levels of public opinion often have to resort to work with the probability factor. However, one of the many problems encountered with probability is the way people interpret it: "High probability" is all too often turned by the media into "this will happen," when it should be translated into "this is likely to happen."

The foremost American writer on expertise, Philip E Tetlock, suggests we should view political forecasting by intelligence analysts, independent pundits, institutional specialists or media figures with the same degree of scepticism that the well-informed now apply to stock market forecasting.[3] Tetlock contends that there is no direct correlation between the knowledge or intelligence of our political experts and the quality of their forecasts. To evaluate the prediction of any of these experts we should look at the ways he or she is processing information and the paths along which they are thinking. Experts often are wrong in their forecasts simply because they fail to use good judgment.

The world is becoming far more volatile in this digital age than even most intelligent people realize. Such volatility makes evaluation of our future direction far more risky for the experts. The best approach consequently is to ask provocative questions which might help to clarify the alternatives. For example, as Dr Randall Wray has observed, professional economists actually know less about government budgeting today than they did 50 years ago.[4]

Another contributor to *The World Economic Review*, maintains, "The bottom line is that there is no fiscal debt crisis... The world is faced with enough problems as it is without us fabricating one. It is high time that we put the myths to bed and started basing policy on fact and not on fiction."[4] What haunts most experts is that what appears most likely often does not happen, while what actually occurs is quite unexpected -- as in Brexit!

---

[1]Dan Gardner, *Future Babble*, (2010) pp.87 and p. 67
[2]Philip Tetlock, *Expert Political Judgment* (2005)
[3]L. Randall Wray, "Taxes are for Redemption not Spending," *World Economic Review* No.7, July 2016
[4]John T. Harvey, "Worldwide Fiscal Crisis: Fact or Fiction," *World Economic Review* No.7, July 2016.

## Respecting The Truth

Posted on November 30, 2016

The day before the election, I posted the long entry about optimism. I believe in it now as much as when I wrote it, but I am most discouraged by the election to the Presidency of a business man who has no interest in, nor respect for, the truth, facts, nor the written word. In this context, much of the American electorate seems equally unappreciative. Much as in Roman times, the populace wants entertainment and distraction.

We are, alas, all entering a new era of mass communication on the Internet with such social media sites as Twitter and Facebook where celebrity is of the essence and wealth greedily clothes ignorance. The lack of values is most evident in the way truth is distorted. Facebook distributed "fake news" such as the falsified presidential endorsement of Trump by Pope Francis. Twitter, encouraged by Trump's addiction, became a focus of disinformation. As a consequence, ever-increasing doubt was sown about how the media processed information.

What the masses in our time have lost is respect for truth, for facts, and for journalism. A blog like mine is typically viewed as a minor eccentricity. (Most fortunately, we still have exceptional newspapers like the *New York Times* and *The Guardian* as well as excellent magazines like *The New Yorker* and the *Atlantic.*) But this election has shown that what the best have written directly and with brilliance ultimately had little impact on the majority when it came to the ballot box. The people obviously did not read, follow, nor understand the printed word. Never in history has any political contender for power faced such a focused rejection by the printed media as Donald Trump. And yet he emerged triumphant.

Journalism, as well as politics, has been unable to keep up to the speed with which change is altering the world. Technology has advanced this phenomenon through the Internet, computers and cell phones. Thus far, it has developed without any social responsibility. I have tried my best to keep my blog factual (even using out-dated footnotes) which has suggested ways to overcome the shock which has overwhelmed all those who respect such values as truth and integrity.

Yes, as a child I experienced the repetition of lies by Hitler and Goebbels whose Wagnerian preference for death over justice, freedom, or the truth climaxed in their own violent ends. Seventy years later, Trump paraded the repetition of lies most effectively, winning by any means at his disposal. Then, victorious, he shifted his position on matters of state without recognition of any discrepancy.

Philosophers, writers, thinkers and politicians have struggled over many centuries to define "the truth." I have selected some quotations which I feel might re-enlighten those who deplore the descent of truth over the past year. Alas, Donald Trump is one of those rare, exceptional figures who seem unable to differentiate between truth and lying. The speed with which he has shifted positions, combined with his lack of experience, has evidenced his lack of interest in and understanding of "the truth." Perhaps the circulation of my listing below could suggest to those around the President-elect that the truth is ultimately fundamental to his survival in office.

## ON TRUTH

Every violation of truth is not only a sort of suicide in the liar, but a stab at the health of human society.
— Ralph W Emerson, *Prudence*, 1841

We arrive at the truth, not by the reason only, but also by the heart.
— Blaise Pascal, *Pensees,* 1670

The exact contrary of what is generally believed is often the truth.
— Jean de La Bruyere, *Caracteres,* 1688

To love truth for truth's sake is the principal part of human perfection in this world, and the seed-plot of all other virtues.
— John-Locke, *Letter to Anthony Collins*, Oct 29, 1703

There are certain times when most people are in disposition of being informed, and 'tis incredible what a vast good little truth might do, spoken in such seasons.
— Alexander Pope, *Letter to William Wycherley*, June 23, 1705

When fiction rises pleasing to the eye,
men will believe, because they love the lie;
but the truth herself, if clouded with a frown,
must have some solemn proof to pass her down.
— Charles Churchill, *Epistle to William Hogarth,* 1763

If we would only stop lying, if we would only testify the truth as we see it, it would turn out that once that there are hundreds, thousands, even millions of men just as we are, who see the truth as we do, are afraid as we are of
seeming to be singular by confessing it, and are only waiting, again as we are, for someone to proclaim it.
— Leo N. Tolstoy: *The Kingdom of God is within you*, 1893

If one tells he truth, one is sure, sooner or later, to be found out.

— Oscar Wilde, *Phrases and Philosophies for the Use of the Young*, 1894

The best test of truth is the power of the thought to get it accepted in the competition of the market.
— Justice O W Holmes, *Dissenting opinion in the Abrams vs. United States,* 1919

If you tell the same story five times, it's true.
— Larry Speakes, White House Press Secretary, December 16, 1983

In this crazy political business, at least in our times, a lie unanswered becomes truth within twenty-four hours.
— Willie Brown, quoted in the *New York Times*, October 31, 1988

Each man has in him the potential to realize the truth through his own will and endeavour and to help others to realize it.
— Aung San Suu Kyi , *In Quest of Democracy*, 1991

In a free society, there comes a time when the truth — however hard it may be to hear, however impolitic it may seem to say — must be told.
— Al Gore, fundraising letter, May 2006

He who has the truth is in the majority, even though he be one.
— Arab Proverb

## #affectsourspirits

Posted on February 22, 2017

My relative isolation from the digital world recently became painfully evident while looking at "PETRIe" an offbeat cultural site on the Internet which deals with various social and cultural domains ranging from fashion to protests. What struck me was a short essay by PETRIe's feature writer, Elena Stanciu, on "Hashtag Protest." I had come across both the symbol and the word, but I had never viewed the hashtag as an important developmental aspect of the new media. I was bowled over by her text which I now take the liberty of introducing you to hashtags with a couple of her dense paragraphs:

Digital platforms feed into the structural fragmentation and individualisation of societies today, paradoxically enhancing connectivity and mirroring the spatiality of protest: the public square is now the platform, and groups of activists are now digital enclaves, linked by tracking algorithms. An artefact of this digital culture of protest is the hashtag, which becomes a social movement instrument, ensuring a successful deployment of tangible realities of protest across connective platforms.

As part of last year's protests against racial injustice and police brutality in the US, the hashtag played a central role in claiming portions of digital space for specific causes, and operating a mirroring of the physical demonstrations, as stand-ins for instances of social injustice, and valid calls for policy change. The epitome of this, #blacklivesmatter transformed the role of the activist digital handle, by pushing a critical re-framing of discourse around the tragedy of extrajudicial violence against black people. By being both inclusive and descriptive of the content it "tags," the hashtag operates a process of negotiating cultural realities, beyond the mere dissemination and immediate conversion of events. With every reposting, #blacklivesmatter negates the implied "black lives do not matter," thus attempting to exclude racism as a viable component of social reality.

In this new architecture of symbolic significance, the hashtag would appear to deliver order to the different forms of organized dissent we are currently experiencing. Stanciu goes on to assert that "the hashtag describes, sums up, re-plays, while it simultaneously produces and reproduces new meanings." Apparently the hashtag now plays a significant part in enhancing the flow of the narrative of events taking place such as the recent women's global marches on January 21st. She views the hashtag as "bringing order in what would otherwise be indistinguishable clutter." In doing so Stanciu believes the hashtag is "launching a dialogue between message and medium, content and channel, existing realities and imagined realities." She quotes two 'theorists' in this field, if one can thus describe the experts who, reflecting on hashtags, embrace a logic that "transforms collective action into connective action."[1]

Much of this analysis seems forced, artificial and somewhat pretentious to me, but then I am not a #twitterthriller. I will not try to guess where this new format is headed, but the way hashtags have swept the world in just a decade is truly astonishing.

The widespread discursivity of the hashtag apparently extends beyond both time and space. It has become a cultural phenomenon of the new millennium with writers like Stanciu viewing it as "the raw material to be used in the forging of a new order of space, action, and life." I find such a conclusion rather incredible, but then I come at this as an outsider who finds it hard to understand the power of such perceptions, riddled as they are by confusion, and leaves me scratching my head. I am not alone.

When Melania Trump, shortly after entering the White House, began sharing her hashtag #Powerofthefirstlady confusion reigned as to what it meant. One reader thought it sounded like an advertising tagline for an antiperspirant. Another thought it could be what a teenage girl in an anime cartoon might shout to transform into an adult. What seems evident is that interpreting hashtags could soon be classified as having a professional status. It is now recognized that the # can convey a full range of emotions from sarcasm to humor.

The hash symbol or [called the pound sign in the USA] has grown in meaning since Chris Messina first used it while camping in California in August 2007 for groups, as in #barcamp.[2] It was then appropriated by Twitter as a way to categorize messages and rapidly became the principal site for advancing its popularity. An etiquette swiftly arose to prevent the misuse of hashtags: Twitter warned that three hashtags were an "absolute maximum" in any 140 letter conversation and that exceeding that number could cause an account to be suspended. Moreover, a hashtag that is not picked up by another user will be regarded as a failure by the media's experts. However, hashtgaggery, or the academic or scholarly study of such phenomena, is still in its infancy.

I shall try not to nurture this fledgling art form in this blog, but its spread is phenomenal. Among its highest promoters #realTrumpIsKing. *The New York Times* closed an amusing entry on the hashtag: "We just have to venture forth and find it, exploit it and perfect it. #Letathousandhashtagsbloom."[3]

I have not yet learned how to appreciate the literary pretensions of the hashtag. The wordplay of its "trending topics" which tend to be event driven by punch phrasing which would seem to be searching crowd-sourced setups such as: #christmascheer, #orgasmicclutter, and #robotjobs — all of which could generate a massive response on Twitter. Some hashtags have gained fame in different ways:

- #jesuischarlie in English #iamcharlie) expressed global solidarity with those who were assassinated in the offices of *Charlie Hebdo* in Paris.
- #OccupyWallStreet became the hashtag of the protesters not only in New York but around the world.
- The "Tonight Show Hashtags" became among the most tweeted on Twitter which promoted this television program on NBC in the US. It is to be noted here that the television formatted hashtags are used to identify a series being broadcast as well as to measure the immediate response from the viewers to the topical hashtags issued by the presenters. Hashtag "bugs" on the home video screens also are being used in television commercials to promote

- branded products as well as to gauge the topical reactions of their audiences.
- Hashtags are also used on social networks like Instagram where users can post a picture and then tag it with a subject. However Instagram can block or censor hashtags which could be linked to illegal activities such as drug use.
- Ultimately the spoken hashtag can work as a joke, or express complex sarcasm, for example to comment on Donald Trump's aside to a British reporter at his over-lengthy press conference: #theBBCanotherbeauty.

Perhaps one of these days @, the "at" sign, will enjoy similar popularity as the #- although currently it is mostly restricted to names, addresses and connections. Frankly, as a writer, the dash "–" has always exerted a greater attraction for me. It seems to possess more meanings, embraces a stronger sense of space and time, as well as inspiring a strange metaphysical continuity. Yet another popular social media may arise someday soon – how shall I put it ? – with dash!

---

[1] W.Lance Bennet and Prof. Alexandra Segerberg, The *Oxford Handbook of Social Movements*, (2015)

[2] Wikipedia gives a brief history of the hashtag

[3] Julia Turner, "In Praise of the Hashtag," *The New York Times*, November 2, 2012 (Magazine section)

## NEW DIRECTIONS FOR RIGHT AND WRONG?

Posted on July 14, 2017

Even before this era of "fake news" and the easy willingness to mix lies and truth, I already was deeply concerned about the swift decline in our belief in ethical rights and wrongs. I accept that we may find it increasingly difficult, given the distractions of social media, to live by our traditional ethical guidelines. However, I feel strongly for the universal need to accept the principles of right and wrong which resonate within us.

Historically, morals, affiliations, and religions have all been dependent on strongly held convictions in right and wrong. Philosophers, beginning with Socrates (469-399BC), have long debated the foundations of moral decision-making. Socrates was one of the earliest of the Greek philosophers to focus on self-knowledge in such matters as right and wrong. He advanced the notion that human beings would naturally do good if they could rationally distinguish right from wrong. It followed that bad or evil actions were the consequence of ignorance. The assumption was that those who know what is right automatically do it. Socrates held that the truly wise would know what is right, do what is good, and enjoy the result. However his most famous pupil, Aristotle, held that to achieve precise knowledge of right and wrong was far more unlikely in ethics than in any other sphere of inquiry. Aristotle thought ethical knowledge was dependent on custom, tradition and social habits in ways that made it distinctive.

Only much later did John Locke, strike in a new direction with his determination to establish a "science of ethics." He went astray in his search but, as we shall see, this was to be picked up again by neuroscientists hundreds of years later. David Hume, a philosophical contemporary then went on to assume that empathy should guide moral decisions and our ultimate ideals.

John Stuart Mill in the mid 19<sup>th</sup> century advanced liberalism in part by advocating that following what is right would lead to an improvement of our lives. "Actions are right in proportion as they tend to promote happiness; wrong as they tend to produce the reverse of happiness," Mill wrote.[1] Admittedly many actions in this colonial era increased the well-being of some while inflicting suffering on others. "Wrong" often boiled down to selfishness while "right" encompassed willingness to take personal responsibility for considering the consequences that such actions might have for others.

Today "right" and "wrong" are generally assumed to have come from schooling, parental teaching and legal and religious instruction. However, primatologists like Marc D Hauser, a Harvard biologist, contend that the roots of human morality are also evident in such social animals as apes and monkeys who display feelings of reciprocity and empathy which are essential for group living. Hauser has built on this to propose that evolution wired survival among other social factors into our neural circuits.[2] The swift decisions that had to be made in life-or-death situations were not accessible to the conscious mind. Hauser's ultimate objective is to get morality accepted as being objectively true. This counters what most people in the northern hemisphere believe: that ethics are relative to time, cultures and individuals. Thus questions like gender, abortion, capital punishment and euthanasia waver in the winds of right and wrong.

The prolific Anglo-Irish writer, Brian Cleeve (1921-2003) asked: "Has the time arrived again when people must make moral standards a personal crusade? Has the time come to stand up and be counted for the difference between right and wrong?"[3] Cleeve contended that "In our modern eagerness to be tolerant, we have come to tolerate things which no society can tolerate and remain healthy. In our understandable anxiety not to set ourselves up as judges, we have come to believe that all judgments are wrong. In our revulsion against hypocrisy and false morality, we have abandoned morality itself. And with modest hesitations but firm convictions I submit that this has not made us happier, but much unhappier." In his book on *1938: A World Vanishing*, he held that at that time the average man and woman in Britain "possessed a keen notion of what was right and what was wrong, in his and her own personal life, in the community, and in the word at large."

The entry of neuroscientists, experimental psychologists, and social scientists into the search for understanding a possibly physical basis for such philosophical challenges as right and wrong has led to experiments with brain-scanning technology. The work of Harvard professor, Joshua Greene, has led him to conclude that "emotion and reason both play critical roles in moral judgment and that their respective influences have been widely misunderstood."[4] Greene's "dual-process theory" posits that emotion and rationality enter into moral decision-making according to the circumstances. Using functional magnetic resonance imaging (fMRI) to examine specific areas of the brain as it functions: The flow of blood to the amygdala (the seat of emotions) is compared to the flow to the prefrontal cortex (which houses deliberative reasoning.) The results Green believes illustrate that even when humans are calculating abstract probabilities, they also may rely on emotions for guidance. "Reason by itself doesn't have any ends, or goals," Greene concludes. "It can tell you what will happen if you do this or that, and whether or not A and B are consistent with each other. But it can't make the decision for you." Greene believes that by learning more about the neurological mechanisms involved in moral decision-making, people could eventually improve the way they make their judgments. Rationality cannot function independently of emotions, even in those who are utilitarian or rational decision makers.

Globally we have come to separate ethics and politics. No group can impose its moral conceptions on the society at large. Social media are powerful in creating herds of subscribers to groups with facades of universal values which mask narrow interests and replace ethics. Members need to be "right" in order to feel popular. The divisions between those who believe they are right sharply divides them from those perceived to be wrong. Most people want to be right as an indication of their intelligence, their power, their vision and ultimately of their desire for admiration and acknowledgment of their status. Like exhibitionist peacocks, some almost seem desperate to display their "superiority." Our psychological make-up traditionally strengthens such positions. William Hazlitt wrote some 200 years ago that, "We are not satisfied to be right unless we can prove others to be quite wrong."[5]

Some three generations ago Adolph Hitler insisted that "Success is the sole earthly judge of right and wrong." I suspect there are contemporary leaders would might agree with such an extraordinary assumption. I feel that the requirements of a moral life are unlikely to be promoted by the current political leaderships. The sociologist Max Weber held that the ethic of responsibility in politics only could be resolved if we demand the minimal of internal and external danger for all concerned.[5] I regret to say that this demand seems unlikely to be followed, but personally I believe that individual responsibility, which must entail a good measure of rationality, is absolutely essential if there is to be a reversal of the fast-fading social significance of human Rights and Wrongs.

---

[1]John Stuart Mill, *Utilitarianism II*, (1863)
[2]Marc D. Hauser, "Moral Minds" (2006)
[3]Brian Cleeve, "1938: A World Vanishing," (1982)
[4]Peter Saalfield, "The Biology of Right and Wrong" *Harvard Magazine*, January (2012)
[5]William Hazlitt, "Conversations of James Northcote," 1830.
[6]Max Weber, "Politics as a Vocation," *Essays in Sociology*, (1946) p.119

## ON RIGHTS AND WRONGS

Posted on November 8, 2017

There should be no shame in changing one's mind on issues or apologizing for being wrong. These rigidly polarizing days, however, saying "sorry" or admitting one's errors has become almost prohibited for politicians. As the *Economist* has noted it is in the interest of those who are in power to pretend that they are never wrong.[1]

In writing this blog I freely admit that I have been wrong on a number of occasions. I feel that unless one admits to the possibility of being wrong, there is less chance for change or improvement. I have been wrong on a wide variety aspects of life's challenges. Although there is often not as much distance between right and wrong as I imagine, being "right" does not always lead to desired results and I know that what I consider to be wrong often can have positive consequences. I have to admit that while there is usually a right way and a wrong way, the wrong path sometimes seems more attractive to me.

I was seriously wrong, for example, when it came to the referendum in the UK on leaving Europe, but I felt at that time that the only way Europe could change and advance on such major issues as that of refugees or the rescue of the Greek economy was to shake up the overly bureaucratic and inept administration in Brussels. My argument, however, was quite different from that of the Brexit enthusiasts in the UK who thought this was the only way to liberate their country from the demands of the European Community. I speculated that if there was a strong voice to protest what was happening, change might occur without an unlikely vote for an exit. In being so seriously wrong, I did not recognize the negative effect the departure would have on all of Europe as well as on the UK.

I was equally wrong about Donald Trump's chances of becoming President. I truly did not believe it was possible. I still can't believe that such a large number of the American electorate could be so desperate and manifestly uninformed. Yes, I was wrong about the mental perspective of Americans living in the "rust-belt" of the United State. I was unaware how these people felt neglected, full of anger, painfully frustrated in their hopes for a better livelihood, and unable to come to terms with the intelligence of a black President. This exposed ignorance on my part and a lack of insightful reporting on the part of the media. Yes, I find it hard to recognize that 8 percent of America's high school graduates can't read or write.

It is also true that I have never been capable of appreciating the comparably miserable situation of the jobless German workers in 1932 who saw Adolf Hitler as the leader who could revitalize Germany. This mad Austrian, whose background was entirely alien, seemed preferable to the far more intelligent politicians of the time. I find it hard to accept that the electoral masses often find it difficult to cope with intellectuals. True, we all seem ready to disregard information or facts, which conflict with our strongly held views. Today, whatever economists or scientific experts demonstrate as being right has little effect on large segments of the population. This has become increasingly evident in the case of beliefs about climate change. It is not that people are blind or deaf, just that they don't want to follow facts which run counter to their own beliefs.

I feel that I have been right about my opposition to and rejection of smoking and the use of brain destructive drugs. My concern with antibiotics, my fears of pollution, and my objections to nuclear weapons have all been evident in my blogs. I believe that our actions are right in proportion to the degree to which they improve the planet and produce happiness for human beings. Such actions are wrong when they result in wanton destruction, pain and misery. The nightmarish stockpiles of atomic and hydrogen bombs being held are insane. They may know it is wrong but the political leaders of this world are convinced that the only way to preserve their national positions is by holding masses of such weapons. Ultimately such a massive wrong may spell the end of mankind.

[1]"How to be wrong," the Economist, June 10, 2017, p.74

# THE PROMOTIONS OF DEATH

Posted on June 5, 2017

I was just starting thinking about the commercialization of death about a year ago when I was bowled over by a promotional leaflet sent to me by the UK's Cooperative Society suggesting what fun death could be! (See above.) My instinctive reaction was: How inappropriate can you get? In my experience, death has brought an end to the fun we could expect to have from life. Indeed, the lyrics of the 'Grateful Dead' have not been ringing in my ears.

Now, a year later, I find a long article starting on the front page of the *New York Times* "Celebrating at his own wake." Reported in detail by a correspondent, she describes how a fatally-ill, former priest, John Shields, carefully planned his last hours before having a lethal injection administered by his doctor. What he wanted was a wonderfully boozy Irish wake celebrated by some two dozen friends while he was still alive.[1]

At his ultimate party, Shields' friends proclaimed their love, gratitude and admiration for their host. Without the increasingly invasive promotional efforts of the funeral trade, the small group expressed their thanks for his friendship and his courage. When one of them planted a kiss on his lips, Shields aroused much laughter when he quipped, "I was just thinking. 'I'd like more of that.' then thought, 'That's not a good idea.'"

Towards the end of his own wake, Shields had wanted to join in the singing of the verses of a special departure song with the classic Celtic folk lyrics of "The Parting Glass"

But since it falls, unto my lot,
That I should rise and you should not,
I'll gently rise and I'll softly call,
Good night and joy be with you all.

However, a tired and sick Shields was drifting off to sleep, and later managed to wave to his friends as he was wheeled out of the party smiling and telling everyone, "I'll see you later."

Perhaps our social attitudes are changing. Maybe it is time to put fun back into our funerals? Could we turn the wake into the party of a lifetime? Promoters suggest a special day themed for the ancient Scots, or New Orleans Jazz, or even a Dadaist celebration? The happy ending of such a wake would be one way to evade our fears of the unknown. Evasion, as well as denial, have been the classic psychological ways of cheering up gatherings which are overcome with grief. As George Bernard Shaw declared: "Life does not cease to be funny when people die any more than it ceases to be serious when people laugh."

At my own father's rushed funeral in an over-populated Italian cemetery on the outskirts of Rome (where myself and my father's assistant were the sole mourners on a hot July afternoon) I was informed by a brusque Mafia undertaker that my father was being buried in an all-male section of the cemetery. This was because the law forbade any intermingling of the sexes underground! I almost felt sorry for my departed father, but was certain that even in these circumstances he would find ways to circumvent such mafia-bound, Catholic driven restrictions.

"Not everyone will be in a condition to toast Death's imminence with champagne, as Anton Chekov did," wrote *The Economist* in a recent cover story on "How to have a better death."[2] Perhaps our social attitudes are advancing? Perhaps we are beginning to accept that birth-life-death is a unity to be celebrated? The traditional weak jocularities of funeral orations do appear to be gradually vanishing.

Writing for *The Guardian*, a part-time observer noted that "Just as weddings have gorged themselves into inflated self-promotion, so funerals are now doing he same. They are becoming extravagant forms of self-expression, designed to articulate our individuality."[3] Certainly the burial costs, not including the catering fees of a good wake, are soaring. Being buried in London's Highgate cemetery (along with Karl Marx and other celebrities) will cost more than £18,000 (over $20,000). This reminds me of the marvelous observation of Woody Allen, "My grandfather had a wonderful funeral... It was a catered funeral. It was held in a big hall with accordion players. On the buffet table there was a replica of the deceased in potato salad."[4]

Funerals were not always as somber as those of the Middle Ages or even of the 19th century. In the time of Homer, for example, the Greek funeral was a three act drama. The body was laid out in the first act, the transport to internment was the second act and the third was the lowering of the body or the ashes into the grave. This scenario presented opportunity for the display of family pride, wealth, solidarity and power.[5] However, in those days there was a closer intimacy between the living and the dead. Homer described the dead as "ghosts of worn out mortals." The dead had to be fitted with their obol, or boat fare, fixed between their teeth. This was a payment for being ferried across the river Styx by Charon, the boatman.[6] It was also customary to place a laurel crown on the head of those deceased who had "bravely fought their contest with life."

The classic Greek ceremony around the grave featured the singing of ritualized lamentations. Sometimes hired mourners dressed in long robes also participated. A chorus of women traditionally uttered a refrain of cries to accompany the sung lamentations. At the end of such burials the women left first to go to the house of the deceased to put the finishing touches on the banquet. However, it was Christianity that truly promoted the belief in life after death which had merely been hinted at by the Greeks.

Of all the global ceremonies surrounding death, none can surpass the creative ways Mexicans celebrate rather than mourn the departed. The Mexican "Day of the Dead" originated with the Aztecs, who before the landing of Columbus, had for centuries spent 30 days every August dedicated to death. The invading Spanish, when introducing Christianity, contracted these lengthy festivities into one day around the All Saints' and All Souls' days in November. Today, *El Dia de los Muertos* continues to be a national celebration to honor those who have passed away.

Gravesites are decorated with flowers, *angelitos* (little papier-mâché angels) balloons and small altars decorated with candles, memorabilia, photos, as well as food in honor of the dead. The same happens at home where those who have died can be reassured that they have not been forgotten and can enjoy a welcome homecoming. All of this is fun. The family may gather at the gravesites of their loved ones and enjoy a picnic in the presence of the departed. Some may play guitars, sing and even dance. The celebrations can continue with an all-night candlelight vigils where good times will be recalled and toasted with a drink or two.

The tragedy of the shortness of life is tempered not only by sorrow but also by pathos and extraordinary creativity. The *pan de muertos* (Day of the Dead bread) is a loaf sprinkled with cinnamon and decorated with "bones" especially baked for the occasion. Sugar candy in the shape of skulls and bones are also common. For the family it may be a way of saying "We cheated death because we are now eating you!" More serious papier-mâché skulls and skeletons, as well as clay, wood and plastic representations of the dead come in different sizes and are even esteemed for their artistic craftsmanship. I have collected a small but charming group of such Mexican memento to the dead.

These Mexican celebrations are untainted by the promotional intrusions of large corporations. Exploiting loss for commercial gain still seems most inappropriate to many. Inevitably, death in the capitalist world sells these days: Virgin Holidays suggests flying your way out of grief. Indeed, travel therapy may offer a faster escape from sorrow than some contemporary form of "sociotherapy." I do recommend drawing on the profoundly celebratory aspects of the Mexicans. As *The Economist* concluded in its cover story: "A better death means a better life, right until the end."

---

[1]Catherine Porter, "Celebrating at his own wake," *The New York Times*, May 29, 2017.
[2]April 29, 2017.
[3]Giles Fraser, "The rise of so-called happy funerals..." *The Guardian*, May 12, 2017
[4]*The Nightclub Years*
[5]Robert Garland, *The Greek Way of Death*, (1985) p.23
[6]Yorick Blumenfeld, *The Waters of Forgetfulness*, (2006)

## WHAT KIND OF A WORLD DO WE WANT TO LIVE IN?

Posted on April 28, 2017

Should the market and the continuing advances in science and technology be the ultimate arbiters of where we are headed? Neither are experiencing controls, and politicians are most reluctant to intervene in the innovations in robotics or the internet. As a writer, the internet has proven to be both a great assistant and a serious enemy: It distracts me from concentrated attention, steals my time and space to think, degrades my memory, and tends to attack my eyes, my spinal column and even my social life. I know I am not alone in these observations. I have not joined Facebook nor do I spend my nights tweeting, like the US President, but the younger generation will simply say that I am out of touch. I counter this by pointing out that technology is undermining bookshops, printed newspapers and human touch.

So where are we headed? Do we really want to transform human nature so that in the 21st century consciousness will be uncoupled from intelligence? Yuval Noah Harari, the popular new writer/philosopher, suggests three more mundane developments in the 21st Century which are likely to overwhelm our human experience on this planet:

1. Humans will lose their economic and military usefulness. This will lower their value in economic and political terms.
2. The human collective will retain its values, but not unique individuals.
3. A new elite of upgraded humans will arise.  1

Harari suggests that "The most important question in 21st Century economics may well be what to do with all the superfluous people?" Contending that humans have both physical and cognitive abilities, he points out that taxi drivers are likely to go the way horses did during the Industrial Revolution. He asks, "What will happen once algorithms outperform us in remembering, analyzing and recognizing patterns?" I tend to agree with him that in the dystopian world which may be facing us, real jobs and full-time employment will be reserved for an educated, technology literate elite. The new wave of top corporations such as Amazon, Apple, Facebook, Google and Microsoft simply are not mass employers like Ford, General Electric, GM or Kodak used to be.

The progression of humans on this earth, from tilling the soil in 5000 BC to toiling in an Amazon warehouse, is not always obvious. Early in the 20th Century, Frederick Taylor in his celebrated book, *Principles of Scientific Management*, regarded workers as cogs in the industrial mass production machine. A century later we are asking why turn workers into machines when robots can do their jobs at a lower cost? Technology has produced ever more efficient ways of monitoring human capabilities and comparing these with the costs and greater profits from robots. Alas, money and profits in the capitalist system are becoming more important than human labor.

Some seventy millennia ago the improved capacity of the Homo sapiens mind started the revolution in which the DNA of one living species was able to dominate the planet. Now a second revolution may be on hand in which the scientific and technological advances of artificial intelligence will triumph over the genetic. Indeed such progress will succeed because of the collaboration between people and algorithms suggests Demis Hassabis the co-founder and CEO of DeepMind. He stated that "If we want computers to discover new knowledge, then we must give them the ability to truly learn for themselves."[2] Please note the personification of the computers!

Harrari adds that "high-tech gurus and Silicon Valley prophets are creating a new universal narrative that legitimizes the authority of algorithms and Big Data." Just as free-market capitalists believe in the invisible hand of the market so Dataists believe in the invisible hand of the data flow. As the global data processing system becomes all-knowing and all powerful, so connecting to the system will become the source of all meaning. I hesitatingly accept Harrari's proposal that "We are already becoming tiny chips inside a giant system that nobody really understands."[3]

We are now at the stage of accepting that neurons, genes and hormones all obey the same physical and chemical laws of life on earth. However, it will take transcranial stimulators to enable us to decode the electrochemical brain process which determine our perspective, because the two separate brain hemispheres are not always in touch with each other. It is the left hemisphere which is the seat of our verbal abilities including our power to interpret the information that makes sense of our thoughts and experiences. it controls the right hand. The right side is more creative and is crucial in the areas of music, imagination, and intention as well as control of the left hand.

I suspect that ultimately spending untold billions on exploring the brain might be more productive than trillions invested in space exploration. The motivation which underpins the competitive advance of this new technology is in large measure an economic one, as evidenced by the market for shares in high tech. Of course there is also the drive of scientists rushing to publish their pioneering breakthroughs and getting these patented. The growth of technology in many ways resembles that of the market. The market is as blind as it is invisible. However, supply and demand cannot guide all of society. Neither can technology. If everything was determined by the market, the courts, the police, and the army would vanish. So would the entire economy. Mark O'Connell, who had studied this proposition, recognized that growth was mediated by corporations whose real interest was to make eventual profits out of reducing human life into data.[4]

The efforts of a future in which human minds might be uploaded to computers, is one aspect of Carbon Copies, a "nonprofit organization with a goal of advancing the reverse engineering of neural tissue and complete brains ...creating what we call Substrate Independent Minds." This non-profit group is funded by a number of adventurous millionaire investors who are seeking scientists who work "towards quantum leap discoveries that might rewrite the operating systems of life."

Somehow I feel human cognition is demeaned when we reduce it to mechanic operations and along computational lines. The internet is proving to be the single most powerful mind-affecting technology ever.

As it is the overwhelming flood of new data is extraordinarily disruptive. Many acquaintances suffer from neural addiction to Facebook, Twitter, the latest news and stock market results on top of the steady flow of emails. Studies have shown that cognitive losses from multi-tasking are higher than the cognitive losses from smoking pot. Aided by our smart phones and computers, we are able to multi-task. Apps on our smart phones serve as a calendar, a watch, voice recorder, alarm clock, GPS, camera, flashlight and news headliner. However, there is a cognitive cost for every time we are rapidly switching from one task to the next.[5]

Surveys show that almost a third of every working day is lost to keeping up with the information flow. The impact on the brain is barely understood and nobody knows how it will affect us socially. What seems certain is that it will transform our existence as homo sapiens has thusfar experienced it. Attention deficit disorders are affecting more and more children. Part of this is ascribed to the swift sequencing of images on the internet. The result is that 3 seconds is about as much time as will hold the attention of kids. How will this affect them in later years?

The universal change of pace already has had extraordinary effects in terms of consumption, obsolescence, renewal, inequality and lots of other conditions. I don't believe the brain was built for the swift and continuing change that we are currently experiencing. The brain is adaptable and can accommodate small changes here and there, but not the continuity of alterations which are changing the face of the earth, employment, wages, round-the-clock news, ringing mobiles, blogs, and communications. Cyberspace has invaded our public and private lives, our economy and our security as well. While everything is changing, politicians have not appreciated nor understood the social revolution taking place. Few can accept the fundamental and rapid shifts in power. Currently there is no comprehension of who and how would control the new constructs as these arose. AI is certainly going to transform the lives of architects, lawyers and medical professionals. Indeed, it threatens to overwhelm us all. Because we have no idea what the job market will be in 2030 or 2040, we have few notions of what to teach our kids today.

Such realities are far from what may come next: The founder of the 2045 Initiative, Dmitry Itskov, a Russian high tech multimillionaire operating in Silicon Valley, wants "to create technologies enabling the transfer of an individual's personality to a more advanced nonbiological carrier and extending life, including to the point of immortality." One of the projects of the 2045 initiative is to create artificial humanoid bodies that would be controlled through brain-computer interface.

A conference in New York by Global Futures 2045 was focused on "a new evolutionary strategy for humanity." The organizer, Randall Koene, a "trans-humanist," sees the mind as a piece of software, an application running on the platform of human flesh. The complex transformation starts with the scanning of the pertinent information stored in the neurons of a person's brain. Although incredibly complicated because of the seemingly endless connections between the neurons, the scan becomes a blueprint for the reconstruction of neural networks which are then transformed into a computational model." Ultimately this would allow scientists to create any material form which technology permits. The human could choose to become large or small, with feet or with wings, like a tiger or a tree. The prospects may challenge the human imagination, but such projections of AI advances overfill me with forebodings of ultimate horror.

Ultimately, it is the arts that may become our human sanctuary when AI and robots will have replaced teachers, doctors, lawyers and policemen. Creating new jobs will not be the challenge, it will be creating ones where humans can outperform robots. The world we want will be one advancing direct experience, such as all the arts: music, dance, singing, painting, sculpting, writing , and acting . It would also endorse all the sports, running, swimming, , hiking, climbing, walking, and exercising as well as cooking, gardening, keeping pets, caring, loving, and travelling . The joys of all these activities will go far beyond the speculations of Alan Turing and his successors on the connections between randomness and creative intelligence. There is an urgent need for a re-evaluation of our relationship with the wonders of the new technology. *

Currently there is a widespread belief that the advances of technology, the internet and science are both unstoppable and to a large extent, desirable. Silicon Valley's most prominent figures hold self-serving views that anything which slows scientific innovation is an attack on the public good.[6]

I liked Rutger Bregman's outlook in, Utopia for Realists. This young Dutchman suggests that we can construct a society with visionary ideas that could be implemented, like the plans for a universal basic income. As an aging Utopian,
I have always endorsed building castles in the sky. Shocking ideas which are usually rejected out of hand, often return to become popular and even accepted. The questions of ethics in a world that will be so different are daunting. Optimistically, crises- real or perceived- can spark genuine change. Sometimes this can be mind-blowing: As Harari cautioned, human nature is likely to be transformed in the 21st Century because intelligence is uncoupling from consciousness. The countering encouragement he provides is that ultimately" It is our free will that imbues the universe with meaning."[7]

——————————————————————

[1]Yuval Noah Harari, Homo Deus, (2016)p.356
[2]Demis Hassabis, "The Mind in the Machine," The Financial Times Magazine, April 22, 2017
[3]Yuval Noah Harari, "In Big Data We Trust," The FT Magazine, August 27, 2016, p.14
[4]Mark O'Connell, "Goodbye Body, Hello Posthuman Machine," The Observer, March 26, 2017
[5]Daniel J. Levitin, "Why the Modern World Is Bad for Your Brain," The Observer, January 18, 2015.
[6]"Computer Security," The Economist, April 8, 2017, p.75
[7]Homo Deus, op.cit

- Regulating the internet would require a change in the political mindset in both Europe and the United States. The invasions of privacy and security as well as the massive tax evasion by the largest internet companies have not sufficed to bring about the essential changes. The two prime decisions made by the creators of the internet and principally by Tim Berners-Lee were that there would be no central control or ownership and that the network could not be dominated by any particular application.

# Blog Afterthoughts: Summer  2018

It seems incredible to me that just five years ago I decided to write a blog which would look at the world from a generally positive perspective. I was encouraged by Martin Rees, the Astronomer Royal, who had for many years been fascinated by the optimism of my writings  But it was not easy to come up with a theme every ten days or so which would enlighten my readers and make them aware of possible improvements and hopes for a brighter tomorrow.

Initially it was encouraging that a capable and highly intelligent President, Obama had taken the US out of its 2008 economic crisis and was doing his utmost to bring common sense into global affairs. Then three years later came Trump and the prospect swiftly turned so bleak that I halted writing about politics. Nausea was never an optimistic reaction. Indeed, I could not have imagined some 500 days after his inauguration, that about 40% of the American electorate would give  this compulsive liar their approval. This seemed like a throwback to my infancy when a similar proportion of a nation gave their endorsement to Hitler. It has been painful for me that such dangerous leaderships occurred in generally literate and educated countries. Alas, the passage of the years does not suggest great advances.  As Amy Sullivan suggested in the New York Times: "80% of white evangelicals would vote against Jesus Christ himself if he ran as a Democrat."

In the long term the prospects for the environment do not look good:  The fast melting glaciers in Greenland and the Antarctic can flood major cities around the world. Our waters can become polluted by plastics,  agricultural run-offs, and hormonal and other medicinal products. The air we breathe is also likely to be polluted by ever increasing road traffic  and partially combusted jet fuel.

Theoretically the results of "knowledge engineering" (AI) could  be positive but a dark new era of algorithms  seems likely to dominate the shape of events. I sense there is an increasingly threatening relationship between the complex mechanics of "the Cloud" which is fostering global forms of populism,  insecurity, fears, as well as social and economic inequalities.

This week I observed a  delightful 16 months old toddler who was becoming hooked on operating her mother's Apple6 mobile. The effects of such early addictions are as yet unknown and unstudied- but I do feel that the addictive design features of Facebook, Fortnite, Snapchat, et.al., may ultimately lead to generations with diminished social and ethical concerns. The fading social responsibilities of commercially focused creators leaves little room for long term optimism. I fear that in coming generations weird alterations are likely to occur in the ways of thinking, seeing and reacting.

Not only are our cars becoming increasingly computerized, but most of the elements in our homes and offices, from the security systems to the lighting, are now electronically controlled. So where are we headed? It would seem that an increasing inability to grasp the wider impact of techno-driven technology is already upon us. As James Bridle has written in his *New Dark Age*, "We cannot unthink the network; we can only think through and within it. The technologies that inform and shape our present perceptions of reality are not going to go away..."

Looking back some 20 years ago in my book, *Optimistic Visions For Change,* I wrote that "The principal obstacle to positive new directions for the 21$^{st}$ Century is that we lack the vision and the clarity to see that things could be both different and better." At that time I thought that our culture, from a global perspective, could be viewed as a historical process of progressive liberation. Now I see that our social structure is being overwhelmed by the relentless push for growth and ever greater profitability and efficiency in an increasingly crowded planet.

I am also struck by our failure to develop a vision for the future. Long term goals could nourish us by providing objectives beyond ourselves towards which we could work. Except for the Chinese, the world seems completely stuck on the short term. Our political conservatives, because of the nature of their outlook , are unable to offer any programmed alternative to the direction in which their country may be moving. Neither foot-dragging nor nostalgia can serve as a program for tomorrow.

The importance of transforming (or perhaps transcending) our desires is also crucial. Pandering to our consumer instinct is not only destructive of the environment and depleting our resources, but also is neither sustainable nor satisfying. Materialism does not serve the enhancement of life in all its fullness. Capitalism because of its exclusive focus on profits, has failed to concern itself with ethics, inequalities, injustice, community values or morals. As such, capitalism has relentlessly undermined family life and the market has undermined the moral foundations of society. Critics consistently rejoin that capitalism is the best alternative going, but the truth is that its effects are rapidly destroying the planet and that our spiritual and moral collapse lag not far behind. In my blogs I steadily tried to promote a new socio-economic order through a democratic form of communitarianism.

As humans, our challenge lies as much in trying to escape our old imprisoning ideas as in accepting new configurations. We find it almost impossible to imagine a world that is essentially different from our present chaotic one and at the same time a better one. We need charismatic public figures who, like Martin Luther King, have a dream. They must hold out a burning torch which combines a utopian compound of enthusiasm and prophetic vision. As I concluded in my book, in the time to come I hope that the human race will be able to recover the purity, the directness and the sheer joy of a child's perceptions.

"All mine! And seen so Easily! How Great! How Blest!
How soon am I of all possessed!
My infancy no sooner Opens its Eyes
But Straight the Spacious Earth
Abounds with Joy Peace Glory Mirth'
And being Wise
The very skies
And Stars do mine become, being all possessed
Even in that Way that is the Best."
Thomas Traherne (1636-1674)

## LIST OF BLOG SUBJECTS

#0015 - 210818 - C0 - 297/210/22 - PB - 9781784565930